197

Reading the West is a collection of critical essays by writers, independent scholars, and critics on the literature of the American West. The essays in this volume enrich our understanding of western writing by reemphasizing the importance of "place" in literary studies. Whether focusing upon gender, genre, class, or multiethnic and environmental concerns, these essays seek to reinvigorate an interest in regional artistry. Aimed at a general audience as well as an academic readership, this volume conveys a sense of the true depth and complexity of western writing, from the nineteenth century to the present.

Reading the West touches upon "literary" western works as well as popular formula art (in literature, movies, and painting). It investigates both the continuing popular fascination with the "Wild West" and new revisionist understandings of the complex ecology and multiculturalism of the American frontier. Critics from diverse backgrounds – literary criticism, drama review, novel writing, naturalist research – have come together in this volume, suggesting the variety of interest in western literature. Their essays address not only such well-known western writers as John Steinbeck, Wallace Stegner, Mary Austin, Robinson Jeffers, Edward Abbey, D'Arcy McNickle, and Jean Stafford but also such lesser-known figures as Isabella Bird, John C. Van Dyke, Nina Otero, and Laurence Yep. By showcasing the full range of western American writing, this collection attempts to gain a new, wider audience for a distinguished body of literary work that has not always received its critical due.

CAMBRIDGE STUDIES IN AMERICAN LITERATURE AND CULTURE

Reading the West

Continued on pages following the index.

READING THE WEST

NEW ESSAYS ON THE LITERATURE
OF THE AMERICAN WEST

Edited by

MICHAEL KOWALEWSKI

Carleton College

CAMBRIDGE
UNIVERSITY PRESS

Published by the Press Syndicate of the University of Cambridge
The Pitt Building, Trumpington Street, Cambridge CB2 1RP
40 West 20th Street, New York, NY 10011-4211, USA
10 Stamford Road, Oakleigh, Melbourne 3166, Australia

First published 1996

Printed in the United States of America

Library of Congress Cataloging-in-Publication Data
Reading the West : new essays on the literature of the American West /
edited by Michael Kowalewski.
p.   cm. – (Cambridge studies in American literature and
culture ; 98)
Includes bibliographical references and index.
ISBN 0-521-45061-6 (hardback)
1. American literature – West (U.S.) – History and criticism.
2. Western stories – History and criticism.   3. West (U.S.) –
Intellectual life.   4. West (U.S.) – In literature.   I. Kowalewski,
Michael.   II. Series.
PS271.R43   1995
810.9'3278 – dc20   95-32384
CIP

A catalog record for this book is available from the British Library.

ISBN 0-521-45061-6 Hardback

for Richard Dalrymple
and Wayne Carver,
native sons of Utah

CONTENTS

vii

CONTEMPORARY WESTERN WRITING: A MOSAIC

ACKNOWLEDGMENTS

First and continuing thanks go to all the contributors for their patience and understanding in accepting the delays to which this volume was heir. Numerous friends from the Western Literature Association also deserve to be mentioned here: Glen Love, David Fine, Gerry Haslam, Charles Crow, David Robertson, Nancy Cook, Sean O'Grady, Don Scheese, Charlotte McClure, Scott Slovic, Cheryll Burgess Glotfelty, Susan Shillinglaw, Stephen Tatum, Michelle Potter, Bonney Macdonald, and Len Engel. They have had nothing specifically to do with this volume, but along with those contributors who are members of WLA, they have all helped make Western Lit meetings a model of humane exchange, good humor, and unintimidated thinking: everything the life of the mind ought to be.

I'm grateful as well to Terry L. Anderson for inviting me to participate in a very stimulating Liberty Fund seminar on the history of the American West at Mountain Sky Guest Ranch in October of 1993. I learned a great deal there from Alston Chase, Clyde Milner, Karl Hess, Wilcomb Washburn, and Tom Wolf, and I enjoyed meeting them all. (I learned some different kinds of things with Bill Mulligan on horseback during my stay.)

This collection would never have gotten off the ground without Julie Greenblatt's initial inspiration and support at Cambridge University Press and she has my heartfelt thanks for that. T. Susan Chang's patience and kindness at Cambridge have also been all an editor of such a volume could ever hope to encounter. I'd also like to acknowledge Vern Bailey's interest in this project as well. He was kind enough to ask after it often and then to remind me why I was doing it with stories of his latest flyfishing trip. Alan Hillesheim helped keep western fires burning with his completely unreasonable love – and animated readings – of Bernard DeVoto's work. Drayton Nabers III deserves recognition here for not finding a

Rhodes Scholarship and an interest in western writing mutually exclusive. His omnivorous reading has kept me supplied with western titles I need to read. I have Andrew Moe to thank for introducing me to Cormac McCarthy's work and for his unlikely letters from Telluride. I owe all the students in my spring 1993 "Literature of the American West" class at Carleton a special nod of thanks for lively discussion. And finally, I greatly appreciated Wallace Stegner's interest in this book, even though he couldn't himself be a part of it. His kind words of encouragement at an early stage meant a great deal to me. I count myself lucky indeed to have finally met him before his untimely death in 1993 and I miss his wit, warmth, and insight as much as anyone who cares about western writing.

Dick Dalrymple might find himself surprised to be a dedicatee of this volume, as he isn't a declared fan of western writing (the Virginian doesn't have much on the Wife of Bath). But more than anyone else I've known, he (and his extraordinary mother, Louise Dalrymple) introduced me to the "idea" of Utah, especially Utah basketball, and then made sure I was warm and well-fed when I visited there.

Wayne Carver – former editor of the *Carleton Miscellany,* author of *A Child's Christmas in Utah,* and the man who simply *was* American literature for so many Carleton students for so many years – continues to teach me about the West over the copy machine, in the halls of Laird, or in conversations after readings on campus. He may remember giving me a paper placemat from the Outlaw Inn in Rock Springs, Wyoming (Restaurant, Saloon, Pool, and Drive-In Liquor Store) – with potted biographies of Cattle Kate, Poker Alice, and Big Nose George Parrotti – during my first year at Carleton. He helped me understand that I wasn't in Princeton anymore.

As always, Cathy Kowalewski (along with Nicholas and Sarah) underwent this book with me, and she, more than anyone else, understands its true genesis over the years: at Acoma Pueblo, on top of Mt. Lassen, at the Ashland Shakespeare festival, or camping in Montana and South Dakota. I can't imagine the West (or anything else) without her.

INTRODUCTION

MICHAEL KOWALEWSKI

What images or associations come to mind when one thinks today of the American West? Pearl-buttoned shirts? Wagon-wheel light fixtures? Neon-rainbow casinos? Red-rock desert? Nuclear test ranges? John Wayne tall in the saddle? Kevin Costner in feathers? A mountain ski-lift? A clear-cut hillside? Four-wheel-drive Border Patrol vehicles? A brigade of RVs in Yellowstone? Devil's Tower? Anasazi ruins? The Houston Astrodome? The Hollywood Bowl? A Russell Chatham painting? Mt. Rushmore? The Golden Gate? A Great Basin ghost town? A Seattle microbrewery? The Utah Jazz? Clearly, no one image – nor even one clump of images – can adequately characterize a region whose geographic and cultural features are so richly bewildering in their contradictory variety.

One image I would throw in the mix is a photograph by Richard Olsenius that accompanied a 1993 article on "Wide Open Wyoming" in *National Geographic*. The picture is a full-page photograph in a series of shots chronicling rancher Bob Britain's eight-day trek, with a flock of 300 sheep, to his winter range near Muddy Creek. It is January and shortly after the drive ended, twenty ewes died while lambing, forcing Britain to shelter the motherless orphans in his camp trailer. The photo shows Britain struggling to put a disposable diaper on a young lamb to help control the mess. A half-dozen lambs mill at his feet in the crowded camper, their back halves swaddled in baggy diapers held on with velcro strips. "They stank," Britain says, "but not as bad as a baby's." This image brings to mind one Louise Erdrich remembers in writing about her female forebears on the Turtle Mountain Indian reservation in North Dakota.

A portion of this introduction appeared first in *American Literary History* 6, No. 1 (Spring 1994): 171–83.

As if in another time and place, although it is only the dim barrel of a four-year-old's memory, I see myself lying wrapped under smoky quilts and dank green army blankets in the house in which my mother was born. . . . my grandmother Mary LeFavor, kept that house of hand-hewed and stacked beams, mudded between. She managed to shore it up and keep it standing by stuffing every new crack with disposable diapers. Having used and reused cloth to diaper her own children, my grandmother washed and hung to dry the paper and plastic diapers that her granddaughters bought for her great-grandchildren. When their plastic-paper shredded, she gathered them carefully together and one day, on a summer visit, I woke early to find her tamping the rolled stuff carefully into the cracked walls of that old house.

I cite these two images not to suggest a new thematic category in western criticism called "Diapers West," but because this most homely of domestic implements reflects pertinently on both the traditional and the new, revisionist visions of the West. One important way in which historians have been reinterpreting western history is by altering a paradigm of single-handed masculine conquest and resistance and emphasizing the neglected domestic elements of family and community. "At the heart of American western history," Kathleen Neils Conzen says in *The Oxford History of the American West* (1994), lies "a family story," one marked by the "insistent themes of family, kinship, and community," one that focuses not solely on saloons, dance halls, and poker games, but on "wives working alongside husbands to erect a log cabin, warriors setting their hands to the plow, children trudging to a one-room schoolhouse, a community building a church." As Shannon Applegate, Susan Rosowski, and Margaret García Davidson all suggest in this volume, many of the most engaging images of western literature have to do with families – families of all nationalities – involved in unheroic but sustaining domestic rituals like recycling a diaper as insulation or keeping newly born lambs alive in a trailer.

The refreshing part of seeing a grizzled ranch hand in muddy Levis diapering lambs, of course, is that it seems so incongruous with the more potent images in the popular iconography of the West. "Take 'em to Missouri, Matt," crusty Tom Dunson (John Wayne) yells in Howard Hawks' *Red River* (1948). The orchestral music swells, the dust rises, the adrenaline starts to pump, and that classic sequence from how many cattle-drive westerns begins, with cowboys yelling "Hee yaa. Hee yaa. Whoopee. Yahoo. Yaa Yaa," as they ride herd and head for open range. The visceral power of this kind of moment has been relentlessly parodied, yet it never quite loses its power. A black dentist on a dude ranch in the film *City Slickers* (1991) mentions this scene from *Red River*, calling it the "Yeehah scene." Yet no sooner have the self-conscious greenhorns he addresses laughed about the absurdity of their playing out this aspect of the legendary West, then they too gallop off, in a slow-motion salute to Hollywood's horse operas. (The tribute to a different kind of western, from the Clint Eastwood era, is there as well in this film in some of the squint-eyed, leatherneck dialogue we hear from Jack Palance. "Hi Curly, kill anyone today?" Billy Crystal asks Palance with a jaunty sarcasm meant to render the suggestion unlikely. "Day ain't over yet," Curly remarks with genial malice as he sharpens his knife.)

The extraordinary resilience of popular visions of the West, the majority of them perpetuated by movie westerns, should not be underestimated. The phenomenal success of the eight-hour 1989 television mini-series of Larry McMurtry's *Lonesome Dove* was a textbook example in this regard. Though McMurtry refused to glorify the West, stressing an antiheroic trail-drive full of snakebite and personal grievances, his antimythic efforts served only to reinforce the legendary aspects of the film. The more credible his characters were, the more they seemed larger than life. *Lonesome Dove* was an anti-western that was heroic in spite of itself, "a kind of *Iliad* for losers," as one reviewer put it.

"Now and then I used to put on my armor and break a lance against the windmill of the cowboy myth that dominated not only much Western writing, but almost all outside judgment of Western writing," Wallace Stegner said in accepting a PEN Center West award in 1990 for lifetime achievement. "As a writer from the West, I had already discovered how it felt to be misinterpreted. Even well-intentioned people who wanted to praise me often saw in me, or expected from me, things that I was not prepared to deliver, and misread things that I *was* prepared to deliver. . . . We rode under the shadow of the big hat. As they used to say of Ronald Reagan, we were big hat, no cows. Nothing could convince them in New York or Massachusetts that there was anything of literary interest in the West except cowboys."

Times have changed. In the past decade and a half, writers of all stripes in the American West have finally begun to receive some of the national acclaim they have been unjustly denied for far too long. No longer – or perhaps, more rarely – do western writers encounter responses like the rejection note Norman Maclean received from one publisher who turned down his manuscript for *A River Runs Through It* (1976). These stories, the note complained, "have trees in them."

The remarkable popularity of Tony Hillerman's fiction, the critical acclaim and bestseller status of Cormac McCarthy's western work, and the surprising success of small-press works like Larry Watson's *Montana 1948* (1993) – to say nothing of popular, critically touted films such as *The Milagro Bean Field War* (1988), *A River Runs Through It* (1992), and *Unforgiven* (1992) – would itself be enough to suggest a continuing popular fascination with western characters and landscapes. Classes in western literature now routinely include books with a sizable following of appreciative readers: Lewis and Clark's journals; Mark Twain's *Roughing It* (1872); Frank Norris' *The Octopus* (1901); Owen Wister's *The Virginian* (1902); John Steinbeck's *The Grapes of Wrath* (1939); A. B. Guthrie, Jr.'s *The Big Sky* (1947; voted the best novel of the American West in a 1991 survey in *North Dakota Review*); Mary Austin's *The Land of Little Rain* (1903); Frank Waters' *The Man Who Killed the Deer* (1947); John Muir, Willa Cather, and Raymond Carver's work; Wallace Stegner's *Angle of Repose* (1971); M. Scott Momaday's *House Made of Dawn* (1968); Robinson Jeffers, Gary Snyder, and William Stafford's poetry; Jean Stafford's *The Mountain Lion* (1947); Larry McMurtry's *The Last Picture Show* (1966); Edward Abbey's *The Monkey-Wrench Gang* (1975); and Leslie Marmon Silko's *Ceremony* (1977).

These works are now also frequently joined on course syllabi by such novels as Marilynne Robinson's *Housekeeping* (1980), Maxine Hong Kingston's *Tripmaster Monkey* (1989), Rudolfo Anaya's *Bless Me, Ultima* (1972), or Sherman Alexie's *The Lone Ranger and Tonto Fistfight in Heaven* (1993); by fictional and nonfictional works by Victor Villaseñor, Ivan Doig, William Kittredge, Gretel Ehrlich, Richard Ford, Arturo Islas, Louise Erdrich, James Welch, Sandra Cisneros, Barbara Kingsolver, Frank Chin, Gerald Vizenor, Thomas McGuane, and Ursula K. Leguin; by the poetry of Garrett Hongo, Cathy Song, Gary Soto, John Haines, Wendy Rose, and Sharon Doubiago; by the drama of Sam Shepard, Luis Valdez, and David Henry Hwang; and by the work of a burgeoning corps of talented western nature writers (many of whom dislike the term "nature writer"): Barry Lopez, David Rains Wallace, Terry Tempest Williams, Gary Nabhan, Linda Hasselstrom, John Daniel, Rick Bass, Richard K. Nelson, and Ann Zwinger. This is but the most abbreviated of lists, and the fact that some will immediately tote up the authors or works I have not mentioned simply underscores the vertiginous complexity and depth of western American writing.

Another kind of revealing example also jumps to mind. *A Literary History of the American West* was published in 1987, and weighed in at 1,353 pages. That was one hundred pages longer than the *Columbia Literary History of the United States* (1988), a work which barely acknowledged the existence of western writing. As several western states have celebrated their centennials in the late 1980s and the 1990s, literary anthologies such as *The Last Best Place: A Montana Anthology* (1988) remind us that much of this country's most vital and challenging writing continues to emerge from places like Denver, Seattle, Salt Lake City, El Paso, and Missoula.

Important new critical studies such as A. Carl Bredahl's *New Ground: Western American Narrative and the Literary Canon* (1989); William Bevis' *Ten Tough Trips: Montana Writers and the West* (1990); Harold P. Simonson's *Writers, Western Regionalism and a Sense of Place* (1989); Stegner's *Where the Bluebird Sings to the Lemonade Springs: Living and Writing in the West* (1992); Vera Norwood and Janice Monk's volume, *The Desert Is No Lady: Southwestern Landscapes in Women's Writing and Art* (1987); and Leonard Engel's collection of essays, *The Big Empty: Essays on Western Landscapes as Narrative* (1994); along with new studies of multiethnic western writing by Genaro Padilla, Stephen Sumida, Cecil Robinson, Kenneth Lincoln, Louis Owens, Ramón Saldívar, Greg Sarris, and Amy Ling, and new investigations of environmental writing by Scott Slovic, James McClintock, and John P. O'Grady have all illuminated various dimensions of western American writing. (The bibliography to this volume amplifies this initial listing more fully.)

Yet despite this seeming embarrassment of riches, a fully informed criticism of western writing as a whole has remained fitful and infrequent. Many of these studies are not as well-known as they deserve to be, and if they are well-known, they often are so because they are thought of as studies of subjects other than western writing. The criticism of western writing one encounters in various places – literary quarterlies, critical journals, and middle-brow magazines – is of uneven quality and often lacks an innovative, inquiring spirit capable of matching that of the literature it considers. "The West doesn't need good writers," Stegner said in his PEN speech, "It has them. It could use a little more confidence in itself, and one way for that to come about is to breed some critics capable, by experience or intuition, of evaluating Western literature in the terms of western life. So far, I can't think of a critic who has read

Western books 'in the same spirit as its author writ.'" What Larry McMurtry said in 1968 about the adulation lavished upon the Big Three of Texas letters (Roy Bedichek, W. P. Webb, and J. Frank Dobie) is, unfortunately, too often still the case today: "they were paid every homage but the homage of acute attention. Such criticism as they got they probably got from one another, for during the years of their prime there was no reviewer in the state with either the guts or the insight to say them nay."

Reading the West seeks to extend the homage of acute attention. With essays by western novelists, naturalists, drama critics, and freelance writers, as well as academic critics like myself, this volume is meant to help establish a national awareness – among general readers as well as specialists – of just how rich, complicated, and rewarding the literature of the American West has been and continues to be. It also seeks to address some of the critical barriers which still keep such an investigation from taking place more readily than it should.

* * * * * *

Barry Lopez has used the term "false geographies" to refer to a congeries of romantic preconceptions by means of which the "essential wildness" and "almost incomprehensible depth and complexity" of the American landscape have been reduced to "attractive scenery." Many Americans, he says, now think about this country in terms of a "memorized landscape" (visually memorized before it has been actually experienced). It may seem unduly harsh to assert that mainstream literary criticism has similarly reduced the complexity of the American literary landscape – especially the literature of the American West – but this seems to be the case. At the very least, certain critical categories seem "memorized" ahead of time such that their premises frequently dictate many of their conclusions.

A lively new interest in recent years in the analytical categories of class, race, ethnicity, and gender has provided insight into the past lives and imaginations of Americans, especially those of blacks, women, and blue-collar workers. All of these categories bear importantly upon the study of western writing. To take only the example of class, one need look no further than Craig Lesley's introductory remarks to his fine new anthology, *Dreamers and Desperadoes: Contemporary Short Fiction of the American West* (1993). "The West I know contains working people living a hardscrabble existence and trying to stay ahead of the bills and banks," Lesley says. He was determined to make his anthology reflect that knowledge and to include stories about characters who are "tough, funny, and *union*." "Driving through the semi-arid high desert of the West," he notes,

> one sees weathered wooden gates along the backroads, marking the entrances to vast ranches. Usually, the ranches themselves are not visible from the highway, and one can see only the two dirt tracks winding to the distance. It's desolate country at first glance – sagebrush and scattered junipers, an occasional loping coyote. But there's beauty here, too, in the shadows and sunsets. The ranch's brand adorns the gate, and frequently it has another marker – a worn-out workboot nailed to a post, a testimony to hard work. In spring and summer these boots serve as vases, holding a variety of desert flowers that bloom after seasonal rains.

Lesley's dry-land realism and his finely honed sense that working-class lives are indelibly marked by the environment in which they take place are not, unfortunately, qualities that typically characterize literary criticism. The new critical diversity is often not quite diverse enough. Why has "region" been neglected as a critical category? The critical assumption seems to be that region or "a sense of place" is not an imaginative factor that can be internalized and struggled with in the same literarily rewarding ways that writers struggle with issues of race, class, and gender.

Though less charitable explanations are possible, region may be condescended to by critics or ignored as a category because many of them simply lack a vocabulary with which to ask engaging philosophical, psychological, or aesthetic questions about what it means to "dwell" in a place, whether actually or imaginatively. "We have the terms *enculturation* and *acculturation*," Gary Snyder notes, "but nothing to describe the process of becoming placed or re-placed." This despite the fact that cognitive scientists are now suggesting that memory itself cannot function without place, that we can have no awareness of past events in our lives without a sense of the place in which they happened. And despite the fact that one of the central impulses in American literature – one shared by Thoreau and Cather, Faulkner and Silko, Stevens and Didion, Hurston and Williams – has been to evoke what Frederick Turner (echoing D. H. Lawrence) calls a "spirit of place."

If critics cannot ask rewarding questions about the impalpable, subtly defined properties of "place," they often simply imply that such features are not actually influences at all. Many critics still seem to feel that landscape and nonhuman environments do not crucially influence writers or their characters. Writers can write, the implication seems to be, wherever they set their typewriters or their laptops. Their primary struggle in writing is not with landscape but with words. "I did not choose to be born in Lowell": the painter James Whistler's arch rejoinder might serve as an epigraph for much contemporary criticism, though perhaps some might prefer a line by Terry Malloy (Marlon Brando) in *On the Waterfront*. "I don't like the country," he says on the docks of Hoboken, "the crickets make me nervous."

An intimate connection between landscape and writing can sometimes, it is true, be more a wished-for condition than an actuality, and it is not always clear what kind of causal relationship can be established between the two. "Our country is so fluid for travel and access," William Stafford said in a 1993 *Paris Review* interview, "that a regional recognition is more a matter of convenience than it is any kind of valid movement." Yet he then went on, in thinking about the importance of natural sounds in his poetry, to mention precisely the kind of detail regional writers so often evoke: "there is a mossy, deadened sound here [in the Northwest]. So you listen more carefully: you're an owl. You don't have to put on earmuffs to keep from damaging your hearing. . . . We need to hear more, see more, smell more, feel more."

Not knowing what kind of link can be established between self and environment is clearly not the same as denying that there is nothing there to be known. Having self-doubts about the possibility of adequately defining regional identity is not the same as asserting that it does not exist. Yet you would never know this from much contemporary criticism, for finding region an important factor in literary studies is still often seen as the equivalent of being an overenthusiastic salesman with a special marketing territory. Regionalism, it seems, is often next to boosterism, a puffing of "merely" local talent – a kind of literary chamber of commerce juxtaposed to the three national congressional houses of race, class, and gender. (Criticism in this regard seems to take its cue from the literary marketplace, where being identified as a "regional writer" usually represents a kind of literary kiss-of-death, one that usually denotes small-press status and the chance for only local recognition. "Regional fiction at its best" is a blurb emblazoned on any number of remaindered novels.)

When certain works of western literature are taken seriously in the academy, they tend to be thought of in nonregional terms; they tend to be legitimized under the aegis of, say, Chicano Studies, Native American Studies, or, more broadly, Environmental Studies. Again, I do not mean to impugn the value or legitimacy of such areas of critical study. I would suggest, however, that one can fruitfully think, write about, and teach the literature of the West without reverting to these particular zoning restrictions. This collection of essays suggests that region and place can be seen, in history, as encompassing a far broader range of critical interests and issues than most individual critical perspectives usually include. Whether dealing with corporate capitalism, bicultural identity, competing conceptions of nature, or the role of genre, gender, and audience, these essays enrich our understanding of western texts by addressing them *in place*. Rather than championing a more abstract, free-floating conception of diversity, the contributors to *Reading the West* share a conviction that "deterritorializing" western writers can lead one to miss much of the vitality and complexity of their work.

* * * * * *

The critic Pierre Sansot suggests that instead of asking "what is the essence of a place?" we should substitute the question, "what can one dream about it?" That question seems especially appropriate in terms of the American West, whose varying landscapes (the Rocky Mountains and the Pacific Northwest, Monument Valley and Malibu) have continually inspired an imaginative projection of desire and freedom Wallace Stegner once lovingly termed "the geography of hope." That central metaphor for the region – the impetus for the westering impulse of eastern Americans – continues to retain its potency. But it is now also being complicated and reconceived as other cultural "directions" come into view.

Many writers of color have explored the implications (in the words of California playwright Luis Valdez) of "crossing the 'T'" when imagining the West. "The winning of the west," Valdez reminds us, "was the losing of the north." The ethnic and cultural complexity of the West cannot be fully imagined until the idea of a westward-moving frontier for people coming from the East can be seen as but one of a series of migrations that helped populate the region: from the west, south, and the north, as well as from the east. Likewise, reenvisioning the cultural variety of indigenous peoples already inhabiting areas that arriving immigrants thought of as empty and forsaken also allows a new vantage from which to evaluate western writing. The idea of the West changes significantly when we think of it as *el norte* or *el otro lado* (the other side) or, simply, as "home" or "the world" for tribes whose spiritual connections with their natural surroundings – through oral traditions, communal rituals, and everyday interactions – were long established before Europeans arrived and decided these tribes had been "discovered."

Estimates of the precontact Indian population north of the Rio Grande have recently been revised upwards from four million to twelve million. In California alone as many as 100 native languages were spoken when white explorers first arrived, 70 percent of them, Malcolm Margolin notes, "as mutually unintelligible as English and Chinese." That prodigious linguistic complexity was matched as well "by a great variety of customs, technologies, beliefs, and physical characteristics." Recognizing this kind of cultural diversity, along with the social and moral complexities of encounter and exchange on the American frontier, many historians and an increasing number of literary scholars have called for a newly conceived literary history that emphasizes multilingual, hybridized tropes and forms of intercultural communication. What is called for, in Annette Kolodny's words, is a new vision of a "liminal landscape of changing meanings on which distinct human cultures first encounter one another's 'otherness' and appropriate, accommodate, or domesticate it through language." This kind of study will be inherently interdisciplinary, she says, and it will call for "comparative cultural and literary analyses in which anthropology, geography, ecology, and literary history can work together in new ways." It will envision the frontier "as a multiplicity of ongoing first encounters over time and land," some of them "seriatim first encounters" in the same place, "rather than as a linear chronology of successive discoveries and discrete settlements."

I find this palimpsest of cultural trace elements and narrative designs an appealing model because it seems capable of suggesting some of the true complexity of the American West, which can no longer be definitively spoken of as a single entity. William Bevis, Philip Burnham, Misha Berson, and Margaret García Davidson's essays all address new ways of discussing the literature of a multiethnic West. They suggest not only the bicultural or even tricultural complexity of this literature, but also the ways in which certain critical models (like the paradigm of "cultural resistance" Davidson discusses) can actually limit rather than enlarge our understanding of certain literary traditions. A new multiracial, intercultural vision of the West will only be valuable insofar as it avoids exoticizing marginality and caricaturing so-called mainstream culture. Little will be served, the novelist Marilynne Robinson rightly notes, by a "new and improved version of the myth of settlement [which] has blond beasts with hegemony in their eyes indulging the appetites of conquest." "Grief, waste, shame – history. Americans act as though they should have been immune to these things," she says. "They also act as if they invented them."

The most fruitful recognition of cultural diversity in the West will be one that complicates our conception of both mainstream *and* marginal cultures – questioning along the way the usefulness of thinking about centers and margins in western writing rather than about interdependence, hybridity, and overlap. The principle that guides Fred Erisman's remarks about the confluence of geography and population in the Southwest might usefully hold true for every subregion of the West in this regard:

> It is here that one finds the sweeping landscapes that the cinema has trained us to think of as "western" – the deserts and cacti of Arizona, the volcanic monoliths of New Mexico and Utah. It is here that one finds the cultural mix tradi- tionally associated with "the West" – Anglo, Spanish, Native American. And it is here that one finds the mythic occupa- tions of "the West" – the vast cattle ranches of the Old West, the Texas oil developments, and the burgeoning cities of the New. Yet one finds other elements as well: the forests and farms of east Texas cannot be denied; the Mormons of Utah are as much a part of the region as the Catholics of New Mexico; the Germans of the Texas Hill Country must be con- sidered alongside the Native American tribes of Oklahoma.

One could do worse, in searching for new ways of imagining a cultural hospitality capable of entertaining multiple viewpoints of western writing, than look to the communal storytelling of New Mexico's Pueblo Indians. "Implicit in the Pueblo oral tra- dition," Leslie Marmon Silko says, "was the awareness that loyalties, grudges, and kinship must always influence the narrator's choices as she emphasizes to listeners [that] this is the way *she* has always heard the story told. The ancient Pueblo people sought a commu- nal truth, not an absolute. For them this truth lived somewhere within the web of differing versions, disputes over minor points, outright contradictions tangling with old feuds and village rival- ries." It seems appropriate that this kind of model for cultural interaction springs from an animistic sense of consciousness with- in, not outside or separate from, nonhuman forms of life, because it mirrors the new emphasis upon "deep maps" (to borrow William Least Heat-Moon's term) in so much environmental writing in the West.

This new writing exemplifies richly textured understandings of human interaction with the land and with other life-forms and it emphasizes an awareness of "place" as a living force in human identity. "The *depth* of a wilderness interests me far more than its height," David Rains Wallace avers in his classic study of wilderness, myth, and evolution, *The Klamath Knot* (1983). Illuminating the complex ecology of local environments and the way those environments have affected the life of those inhabiting them, these new writers often superimpose the temporal depth of history and human development on the spatial depth of particular ecosystems to create a kind of fourth dimension in which "deep" descriptions of local ecology become depth soundings into the origins of spirit and consciousness.

Though it has received less national attention than multiculturalism, the newly revived interest in nature writing may well be the most exciting development in the study of western American literature. Nature writing is not, of course, restricted to works about the West. But it is no accident that ASLE, the Association for Study of Literature and Environment (an organization that attracted more than 500 members in less than two years) originated in an open forum at the 1992 Western Literature Association conference in Reno.

Landscapes that to the untutored eye look, in Jim Garry's words, like "mile after mile of nothing but mile after mile," have long played an integral part in the literary imagination of the West. Western landscape was typically seen by arriving European settlers as both awe-inspiring and unforgiving. Though often admired for its rich mineral wealth and for its supposed capacity to restore good health, the West was also seen as in need of "reclamation" by mammoth irrigation and engineering projects and by devastating extractive industries. Peter Wild and David Rains Wallace's essays trace some of the multiple elements – social, political, scientific, and aesthetic – that have shaped western nature writing and that have increasingly inspired closer, more attentive accounts of natural environments in the West. Examining what might be called the "history of nature," both ancient and recent, Wild and Wallace use the insights of recent environmental thinking to emphasize the complex interconnections between societal beliefs and biophysical processes.

The form as well as the content of western writing has attracted new attention, and *Reading the West* is meant to reflect an increasingly sophisticated sense of the generic diversity of western literature. Shannon Applegate's essay, and my own, focus on nonfictional western works: letters, diaries, and travel books. Misha Berson considers contemporary Asian American drama in the West, while

Linda Hamalian focuses on the different facets of western poetry in the form of the San Francisco Renaissance. No longer should the novel (or even fiction more generally) overshadow other literary forms when one assesses the accomplishments of western writing. The essays in this volume fully demonstrate that western writers have attempted to absorb, celebrate, or satirize the West's landscapes and its cultural heterogeneity in all literary genres, not just in fiction.

The ability to read across cultural boundaries or across the disciplinary boundaries of science, history, literature, and art may, as Kolodny suggests, prompt a reconsideration of what constitutes "literariness" in western writing and what distinguishes it from the solely historical or ethnographical. This seems to me an intriguing challenge but not one that will automatically result, as some exponents seem to feel, in a quick dismissal of a traditional "canon" of western texts. As Tom Lyon suggests in his essay, serious or "literary" westerns were engaged in historical revisionism long before the term became popular. Even the formula writing about the West (first mass-produced by Erastus Beadle's New York dime-novel scribes at the impossible rate of one thousand words per hour in twelve-hour shifts), which has convinced so many that the West consists only of crooked sheriffs, schoolmarms, and stone-jawed plainsmen, has been read with fresh critical eyes. Scholars like Forrest G. Robinson, Christine Bold, Jane Tompkins, and Robert Murray Davis have variously illuminated our views of the formula western, and Lee Mitchell, who has done the same elsewhere, turns his attention in this volume to the surprisingly complicated narrative logic of melodrama in Bret Harte's fiction and Albert Bierstadt's painting.

* * * * * *

Another unduly restrictive idea the essays in this collection implicitly challenge is the notion that western literature is restricted to rural landscapes. (This is an idea inherited from a late nineteenth-century conception of "local color," which conceived of regional writers as provincials writing at a remove from the centers of commerce and culture.) No longer must we claim that when we are discussing western writers we are *really* talking about Ivan Doig and Louise Erdrich and Willa Cather, not Raymond Chandler or Ishmael Reed: that what we are discussing are writers close to unpaved roads and open prairie, not freeways, malls, gangs, and swimming pools.

The distinction here is not between a new technologized West and an older rural region and it is not a question of saying Chandler and Reed are somehow "better" than Cather and Doig – it is possible to like all these writers equally, though for quite different reasons. What is at issue are habits of perception and categorization that prevent us from seeing how rich and varied western writing actually is. We should be careful, David Simpson reminds us, about seeing country life as consisting of comfortable localities where "there has never been any migration within the rural economy itself, as if coming and going were simply the result of some avoidable metropolitan contagion." James D. Houston's essay recognizes as much, for although he shows that the literature of California has been profoundly influenced by the presence of the state's natural landscape, he also suggests that it reflects the fact that California, like many other areas of the West, has become an increasingly urbanized realm.

There is no denying that much western writing retains and continues to celebrate what Gretel Ehrlich calls "a landbound sense of place." A firm sense of orientation and rooted identity are prominent in much western literature: John Muir in the Sierras, Mary Austin in the Mojave desert, Mari Sandoz in the Nebraska panhandle, Ehrlich herself in Wyoming. Gary Snyder suggests the term "bioregionalism" to describe a kind of writing and thinking which defines a region using biotic and pre-white boundaries and markings rather than recently imposed artificial political boundaries. Bioregional writers are less concerned with human oddities than with the biological qualities of a place; they define their territory in terms of watersheds and habitats rather than city limits and waterslides.

Yet as important as this emphasis upon rural rootedness and proximity to the land is in relation to western literature, it cannot exclusively define that writing. If one imagines the West in ecological terms, Stegner argues, one sees primarily arid country. Dry space, not rooted place, is the region's determining factor. Aridity enforces space – limited amounts of water support fewer numbers of people, who have to spread out – and space enforces mobility. "The principal invention of western American culture," Stegner says in *The American West as Living Space* (1987), "is the motel, the principal exhibit of that culture the automotive roadside. The principal western industry is tourism, which is not only mobile but seasonal. Whatever it might want to be the West is primarily a series of brief visitations or a trail to somewhere else; and western literature, from *Roughing It* to *On the Road*, from *The Log of a Cowboy* to

Lonesome Dove, from *The Big Rock Candy Mountain* to *The Big Sky*, has been largely a literature not of place but of motion." One might propose any number of counterexamples to Stegner's assertion here (especially by women writers in the West, who were often denied the chance to roam and explore), but his point is well taken. The West, Stegner contends, is still badly in need of a "society to match the scenery."

A lingering defensiveness about this situation among western writers and critics can be seen in the "outpost mentality" that still occasionally surfaces in criticism. When James M. Cox wrote an essay for the *Columbia Literary History of the United States* entitled "Regionalism: A Diminished Thing," it became fashionable at meetings of the Western Literature Association to publicly denounce the essay and start sounding like the Virginian. One keynote speaker (James Maguire) took the lack of western writers listed in the *Columbia Literary History* as an insult to the entire region. "Just remember," he proclaimed, "you may . . . find it difficult to persuade more than fifty million Westerners if your preconceptions and new histories say that the region we inhabit does not exist. When you call us nonexistent, partners, smile!"

I admire the feistiness of this defense, especially its evocation of fifty million western readers arising, with a copy of *O Pioneers!* in hand, to redress a cultural slight. It *is* important to remember that many western writers (and critics) have good reason to feel touchy about such matters. Critical and editorial practices which constantly suggest there is no "there" there in the West are often rightly taken by westerners as instances of insensitivity, eastern bias, and cultural chauvinism. In the opinion of a nameless customer in a Strong City, Kansas, café in William Least Heat-Moon's *PrairyErth* (1991), even those who allege an interest in the West are suspect. The Strong City resident has no patience with a visiting history professor in Hush Puppies from Back East: "Couldn't tell a sycamore from a cottonwood, hadn't the least idea of what kind of tree to cut a wagon axle out of. He wasn't exactly sure what an ox is. He didn't know how to make hominy, hadn't ever skinned a squirrel or milked a cow – and he got paid fifty thousand a year to tell college kids about the West."

However appealing this kind of combativeness may be on occasion, critics feeling thus embattled run the danger of letting serious criticism degenerate into a sparring match with caricatures. They might be better served by taking Edward Abbey's epitaph as a bemused reflection on western letters. He was buried by his wife and friends in a secret ceremony in an unidentified Southwestern canyon, and Abbey's grave is reportedly marked by a chiseled inscription that reads:

EDWARD PAUL ABBEY

1927–1989

NO COMMENT

(Charles Bowden followed up on this sentiment by dedicating his western travel narrative, *Desierto: Memories of the Future* [1991] with the following epigraph: "Edward Abbey/ R.I.P./ But I doubt it.") Western writers and critics might also turn for solace to Marilynne Robinson's brilliant redaction of what others, from elsewhere, have often found recalcitrant or annoying in western life and letters:

> fecklessness of a kind is built into the Western personality, as a form of moral and physical courage. It is a nod to human frailty, without which, after all, courage would be meaningless. And it is the sign and seal of a kind of orneriness that recognizes in self-interest yet another form of coercion. . . . [westerners] are descended from self-exiled people, who dealt with their quarrels with society by walking away from them. So they are less inclined than others to look to society for guidance or remedy. . . . They are of all people most likely to know things to which aesthetic pleasures attach, things to do with geology, astronomy, the ways of animals. Southerners are unsurpassed for humor and anecdote, but Westerners beat anyone at the remarkable, and they own the style of serious pleasure in which they confide it.

The challenge *Reading the West* seeks to meet is twofold: how can literary criticism propose new ways of exploring the true complexity and range of western writing while still remaining true to its style of "serious pleasure"? Any truly candid evaluation of western culture and writing will have to describe both ancient forests and missile silos, both indigenous folk art and the tourist emporiums that merchandize it. It will emphasize not only multicultural diversity and pride but cultural estrangement and aimless drifting as well. It will, in other words, need to include the volatile and exploitative elements of western life as well as the lyrical and sustaining ones. That these tensions and contradictions seem abiding and unresolvable in the West simply means that they will continue to provide a germinal ground for literature.

Whether attempting to fashion marveling accounts of the out-of-scale western landscape or simply trying to keep one's bearing in places devoid of familiar cultural orientations, the search for a vantage and style commensurate with western subject matter continues to pose challenges and difficulties for western writers that are distinctly different from those faced by writers in other areas of the country. Reinvigorating the importance of "place" in literary studies and helping to define and enrich our sense of western regional identity and expression will not, it is hoped, lead to defensiveness or isolation, for as William Kittredge says, "we begin to die of pointlessness when we are isolated." What such a new perspective can lead to is a richer, morally complex understanding of our national literature, one that leads to what Kittredge says we all need most: "What we need most urgently, both in the West and all over America, is a fresh dream of who we are that will tell us how we should act, . . . We want the story of our society to have a sensible plot. We want it to go somewhere; we want it to mean something. We must define some stories about taking care of what we've got, . . . stories about making use of the place where we live without ruining it, stories that tell us to stay humane amid our confusions."

Works Cited

Abbey, Edward. "Epitaph." Qtd. in Charles E. Little. "Books for the Wilderness." *Wilderness* (Summer 1994), 34–35.

Abercrombie, Thomas J. "Wide Open Wyoming." *National Geographic* (January 1993), 54–79.

Bowden, Charles. *Desierto: Memories of the Future.* New York: Norton, 1991.

Conzen, Kathleen Neils. "A Saga of Families." In *The Oxford History of the American West.* New York: Oxford UP, 1994, 315–57.

Ehrlich, Gretel. *The Solace of Open Spaces.* New York: Penguin, 1985.

Erdrich, Louise. "The Names of Women." *Granta,* 41 (Autumn 1992), 132–38.

Erisman, Fred. "The Changing Face of Western Literary Regionalism." In *The Twentieth-Century West: Historical Interpretations.* Eds. Gerald D. Nash and Richard W. Etulain. Albuquerque: U of New Mexico P, 1989, 361–81.

Garry, Jim. *This Ol' Drought Ain't Broke Us Yet (But We're All Bent Pretty Bad): Stories of the American West.* New York: Orion Books, 1992.

Heat-Moon, William Least. *PrairyErth: A Deep Map.* New York: Houghton Mifflin, 1991.

Kittredge, William. "Doing Good Work Together." In *The True Subject: Writers on Life and Craft.* Ed. Kurt Brown. St. Paul, MN: Graywolf P, 1993, 52–58.

Kolodny, Annette. "Letting Go Our Grand Obsessions: Notes Toward a New Literary History of the American Frontiers." *American Literature*, 64, No. 1 (March 1992): 1–18.

Leonard, John. "Plains Fare." Rev. of *Lonesome Dove. New York*, February 6, 1989, p. 86.

Lesley, Craig. "Introduction." *Dreamers and Desperadoes: Contemporary Short Fiction of the American West.* New York: Laurel, 1993, 1–7.

Lopez, Barry. "The American Geographies." In *Finding Home: Writing on Nature and Culture from Orion Magazine.* Ed. Peter Sauer. Boston: Beacon P, 1992, 116–32.

Maclean, Norman. *A River Runs Through It and Other Stories.* Chicago: U of Chicago P, 1976.

McMurtry, Larry. "Southwestern Literature?" In *In a Narrow Grave: Essays on Texas.* 1968. Rpt. New York: Simon & Schuster, 1989, 31–54.

Maguire, James H. "The Canon and 'The Diminished Thing.'" *American Literature*, 60, No. 4 (December 1988): 643–52.

Margolin, Malcolm. "Introduction." *The Way We Lived: California Indian Stories, Songs, and Reminiscences.* Berkeley: Heyday Books, 1993, 1–9.

Robinson, Marilynne. "Hearing Silence: Western Myth Reconsidered." In *The True Subject: Writers on Life and Craft.* Ed. Kurt Brown. St. Paul, MN: Graywolf P, 1993, 135–51.

Sansot, Pierre. Qtd. in Gerald Kennedy. "Place, Self, and Writing." *Southern Review* 26 (1990): 496–516.

Silko, Leslie Marmon. "Landscape, History, and the Pueblo Imagination." In *On Nature: Nature, Landscape and Natural History.* Ed. Daniel Halpern. San Francisco: North Point P, 1986, 83–94.

Simpson, David. "Literary Criticism, Localism, and Local Knowledge." *Raritan*, 14, No. 1 (Summer 1994): 70–88.

Snyder, Gary. *The Practice of the Wild.* San Francisco: North Point P, 1990.

Stafford, William. "The Art of Poetry." (Interview) *Paris Review*, 129 (Winter 1993): 51–78.

Stegner, Wallace. *The American West as Living Space.* Ann Arbor: U of Michigan P, 1987.

———. "The New Literary Frontier." *San Francisco Examiner*, August 5, 1990, E1, E4.

Turner, Frederick. *Spirit of Place: The Making of an American Literary Landscape.* San Francisco: Sierra Club Books, 1989.

Valdez, Luis. "Envisioning California." *California History* 68, No. 4 (Winter 1989/90): 162–71.

Wallace, David Rains. *The Klamath Knot: Explorations in Myth and Evolution.* San Francisco: Sierra Club Books, 1983.

NATURE AND PLACE
IN WESTERN WRITING

REGION, POWER, PLACE

WILLIAM W. BEVIS

"Place" and "region" permeate western literature, from James Fenimore Cooper's *The Prairie* in 1825 to Mary Austin's *The Land of Little Rain* (1903) to Ivan Doig's *This House of Sky* (1978), subtitled "Landscapes of a Western Mind." Yet, says current wisdom, does not modern civilization render all talk of place obsolete? Could not Montana be astrodomed, and so become a different place entirely? Even before postmodern theory (itself aggressively urban) dislocated voices while paradoxically arguing for pluralism, the presence of "place" often seemed an embarrassment to western literature in particular and to "regionalism" in general.

Why did the "regional," a "sense of place," come to seem hopelessly nostalgic? Because, as Octavio Paz says, all cultures are "condemned to modernity"? One then wonders, does not modernity have a culture or a place? Perhaps this is simply a question of power: "provincial" means "marginal." But if that is the case, we may not infer the cultural inferiority of a "region." Why, then, should the term "regional" seem derogatory in literature, unless one wishes to speak from the point of view of the center of power and indeed serve that status quo? These are the questions I would like to address in a reconsideration of the literature of Montana and the American West. The questions will lead us to challenge the terms in which the debate has been conceived. Just as the emphasis on place once seemed nostalgic and agrarian, so the current erasure of place seems to me capitalist and modern – in that sense of the modern rooted in the Renaissance and blooming in the eighteenth century.

I will argue that capitalist modernity seeks to create a kind of no-place center, compared to which all "places" or "regions" are marginal. The no-place of capitalist modernity is a kind of culture, and we will call its dominant trait "liquidity." Two huge and unrelated movements, both prominent in western American literature, have been resisting the culture of liquidity.

The first counter-liquidity movement is ecological. Buckminster Fuller's "spaceship earth" spelled the end of liquidity: the biosphere cannot be exchanged, since nothing else is equivalent to it, nor can local places, since each ecosystem is unique. Suddenly the bottom line again becomes "place." This kind of limitation to our choices has a long history beyond the hundredth meridian, as I argued in *Ten Tough Trips: Montana Writers and the West* (1990); call it "dry land realism," from Cooper to the present.

The second counter-liquidity movement I will call tribalism. Since liquidity (capitalist and socialist) cannot confer identity, we are seeing – for better or worse – a worldwide resurgence of regionalism, nationalism, and ethnic identification. These movements, which I am loosely calling "tribal," have been explored and predicted by Native American literature of the West. To sketch the outline of tribal resistance to liquidity, I will focus on the work of D'Arcy McNickle, a Native American author of two novels from the thirties and the seventies, who had a remarkably balanced knowledge of both the white and native worlds.

The stakes are higher, however, than the above implies, for this essay does not constitute an attack from the left on the center of capitalism. Liquidity defines the left as well as the right, suggesting not only commodification of material assets, but abstraction, variety, mobility – in short, freedom. Conversely, "place," tribe, identity – all suggest fate. The Enlightenment seeks to erase place, and free us all. In this paradigm, most postmodern critics are themselves speaking from within liquidity, from within a bias towards freethinking, mobility, and variety. Therefore I will also be arguing that Native American and third-world critiques of modernism, along with the implications of ecology, are often profoundly "other" to our Enlightenment modernity in ways that new leftists and postmoderns are not.

Finally, I will suggest that some contemporary western literature, such as memoirs by William Kittredge and Mary Clearman Blew, can be seen as a kind of "mixed blood" examination of a troubling double heritage: liquidity versus identity.

The prejudice against "place" issues from modernist tradition and expresses it; the time is ripe to redefine terms, to identify the modern culture of the center – "liquidity" – to look at the inherent subversiveness of the "regional," and to ask again who owns the future.

* * * * * *

There are good reasons for our current prejudice against "place" and against critical attention to place. Regionalism and the idea of the uniqueness of place share a rich, escapist history in an American pastoral/agrarian tradition. The country place, say Maine or Vermont, is attractive, quaint, relaxing, because of its distance from power and from the present time of power; being impotent, it is unthreatening and easy to love. And just as we call Vermont, Maine, or Montana "places" or regions partly because of their absence from power and time, so the World Bank calls such places "underdeveloped nations"; they are then "doomed to modernity," but the hand of doom is not the hand of God.

Conversely, the seat of power aspires to be a no-place: neither quaint, since it lives in the present, nor charming, since it has no distance from reality. The idea that the center of power is a no-place has its own rich traditions in liberalism (the law is no respecter of places), progressive capitalism, and modernism. Let us begin our ruminations here, with the marginality of place and the supposed neutrality of power.

The U.S. National Public Radio on October 14, 1991, carried an interview with an Indian leader in a remote part of the Amazon threatened by development. He was concerned with his place in tribal history. He said he wanted to be remembered for a hundred years, he wanted his words remembered, and then he said: "We will never be white, or join with whites, or drink their alcohol, and we will keep this land which is our blood."

That spirit of Crazy Horse, a spirit willing to go down in flames to keep an identity of place and tribe, made me think of another respected tribal elder, my father, who during the Depression got a scholarship and left the Bevis tribe on the Tennessee frontier to try his luck in a classroom at the Harvard Business School. The first time he raised his hand and spoke, the professor interrupted him: "Mister Bevis, when you learn to speak without that accent, you may enter our discussion." My father loosed no arrows, shot no blow-gun darts. They were all in that classroom for the same reason, to make money, and money had no accent. A month later he raised his hand again; the professor noticed and called on him right away. The drawl was gone.

My father was as tough in his way as the Amazon Indian or the Sioux Crazy Horse, but clearly he served some opposite ideal; if the two Indian leaders were rock solid in their identity, my father was equally devoted to assimilation. This was never felt by him as treachery to Tennessee, or abandonment of drawling kinsmen, nor would it be fair to say that he was willing to change anything to pursue self-interest. Assimilation, after all, *is* our tribal identity: my father was surrounded by a nation of people – especially in 1931 – who had left their places, changed their languages, lost their accents, in order to start over, and get ahead.

So what accent would they learn? Where would they live in this brave new world of industrial wealth? In important ways, I believe, they were taught to think they would have no accent, and live nowhere. Indeed, my father had been taught at Harvard to become first a nobody, from nowhere, in order to make himself over and become somebody defined only by vocation. Another American Adam. In our culture, in marked contrast to most of the world, the ruling class aspires to a kind of neutrality: they would speak with no accent, and come from that not-region, the establishment, to which all unique regions are subordinate. This is very different from, say, the Han Chinese controlling China, or the Malays Malaysia, or the Hindus India, while retaining the specific language, traditions, and characteristics of a ruling class that is also a culture.

To put it another way, I remember the shock – followed immediately by delight – when first addressed as a WASP in Berkeley in 1963. I felt fenced in, like the cowboys in Charlie Russell's "End of the Open Range." Others had ethnic identity; I had been free. The usage of "ethnic" still perpetuates this myth, as if Emerson were not an ethnic writer. Again, this is a particularly American and quintessentially western version of freedom ("Don't ask where I'm from, mister"). Few Chinese, Malays, or Hindus of a ruling class would be shocked to be identified (fenced) as members of a bounded culture.

"Assimilation" is not a big enough word for what we do here in mainstream America, in this strange amalgam of eighteenth-century liberty, twentieth-century industrial capitalism, and radically modern freedom. Let us call it "liquidity."

When the head of General Motors says that if American workers price themselves out of the market, GM will move its operations elsewhere, one has to ask: what is an international manufacturing firm? It seems a money-making system remarkably divorced from family, tribe, nation, and place. It apparently serves nothing but profit. Now hear that not morally, as a pontification against greed, but anthropologically, as a description of an entire group of people willing to be divorced from their history, family, place. It is the liquidity, not the greed, that seems fascinating.

The basis of capitalism is liquidity. Things become "commodities" in reference to their potential value on the exchange. The medium of exchange is money; the more commodity/money units that can be put into circulation, the better. The natural tendency of capitalism is to liquify assets, and liquidity – abstracting things to equivalent units that can be exchanged – lies at the core of capitalism as a culture. We have traveled far in that direction from our early phases of manufacturing, to credit capitalism and leveraged buyouts.

By unfreezing assets, liquidity puts enormous markets into motion. Furthermore, this industrial-economic liquidity arose within the European democracies during the exfoliation of other kinds of liquidity: the ideals of liberty, liberal humanism, and progressive notions of the modern. "Capitalist democracy" seems to many a natural yoking, and usually implies more, a "modern industrial capitalist democracy" wed to "progress," as if economic liquidity were necessarily linked to political freedom, social mobility, and individualism. Contemporary observers from many points of view – Peter Drucker, John Lukacs, Christopher Lasch, Edward Said – feel the need to understand capitalist industrialism as a culture, modernity as an economics, and both as a politics; that is, to describe what seems to be a "first world" culture, above or beyond or permeating various national and local traditions, and vigorously exported.

And vigorously resisted, by much of the world, by Native Americans, and by "regions" in the literature of our West. Just what these various groups are resisting, however, and the terms of their resistance, have not been clear. One interesting man, a western Native American who went East, may help define the opposition between power and place. By 1936, D'Arcy McNickle apparently thought that liquidity – abstraction, exchange, market values – defined white culture.

* * * * * *

D'Arcy McNickle, the Métis-Irish man from St. Ignatius on the Salish-Kootenai (Flathead) reservation in Montana, and later a Bureau of Indian Affairs (BIA) administrator and a founder of the National Congress of American Indians and the Newberry Library in Chicago, saw clearly the irony of liberalism substituted for place and located tradition. In his novel *Wind from an Enemy Sky* (1978), written from the late thirties to the late seventies, he presented a rich white liberal, Adam Pell from upstate New York, a kind of Rockefeller figure based on George Heye. Pell is a museum owner and engineer who masterminds the building of a dam on the Flathead reservation to give the Indians an irrigation system, to make them farmers. Pell loves native peoples. He collects their artifacts.

The Indians think he has killed the water by imprisoning it; moreover, they have lost their sacred medicine bundle, Feather Boy, which has disappeared into the basement of Pell's museum in New York. Things are not going well; if only they could get Feather Boy back . . .

Pell is happy to oblige; unfortunately, the museum's curator was sloppy, and with all the water damage and the rats in the basement, there's not much left of Feather Boy. Pell arrives at St. Ignatius at the end of the book intending to give the Indians everything that liberalism can offer.

The construction of chapter twenty-nine is wonderfully apt. "Ordinarily, Adam Pell was intolerant of delay," we are told in the opening sentence. "Thus it was quite out of character for him to accept calmly the word that the Little Elk leaders were going to look for some horses before coming in for a meeting." He intends to adjust to Indian time. He not only means well; he has been reading the Little Elk history, he tells Rafferty, the local Indian agent, "the whole bloody documented history. And it mortified me to discover that I had been part of the fraud against these people. That dam in the mountains had its place in the pattern of exploitation promoted by government policy." Pell talks like a good man, a man who can learn, capable of radical insight – a man like us.

In a few minutes he is fuming about "the idea of the grid survey. . . . Settlement of the Great Plains was responsible for the monstrous custom of applying straight lines and right angles to the earth." Pell is practically quoting John Wesley Powell's 1877 report to Congress on the arid lands of the West – a touchstone for western liberals, revisionists through Wallace Stegner, and now, ecologists. In McNickle's book, the Indians' enemy is no redneck or loose-cannon colonel; Pell does not think nits make lice. The enemy is me, maybe you – McNickle's educated white readers. Pell stares at the fence-lines in the valley and correctly blames allotment as well as geometry; the parceling out of private land "makes him sick." They drive off, and having finished his considerable lecture on straight fence lines and white guilt, he tells the Indian driver, "Boy," to relate to the Little Elk leader his sentiments. "The Boy glanced sideways, trying to put together the feelings he had about the thin man, whose long legs were jackknifed between the front seat and the cowl. 'I tell him you gonna tear down fences.' The quick smile implied the joke." McNickle knows how liberalism works; he also, in one graceful sentence, has sketched in native humor, irony, and distrust.

It is the native driver "Boy" who turns the conversation to the reason for Pell's visit: "The people say what brought the bad times was when they lost the medicine bundle, Feather Boy bundle. They say it would be alright again, they wouldn't care about the fenced-up land and the hard times if they had Feather Boy." Pell "paled slightly."

A little later, with the local white elite – the doctor and his wife, the agent – Pell shows his hand; that is, what the victorious first world has to offer the overrun, studied, collected, and impoverished third. Pell opens the mysterious wooden chest he has brought on the train. He hopes to restore to these Indians "something of the world they knew" by giving them "a Peruvian piece, probably pre-Inca, possibly a thousand years old." A "gold statuette." "Gold" is used three times in a half page, the irony compounded by Pell's unconscious comparison of himself to conquistadors: "It is one of the relatively few larger pieces that the Spanish invaders failed to discover and melt down for bullion."

Pell seems oblivious that he has discovered the statue himself (he found it at Christie's in London), and is using it for exchange. At least the Spanish were liquifying material assets; Pell is melting down a culture – and thereby unwittingly defining his own, a liberal's cultural imperialism. The figure's value is established in the mind of the individual connoisseur/collector, as he explains to his astonished audience: "'It grows on you, just study it.' Adam's voice was a disembodied sound hanging in the air." McNickle knows exactly what he is doing. Liberalism is inseparable from abstraction ("a piece . . . study . . . disembodied . . . in the air") and individualism ("grows on you"). As Pell continues, it is clear that liberalism is inseparable also from capitalism: "I have to add that I prize this little piece above all the rare, even priceless, objects in my collection. And in that sense I suppose it might be comparable to the priceless thing they lost."

There it is: prizing by individual consumers – demand – sets price, things are comparable in relation to that abstraction, and paradoxically, the greatest value, "priceless," means, as we all know, very expensive, for in our culture everything has its price. The "artifact," Feather Boy, was the tribe's identity and power; for Pell, with the very best of Enlightenment intentions, their assets as well as his own are liquid: values are commodified while place is annihilated by structuralism. "I intend to tell them about the Indians of the Andes," Pell says to the stunned agent, Rafferty; "I hope they will understand the brotherhood." Columbus has landed again. All Indians – East Indies, West Indies – are one in relation to trade. Rafferty, no less white but a good deal more knowledgeable and cynical, says Pell is trying to "restore a lost world by a simple substitution of symbols."

Clearly the ground of McNickle's opposing of cultures extends far beyond conquest, or primitivism, or a narrowly Marxist "capitalism," or tribalism as a kind of communalism. Pell thinks of things in relation to other things and how they are comparable. "All thought is by analogy," as the white Alfred Whitehead said. The natives, according to native author McNickle and many others, think of things as unique in relation to other unique things. Things are incomparable, and therefore, cannot be exchanged. Their tribe, their bundle, their place ("we will keep this land which is our blood") – the Indians are regionalists. Pell has mobility, individual achievement, and freedom; the Indians have location, identity, and fate.

There may be, then, a kind of merit to the center's claim to neutrality. What kind of region is the center? In America, it is the region that denies place in favor of commodity. The center has liquified all its assets, so that it does live nowhere, or at least its "where" is interchangeable with any other where or can be traded up. McNickle's view of this center is fatalistic; liquidity has its virtues, but cannot be reconciled with traditional, located values. Thus his plot becomes tragic. What might interest us is that for McNickle and other third-world commentators, liquidity, embodied (or disembodied) in Pell, includes the Enlightenment virtues – individualism, reason, free-thinking, freedom – favored still by Anglo radicals, including neo-Marxists and postmodernists. Later we will return to McNickle versus the avant-garde in subversions of the center. First, however, let us establish that McNickle's story typifies Native American dissent.

I argued in *Ten Tough Trips* that a huge resistance to white mobility and assimilation characterizes Native American novels from McNickle to N. Scott Momaday, James Welch, Leslie Silko, and Louise Erdrich. The terms of that resistance defy both postmodernism and the Enlightenment.

American whites keep leaving home: *Moby-Dick*, *Portrait of a Lady*, *Huckleberry Finn*, *Sister Carrie*, *The Great Gatsby* – a considerable number of American "classics" tell of leaving home to find one's fate farther and farther away. The story we tell our children is of Huck Finn lighting out for the territories. A wealth of white tradition lies behind these plots, beginning with four centuries of colonial expansion.

Such "leaving" plots embody quite clearly the basic premise of success in our mobile society. The *individual* advances, sometimes at all cost, with little or no regard for family, society, past, or place. The individual is the ultimate reality; hence individual consciousness is the medium of knowledge, and "freedom" is a matter of distance between one's self and the smoke from another's chimney. Isolation is the poison in this world of movement, and romantic love seems to be its primary antidote. Movement, isolation, change, personal and forbidden knowledge, fresh beginnings: these are the ingredients of the American Adam, the man who would start from scratch. His is the story we tell and always in our ears is Huck Finn's strange derision: "I been there before."

In marked contrast, most Native American novels are not about going out, diverging, expanding, but about zooming in, converging, contracting. The hero comes home. "Contracting" has negative overtones for us, "expanding" a positive ring. These are the cultural habits we are considering. In Native American novels, coming home, staying put, contracting, even what we might call "regressing" to a place, a past where one has been before, is not only the primary story, it is a primary mode of knowledge and a primary good.

In McNickle's *The Surrounded* (1936), Archilde comes home from Portland, where he "can always get a job now any time" playing the fiddle in a "show house," to the Salish and Kootenai reservation. He has made it in the white world, and has come "to see my mother . . . in a few days I'm going again." From the very beginning, however, family ties, cultural ties, ties to place, and growing ties to a decidedly "reservation" (versus assimilated) girl are spun like webs to bind him down. He does not leave and finally is crushed by the white man's law. It seems to be a "tar baby" plot; Archilde takes one lick and then another at his own backward people, and suddenly he is stuck. At first, being assimilated into a white world, he had expected to remain mobile, thinking of "wherever he might be in times to come. Yes, wherever he might be." McNickle's repetition underscores the plot: whites leave, Indians come home.

Although whites would usually find in such a homing-as-failure plot either personal disaster or moral martyrdom, McNickle's point of view is more complex. His novel does not present Archilde as simply sucked into a depressing situation, although he certainly is; the novel applauds his return to Indian roots.

In McNickle's two novels, Momaday's *House Made of Dawn* (1968), Welch's *Winter in the Blood* (1974) and *The Death of Jim Loney* (1979), Silko's *Ceremony* (1977), and Erdrich's *Love Medicine* (1984), the "homing" plots present a tribal past as a gravity field stronger than individual will. These novels suggest that "identity" for a Native American is not a matter of finding "one's self," but of finding a "self" that is transpersonal. They depict Indian individuals coming home while white individuals leave, but also they suggest – variously and subtly and by degrees – a tribal rather than an individual definition of "being."

Henry Jim in *Wind* tries assimilation, which means being a free individual, by farming his own land and living in his own frame house: "The government man said it would be a good thing. He wanted the Indians to see what it is like to have a nice house like that. In those days I had the foolish thought that a man stands by himself, that his kinsmen are no part of him. . . . I didn't notice it at first, but one day I could see that I was alone. . . . Brothers, I was lonesome, sitting in my big house."

To white Americans, then, the individual is often the ultimate reality; therefore individual consciousness is the medium of knowledge, and our "freedom" can be hard to distinguish from isolation. In contrast, Native Americans value a "transpersonal self" and this transpersonal self composed of society, past, and place confers identity and defines "being." That an individual exists is not contested, and Native American life and novels present all the variety of personality expected in our species, but the individual alone has no meaning. Individuality is not even the scene of success or failure; it is nothing.

In all these novels the protagonist ends where he began. Even in Welch's work, the most contemporarily realistic of the novels, the reservation is not just a place where people are stuck; it is *the* home. Curiously, all seven of these Native American novels are from Inland West reservations and come from tribes not drastically displaced from their original territories or ecosystems. Place is not only an aspect of these works; place may have made them possible. As McNickle and Harold Fey phrased the Indian position in 1959: "One cannot grow a tree on a pile of money, or cause water to gush from it; one can only spend it, and then one is homeless."

So these novels depict Indians coming home and staying home, but "home" is not the "house" of white heaven as dreamed by Catherine in *The Surrounded:* "everything they wanted, big houses all painted, fine garments . . . rings . . . gold." The heaven-home to the Indian is a society: "Then I went to the Indian place and I could hear them singing. Their campfires burned and I could smell meat roasting." In all of these novels the protagonist succeeds largely to the degree that he reintegrates into the tribe, and fails largely to the degree that he remains alone. Such aspirations toward tribal reintegration may be treated by a novelist sentimentally, or romantically, or as fantasy, but these aspirations are not *inherently* sentimental or romantic. Rather, they constitute a profound and articulate continuing critique of modern European culture, combined with a persistent refusal to let go of tribal identity, a refusal to regard the past as inferior, a refusal – no matter how futile – of even the wish to assimilate.

For over twenty years, Vine Deloria and others have been saying that Indians still do not accept white "progress" as the only future, still do not believe they are "doomed to modernity." This is not necessarily head-in-the-sand primitivism; Indians in law school, tribal councils, sending signals by E-mail, can hold this view. They are skeptical of the long-term efficacy of unbridled individualism and of the war on the environment. For a superlative of skepticism, see Silko's *Almanac of the Dead* (1991).

What the Native Americans are rejecting I am calling liquidity, a culture of individualism, freedom, mobility, change. This culture surrounds and nurtures contemporary liberalism as well as capitalism.

Liquidity suggests, in economics, unfreezing as many assets as possible, to make everything part of the market; in our social life, it suggests mobility, moving away from family, kin, background, and therefore it suggests individualism; in our culture, liquidity suggests the liberal substitution of principle and abstraction for specific belief, and is related to proceduralism, or the way eighteenth-century rationality has become rule by bureaucracy and law; such abstraction is related to cherished political ideals, especially to freedom in the form of license, the right to do anything one wishes, free of background, race, kinship, place, and fate.

Outside of America and Europe, however, Indian skepticism does not look strange, extreme, or marginal. To the Muslim world, to Iran, for instance, or Malaysia, whether industrial development must come with the other freedoms of "progress" is a clear and pressing question. Furthermore, they are painfully aware of our first-world derision at anything less than the whole package – all freedoms, a liquidity of values.

In 1988, Malaysia banned "the Asian face" from television. The Asian face was a generic look favored by models who might pass, in advertisements, as Malay, or Chinese, or even Indian – the major ethnic groups of Malaysia. The government said models had to be identifiably Malay, or Chinese, or Indian. The nation decided that the interchangeability of parts and liquidity that made the new factories and international banking system possible was not a sufficient foundation for a culture. The models would have to choose a local look, a background, a tradition – presumably their own.

Why did Malaysia do this? Because industrial consumer capitalism has absolutely failed to address problems of identity. People need not only to *have* something; they need to *be* something. That "being" is in a social, historical, and often geographical context: we need to be someone beyond our name; of a people, a tradition, a place, even if, in America, it is sometimes a background we choose. For all its virtues and achievements, industrial capitalism does not deal with these issues. The bottom line is not money; it is identity.

One region – very much a region – has already shown, however, that liquidity is not necessarily the same as capitalism. In Japan, the national community, not profit, is the bottom line. James Fallows states clearly what many observers find:

> Soda ash is a staple chemical used for making glass, other chemicals, and detergents. Because soda ash is produced in big petroleum-fed cookers, Japanese suppliers, with their very high energy costs, are at an inherent disadvantage compared with American suppliers. Nonetheless, Japanese customers buy five sixths of their soda ash at home. An executive of Asahi glass, a major purchaser, announced in 1986 that he would never leave his high-cost Japanese supplier. After all, they'd been friends in school. "This isn't exactly collusion," an American diplomat told me. "It's just a refusal to act on price." . . .
>
> For most of its history, the United States has behaved more or less in accordance with the proconsumer capitalist model. Japan has not. The welfare of its consumers has consistently taken second place to a different goal: preserving every person's place in the productive system.

For "proconsumer," read individualist; for "productive system," read tribe. My government seems to consider the Japanese preference for national strength over low-cost goods un-American, and unfair. It may be the spirit of Crazy Horse in a new guise.

While Japan may be in ways unique, its rejection of liquidity is not. In Southeast Asia, at least, the Muslim movement is in part a conscious declaration that not everything should be tolerated, that not everything should be for sale. For much of the world, opposition to the industrial culture of the United States is an opposition to loss of values, an opposition to the chaos which seems to be the dark side of freedom.

The postmodernists are relevant to this discourse, since most consider themselves anticolonialist, yet welcome the notion of liquidity; therefore whether liquidity is itself a cultural colonialism – the end of culture, perhaps, as well as the end of nature – becomes an interesting question. The defining modern and postmodern metaphors of flux and float suggest all context with no bottom to touch, the need for constant treading to stay on the surface, and the possible fun of it all. The post-Nietzschean comic mode (it is not black humor) has often been overlooked, from Wallace Stevens to Gerald Vizenor. In the critique of modernity, many postmodernists describe something like liquidity, then leap in. Here's Marshall Berman:

> There is a mode of vital experience – experience of space and time, of the self and others, of life's possibilities and perils – that is shared by men and women all over the world today. I will call this body of experience "modernity." To be modern is to find ourselves in an environment that promises us adventure, power, joy, growth, transformation of ourselves and the world – and at the same time, that threatens to destroy everything we have, everything we know, everything we are. Modern environments and experiences cut across all boundaries of geography and ethnicity, of class and nationality, of religion and ideology: in this sense, modernity can be said to unite all mankind. But it is a paradoxical unity, a unity in disunity: it pours us all into a maelstrom of perpetual disintegration and renewal, of struggle and contradiction, of ambiguity and anguish. To be modern is to be part of a universe in which, as Marx said, "all that is solid melts into air."

The ecstatic postmodern is describing modernity as a frontier – a mining camp – a maelstrom of immigrants, "adventure, growth, transformation," opportunity. He is also quoting from a remarkable passage in *The Communist Manifesto,* in which Karl Marx describes what I am calling the liquidity of the modern age:

> Constant revolutionizing of production, uninterrupted disturbance of all social relations, everlasting uncertainty and agitation, distinguish the bourgeois epoch from all earlier times. All fixed, fast frozen relationships, with their train of venerable ideas and opinions are swept away, all new formed ones become obsolete before they can ossify. All that is solid melts into air, all that is holy is profaned, and men at last are forced to face with sober senses the real conditions of their lives and their relations with their fellow man.

Marx shows his own Enlightenment bias by finishing with the progressive epiphany of a realist: in this chaos, with lies of the sacred gone, we will discover – "face . . . sober . . . real" – our true power relations, and thus correction may begin.

John Tomlinson objects to those who easily assume that the spread of modern capitalism is an "imperialism." Yet, as Tomlinson concedes, a powerful capitalism/modernism (that brought Adam Pell to the Flathead valley intending to help Indians) seems to spread relentlessly and systematically, and it is very naive to think that each individual in the world is making free choices in an open market, and therefore is in control of his or her life, much less his or her culture. Tomlinson concludes his own review of "cultural colonialism" with Habermasian terms and systems theory, postulating that we are all "'colonized' by 'system imperatives' belonging to the major institutions of capitalist modernity." Tomlinson doubts "the capacity of a collectivity to generate any satisfying narratives of cultural meaning in the conditions of social modernity."

Tomlinson and Jürgen Habermas are so depressed, perhaps, because they themselves will not question certain key Enlightenment assumptions: individualism, freedom, variety, and reason. Therefore they are within modernism, and cannot see their way out. Tomlinson passes on to us, from Habermas and Theodor Adorno and the Frankfurt school, an unexamined bias towards "individual autonomy" versus "the unfreedoms of traditional societies." Remarkable assumptions. Tomlinson says that for Habermas, to be modernized is to be "emancipated from the pre-rational forces of tradition." What is being emancipated is, of course, the individual and his or her thought and feeling, although whether that is the only, the most, or the best freedom could be argued. The doctors are prescribing the disease – or at least the condition of unbridled individualism – and wondering why it is not a cure. The extreme of Enlightenment emancipation is itself liquidity, a form of commodification that enhances change and exchange. This may work very well for many individuals, but what of society? Does society, if it is capable of choice, have to choose between liquidity and identity, freedom and fate, consciousness and meaning? "Give me liberty or give me culture." Not a pretty thought.

* * * * * *

The American West has long been seen as both progressive and antiprogressive, a sensational, almost schizophrenic drama starring those building the brave new world – mining camp mayors, boosters, railroaders (mainly owners) – and those lamenting the loss of the old – mountain men, cowboys, Romantic primitivists (mainly workers). The Daniel Boone paradox, that those who escape to the wild destroy it by bringing civilization, was enshrined in Guthrie's

The Big Sky in 1945: "She's all gone now" still tops the country-western charts.

I am suggesting, however, that the antiprogressive West was not always primitivist, nostalgic, or anti-civilization. Specifically, Native Americans and dry-land realists offered critiques of liquidity from marginal but informed cultural points of view, and so prefigured contemporary attacks on liquidity by ethnic groups and ecologists. The problems of capitalist modernity are problems of identity, not just of ownership of production or distribution of profits.

D'Arcy McNickle knew a good deal about liquidity and identity before he went to Paris in the twenties or met communists, and in his writings the critique of capitalism springs more from his Native American background than from the liberal left, with which he was well acquainted. As Dorothy Parker's fine biography reveals, McNickle knew the particular ironies of the mixed blood, or as he called himself when it was very unfashionable, the "breed." The mixed blood, part Indian, part white, has come to stand – in Welch, Silko, Erdrich, Vizenor, and others – for the figure of agony between two cultures, or in the works of Vizenor, for the postmodern trickster, swimming in the float of all possibilities, himself mutating: coyote. The mixed-blood novels are regarded as the ground where the two cultures, white and Indian, clash; but these novels are the meeting ground also of the first and third worlds, of the modern and antimodern, of the liquid and the regional. By the 1930s, McNickle had seen these possibilities.

The young McNickle had his tribal allotment of land in western Montana from his Métis mother, but as for identity, "all that is solid melts into air." McNickle was French/Cree/Métis/Irish/Salish (each implies a different class and role as well as race), went to the Catholic Mission school in St. Ignatius, and after his parents' stormy divorce and custody suit (a white ceremony of dislocation) was sent off to Chimewa school in Oregon. His life predicted the mixed-blood novels of today; he would have to invent himself.

He invented a man who was not an Indian, who studied writing under H. G. Merriam at the University of Montana, went off to Oxford by selling his allotment, then to Paris in 1925–26, became a connoisseur of wine, returned to New York, and lived there writing novels about being Indian on the reservation he had left and would not visit for forty-five years.

In his diary of the New York years he lamented the American obsession with "things." A job in Philadelphia selling cars made him feel Indian: "a daily betrayal of my birthright in opposition. . . .

Everything I was called on to do was a violation of instinct and desire." He turned easily to the white leftist vocabulary of the thirties, for the communists, like the Christians of old or the new communitarians of today, were constantly seeking to define the limits of individualism: America was "bent on exploiting every inch, every microscopic entity, of the known world in the interest of money," he wrote. In 1932, he thought the crash had neatly exposed the captains of industry for what they were: "blundering opportunists."

McNickle in his diary saw himself as melted, "an undesigned, unaccountable, unwitting accident in the laws of causation." He could not have been less tribal; he had thrown himself into the float; he did not know his mother's whereabouts, nor she his; he had no news of his father's death – his sister told the local paper she thought D'Arcy was in Chicago. Meanwhile, he was writing his first novel, *The Surrounded*, about a wandering boy, a fiddle player in the white world, who comes home and relocates within family and tribe. By 1936, McNickle had considered that in America, identity might be the opposite of success.

The first drafts of both novels, as Louis Owens has shown, are white. Archilde, in the manuscript version of *The Surrounded*, is lectured at his murder trial by a white prosecutor on the "sturdy Pilgrim fathers who owned the virtues of discipline. They built us a great nation on that very principle." The white judge decides in Archilde's favor and commends his "stolid qualities," a "splendid citizen." Archilde inherits his white father's farm and, rejecting relatives, makes a go of it alone. "All this world would be his. . . . He must . . . make a survey of everything, asserting his command once more." In the white tradition of land use, Archilde is envisioning the very fence lines which in McNickle's second novel will be so offensive to Pell. As John Purdy says, Archilde is "assimilated and happy at last." And more: Archilde marries the beautiful, sophisticated, white Claudia, from New York.

These are not isolated scenes. Both of McNickle's novels have happy resolutions in manuscript draft, and tragic endings as published. In the first draft of *Wind*, Henry Jim in fact remains a yeoman farmer; at the end, Feather Boy is restored instead of lost, the old leader Bull is shaking Pell's hand instead of murdering him, and with the opening of the sacred bundle, the rains come.

Why the changes? As he was writing these drafts in the thirties, McNickle combined extensive new experience in the white world with his Native American background, and began to doubt that the two cultures could come together, or even understand one another. He developed an unusual perspective, different from the white reformers he worked for. In *The Surrounded* (1936), the white world is only implied; in *Wind,* however, there is a full-blown opposition of native life to a liberal establishment.

McNickle officially began working for the BIA under George Collier in February of 1936, three days after *The Surrounded* was issued. Collier, like Adam Pell, was a model liberal – he fought allotments and tried to strengthen reservations in every way he could. However, as Dorothy Parker points out, "Collier was a visionary. He had dreamed for years of an ideal human community grounded on non-material values. . . . He thought he saw this kind of social organization among the Pueblo Indians of the Southwest, and he extrapolated from them to all Indian communities in the western world . . . thereby denying their great cultural diversity." Collier's vision was one of liquidity.

During those years, as McNickle mingled with the Washington elite, met anthropologists, joined Collier and the American Civil Liberties Union defending the BIA in Congress against right-wing attacks, and gained valuable field experience among Southwest tribes, he became increasingly and professionally aware of problems within the liberalism he served, problems of cross-cultural communication.

Adam Pell's substitution of the gold statue for Feather Boy is rooted in a number of issues McNickle had been considering – by 1970 – for over thirty years. He had been very interested in the debate over a hydroelectric plant at Muquiyauyo, Peru; well-intentioned anthropologists, rather than capitalists, built the plant and then turned it over to the peasants. "We used our power to share power to a point where we no longer held power," the leader Allan Holmberg said. This is pure liberalism, modernization pursued altruistically (if we assume that money is the important thing to give, and that culture is not an important thing to take). Nevertheless, as Parker notes, McNickle worried about Holmberg's "control and manipulation" of the Indians, and of course, one kind of power had been substituted for another, even if locals owned the means of production.

In chapter eighteen of *Wind,* McNickle retells the Peru story through Adam Pell. With another character, a mestizo friend named Carlos, Pell had built a hydroelectric plant in the Andes. Carlos "had transformed one of the most fertile of the family holdings into a cooperative farm," and he and Pell helped build a leftist utopia of equality by giving the miners and peasants the power plant. The lights came on; Pell was honored in the Collierian community. Yet McNickle saw this as the seed of Pell's folly.

McNickle's editor at Harper & Row, Douglas Latimer, wanted the sequence cut severely. McNickle tried, and couldn't do it: "I have had to conclude that it stands on its own feet and the detail is essential to an understanding of the basic theme of cross-cultural confrontation." McNickle was well beyond any Marxist revisionism, and no one will accuse him of romancing the old days. The very best of progress, liberal industrial capitalism, even with workers owning the means of production – the professional elite and the landed patriarchs having jovially abdicated – was still a problem. Why?

In a curious wrinkle of history, McNickle understood more of America's project by watching the treatment of another communal group – also more tribal than communist – during the Second World War. Japanese Americans were interned at Poston on the Navaho reservation, where McNickle had worked. Their treatment became a bone of contention between McNickle's boss, Collier, and the midwestern conservative Dillon Myer, who had taken over the War Relocation Authority in 1942, and who would later become Collier's successor at the BIA. According to Parker, "Myer was convinced that communities that differed culturally from mainstream society were inherently 'un-American,' and that their existence weakened the fabric of American life."

The Japanese Americans placed at Poston immediately went to work doing what they do best, cooperating and adapting. Collier, visiting the Japanese as they arrived, wrote "I have never had in all my life as moving an experience . . . the esprit of the Japanese is superb." In September McNickle came and noted the flower and vegetable gardens everywhere; Collier in November mentioned their "psychic or spiritual adjustment."

Myer, however, apparently did not like the idea of Japanese Americans becoming even more Japanese, in isolation. They looked settled, and discrete. He came a few days after Collier and told them they would soon be scattered and relocated where they might mingle and work with the local population. All along his aim had been, after the war, to have the Japanese Americans split up, melting into the pot, no longer in coastal enclaves.

Eight years later, as new head of the BIA and McNickle's boss, Myer was proposing dereservation for the same reasons: liquidity versus identity. Indians and Japanese Americans should not set themselves apart with distinct ethnic values; they should melt into that capitalist/modern neutrality which is America. McNickle had watched these oppositions play out, and he was still revising *Wind*.

As he deepened his knowledge of both white and Indian cultures, McNickle became increasingly pessimistic about any reconciliation. In 1934, in a series of letters with the anthropologist William Gates, McNickle wondered how Gates, or he, could attempt to translate from an ancient Mayan language into English. Was there a "missing link" which allowed you to get into another culture's mind-set, and then communicate it? He became disillusioned about his own Mayan poetry project. As he wrote in a letter in July 1934, "I was perhaps contemplating doing the very thing which, in reading, I have distrusted and felt antagonized by: I mean those 'translations' one finds of Indian poetry in which the 'translator' has made the Indian singer over into a kind of sonneteer or at worst a *vers librist,* and on top of that has asked us to admire the individuality of Indian poetry." McNickle's disgust with Pell's easy transformation of the Peruvian statue into a Salish artifact has its origins perhaps in McNickle's own self-doubts concerning his aborted project on Mayan poetry, as well as in the liberal modernization of Peru. Neither language, nor equipment, nor money in a bank, nor objects collected in a museum constitute a neutral ground where cultures can meet.

Louis Owens is particularly perceptive concerning this crisis, "the difficulty, verging on impossibility, of communication and the tragic consequences this entails" in *Wind from an Enemy Sky*. He details the many instances of missed communication even between Indians (Bull and Henry Jim) or for Feather Boy ("the only one he could talk to was his own mother"). Owens concludes, "In the beginning, Henry Jim had tried to decode the invader's discourse, 'to discover what the white men were saying, and what they meant beyond the words they used' . . . Henry Jim's final rejection of the white world is indicated by the fact that before he dies he can no longer speak English." Cross-cultural communication ceases.

Finally, the most traditional of Indians, Bull, murders the best of liberal reformers, Pell. Thunderbird is not replaced by abstraction; Pell and Bull do not understand each other. The book rejects not just imperialism, or capitalism, but the Enlightenment – liberal modernity – in a way that whites still can hardly imagine. Pell and Bull cannot represent each other's points of view; the gap cannot be crossed by good intentions, and the Indians have to speak in their own way. "No people," McNickle wrote to Matthew Lowman, "should have to depend on another and possibly hostile party to give its account to the world." McNickle's changes of his novels' plots reflect not so much aesthetic considerations as an entirely different approach to economic/cultural issues. The end of *Wind* is not about a failure of negotiations; it is about a culture that believes in the negotiable, trying to destroy through modernization a culture that does not.

* * * * * *

I would like to end by briefly sketching how these issues might apply to some contemporary western writing. Two recent memoirs by William Kittredge (*Hole in the Sky*, 1992) and Mary Clearman Blew (*All But the Waltz*, 1991) can be seen as arguing location and identity versus mobility and liquidity. They too are mixed-blood novels, that is, predicated upon a voice that stands in two worlds: the located and the modern.

Kittredge says that his ranching family in Oregon failed to make any meaningful connection to the past or to each other:

> the stories died, and nobody told us anything revealing from the history of our family, or our neighbor's families. It was right there, as I understand it, that our failures, in my family, began. Without stories, in some very real sense, we do not know who we are, or who we might become. We were deprived like that.

Readers sense that this isolation is connected to dislocation – the destruction of a marsh, the "heedless people in a new country" who "plowed a lot of ground while we were there." They were separated from each other, and from their natural world; that is, from the people, past, and place that dominate tribal mythologies. Kittredge says if he cannot now locate himself by reconstructing a story of his people and place, through memory – "I am lost."

On the other hand, this background of located dislocation has its own gravitational field, and Kittredge, back home looking at a man who stayed, feels its pull:

> That man is home, where I could have been. I was born to it, but I left. As a consequence I carry a little hollow spot inside of me. Part of me despises that man – he settled so easily, in such an unquestioning way – while in another part I despise myself for having given away that possibility. . . . I have to keep telling myself . . . that it's alright, I get to be what I want. It's a free country.

Kittredge's leaving was an act of mobility, of freedom in a free country, an act of individual desire – "what I want." Like McNickle, he got out, and in the float of the modern, made himself something else. And like McNickle, he now looks back with a kind of longing – for what, Fate? Not questioning? Identity? – and yet there the parallel ends. For unlike McNickle's past, Kittredge's was itself liquid, the imposition of capitalist modernity on the desert. Without stories, without ties to people, past, and place, Kittredge's people were lost.

Mary Clearman Blew's *All But the Waltz*, coldly eloquent, chillingly accurate, wrestles with a similar tale of mobile individuals who came west and settled into patriarchs who despised those who might leave. "Within the terms of Abraham's conversion of place from habitat to real estate, with all its concurrent assumptions about patriarchy and patrimony," Blew was lost – "a runaway daughter, a failed 'little wife,' an uppity woman." Although Blew was not in the line of succession, her love/hate story of family and land is in many ways similar to that of Kittredge, who inherited the ranch, and both recall Doig's reconstruction of the frontier which he loved yet left.

These works encapsulate much American frontier literature, which increasingly we appreciate as part of world colonial history: the mobile/modern society moved people onto the frontier (lobbed them, like incoming rounds) where they became stuck, or as Nannie Alderson said, they began "to pioneer in earnest." In Montana especially, the white fringes of capitalist modernity grew roots, and became truly located, tied to past and place. The talented young – such as Kittredge, Blew, and Doig – break out to mainstream America as free individuals, and then look back on their family tribe with strange longing. Strange, because in this case the mixed blood of two cultures has occurred in both phases – on the ranch and at the computer.

The ranch is itself a hybrid, and there begins the paradox. It is an imposition of modern capitalism on the plains and yet, in the experience of the children grown into these remote kingdoms, it is a more located, family-tribal, fated past – with all the strength of those conditions – than most Americans can dream. So it is both a slice of the capitalist/modern problem, and a counterculture, profoundly alternative to the mobile, the various, the free. Conversely, the writer/professor looking back sees both a strength of background, located in a regionalism he or she respects as a kind of harsh truth, conferring identity, and yet also sees liquidity: drifting, aimless lives, an economic disaster, a failed modernism. To put it another way: they had place, but not culture.

These issues cannot be approached by the old "regional" versus "establishment" terms; the point is the choice between freedom and identity. Our Native American literature has consistently chosen identity over the liquid assets of freedom as the center conceives it, and new ecological thought gives form and urgency to the rethinking of place. Our biosphere is non-negotiable. Much of the contemporary "regionalism" of the West contains a profound critique of our own Enlightenment values – mobility, individuality, exchange, freedom – and so rather than representing a "region" which is marginal to a neutral center, this literature defines the limits of the center, makes of the center a "region" increasingly marginal to reality, and joins much of the third world in predicting an end to the imperialism of liquidity, and, for better or worse, a return to the fate of place.

Works Cited

Alderson, Nannie T., and Helena Huntington Smith. *A Bride Goes West.* Lincoln: U of Nebraska P, 1942.

Berman, Marshall. *All That Is Solid Melts into Air: The Experience of Modernity.* London: Verso, 1983.

Blew, Mary Clearman. *All But the Waltz.* New York: Viking Penguin, 1991.

Fey, Harold, and D'Arcy McNickle. *Indians and Other Americans.* New York: Harper, 1959.

Fallows, James. *More Like Us: Making America Great Again.* Boston: Houghton Mifflin, 1989.

Kittredge, William. *Hole in the Sky.* New York: Knopf, 1992.

Marx, Karl. *The Communist Manifesto* (1848). Qtd. in Berman, *All That Is Solid Melts into Air.*

McNickle, D'Arcy. Diary entries, August 1932. Qtd. in Dorothy Parker, *Singing an Indian Song.*

———. Letter to William Gates, 26 July 1934. Qtd. in Parker, *Singing an Indian Song.*

———. Letter to Douglas Latimer, 6 July 1976. Qtd. in Parker, *Singing an Indian Song.*

———. Letter to Matt P. Lowman III, 1 February 1971. Qtd. in Parker, *Singing an Indian Song.*

———. *The Surrounded.* 1936. Rpt. Albuquerque: U of New Mexico P, 1964.

———. *Wind from an Enemy Sky.* 1978. Rpt. Albuquerque: U of New Mexico P, 1988.

Owens, Louis. *Other Destinies: Understanding the American Indian Novel.* Norman: U of Oklahoma P, 1992.

Parker, Dorothy R. *Singing an Indian Song: A Biography of D'Arcy McNickle.* Lincoln: U of Nebraska P, 1992.

Paz, Octavio. Qtd. in Berman, *All That Is Solid Melts into Air.*

Purdy, John. *Word Ways: The Novels of D'Arcy McNickle*. Tucson: U of Arizona P, 1990.

Tomlinson, John. *Cultural Imperialism*. Baltimore: Johns Hopkins UP, 1991.

Twain, Mark. *Adventures of Huckleberry Finn*. *Mark Twain: Mississippi Writings*. Ed. Guy Cardwell. New York: Library of America, 1982, 617–912.

BURROS AND MUSTANGS:
LITERARY EVOLUTIONISM
AND THE WILDERNESS WEST

DAVID RAINS WALLACE

Usually associated with science and religion, creationism and evolutionism also have their literary side. A creationist outlook derived from Puritanism was fundamental to classic American literature (and persists in the mainstream), while an evolutionist one derived mainly from nineteenth-century science has played a counterpoint to it. Neither literary outlook has been as overt or dogmatic as the scientific or religious antagonists in the evolution controversy. Many writers have manifested either outlook (or both) without much awareness of their ideological implications. Yet two very different ways of regarding humanity and nature are involved.

Based on a redemptionist, millennial interpretation of the Bible, the creationist outlook sees separate origins and destinies for human and nonhuman life. Classic American literature is to some extent the story of the creationist outlook's response to a continent where nature was threateningly free and powerful, where separation of the human and nonhuman was much less of a given than in long-subdued Judeo-Christian homelands. This is not to say that classic American literature is a celebration of Puritan Euro-America's triumph over Native America. In fact, it is largely a story of the anxiety that arose from the conquest of a continent that was ambiguously perceived as an Eden as well as a fallen wilderness. Yet there is always a sense in Hawthorne, Melville, and Poe – even at their most pessimistic – of the necessity of that conquest.

Classic American writers were in a double bind with the creationist outlook they inherited. They *felt* separate and superior regarding nature, but many did not feel (as their ancestors had felt) that a reliable divine presence upheld them in that privileged position. What clearly *did* uphold them was their rapidly industrializing American civilization. Yet that civilization was disturbingly deficient in the qualities that were supposed to make humans superior

44

to raw nature – civility, charity, piety, amity – the qualities of the Puritan commonweal. The writings of Melville, Hawthorne, and Poe, and later of Henry James, Henry Adams, and Mark Twain, are suffused with horror at the disintegration of sustaining divinity in the face of socioeconomic machinery, and with nostalgia at the loss of the Puritan village. Their fictional heroes were unwillingly torn from the village and pressed into biblical projects – confronting the leviathan, seeking the Promised Land – in a world where divinity was silent.

Other classic American writers were less inclined to cling to human separateness after the decay of Puritanism. Puritanism itself contained an element of admiration for creation as well as for the Creator. As the Creator faded into Deism and Unitarianism, and as the physical universe expanded in scientific discovery, the evolutionist outlook, which sees human life as growing from the nonhuman, brought some new implications to Euro-American thinking. If humanity and nature shared the same origins, they might share a destiny as well. Evolutionism did not rule out the possibility of divinity behind a unity of humanity and nature, but it questioned the creationist assumption that humanity would somehow outlive nature.

The evolutionist outlook appears in American literature before Darwinian theory. (In fact, evolutionism as defined here is not synonymous with Darwinian theory, since many Darwinians have had a creationist outlook in believing or hoping that humanity would "evolve" beyond a dependence on this planet's biosphere.) Early naturalists such as John and William Bartram were creationist in theology, but evolutionist in their sense of emotional and ethical engagement with nonhuman life. A generation later, Ralph Waldo Emerson became the first American writer to break consciously and publicly with the creationist outlook when he left the Unitarian pulpit.

The psychosomatic illnesses that Emerson suffered in breaking with the church suggest he felt a double bind like that of Hawthorne and Melville – a sense of separateness from the living world without a sense of sustaining divinity. Unlike them, Emerson chose to drop separateness (to a degree) and place his faith in an optimistic view of nature as a sustaining condition and process.

Much has been written about the intellectual influences that led Emerson to renounce Christianity. Pagan philosophy and European romanticism obviously played a significant role. Yet Emerson sounds more like Chief Seattle or Black Elk when he writes about nature than like Socrates or even Wordsworth. "I have no hostility to nature but a child's love to it," he says in *Nature*. "I expand and live in the warm day like corn and melons. . . . I do not wish to fling stones at my beautiful mother, nor soil my gentle nest." There is no evidence that Emerson paid much attention to Native American ideas about nature, but his own have a striking resemblance to them. The reasons for this are obscure. Europeans made a fashion of seeing "Red Indian" characteristics in Americans like Emerson, but there is more to his attitude than romantic patina. Emerson's sense of a benevolent, nurturing spirit in nature is characteristic of Native American religion: "The greatest delight which the fields and woods minister, is the suggestion of an occult relation between man and the vegetable. I am not alone and unacknowledged. They nod to me, and I to them."

Emerson's thinking also resembled Native American responses to nature in its pragmatism and anthropomorphism. Neither saw it as separate or inferior, but both saw it as existing for human use, although not in the narrowly utilitarian and economic sense current in the Euro-American mainstream. For Emerson and Native Americans, the satisfaction of physical wants was only the first level in a hierarchy of uses which led toward participation in a spiritual world of which nature formed the physical manifestation. "Nature is made to conspire with spirit to emancipate us," Emerson asserts. "The only true wisdom lives far from mankind, out in the great loneliness," said the Eskimo shaman Igjugarjuk. Participation in the spirit world is to be pursued through nature, and in that world, nature has human qualities. Animals, plants, and minerals talked and thought like people.

Emerson's pragmatism and anthropomorphism differ from Native American practice in his enthusiasm for science and technology. "How calmly and genially the mind apprehends one after another the laws of physics!," he exclaims in *Nature*. "Nature is thoroughly mediate. It is made to serve. . . . It offers all its kingdoms to man as raw materials which he may mould into what is useful." Yet Emerson did not confound science with wealth and power, or with knowledge for knowledge's sake. "Empirical science is apt to cloud the sight, and . . . bereave the student of the manly contemplation of the whole," he says. "Nor has science sufficient humanity, so long as the naturalist overlooks that wonderful congruity which subsists between man and world; of which he is lord, not because he is the most subtile inhabitant, but because he is its head and heart, and finds something of himself in every great and small thing." As a naturalist, Emerson resembled a Native American shaman as much as a Newtonian scientist.

Emerson's position as a naturalist-shaman offers another difference between his thinking and that of Native Americans. The shaman is a traditional being, an eternal figure. The naturalist-shaman is a historical figure. Emerson's historical enthusiasm for novelty was as boundless as mainstream America's. "Why should not we have a poetry and philosophy of insight and not of tradition," he asks in *Nature*. "It is essential to the true theory of man and nature that it should contain something progressive. Uses that are exhausted or that may be . . . cannot be all that is true of this brave lodging wherein man is harbored."

Emerson's technological progressivism shows that he never entirely let go of a sense of separateness from nature. He let go of the disagreeable parts, but like some evolutionary theorists he held to the pleasant option of a vague higher destiny. Emersonian enthusiasm for the spiritual potentials of railroads and telegraphs did not contribute as much to the dismantling of North American ecosystems as did more materialistic motives, but it did provide an inadvertent justification for that dismantling.

Yet Emersonianism flowed not only into railroads, but into another form at which Emerson himself looked askance. One of his naturalist-shamans, his handyman Thoreau, began writing unexpected things. Thoreau entered the Concord woods with an Emersonian outlook – pragmatic, anthropomorphic, and progressive – but emerged with kinks in his transcendentalism. Social responsibility formed an important element of Emersonian (and Native American) spiritual practice – knowledge and power acquired in the woods was to be devoted to the community. Thoreau did not devote his knowledge and power to Concord society – he rebelled, instead, against it. "It cost him nothing to say No," Emerson complained at Thoreau's funeral, "with his energy and practical outlook he seemed born for great enterprise . . . I cannot help counting it a fault in him that he had no ambition. Wanting this, instead of engineering for all America, he was the captain of a huckleberry-party."

What Emerson saw as a lack of ambition actually amounted to a difference of perception. Although he went to the woods with Emerson's acceptant enthusiasm, Thoreau found not an anthropomorphic, spiritual world there, but the unknown. "Talk of mysteries!," he writes in *Ktaadn*, "Think of our life in nature, – daily to be shown matter, to come in contact with it, – rocks, trees, wind on our cheeks! the *solid* earth! the *actual* world! the *common sense! Contact! Contact! Who* are we? *where* are we?" Thoreau saw a mother in nature, but his, as he said in "Walking," was "vast, savage, howling . . . as the leopard."

Useless bugs and weeds interested Thoreau more than game and medicinal plants – *because* of their uselessness, their unknown quality. "The meaning of Nature was never attempted to be defined by him," Emerson – who expected bugs and weeds to disappear as nature progressed – sighed in "Thoreau." Emerson did not see a meaningless nature in the woods. But Thoreau looked at the woods much longer and harder than Emerson had. "We have heard of a Society for the Diffusion of Useful Knowledge," Thoreau says in "Walking." "Methinks there is equal need of a Society for the Diffusion of Useful Ignorance." Emerson asserted that nature needed the human; Thoreau, the contrary. Emerson likened his disciple, in a journal entry, to "the woodgod who solicits the wandering poet & draws him into antres vast & desarts idle, & bereaves him of his memory, & leaves him naked, plaiting vines & with twigs in his hand."

Like many lovers of novelty, Emerson was uncomprehending when he stumbled on it. He sought a new compound of Euro- and Native Americanism, but Thoreau departed from both. Thoreau devoted his knowledge and power to the woods, an "alienated" devotion that had never quite existed before, not in the old pagan cultures, certainly not in the new Judeo-Christian ones. As he put it in "Walking," "a town is saved, not more by the righteous men in it, than by the woods and swamps that surround it." He coined a new meaning for "wild," a word hitherto defined in terms of the disorder and desolation central to the creationist sense of separation from nature. The Emersonian and Native American viewpoints underplayed the wildness of nature because of the opposition to humanity it implies. Thoreau did a kind of jujitsu flip with the concepts of wild and tame, raw and cooked. Rather than forming the opposite of "tame," wildness formed its complement – "the preservation of the World." Nobody had expressed a link between humanity and "unredeemed" nature so graphically before. "A township where one primitive forest waves above while another primitive forest rots below – such a town is fitted to raise not only corn and potatoes," he says in "Walking," "but poets and philosophers for the coming ages." Thoreau transformed natural constraints into potentials. A tree "is as immortal as I am," he contends in "A Moose Hunt," and "perchance will go to as high a heaven, there to tower above me still."

Thoreau wrote that he usually walked west toward the woods,

and that was the direction his influence took. Eastern nature writing reverted to bucolic Emersonianism after his death, as with John Burroughs's tranquil essays. The vast expanses of empty land west of the Mississippi encouraged Thoreau's literary offspring to practice the contrary outlook that arises from a sense of the unknown and previously unexperienced in nature. Such practice did not come easily, since the western population was no less utilitarian and anthropocentric than the eastern, merely sparser. Thoreau himself had never really practiced his expressed devotion to the woods in Concord. Saving some of the woods from the axe and grub-hoe would have required some compromise, some "yessing" and flattering uncongenial to the Thoreauvian temperament. Particularly in the West, saving the woods came to involve a kind of dialectic between Emersonian *yeses* and Thoreauvian *nos,* and the most successful savers have been the nimblest synthesizers.

The expansionist, progressivist Emersonian *yes* prevailed in the earliest western writing. Explorers from Lewis and Clark to John Frémont had no doubt that farms and cities formed the West's raison d'être, regardless of any wayward Thoreauvian impulses that might have propelled them beyond the frontier. Even the one American explorer who suggested leaving at least part of the West as it was, George Catlin, saw it in Emersonian terms of human use – by Indians. Catlin's proposal for a Great Plains National Park to preserve the buffalo-hunting cultures out-Emersoned Emerson in its visionary optimism, and in its naiveté. (Emerson's own optimism did not extend to a perpetuation of "savage" lifeways; he complained that Indians were hard to talk to. Thoreau admired Indians, although even they did not escape his contrariety, as when he wrote that a farmer submerged in a swamp while surveying it got more of its wildness than an Indian hunting over it.)

The Thoreauvian *no* was not heard in the West until the first boom decades of mining and landgrab had passed. It needed such things to negate. John Muir had to say no to the San Francisco streets before he could say yes to Yosemite, and he spent the rest of his life vacillating between the two. Muir was the first of many Emerson/Thoreau hybrids who could not decide if they were burros or mustangs. After running from the city to the Sierra Nevada, Muir realized that the city would devour the Sierra if not convinced of the Sierra's undevoured value, so he ran back to the city, as writer and gentleman farmer, to save the Sierra. The agenda was stressful, as evidenced by Muir's psychosomatic complaints (oddly like Emerson's), but it convinced much of the public that the Sierra was for them, despite Muir's deeper belief that the Sierra was for itself. The city saved the Sierra as far as convenience went – the Yosemite Valley *yes*, the Hetch Hetchy Valley *no*.

Muir's approach to writing about nature was rather the opposite of Thoreau's. Thoreau shed anthropomorphism and spiritualism as he looked longer and harder at the woods. Muir used anthropomorphic and spiritualist rhetoric to transmit his long, hard observations to a genteel, biblically minded magazine audience. Thoreau had been content to observe nature as an incomprehensible array of phenomena. Muir was driven to promote it as a comprehensive order wherein the most minute, mechanical events – like the fall of snowflakes on granite – were both useful and spiritual.

Such yessing and flattering evidently was hard for Muir, since he was more passionately set against the creationist outlook than Thoreau. Having spent his youth as the virtual slave of a Calvinist father, he had a visceral hatred for human arrogance, and a sharp eye for human degradation, whether of overfed tourists at Yosemite or malnourished freedmen in Florida swamps. Thoreau never called humans "sticks of corruption." Yet Muir's life was much more that of an "engineer for all America" than Thoreau's life had been.

Muir's literary successors in the late nineteenth and early twentieth centuries succeeded in saving the woods to the extent that they convinced the public that the woods were for them. Enos Mills succeeded in creating Rocky Mountain National Park by presenting himself in the popular role (popularized by Muir) of the robust but sensitive mountain man, and by writing about beavers – industrious, familial rodents of great anthropomorphic appeal once the value of their pelts had declined sufficiently. Mary Austin failed to stop the draining of the Owens Valley and the damming of the Colorado river by presenting herself as a set of clear but dispassionate sense organs, and by writing about the desert, for which contemporary audiences had fascination but little affection.

Only Thoreau had antennae comparable to Austin's for the comings and goings of the nonhuman landscape. "Venture to look for some seldom-touched water-hole," she says in *The Land of Little Rain* (1903), "and so long as the trails run with your general direction make sure you are right, but if they begin to cross yours at never so slight an angle, to converge toward a point left or right of your objective, no matter what the maps say, or your memory, trust them; they *know*." Like Thoreau, Austin accomplished little socially with her gift, except to make people uncomfortable, as when she left Los Angeles water czar William Mulholland staring at the wall after an interview about the Owens Valley. (Asked by an aide what was wrong, Mulholland said Austin was the only person he had met who realized what he was up to.)

Aldo Leopold was the next writer after Muir to develop a powerful synthesis of the Emersonian and Thoreauvian temperaments. He did so by moving in a direction contrary to Muir's. Muir had begun as a solitary observer with a Thoreauvian distrust of philanthropy (unlike the rabidly abolitionist Thoreau, he considered himself neutral in the Civil War) and had ended as a friend of presidents. Leopold began as an ambitious civil servant (supervisor of New Mexico's Carson National Forest) and ended in spirit if not in body (he held the chair in Wildlife Management at the University of Wisconsin at his death) as a hermit in a "Sand County" shack.

It is hard to imagine anyone more energetically pragmatic, anthropocentric, and progressive than the Leopold who drove around the 1920s Southwest promoting a "deer hunter's heaven" by means of predator extermination. He was an exemplar of the "conservation is wise use" philosophy of Forest Service founder Gifford Pinchot. Like Thoreau, however, Leopold eventually spent enough time in the woods to meet the unexpected, including a near-fatal case of nephritis from passing a stormy night in a wet bedroll. During a year's convalescence, this aspiring "engineer for all America" had time to reflect and to read Thoreau.

As the last wolves and grizzlies vanished from the Southwest, Leopold felt an unexpected regret. Doubts welled up through the cracks in his progressivist program. One of the flagstones of that program was the federal wilderness area, which Leopold had conceived as part of his "deer hunter's heaven" – a wild area big enough to accommodate the two-week pack trip that formed the quality deer hunter's beau ideal. He convinced the Forest Service to designate the Gila River watershed in New Mexico as the first such area. With wolves gone and mountain lions "controlled" in the late 1920s, the Gila deer herd grew so rapidly that they over-ate their range and suffered ghastly winterkills. The Forest Service responded pragmatically by building a road into the wilderness so less purist hunters could get their Model-T's in and cull the herd. The wilderness was halved and Leopold (as Curt Meine has shown in his biography, *Aldo Leopold: His Life and Work*) was hoist on his own progressive petard.

Leopold's doubts grew through the 1930s. He visited Germany, where foresters had been practicing "wise use" for centuries, and saw a forest that was deteriorating as artificially maintained conifers and game depleted soils and food plants. He visited Mexico's

Sierra Madre, where Apache guerillas had excluded civilized uses, and found a healthy forest teeming with game *and* predators. Leopold concluded that the only way to maintain the useful and meaningful in nature was to maintain the useless and meaningless as well. "The scientist . . . knows that the biotic mechanism is so complex that its workings may never be fully understood," he wrote in *A Sand County Almanac* (1949). "The first rule of intelligent tinkering is to keep all the parts."

Leopold's conclusion was a pragmatic and anthropomorphic version of Thoreau's *no,* but a "no" nonetheless, because it set strict limits to human power: "too much safety seems to yield only danger in the long run." Leopold ended without much faith in the transformation of nature. Still, his Emersonian side remained too strong to leave it at that. He tried to harness Thoreauvian negatives to Emersonian positives with his land ethic, his proposal that society adopt the principle that "the despoliation of land is not only inexpedient but wrong." The land ethic is Thoreauvian in recognizing nonhuman nature as a "significant other," not simply matter to be manipulated at will. It is Emersonian in optimistically trying to establish an anthropomorphic relationship, a social contract, with nonhuman nature.

Native Americans could make contracts with nature logically because they saw it anthropomorphically. (They also could break them as when they felt justified in exterminating beaver for the fur trade because the animal spirits had failed to protect them from European diseases.) Social contracts with nature are harder for the Euro-American mind to grasp, since it tends to view nature as an insignificant other. Yet Leopold's land ethic prompted some substantive changes in law. The 1964 Wilderness Act empowers Congress to establish areas that will remain "untrammeled by man." The overt reason for this is recreation, a concept arising from the Emersonian ideal of "higher use," but wilderness designation also implies legal and philosophical standing for the existence of wildland and wildlife per se. The Endangered Species Act does not merely imply but mandates a right of existence for native species regardless of economic value or social significance.

Leopold's synthesis has mainly affected public land management (although he saw private morality as the land ethic's main arena, and had conceived it partly from despair at government conservation's ecological ineffectiveness), so it has bulked larger in the West than in other areas of the country. The generation of western writers who followed Leopold saw protecting nature largely in terms of protecting public lands. Robert Marshall, Olaus Murie, Sigurd Olson, Bernard DeVoto, and Wallace Stegner all had a sense of "nature for itself," but they looked to the public good as a justification of intrinsic value, and to public agencies as guardians of both. They had some reason to do so in the 1930s, when the effect of agrocommercial brutality on drought-stricken plains was painfully evident, and business's hold on government was loosened. Before an early death, Marshall had particular influence, publishing such bestsellers on Alaskan wilderness as *Arctic Village* (1933) and *Arctic Wilderness* (1956) and pushing both the Agriculture and Interior Departments to designate wilderness areas.

Another Depression generation writer achieved an influential Emerson–Thoreau synthesis by fictionalizing national park wilderness ecosystems. When employed early in the century by Ernest Thompson Seton and other popularizers, fictionalization had been too sentimental and anthropomorphic even for the general public. In "novels" like *One Day On Beetle Rock* (1944), however, Sally Carrighar imagined the lives of lizards and jays so sparingly, and with such attention to actual behavior, that even Aldo Leopold approved. A solitary like Thoreau, Carrighar looked long and hard at the western landscape yet also infused her observations with an Emersonian warmth and gentleness. Her work gave readers a sense of integration with, and participation in, the wilderness similar to Muir's. Her popularity in the 1950s and 60s rivalled Rachel Carson's, and perhaps did as much to further public acceptance of wilderness protection as Carson's did for environmental protection in general. Disney film adaptations did not do Carrighar's books justice, but they did lead to the television nature films that widely popularized wilderness after 1970.

Wallace Stegner, the most persistent and accomplished western writer of his generation, stressed the relationship between evolutionism and ecological conservation in *Beyond the Hundredth Meridian* (1954), his study of pioneer geographer John Wesley Powell. A founder of the United States' conservation bureaucracy, Powell opposed the millennial frontier optimism that saw a future of unlimited growth for the West, and argued for scaling down population to fit the limited western water supply. Powell was an optimist, Stegner noted, but of a different sort than boosters like William Gilpin who saw the West "blooming as the rose" through a kind of biblical redemption. "Evolutionary science as Powell interpreted it," Stegner says, "denied any and all theories of human degeneration from a perfect state. It repudiated alike the myth of the Garden and the Fall, the iron rigidity of Calvinism, and the sentimental nostalgia for an olden and perfect time with which Arcadian poets

and idealist philosophers had endowed the idea. . . . For Powell the
road led up toward perfection, not down from it." While Stegner
respected Powell's conservationist ethic, however, he doubted
whether Powell's idea of perfection would coincide with the heavily engineered West that federal bureaucracies have subsequently
created.

When business again dominated the government after World
War II, the New Deal writers continued defending public lands
against the raids of commerce. In a *Harper's* magazine column,
"The Easy Chair," Bernard DeVoto combated an Eisenhower Ad-
ministration attempt to turn over the public domain to miners and
ranchers. Yet business now exercised increasing control over resource agencies, and these greatly reduced or terminated many
wilderness areas to accommodate extractive industries. The always
uneasy progressive coalition between bureaucracies and conservationists deteriorated.

Meanwhile, further developments in evolutionary thinking undermined the easy optimism of Emersonian progressivism. As evidence of vast periods of biotic stasis punctuated with mass extinc-
tions accumulated, evolution began to seem a less progressive
process than the nineteenth century had conceived. Loren Eiseley
evoked this growing unease in his essays on fossil-hunting on the
Great Plains. Where Powell had seen a solid if limited world of
farmland in "America Deserta," Eiseley saw a kind of mirage landscape, a phantasmagoria of instability as species came and went in
geological strata. In "The Slit" (the first sketch in *The Immense Journey* [1957]), the narrator observes a prairie dog town, then descends
a rock fissure where he confronts the skull of a primate, a distant
human ancestor, which may have lived like a prairie dog fifty million years ago but is now extinct – perhaps pushed out of its bur-
rowing, grassland niche by evolving rodents.

Eiseley's work gives little sense that nature is meant for human
uses, however high, or even that humanity is particularly significant. Eiseley passed up a chance to look for hominid fossils in
Africa, as though the matter was of peripheral interest. For him,
not even *human* consciousness was anthropomorphic in the comfortable Emersonian sense of something familiar and "mediate."
Human consciousness was an unknown quality evolved mysteriously in a not-too-remarkable animal.

Although obscured by Earth Day's flush of optimism in 1970,
this collapse of evolutionist progressivism affected nature writing
rather catastrophically. Whatever their differences of feeling or
thought, earlier writers from Burroughs to Carson had been

united by a belief that limited and destructive traditional ideas of nature were giving way to more comprehensive and creative ones based on science. This belief provided an alternative to a literary mainstream that continued to have a strong creationist orientation, as (for example) when William Faulkner spoke of man prevailing at "the last ding-dong of doom" in his Nobel Prize acceptance speech or Saul Bellow characterized the earth as a graveyard in *Mr. Sammler's Planet.*

Such unity dissolved in the post-Vietnam era. The neoconservatism of the 1970s fostered a kind of ecological creationism, a hybrid of traditional religious attitudes and environmental concerns in which nature is seen as deserving protection although its destiny is still seen as separate from humanity's. The notion of "stewardship," of humanity as a temporary caretaker of nature, is an example of this softening of the old Puritan separation. This hybrid attitude was not really conducive to long, hard looks at the woods, however. Writers like Annie Dillard and Wendell Berry, who had done nature writing early in their careers, moved toward more mainstream genres (autobiography, social polemic) as though uneasy at evolutionist implications for religious sensibilities – or simply from waning interest in nonhuman life.

Without evolutionist progressivism, remaining nature writers tended to become polarized by the Emerson–Thoreau antithesis that Muir and Leopold had once resolved. Neo-Emersonians, viewing nature anthropomorphically and pragmatically, often adopted an essentially Native American outlook, accepting traditional beliefs and practices as authoritatively defining the human–nature relationship. Neo-Thoreauvians took a more nihilist attitude toward that relationship, and tended to see no goal for the ecologically oriented except a drastic and possibly violent reduction of human control over nature. Both groups wrote largely about the West.

Peter Matthiessen and Edward Abbey exemplify this polarization. At the neo-Thoreauvian pole, Abbey tended to see no saving grace in human culture whether traditional or not. He was caustic in his criticism of Native Americans as well as Euro-Americans, mocking the former's burgeoning population and dependence on technology as well as the latter's more numerous vices. Abbey even made fun of pre-Columbian culture, as when one of his protagonists asks some Indians why their ancestors exterminated the Pleistocene megafauna and is told: "We were hungry. Que voulez-vous?"

Abbey took Thoreauvian contrariety farther than any writer

thus far, often seeming to perceive no more in nature than a gorgeous absurdity. His gratuitous killing of a rabbit in *Desert Solitaire* (1968) seems a conscious repudiation of pragmatism and anthropomorphism, of the frugal and the humane. Abbey's advocacy of lawbreaking in defense of nature is consistent with a perception of human culture as incapable of establishing deliberate harmony with nature. Abbey seems to have thought, and not without ample historical justification, that culture could be made to coexist with the biosphere only through reduction of its scope and power. His popularity after 1980 was a measure of progressivism's decline.

At the Emersonian pole, Matthiessen has been largely uncritical in his advocacy of Native American culture as the authentic response to Euro-American destructiveness. In one of his books on this theme, *Indian Country* (1984), he seems to regard his naturalist vocation in the past tense, implying a repudiation of that Euro-American tradition. He explicitly regards government and its scientific bureaus as obstacles to traditional peoples inhabiting land in tried and true ways.

Matthiessen's devotion of literary skills and prestige to the traditionalist cause has been generous and courageous, yet it leaves him in the cultural bind that awaits the Euro-American exponent of the Native American. The main significance it has for Native Americans is its effect on Euro-Americans. As an outsider, Matthiessen cannot (and does not) pretend to lead Native Americans. And while his books have done a great deal to expose the many injustices Indians still face, the prospects for establishment of traditional Native American relationships with nature among the Euro-American mainstream remain poor.

Prospects for an Abbey-style guerilla insurgency against industrial civilization are also poor. Despite the merits of polarized viewpoints, an Emerson–Thoreau synthesis still seems the most practical way of addressing the Euro-American assumption that earth is a throwaway container for civilization. Gary Snyder probably has produced the best synthesis since 1970. Nimble at balancing between the poles of nature for humans and nature for itself, Snyder is never the complete outsider like Abbey, but he never submerges his relationship with nature in any cultural tradition.

Snyder was one of the first American writers to view Native American culture not only sympathetically but as equal to the European. His early poetry and prose probably did as much to validate Native American beliefs for literary culture as any writer's work. Yet while supportive of Native American causes, Snyder did not presume to be a spokesman for them. Although he used anthropomorphic Native American imagery in his writing, he was unlike the Carlos Castanedas and Lynn V. Andrews's who claimed to inhabit a shamanic spiritual world. Instead, Snyder moved to Asia and espoused Zen Buddhism, a religion which perhaps comes closer to the Thoreauvian outlook than any other in its sacralization of the useless and meaningless. The universe, as Snyder puts it in "T-2 Tanker Blues," is "playful, cool, and infinitely blank."

Snyder did not stop at meditative detachment. He leaned back toward Emersonian engagement, returning to the United States in the 1970s to promote a socioecological revolution that might have arisen from Leopold's conclusion that the main hope for a land ethic lay in land-based communities rather than government conservation agencies. With such communities, Snyder tried to include in everyday life the regard for nature itself expressed in Muir's national parks and Leopold's wilderness areas. As he observed in criticizing traditional Asian culture, it is not enough to sacralize parts of nature, because the parts that are not considered sacred will be abused. Snyder's comparison, in *The Practice of the Wild* (1990), of the way traditional (and progressive) cultures treat land with the way they treat women has a Thoreauvian pungency: some land is saved like a virgin priestess, some is worked to exhaustion like a wife, and some is raped like a whore.

Snyder's synthesis is more radical than Muir's or Leopold's – reshaping culture to fit nature instead of merely adjusting culture to let vestiges of nature remain – and it has had less immediate effect. "Counterculture" communities are scattered about the landscape, but their influence on the mainstream has not been large. This is not surprising, since changing a culture is harder work than setting aside some parks and wilderness. Even setting these aside is getting harder as population and artificial demands on land increase. The United States is approaching the condition of the Asian civilizations that Snyder loved and left. Like Shinto or Taoism, the United States' nature-centered Emersonian-Thoreauvian tradition may become so submerged in the hypertrophy of mainstream culture as to devolve into a collection of artifacts and rituals with little actual influence on the human–nature relationship.

On the other hand, civilization is unlikely to hypertrophy much longer if life is really organized according to the evolutionist outlook. If human and natural destiny are one, then the only human cultures within a few centuries will be those shaped to fit the biosphere. This is not encouraging to anyone with an evolutionist outlook today, since nature and humanity will be severely impaired by then if present trends continue. But perhaps twenty-first century society – in the American West and elsewhere – will make a change such as D. H. Lawrence described early evolutionist Walt Whitman making:

> Whitman was the first to break the mental allegiance. He was the first to smash the old moral conception that the soul of man is something "superior" and "above" the flesh. Even Emerson still maintained this tiresome "superiority" of the soul. Even Melville could not get over it. Whitman was the first heroic seer to seize the soul by the scruff of her neck and plant her down among the potsherds.
>
> "There!" he said to the soul. "Stay there!"
>
> "Stay there. Stay in the flesh. . . . Stay in the marsh where the calamus grows. Stay there, Soul, where you belong."
>
> The Open Road. The great home of the Soul is the open road. Not heaven, not paradise. Not "above." Not even "within." The soul is neither "above" nor "within." It is a wayfarer down the open road.

Works Cited

Abbey, Edward. *Black Sun*. New York: Avon Books, 1971.

Austin, Mary. *The Land of Little Rain. Stories from the Country of Lost Borders.* Ed. Marjorie Pryse. 1903. Rpt. New Brunswick, NJ: Rutgers UP, 1987, 1–149.

Emerson, Ralph Waldo. Journal Entry, July–August 1848. In *Emerson in His Journals*. Ed. Joel Porte. Cambridge: Belknap P, 1982.

———. *Nature. Ralph Waldo Emerson: Essays and Lectures*. Ed. Joel Porte. New York: Library of America, 1983, 5–49.

———. "Thoreau." In *Ralph Waldo Emerson*. Ed. Richard Poirier. New York: Oxford UP, 1990, 475–90.

Faulkner, William. "Address Upon Receiving the Nobel Prize for Literature." In *The Portable Faulkner*. Ed. Malcolm Cowley. 1946. Rpt. New York: Penguin, 1985, 723–24.

Igjugarjuk. Qtd. in Joseph Campbell, *Primitive Mythology*. 1959. Rpt. New York: Viking, 1977.

Lawrence, D. H. "Whitman." In *Studies in Classic American Literature*. 1923. Rpt. New York: Viking, 1966, 163–77.

Leopold, Aldo. *A Sand County Almanac*. 1949. Rpt. New York: Oxford UP, 1987.

Snyder, Gary. "T-2 Tanker Blues." In *Riprap and Cold Mountain Poems*. San Francisco: Grey Fox P, 1982.

Stegner, Wallace. *Beyond the Hundredth Meridian: John Wesley Powell and the Second Opening of the West*. 1954. Rpt. New York: Penguin Books, 1992.

Thoreau, Henry David. *Ktaadn. Henry David Thoreau: "A Week on the Con-*

cord and Merrimack Rivers"; "Walden; or, Life in the Woods"; "The Maine Woods"; "Cape Cod." Ed. Robert F. Sayre. New York: Library of America, 1985, 593–655.

———. "A Moose Hunt." In *Henry David Thoreau: Essays, Journals, and Poems.* Ed. Dean Flower. Greenwich, CT: Fawcett Publications, 1975, 83–103.

———. "Walking." In *Henry David Thoreau: Essays, Journals, and Poems,* 518–53.

*REIMAGINING THE AMERICAN
FRONTIER*

THE LITERATURE OF LONELINESS: UNDERSTANDING THE LETTERS AND DIARIES OF THE AMERICAN WEST

SHANNON APPLEGATE

Such is life in the far west, but if it is true that the wester you go the sucher it is, I don't want to go any wester.
— Diary of L. H. Vincent, M.D., Sunday, September 23, 1922

Nothing could feel "wester" than the I.O.N. (Idaho, Oregon, and Nevada) country with its sage-humped deserts, eerily sculpted bluffs, and darkly pocked lava fields that border vast tracts of marginal range lands administered by the Bureau of Land Management. Part of what may rightly be called the "dry" West, the ranches of the Owyhee upland sometimes overreach the nearby, manmade borders of Idaho, Oregon, and Nevada. Ranch families, inconvenienced by the daunting distances between themselves and what passes for civilization, frequently resort to small airplanes instead of autos.

In August of 1865, Major G. G. Kimball passed through this same region "trailing" a band of sheep from Chico, California, to the Boise Mines in Idaho. No ranch would be seen on the horizon for a decade more. In a diary he intended to share with his distant family, Kimball recorded his responses to an ominous landscape:

> I was brought up and educated to believe there is a Hell where all had to suffer for their sins. I now think there was one once, and the country over which I have just passed must have been the place . . . I have seen no boundary lines, but the marks of the heat are still there . . . I hope someone will enjoy reading this for it has been a task to write . . . and [that] you all will never have the same road to travel . . . I am lonely.

The landscape looms intimidatingly large in many of the diaries and letters of the American West. The accompanying themes of

63

isolation and separation – of physical as well as emotional distance – reverberate like coyote howls. I have come to think of these genres as the literature of loneliness.

As I drove alone over thousands of miles of remote highways and rough back roads while finding and photocopying far-flung letters and diaries, nowhere was the sense of the pitiful scale of a solitary human figure more profound than when I passed the same sun-seared, eastern Oregon terrain described by Major Kimball. I was on my way to one of the oldest ranches in the I.O.N. country.

It could well be said that, like desperadoes, hermits, and ne'er-do-wells abiding on literature's borderlands, the precise "whereabouts" of many a letter and diary is often unknown. A surprising number of the American West's diaries and letters have successfully evaded the authorities. Most are still hiding out in shoe boxes rather than box canyons, tucked on closet shelves or bundled up in one newspaper-lined bureau drawer or another.

The reason such texts have survived – although often in settings and conditions that would make an archivist shudder – is obvious enough: diaries and letters are among the most intimate of literary expressions and, as such, are likely to be valued as keepsakes. Considered more artifact than art, a letter or diary may be preserved merely because it is "old." It has been my experience that when such texts are owned by individuals, there is more interest in form than content; the "scratchings" in silvery graphite or the graceful, but not easily decipherable, loops and filigreed capitals inked in black, brown, or fading blue are taken out and admired from time to time but are rarely read. Indeed, whether in the homelier settings already noted, or in acid-free files in the keeping of libraries and other institutions, the majority of letters and diaries have not been transcribed.

Not all such texts contain writing of literary merit in any narrow, canonical sense. As a body of literature, the majority of the West's collected letters and diaries share to the nth degree what scholar and American diary anthologist Steven E. Kagle refers to as the qualities of "greenness" and "presentness." Yet these are the very qualities that make many letters and diaries vivid and engaging. The region's little mined letters and diaries are rich in literature's most essential trace elements, if we mean imaginative, evocative uses of language and the revelation of subjective truths. As expressions of private literacy and imagination, letters and diaries form a unique medium in which to examine new historical conceptions of the American West.

What would I discover at the Swan Ranch, a ranch named, I'd

learned, for its location on the great flyway which arcs over the dry basin and range dotted with shallow lakes and vast tule marshes? The sky, I remember, was devoid of the huge flocks of waterfowl frequently sighted during migration months. All that the heavens held were the streaked configurations of clouds known regionally as mare's tails. It was a long dusty distance from the initial gate, over several cattle crossings, past the airfield, corrals, and metal farm buildings to the cluster of homes Mr. C— had told me to be "on the lookout for." The original farmhouse, he said, had been razed and replaced.

At last I spied two or three mobile homes sheltered from the vast, open plain by a grove of old Lombardi poplars. These manu-factured homes belonged to two younger generations of his family. Mr. C— and his wife occupied a very large and attractive split-level near the site of the original ranch house. Farming equipment, pick-up trucks, flatbeds, and late-model cars were everywhere on the premises. There was not a horse in sight.

On previous expeditions I had got over many of my romantic illusions about ranching. Nowadays, buckaroos – a corruption of the Spanish word, *vaquero*, literally "cow man" – ride motorbikes wearing jump-suits and baseball caps, not chaps and battered Stet-sons. Any affordable device that will make a hard life easier is likely to be pounced upon in ranching country. Perhaps this was one reason why Mr. C— and I got on so swimmingly in our initial telephone conversation many weeks before. He was obviously im-pressed when I told him that he need not worry about my asking to remove documents from his home in order to photocopy them, since I traveled with my own machine and fifty feet of extension cord, all of which fit snugly in the portable office in the back of my van.

As I turned into the appropriate driveway, I hoped Mr. C— had kept his promise and had already retrieved his family papers from their storage places. On more than one occasion, I have been obliged to forage, climbing ladders into lofts and attics that smelled of mouse droppings or assisting in closet cleaning years overdue.

Extended initial phone conversations, I discovered, often served my purposes better than a letter of inquiry. A two-way, metaphori-cal hunkering, with the telephone substituting for squatting on one's haunches in the best rural style, helped establish my credibili-ty. As usual, when speaking with Mr. C—, I probed carefully for any mutual acquaintance or interest. Despite the fact that my fami-ly ties were in the "wet" West on the other side of the mountains, Mr. C— occasionally fished in a river named after one of my ancestors. In his eyes – or ears – this made me less of what a westerner hates most: a stranger.

In due time I gently pressed Mr. C— about the specific nature of his family collection. He was evasive. "Now, it may be that what we've got won't amount to anything. Yes, there are letters among other things. Old ones. But don't come all the way across the state just to see us. It's probably a waste of time." I assured him I was making a series of stops en route, and that I had already made arrangements to visit several families – including two Basque clans – in his general vicinity. This information seemed to satisfy him.

Where, I have wondered since, did I go wrong? Perhaps he saw too much "Eureka!" in my eyes as I read his grandmother's letter. Before that moment I had been treated warmly. I took pictures of him, his wife, and his giggling little granddaughter bedecked in her mother's bridal finery. I was taken to the old, rock-work spring-house built many years before by Basque stonemasons. Mr. C— told me his family no longer referred to the ranch as the Swan Ranch. He couldn't explain why, he said, but the wild swans didn't fly over the place in such vast numbers any more. And when I told him I'd heard wildlife biologists say bird counts were dramatically reduced all over the region, Mr. C— scowled. He didn't know about that. He said he figured all the scientists were out trying to scare people, making things sound worse than they were. In his opinion, the swans had just switched routes, that was all. They were still out there. Somewhere.

I heard family stories about the Paiute Indians he had known in his youth – members of the famous Chief Winnemucca's band – who had worked side by side with Mr. C—'s ancestors for two cold winters in the 1880s, "grubbing" almost two thousand acres of sagebrush-covered rangeland into fields fit for raising hay.

"Yep," Mr. C— said, "those Indians knew how to work just like a white man if you took time enough to teach them. I don't care what other people say about them being lazy."

When it was at last time to sit down and look over the family treasures that he obligingly gathered together and placed in a large dress-box that bore the name of an Idaho department store, Mr. C— chuckled every so often. It was clear he was enjoying himself. He watched my face while I read his grandmother's letter. "It's a doozie, isn't it? Well written, too. Quite an educated woman for those times," he said proudly.

Referring to the portion of the letter in which, with amazing alacrity and thoroughness, his grandmother instructed her son in the art of cattle buying, Mr. C— commented, "She was a widow by then and had a lot of responsibility. But she could run this ranch with one hand tied behind her back even when living a hundred miles away. And she did too!"

As I handed the letter back, I beamed at him. It was exactly the kind of letter I had hoped to find somewhere, I told him. We were both grinning by then. He said, "How about that part when she tells my dad not to be a spendthrift – that he can do his own washing if he has used up his allowance and to forget hiring a girl. Dad was fifteen or so at the time, the oldest kid in the family, and Grandma had no choice but to put him in charge. She held on pretty tight to the family purse strings." To all this he added in a serious and respectful tone, "but I guess it's fair to say, if she hadn't been exactly the way she was, there wouldn't be a family ranch today." He took the letter back. "Yep. We owe her a lot."

It was time to plug in the machine. Mr. C— asked if I would make extra copies of several documents so he would have them to pass around to relatives at an upcoming family reunion. "Say, this machine sure is a dandy, I'm going to look into one of these gizmos," he said. "It beats driving all the way to the one machine in town." Town was thirty miles away.

"What about your grandmother's letter, Mr. C—," I asked. "I don't see it in this pile."

"Oh, no. I can't let you copy that."

I was puzzled. I told him why I thought it was such an extraordinary letter; that it was, in many respects, emblematic of the western experience for women. I pointed out that many women had been ranchers in their own right, only they hadn't gotten credit for their efforts. Few documents substantiated their contributions and his grandmother's letter – well, it was so witty, so interesting and complete in its descriptions of life on a ranch in the 1880s. I'd not seen another letter like it. "That's all true," he said. He even admitted that he could think of several other "outfits" in the I.O.N. country where women, in every sense of the word, had been ranchers. "Grandma wasn't alone in that respect. Still, I can't let you have it."

My frustration must have shown. He seemed to be reconsidering, holding onto the letter, stroking it with one thumb. At length he added, "Well, you see, this doesn't present Grandmother in a very becoming light, now does it?"

* * * * * *

"Becoming." The word rolls around like a strangely colored pebble in my head. I cannot grasp it.

Folding the letter carefully, almost tenderly, Mr. C— replaces it in the dress-box.

Politeness dictates that I say not another word about his grandmother's letter. I drive away noting all the gates, the miles of fences. Thinking: *Now you see it, now you don't.* You old son of a bitch. Or grandson of. Except she wasn't one. By any standard that is just. And later, still seething, eating Basque shepherd's bread and beans, the question will not go away: Unbecoming to whom?

"The impulse to deny," says critic Forrest Robinson in an essay about the New Historicism and the Old West, "may be said to tell the tale, though the denial in turn assures that we will pass this way again."

When such texts are not denied to us, many diaries and letters permit us to observe an American West caught in the act of living out the push and pull of its historical contradictions and cross-purposes. The counter-narrative, never too far beneath the surface, Robinson tells us, reveals what was hitherto concealed: "the grave injustices of the social order, especially as those injustices bear on people of color, and on women."

The "doubleness," the "counter-narrative," evident in so many classic westerns exists, in the first place, within the psyches of flesh-and-blood westerners. Mr. C— and others like him, attempt to hold on to the reins of an outmoded cultural narrative for dear life, lest things get away from them, struggling with the tension that Robinson identifies as "seeing and concealing, recording and denying."

Many westerners – indeed, many Americans for whom the Old West continues to be symbolically important and comforting – long to believe in stock characters inhabiting a world where women do not rescue men or ranches. The tall fellow, whose clear blue eyes are shaded by the brim of a pale Stetson, leans down and takes the arm of a woman – who is, perhaps, as independent and capable as Mr. C—'s grandmother – saying, "Let me help you, little lady." One hand steals while the other attempts to uplift "the savage" by insisting on an unfamiliar work ethic wherein the native is taught to work as well "as any white man."

Billy Chinook, who was taught to read and write by the missionaries living on the Columbia River, wrote to Indian Agent Joel Palmer, on November 3, 1853, expressing how it felt to experience the darker side of the western narrative:

> We are tormented almost every day by the white people who desire to settle on our land and although we have built houses and opened gardens they wish in spite of us to take possession of the very spots we occupy. We remonstrate and tell them that this is our land, they reply the Government gives them the right to settle in any part . . . they desire to take land in

this very spot. Now we wish to know whether this is the land of the white man or the Indians. If it is our land the whites must not trouble us. If it is the land of the white man when did he buy it?

Countering Chinook's plaintive query is a letter written to the same Indian agent but a few weeks later by a settler named Robert Hull:

I was on my claim sometime before I knew that I was on the Indians' camping ground, but the land bill requiring them to be removed I remain satisfied thinking that the Government would soon take them away. I have continually had to suffer from them ever since. Year after year has passed and they are still among us . . . I want to know of you whether I should take the law into my own hands and shoot them down or not . . . ?

Late in his career, Henry Nash Smith, a scholar highly respected by both critics and historians, conceded that his seminal work, *Virgin Land: The American West as Symbol and Myth* (1950), had failed to underscore the "tragic dimensions of the Westward Movement." "I took over from Turner," he said, referring to Frederick Jackson Turner's notions of motion wherein the West was not a place, but a process marked by continually shifting frontiers. Smith expressed regret that his work virtually ignored the role of indigenous cultures, the effects of the national "cult of violence," and the "regional legacies of racism and environmental abuse."

More recently, historians such as Patricia Nelson Limerick have emphasized that violence, racism, and environmental abuse do not roll over a largely symbolic series of shifting frontiers like darkening cumulus; instead, layer upon unholy layer of the western landscape itself is infused with the evidence of unbroken cycles of conquest and subjugation. "Reorganized," Limerick asserts, "the history of the West is a study of a place undergoing conquest and never fully escaping its consequences."

The West: not an idea but a place. Bloodstained. Far from virginal. "A region," as scholar and feminist Lillian Schlissel has observed, "with indigenous cultures in place for centuries."

It is the literary and historical evidence of this reenvisioned West that I have searched for in traveling to the locales where historic letters and diaries have originated. These genres are firmly hitched to the addresses mentioned in their headings: places such as "The Diggins" on Feather River, Glendale Siding on the Southern Pacific

Line, the Bell "A" Ranch, Kam Wah Chung Mercantile Co., Fort Klamath, Warm Springs Indian Reservation, Logging Camp #13, Crooked Finger School, Homestead Lot 72, and the Sunset District P. O. The names themselves invoke the landscapes peculiar to America's West. With the compelling emphasis made possible by the use of the first-person voice, many a western diarist and lettrist tells us: "I am here now, in this *place*."

Within the supple boundaries of these genres, the distinctiveness of each writer's voice is often accented by the fascinating peculiarities of extremely localized speech and cadence. Often, it is as if one were eavesdropping, overhearing highly individualistic diarists and lettrists talking on paper. Yet when all these richly varied letters and diaries are reconceived of as a running story, each text taking its place within a sprawling cultural narrative, the polyphony of the West with its complex amalgam of ethnicity, gender, religion, and class is fully revealed. The West, as Limerick points out, "is not where we escaped each other but where we all met." And soon after meeting, it would seem, the violence began: "Should I shoot them down or not?"

Western letters and diaries describe almost every aspect and variation of the ongoing conflicts on this meeting ground in an extended narrative that overarches three centuries and incorporates the perspective of many nationalities. It is said that historically, at least eight "races" have been oppressed in the West: Indians, Hispanics, Chinese, Japanese, blacks, Mormons, strikers, and radicals. To this list one might add women, for as Schlissel insists, "the task of writing about women in the American West has come to embrace the history of minorities."

What is believed to be the first recorded murder of an African American on the Pacific Slope is described in the 1788 maritime log of Robert Haswell, a youthful ship's officer who accompanied the American sea explorer Captain Robert Gray to the Northwest coast. The murdered man, Darius Lopius, a "young Black man . . . a native of the Cape de Verd Islands," was killed by members of an Oregon coastal tribe. It is ironic that Lopius died by the hands of Native Americans, the West's most oppressed people. Just as the institution of slavery and all its moral and social ramifications textures (and taints) the literature of the American South, so does the conquest of Indian America stain the narratives of the American West. Letters and diaries reveal a particolored lens through which to view the fateful struggles between Native Americans and those who came to the New World intent on conquering.

Instead of finding himself "in a land flowing with milk and

honey, as the West was represented," Second Lieutenant Harry De Witt Moore, a West Point Military Academy graduate, found himself in California near the Oregon border fighting one of America's last Indian wars in 1873. Writing his letter while living in a cave where he slept on a bed of bulrushes gathered from nearby Tule Lake, Moore described what is presently known as the Lava Beds National Monument as "a hundred and fifty square miles of the roughest ground to be found anywhere on the globe. . . . This [place] flows with rattlesnakes and scorpions," he said of his "den of rocks."

He informed a woman friend whom he would never see again, "You have, undoubtedly . . . read accounts in the daily papers of our last fight with the Modocs and of the massacre of the last detachment." In the jagged lava labyrinth – a veritable moonscape – the small band of Modoc warriors glided "like snakes" through the ancient rock channels. And at night, "so intensely dark," native marksmen picked off U.S. Army Officers at will, it seemed, sometimes even calling out the first names of certain Army officers in eerie falsetto voices: "Charlie-ee-ee-eeee!"

For the Modoc chieftain Kintpuash, who the soldiers knew as Captain Jack, the goal was to reclaim the old hunting and fishing grounds the government had denied them. For Harry De Witt Moore, "among these rocks [where] every one must look out for himself," the goal became increasingly troubling and obscure.

> I never realized what a horrible thing war is, until I came out on this trip. I want no more Indian fighting. . . . It is bad enough in Arizona where a troop of Cavalry can surprise an Indian camp, kill fifty or sixty and not lose a man. In fighting there the danger is not much greater than in deer hunting. But among these rocks . . . the officers stand the worst chance of all.

Moore underestimated the indignities awaiting both the conqueror and conquered when they are locked in a mutually degrading struggle. One hoarfrosted morning not long after the Modocs had been defeated, Lieutenant Harry De Witt Moore was found dangling from a wooden footbridge at Fort Klamath; accidentally – or so it was reported to his mother – hung by his own military issue woolen scarf. Captain Jack was also found hanging – although it was no surprise. He and a handful of his warriors were sentenced to the gallows. Lieutenant Moore had a proper burial according to his people's customs. Captain Jack's adversaries accorded him no respect at all. For years, his severed head was to swim in a Medusan tangle of green-black hair. The lead-lidded viewing jar was to be eventually misplaced by a museum in Washington, D.C.

All in all, Native Americans and whites living in Oregon would endure five different Indian wars in a thirty-year period. Other western states suffered similarly. Eventually, those peoples who were "unassimilated" were "removed" for their own good – or so went the argument. Banishing the victim was the solution to the Native American crime of trying to hold on to a homeland. The terms of banishment were particularly harsh for many Modocs who were rounded up and sent to a reservation in distant Missouri – the same state that was the starting-off place for so many white westbound overlanders in their covered wagons.

But despite the subjugated condition of the West's many tribes – in Oregon alone, for example, there were at least forty distinct tribes speaking more than twenty native languages – the violence was far from over. Settlers still had each other to fight with.

In 1882, young "school marm" Eunice Robbins, having come with her parents to live "in the high pure atmosphere" of central Oregon's Ochoco Valley, wrote to her New England grandmother: "Last week a man was shot in our hotel, but there has been so much shooting, stabbing and hanging done here lately that it does not seem to shock people very much."

A year later, Eunice's mother, Kate, who often managed the family holdings alone for months on end while her husband drove sheep and cattle back and forth to California, explained in a letter that, if anything, local violence had increased:

> We have had another dreadful lynching affair . . . and it makes me very nervous. . . . [He was] the ring leader of the horse thieves in this section. . . . He left a wife and three small children. . . . It is getting so that we live in constant dread of some one being killed. A man who was found a week or two ago dead in the hills was shot . . . no one knows who did it or if any one had any thing against him. A few days ago a man was shot at through the window.

Violence of this kind did not abate. The West was "wild" well into the twentieth century – some would doubtless add, is yet – for the white man's "fire stick" continued to exacerbate the worst aspects of human nature. In 1923 Mary McKinley, a forty-five-year-old divorcee, rancher, and rodeo horse trainer, lived "out on the breaks" in a clapboard cabin on Oregon's wind-battered Deschutes-Umatilla plateau. "Last night our homestead was burnt up. . . .

Minnie and I went to The Dalles to get a warrant out for four men, and in the evening we started for home but broke down."

McKinley tersely chronicles a hard-luck life experienced "in a five-cent house out of a nine o'clock town," where women still suffered from, and occasionally engaged in, the West's cult of violence.

4–15 Louisa came up and told us news. That night her and Oscar had a rowe . . .

4–16 Louisa shot herself in the left hand trying to unload a pistol . . .

4–17 I was up nearly all night, Louisa is very sick, her hand hurts awful bad. Her boys came home, I got dinner at Louisa's.

4–21 Dear Louisa died at two o'clock. . . .

4–24 . . . today poor Louisa is in the grave and out of the world, her little boys are left behind alone. Louisa was 27 years old. . . . Two hours before she died she asked me if I thought she would live, she ask me those terrible words five or six times, at last she said, "Well, I give up." . . . and when she died the last words was "Hurry, hurry."

As though words alone could not describe the unsettling circumstances of her life, Mary McKinley sometimes added little sketches to her diary pages. In one drawing two stick figures are in chase. The taller figure, wearing a cowboy hat, is brandishing a revolver. The caption reads: "Eddie went to town but had to leave again to keep from being arrested."

McKinley died in a violent car collision late on the night of November 24, 1934. Until "they went through her things" her relatives were not aware that she kept a diary. What made her do it? Her family believed it was loneliness, pure and simple.

Critic and novelist William Maxwell aptly characterizes the appeal of diaries and ascribes more complex motives to those who, like Mary McKinley and I, have felt a compulsion to keep them: "They [diaries] tell what happened – what people said and did and wore and ate and hoped for and were afraid of, and in detail after often unimaginable detail they refresh our idea of existence and hold oblivion at arm's length."

Maxwell notes that diaries and memoirs, along with other written expressions of personal literacy and imagination, "do not spring from prestidigitation or require a long apprenticeship."

Countless diarists and lettrists, in the manner of Mary McKinley, leap over the boundaries of wealth, station in life, and education. In many respects letters and diaries are the most democratic of all literary genres, for any reasonably literate person, regardless of gender or age, can, as the saying goes, "take a crack at them."

Fortunately, women have been as likely to express themselves in diaries and letters as men or we should have never known, "in detail after often unimaginable detail," how many of them really led their daily lives and what they considered important.

Mary Jane Moffat and Charlotte Painter, in their volume that excerpts the diaries of women of several nationalities, believe that the diary form has been important to women because it is analogous to their lives: "emotional, fragmentary, interrupted, private . . . and restricted." In addition, women's loneliness stems from both physical isolation and psychological alienation from one's milieu because normal outlets of discourse have been denied to them.

In the American West women were particularly motivated, it would seem, to keep the diary type known as the "overland journal," a form that is as connected to the American westering experience as an oxen team is to a Conestoga. It is one of the few subsets of American diary literature that has been exhaustively collected and anthologized.

An eleven-volume series, admirably edited and annotated by Kenneth Holmes, suggests new ways of looking at the experiences of western mothers, daughters, and wives during the difficult four-month trek West. Holmes describes some of these chroniclers as "grave counters." Others, such as diarist Elizabeth Dixon Smith, starkly convey images of unexpected traumatic occurrences. On September 15, 1847, for example, Smith recounts: "layed by this morning one company moved on except one family   the woman got mad and would not budge nor let the children."

For three hours the husband had his oxen hitched attempting to coax his wife to leave camp, "but she would not stur." At length, other travelers gathered up the woman's three youngest children and the exasperated husband drove away leaving his wife behind. Sometime later he sent one of their sons back to camp to collect a stray horse. When the son did not return the father went back to query his wife, whom he discovered had started out on foot:

> her husband says did you meet John   yes was the reply and i picked up a stone and nocked out his brains   her husband went back to ascertain the truth and while he was gone she set one of his waggons on fire which was loaded . . . with value-

able artickles he saw the flame. . . . put it out and then mustered spunk enough to give her a good floging.

Equally steeped in the idiomatic homebrew of rural schooling, the letters and diaries of the West's children are often as tersely descriptive as Smith's. Western violence respected neither gender nor age and took many forms. The punishing unpredictability of the weather is poignantly described in the letter of a ten-year-old Oregon girl named Julia Wilson, who lost her mother and three siblings in a flash flood:

> Well, it rained very hard. Then the water came right to the door. . . . We got to the ditch and then Ma fell down with George in her arms and Autia helped her up. . . . We saw the flood coming down the creek. . . . Then Ma commenced praying for help . . . Autia said to Ma, "If we can get to the hill we will be all right," and Ma said, "we can't do that." Then Autia commenced getting us acrosst the ditch. He had us all across but Ma and Maggie. He went back for them when the water was up to his neck. That was the last time I ever saw any of them. I then ran for the hills. Maggie said, "Oh! We can't live any longer, can we?". . . . The water was up to my waist about halfway to the hill. When I got there I looked back – the house and everything was gone. I stayed on the hill a long time. I could not see any one of them.

Grief-stricken Rachel Colver, a seventy-five-year-old grandmother,wrote of another form of violence that mortified the flesh – disease. Virulent epidemics such as diphtheria and scarlet fever periodically raged over the same western landscapes boosters touted as "the most healthful environs on the planet." Describing the small newly dug graves in a Phoenix, Oregon, cemetery where, "little Frances and Quincy were paled in [fenced] together," Colver added that "poor Quincy died very hard." She closed by saying, "i never expect to see you again only in Memory . . . i have not long to stay."

Mrs. Colver's granddaughter, the recipient of this unhappy correspondence, soon discovered that she, too, had "not long to stay." It would not be death that carried her away but her husband's search for gold. Tens of thousands of families would continually crisscross the West as a result of one or another resource rush. The theme of restlessness, even *after* reaching the Promised Land, resonates in the West's letters and diaries just as it does in the fictional works of Wallace Stegner, H. L. Davis, Vardis Fisher, and many other of the region's best-known writers. Boom and bust economies kept people moving on. Surely, G-O-L-D was the West's first four-letter word, especially for those longing for hearth and home.

Rodman Paul has said, "There was quite enough of the bizarre and dramatic about gold rushes to justify the novels, plays, and movies that have been written about them." "The pursuit of Money, money, is the absorbing object. . . . No longer ago than last night, I saw a man lying on the wet ground, unknown, unconscious, uncared for and dying." So observed gold seeker and superb letter writer J. B. D. Stillman, living out his own version of the West's contradictory narrative, and pondering the physical and moral effects of riches or the lack thereof. In a sense, gold mining set the tone for all of the West's excesses that Limerick and others characterize as get in, get rich, get out. It is still the attitude that prevails in our present era, only slightly ameliorated by the sure knowledge that the West's treasures are diminishing – some, such as old-growth forests and certain wild fisheries, never to be replaced. "Money, money" is still "the absorbing object" of the West's insatiable developers and entrepreneurs.

Stillman's '49er – left to die on a muddy, tented tract of a "diggins town" that would eventually become California's state capital, Sacramento – was a forerunner of a new urban underclass: the working poor. Another stratum would soon be added known as the transient poor, comprised of workers who followed seasonal production cycles or participated in spasmodic smaller natural resource rushes. The introduction of outdoor as well as indoor factories whose owners lived elsewhere created the West's second frontier: industry.

In reality, profit, loss, competition, and consolidation had always undermined the westerner's illusion of self-reliance. Long before 1849, Spanish, Russian, British, French, and American interests had exploited the Far West's resources on behalf of various international corporations. But from the 1850s onward the need for cheap labor pulled like an undertow. Tides of "alien" laborers swelled both urban and rural populations. It was clear that western America shared in the need for a cheap labor force that would result in the transplanted diversity of European and Asian workers whether the so-called nativists (who had successfully overrun the rights of Native Americans and Mexicans) liked it or not. "To an American death is preferable to a life on a par with the Chinaman. . . . Treason is better than to labor beside a Chinese slave." So went the manifesto of the California Workingmen's Party in 1876. Laborers of European extraction would carry a fiery torch quite different than the Statue of Liberty's.

An old Chinese proverb advises: "Better be kind at home than burn incense in a far place." But who could blame the men of poverty-plagued southern China for leaving home, especially when American speculators and capitalists made so many promises about the riches of Gum San – Land of the Golden Mountain? By 1860 nearly 35,000 Chinese had arrived on the Pacific coast. That industry and discipline – only two of the stereotypical attributes of Chinese laborers – moved the West to a new level of economic development was immediately clear, even to those who bitterly resented the fact that "coolies" worked for half as much as whites.

Tediously mining the tailings of gold mines whose white claimants had moved on, Chinese workers left sinuous lengths of low rock walls and hydraulic trenches such as the Eldorado Ditch in eastern Oregon's Blue Mountains, that was one hundred and thirty miles long. "The Chinamen are about to take the country," wrote an Oregonian (Viola Noon Currier) as early as 1857 in a letter to the editor. By the 1880s antipathy had only escalated, especially as Chinese (and other minorities) were used as strikebreakers.

It is generally known that Chinese laborers built many of the West's railroads. In Oregon alone, eight different lines were principally constructed by "coolie" labor. But to truly understand the significance and versatility of the immense bachelor labor force that so altered the West's life and landscape, other tasks should be enumerated: The Chinese strung literally hundreds of miles of telegraph line that, along with the railroads, would serve to connect the West with the rest of the nation and the world. Chinese men mined not only gold and silver but coal, mercury, and borax. They labored in forests and logging mills. They helped drain and clear the vast swamps of central California and the great brushy interior valleys of Oregon. Chinese farmers also produced vegetables and fruits – the famous Bing cherry was named for a pioneer Northwest orchardist's Cantonese assistant. Processing salmon, constructing homes, roads, bridges, and dams, the Chinese provided the principal labor source for many of the West's nascent industries, including textile mills.

Harsh exclusion laws kept Chinese men from sending for wives and other family members. Discrimination took many forms, and violence against them grew commonplace: "I'm shocked by the message that our friend, Mr. Lin was shot and killed by a barbaric American. Grief came with that news. What a miserable act! But what can we do?" wrote Kwang Chi in a recently translated letter to his cousin who was also living in the West.

By the 1880s many of the thriving "Chinatowns" located in more than fifty locations in five western states lost significant portions of

their population or disappeared altogether, sometimes as a result
of fires torched by mobs. Many sojourners expecting to remain
only a year or two in the lonely land of Gum San stayed for a
decade or more because of their indenture that made it almost
impossible to save enough money to return home. A few elected to
remain but for safety's sake struck out on their own to isolated
settings, such as remote mining settlements, where they occasionally found prosperity and qualified acceptance.

An unmailed letter from a nameless Cantonese miner was found
among thousands of scattered documents in the Kam Wah Chung
Mercantile Company building in John Day, Oregon, in the 1970s.
There, in the iron-shuttered gloom, laborers had once lit oil lamps
and joss sticks while mingling with their own kind. Many sought
pungent Oriental remedies from the Kam Wah Chung's owner
Doctor Ing Hay. Others dictated or wrote letters, worshiped at
community shrines, purchased tinned rice, noodles, and tea. Desperate to forget the tedium of their exhausting daily existence,
many men seemed to live only to gamble at fan tan or, perhaps, to
dream vividly with their long opium pipes poised beside them on
the bunk ledge while they seemed to drift home in clouds of sweet-
ly acrid smoke.

Whether the unnamed miner dictated his unfinished letter or
wrote it himself the message is at once timeless and eloquent:

> My Beloved Wife,
> It has been several autumns now since your dull husband left
> you. . . . I am all right. Therefore stop your embroidered
> worries. . . . Yesterday I received another of your letters. I
> could not keep the tears from running down my cheeks. . . .
> Because of our destitution I went out to try to make a living.
> Who could know that Fate is always opposite to man's design?
> Because I can get no gold, I am detained in this secluded
> corner of a strange land. Furthermore, my beauty, you are
> implicated in endless misfortune. I wish this paper would
> console you a little. This is all that I can do for now.

Until fairly recently, the American West's minorities have abided
in the margins of "the story." Frequently portrayed as stock characters by Eurocentric authors, like "extras" on a movie set, representatives of various ethnic groups have only been given a few lines to
say. As poets and novelists who are themselves members of minorities have newly emerged or been rescued from obscurity, more
accurate and respectful literary interpretations of the West's various peoples have found their way into print.

In this sense, Patricia Limerick's "meeting ground" has been illuminated through the manufactured light of fictional descriptions and encounters which may reflect historic or present realities depending upon the author's intentions and abilities. Certainly, the much needed stance of such authors writing from *within* the experiences of their respective cultural groups has served to deepen understanding.

Nevertheless, as scholar Elizabeth Jameson has suggested in reference to American western women, and, by extension, to other minorities as well, history should not be viewed "through the filters of prescriptive literature or concepts of frontier liberation and oppression, but through the experiences of the people who lived the history." Lettrists and diarists "who lived the history" in the context of real as opposed to imagined time may eventually provide the clearest view of ethnic life in the American West.

Unfortunately, it has sometimes been assumed that due to the transient nature of the West's many ethnic laborers – who, of necessity, were historically obliged to move from one western locale to another – it was highly unlikely that their letters and diaries would be found. This has been coupled with another assumption: that most ethnic laborers were illiterate. But one does not find what one does not look for. One can count upon the fact that there will always be exceptions such as the unexpectedly voluminous and complex array of letters discovered at Kam Wah Chung.

Another exception is the informative lyric-laced diary of Greek railroad worker Haralambos Kambouris, who came from his native Thebes in 1912 and kept a diary throughout his sojourn in the wet West as he lay track, dug tunnels, and endured long hungry stints in the ranks of other unemployed laborers in places like Idaho, Washington, and Oregon, where the rains seemed endless.

From the beginning of his journey in 1912, Kambouris's fate seemed linked to the "iron horse." "We boarded the train drenched with tears. We reached Athens and Piraeus. Still we had hope and still joy," he wrote later in his diary in demotic Greek while looking for employment in Oregon on the Southern Pacific Railroad. Increasingly homesick and disconsolate, he described slogging through water-clogged tunnels in danger of collapse; of train wrecks; of strife among Greek, Mexican, and Arab laborers who all tried to make a living in "Xenetia" (a foreign land). Surely, Kambouris spoke for the members of numerous nationalities when he implored, "Countrymen, friends, relatives, if you want to be joyful don't leave your sweet country!"

How much more of the West's polyphonic chorus remains unheard – the voices of people, old and young, talking on paper to the pages of letters and diaries? Men like Billy Chinook, Kwang Chi, and Haralambos Kambouris? Women like Mary McKinley, Kate and Eunice Robbins, and Mr. C—'s grandmother? Until we hear such voices, until we make room for everyone in the American West's story we won't know what the *place* we call the West really was, or is.

Works Cited

Anonymous. "Manifesto" (1876), California Workingmen's Party. Qtd. in Patricia Nelson Limerick, *The Legacy of Conquest.*

Currier, Viola Noon. Letter to the Editor. *Portland Weekly Oregonian,* 31 October 1857. Qtd. in Gunther Barth, *Bitter Strength: A History of the Chinese in the United States.* Cambridge: Harvard UP, 1964.

Holmes, Kenneth. "Introduction." *Covered Wagon Women: Diaries and Letters from the Western Trails, 1840–1870.* Vol. II. Ed. Kenneth Holmes. 1983. Rpt. Spokane, WA: Arthur H. Clark Co., 1990, 9–12.

Jameson, Elizabeth. "Women as Workers, Women as Civilizers: True Womanhood in the American West." *Frontiers: A Journal of Women's Studies* 7 (1984): 1–8.

Kagle, Steven E. *American Diary Literature: 1620–1799.* Boston: Twayne, 1979.

Kimball, G. G. Diary entry (August 1865). Qtd. in Helen R. Fretwell-Johnson, *In Times Past: A History of the Lower Jordan Communities.* Filer, Idaho: The Print Shoppe, 1990.

Limerick, Patricia Nelson. *The Legacy of Conquest: The Unbroken Past of the American West.* New York: Norton, 1987.

Maxwell, William. "Note." *The Outermost Dream: Essays and Reviews.* New York: Alfred Knopf, 1989, vii–ix.

McKinley, Mary. "Mary McKinley's Diary." In Helen Guyton Rees, *Shaniko People.* Portland: Binford & Mort, 1983, 73–79.

Moffat, Mary Jane. "Foreword." *Revelations: Diaries of Women.* Ed. Mary Jane Moffat and Charlotte Painter. New York: Random House, 1974, 3–12.

Paul, Rodman W. "Gold & Silver Rushes." In *The Reader's Encyclopedia of the American West.* Ed. Howard Lamar. New York: Harper & Row, 1977, 445–51.

Robinson, Forrest G. "The New Historicism and the Old West." *Western American Literature* 25, no. 2 (Summer 1990): 103–23.

Schlissel, Lillian, Vicki L. Ruiz, and Janice Monk. "Introduction." *Western Women: Their Land and Lives.* Eds. Schlissel, Ruiz, and Monk. Albuquerque: U of New Mexico P, 1988, 1–9.

Smith, Henry Nash. "Symbol and Idea in *Virgin Land.*" In *Ideology and Classic American Literature.* Eds. Sacvan Bercovitch and Myra Jehlen. New York: Cambridge UP, 1986, 21–35.

Stillman, J. B. D. "Gold Rush Letters." In *Looking Far West: The Search for the American West in History, Myth and Literature*. Eds. Frank Bergon and Zeese Papanikolas. New York: New American Library, 1978, 255–58.

Letters and Diary Excerpts Cited

The following letter or diary excerpts are taken from *Talking on Paper: An Anthology of Oregon Letters & Diaries*. Ed. Shannon Applegate and Terence O'Donnell. Corvallis: Oregon State UP, 1994.

Anonymous Chinese Miner. Letter. Undated.
Chinook, Billy. Letter. November 3, 1853.
Colver, Rachel. Letter. August 3, 1864.
Haswell, Robert. Ship's Log. August 16, 1788.
Hull, Robert. Letter. December 14, 1853.
Kambouris, Haralambos. Diary Entry. February 28, 1915.
Kwang Chi. Letter. Undated.
Moore, Harry De Witt. Letter. April 29, 1873.
Robbins, Eunice. Letter. June 5, 1882.
Robbins, Kate. Letter. January 7, 1883.
Smith, Elizabeth Dixon. Diary Entry. September 15, 1847.
Vincent, L. H. Diary Entry. September 23, 1922.
Wilson, Julia. Letter. Undated [1884].

QUOTING THE WICKED
WIT OF THE WEST:
FRONTIER REPORTAGE
AND WESTERN VERNACULAR

MICHAEL KOWALEWSKI

Language, Walt Whitman reminds us in his remarkable essay "Slang in America," "is not an abstract construction of the learn'd, or of dictionary-makers, but is something arising out of the work, needs, ties, joys, affections, tastes, of long generations of humanity, and has its bases broad and low, close to the ground." It is slang (by which Whitman means colloquial speech in general) that forms the "source-impulse" of "the whole immense tangle of the old mythologies" which language embodies. "Slang, profoundly consider'd is the lawless germinal element, below all words and sentences, and behind all poetry, and proves a certain perennial rankness and protestantism in speech." Slang most flourished in the American West, in Whitman's opinion, "not only in conversation, but in [the] names of localities, towns, [and] rivers":

> Among the far-west newspapers, have been, or are, *The Fairplay* (Colorado) *Flume, The Solid Muldoon,* of Ouray, *The Tombstone Epitaph,* of Nevada, *The Jimplecute,* of Texas, and *The Bazoo,* of Missouri. Shirttail Bend, Whiskey Flat, Puppytown, Wild Yankee Ranch, Squaw Flat, Rawhide Ranch, Loafer's Ravine, Squitch Gulch, Toenail Lake, are a few of the names of places in Butte county, Cal.

Whitman's energetic sense that the life of the West has been shaped not only by mining strikes, cattle drives, and arid landscapes but also by the verbal inventiveness of popular western speech offers but one example of a fascination on the part of American writers with the full range of vernacular idioms, one that extends well beyond western writing. The vernacular tradition in American literature predates nineteenth-century writing, but it flowered there, early and late, with a particular vitality and force.

82

Whether in Emerson's belief that "colleges and books only copy the language which the field and the work-yard made" or in the rip-roaring, wildcat-wrassling, helliferocious dialect experiments of the Southwest humorists, the search for a native idiom in American writing often suggested that linguistic servility to English taste was analogous to feebleness of will.

"The notion that stylistic elegance was the literary counterpart of European political oppression," Leo Marx says, has a longstanding history in the United States. Masters of the vernacular like Whitman and Twain created what Marx aptly calls "a drama of cultural contrast," one that juxtaposed "the possibilities and the dangers of [a] new society." Allowing that drama to spring from the vitality of native idioms in their work, Whitman and Twain created not simply a style, Marx asserts, "but a style with a politics in view," one that contravened "the repeated European sneer against the crudities of American culture" and affirmed "an egalitarian faith . . . [that] sweeps aside received notions of class and status – and of literature." An interest in vernacular speech in the United States has thus involved far more than a diversionary interest in colorful language. The sounds and movements of idiomatic speech have been taken to offer social gestures of personality and expressions of value in American writing which cannot be adequately evoked in standard English or in a genteel literary tradition. In its most provocative or aggressively plebian mode, the vernacular has been used to question not only the necessity of tradition but the very idea of literature itself.

Still, the presence of colloquial speech in American writing is no guarantee in itself of linguistic egalitarianism or the championing of socially marginal groups. It can just as easily be used to encode social condescension and disparagement. As David Sewell points out, Twain himself, who is often taken as a kind of folk hero of the vernacular, had a life-long ambivalence about colloquial speech. Twain was perfectly capable of satirizing pedantic grammarians and "the moral inadequacies of the standard language with which social authority expresses itself," Sewell says. But Twain also never seriously doubted the authority of standard English or prescriptive grammar and he was constantly at pains to call the attention of his eastern readership to "his 'good English,' his 'pure English,' the guarantee of his social acceptability and of his right to join the literary 'rocks' of the Eastern Establishment."

The celebration of an indigenous language and literature in the United States has always been more easily conceived than executed. Even in the first surges toward literary independence, as Richard

Bridgman notes, "the fundamental question for all those working with the vernacular was how to eliminate the taint of vulgarity and of humor that normally accompanied popular speech": "the arbiters of taste generally agreed that the crudities of American common speech were to be barred from any decent writer's style. Vulgarity in writing had to be fenced in with quotation marks, or clearly labeled as comic and therefore not to be taken seriously." The rebellious potential of ungenteel speech, that is, even when that speech was recognized as a literary resource, was often neutered or rendered passive by an innocuous typographical convention that nevertheless carried the authority of a cultural norm, one that established "proper" usages and behavior, on and off the page.

Quotation of spoken speech in writing, even of colloquial speech, does not always call attention to itself. It is often scarcely noted, as a technical device, by a reader. (How much do readers actually *see* quotation marks as they read? They may actually pay more attention when quotation marks are conspicuously absent around dialogue, as in Cormac McCarthy's fiction.) The narrative context in which a person is quoted determines the degree of contrast whereby quoted speech is comfortably assimilated or rendered outlandish and thrown into comic or picturesque relief. The narrative voice which is otherwise in force in a piece of writing – whether a letter, a journal, or a novel – regulates the degree to which we notice how much more conscious or more discriminating a writer is about his use of language than are the speakers he quotes. Quoted speech can easily be countervailed by a writer's idiom and relegated to another verbal world, one in which the speaker quoted conspicuously lacks the powers of descriptive analysis and irony of the writer who has put him in quotes. Colloquial speech can, it is true, take on an imaginative life of its own which often seems better than its verbal occasion: more pungent, more challenging, more grounded in life. But its distinctiveness remains crucially dependent upon the context in which its linguistic difference is accentuated.

* * * * * *

The western frontier had no monopoly on the use of the vernacular in American literature. Western colloquial speech has, however, been granted a special literary exuberance and life, and many writers in or from the West have shared Whitman's sense that whatever the "hasty and grotesque" aspects of western vernacular, it has helped breathe the "breath of life" into the "nostrils" of language. For many early visitors to the American West, the region's dialect geography offered a delicately calibrated means by which to measure the depth and complexity of western culture. In addition to the overpowering landscapes and squalid living conditions they encountered in the West, writers were invariably fascinated with the way people verbally conducted themselves, with how language had been transplanted and had taken to seed. Language, intonation, and idiomatic nuance were taken to be vivid indicators of cultural difference. Western vernacular was seen as exemplifying the most degraded and duplicitous features of western society as well as its most revivifying and imaginative aspects. Dramatizing both the social incongruities and the cultural adrenaline of the West, spoken speech seemed uniquely to capture the spirit of the region for many authors. *Hearing* the West quickly became a crucial component of what it meant to experience it.

Here's Mark Twain – or rather his enthusiastic narrator – reporting on a station master in *Roughing It* (1872):

> "Pass the bread, you son of a skunk!" No, I forget – skunk was not the word; it seems to me it was still stronger than that; I know it was, in fact, but it is gone from my memory, apparently. However, it is no matter – probably it was too strong for print anyway. It is the landmark in my memory which tells me where I first encountered the vigorous new vernacular of the occidental plains and mountains.

The passage is self-consciously knowing on several counts. The greenhorn narrator – who has been reading the Unabridged Dictionary and "wondering how the characters would come out" – suddenly becomes a rogue linguist pretending, with mock-precision, to remember a word he knows he cannot print. The humorous paradox, as Lee Mitchell points out, "is that he claims to have forgotten the word that had affected him so memorably." Twain here pokes fun at an eastern literary decorum concerned with unprintable language even as he flatters it. He demonstrates his affection for the station master's language and for all the lawless, germinal ways of verbally roughing it in the West. But he also invokes a cultural frame of reference here, another way of talking, which is unavailable to the station master. Twain, that is, can use a phrase like "the vigorous new vernacular of the occidental plains and mountains," which offers an "eastern" way of domesticating a vigor which might otherwise put standardized English to rout.

Much of the fun of *Roughing It* stems from the fact that Twain's parody is often most anarchic just when he seems to be striking a moralistic or an aesthetically discriminating stance. The narrator, for instance, complains at one point about "the dislocated grammar and decomposed pronunciation" he encounters in the West. He himself then turns around and uses dislocated syntax, however, claiming, "[our] grammar was faulty, maybe, but we could not know, then, that it would go into a book someday." At another point, the narrator tells of a stagecoach driver on the Southern Overland Express: "He said the Apaches used to annoy him all the time down there, and that he came as near as anything to starving to death in the midst of abundance, because they kept him so leaky with bullet holes that he 'couldn't hold his vittles.' This person's statements were not generally believed." The comic superfluousness of the narrator's soberly informing us that this driver should not be believed is heightened by the quote-unquote way in which the narrator offers up a colloquial phrase as a sign of veracity and exactitude.

The "linguistic vertigo" of Twain's picaresque narrative, Mitchell says, results from the narrator's perverse insistence on imposing "a set of traditional idioms on [western] experience." The strangeness of the West in *Roughing It,* he rightly avers, "depends as much on its language as on its landscape": "for Twain, a tour of the West celebrates not the landscapes and denizens depicted by predecessors like Bayard Taylor, Francis Parkman, and Bret Harte" but "the idiosyncratic locutions and narratives by which the region made sense of itself." Western idioms, in their very boisterousness and cheerful malice, reflected the rough society from which they derived. Thus for Twain and others, an interest in western speech often represented an implicit challenge to the social privileges and pretensions of eastern behavior.

Twain was obviously not in favor of discarding the conventionalized eastern discourse which made it possible to communicate his experiences in the first place, and neither did he simply idealize common language. But he was particularly sensitive to the dreary, neutralizing powers of correct English which could lead to what he calls "chloroform in print" (his description of the Book of Mormon). However much (as Sewell argues) Twain saw the carnivalesque pull of multiple voices as a symptom of social decadence, he was still acutely aware of how "correct" usage could anesthetize the disruptive action of vernacular speech, and bleach it of its original color. The very means by which the vigor of colloquial western speech was recorded – in typographical irregularities and quotation marks – represented, he knew, a kind of verbal leash by which to keep it in check. Like other writers in the West, Twain's exposure to western idioms fostered a desire to make his standard English equal to the playfulness and energy of colloquial speech. The wish to do so places him firmly in the tradition of such otherwise diverse American writers as Cooper, Melville, Thoreau, Faulkner, and Frost: all of whom ask of their readers and of themselves that they be, as Richard Poirier puts it, both "common and literary all at once."

* * * * * *

Twain's attention to the play of voices in the West (his own included) in *Roughing It* offers but one example – an entertainingly disruptive one – of how the quotation of colloquial speech in western texts expresses complicated attitudes toward language and cultural values. The work of two other, lesser-known nineteenth-century frontier journalists – Louise Clappe's *The Shirley Letters* (1854–55) and Isabella Bird's *A Lady's Life in the Rocky Mountains* (1879) – offers a further opportunity for understanding the range of cultural interaction and synopsis involved in recording western colloquial speech.

As was usual in the nineteenth century, these two authors came to the West from the East (or, in Bird's case, from England, though she actually arrives, at the start of the book, from Hawaii and then moves east). The writers who first reported on the West were not usually themselves the ones using western idioms and neither were their readers. The West in the nineteenth century, Stephen Fender says, "could never have expressed itself for itself; it was described by easterners for other easterners who stayed at home." Clappe, Bird, and Twain thus all confronted the problem of how (to borrow Raymond Williams' term) they were to make western characters "knowable" to an eastern or English audience. How could they record the extemporizing verbal gifts of the "wicked wits" of the West, as Clappe called them, without dampening their expressive energy? How could they celebrate the promiscuous wit and humor of western idioms without somehow killing them off? And how could they express their disapproval of the less appealing aspects of western life that speech embodied without sounding overly censorious or unresponsive?

The use of quotation marks to "fence in" the free-roaming verbal life of the West offers an illuminating way of investigating what contemporary theorists call "the politics of representation." That is, who gets to represent whom, and in what terms? The temptation to quote scoffingly or with unsympathetic satire is often strongest in these texts when the cultural barrier is that of a foreign language. With certain groups of people – especially the Chinese and

Native Americans, whose members often spoke little English – what was actually available for quotation were pidgin hybrids or "jargons" that are sometimes made to sound degraded or nonsensical in western texts, whatever the actual complexity of such languages might have been in the context of frontier communication.

Clappe at one point describes the sounds of the "living polyglot of languages" in the gold camps, which strike her as "a perambulating picture gallery, illustrative of national variety in form and feature." She notes "the piquant polish of the French," "the silver, changing clearness of the Italian," "the harsh gangle of the German," and "the liquid sweetness of the Kanaka." She then adds: "To complete the catalogue, there is the *native* Indian, with his guttural vocabulary of twenty words." Clappe is stimulated by the cultural heterogeneity of the camps, but there are clearly limits to what she finds exhilarating. However harsh the German "gangle," Clappe still finds it preferable to the "guttural" sounds of Indian (perhaps mountain Maidu) speech. As often as not, Chinese and Indian characters in these works appear in degraded silence, with no speech at all, as when Bird describes the "Digger Indians" crowded in a train headed for Lake Tahoe: "They were all hideous and filthy, and swarming with vermin."

Yet if certain of the polyglot speech communities of the West did not lend themselves to sympathetic depiction, the Spanish (or, more accurately, Mexican) words that gained a quick currency in western speech were often noted appreciatively by these writers. "A *corral* is a fenced enclosure for cattle," Bird writes in a footnote. "This word, with *bronco, ranch,* and a few others, are adaptations from the Spanish and are used as extensively throughout California and the Territories as is the Spanish or Mexican saddle." Clappe admires Spanish place names and phrases in the California gold camps, and Twain paints an entertaining picture of the "*cayote* (pronounced ky-*o*-te)" and appreciatively watches the Mexicans and "Mexicanized Americans" in Carson who forgo the "jiggering up and down after the silly Miss-Nancy fashion of the riding-schools" and sweep through town "like the wind," with a "long *riata*" swinging above their heads.

Contrary to what some might suggest, quotation of colloquial speech in the nineteenth century did not always represent the subjugation of idiomatic verve to verbal convention and proper usage. It did not always encode a superiority or cultural contempt. It could also, and just as importantly, be used to suggest admiration and imaginative leniency. In fact, as with Twain, colloquial speech often turned back to sting the citified overcultivation and imagina-

tive exhaustion of an "eastern" voice grappling with western characters. The immediacy and spark of common speech was often
presented not as yielding to a cultural norm but as a restorative and
reanimating alternative to the very cultural authority that attempted to quarantine it in quotes. Western vernacular was taken
to embody the possibilities for interaction and understanding,
however strained or awkward, between divergent social and cultural groups on the frontier.

The difference emphasized most strongly for Louise Clappe was
that of gender. *The Shirley Letters*, which Wallace Stegner rightly
called the "finest of all Gold Rush books," is a group of twenty-
three letters written by Louise Amelia Knapp Smith Clappe (writing under the *nom de plume* "Dame Shirley") to her stay-at-home
sister in Massachusetts. Clappe's letters from two crude camps high
in the upper canyons of the Feather River convey a clear-eyed but
tolerant view of the rowdy masculinity of makeshift settlements in
which she was one of only a few women amidst hundreds of men.
Clappe was married when she arrived, but the very fact that she
was a woman counted highly for the miners. A young southerner
"had not spoken to a woman for two years; and in the elation of his
heart at the joyful event, he rushed out and invested capital in some
excellent champagne, which I, on Willie's [a young relative's?] principle of 'doing in Turkey as the Turkies do,' assisted the company in
drinking to the honor of my own arrival."

Clappe was especially sensitive to the sounds of spoken speech
because her position as a woman often relegated her to the role of
an unwilling eavesdropper. "Profanity prevails in California" to a
"mournful extent," she reports in her sixth letter. "Of course, the
most vulgar blackguard will abstain from swearing in the *presence* of
a lady," she adds, "but in this rag and card-board house, one is
compelled to hear the most sacred of names constantly profaned by
the drinkers and gamblers who haunt the bar-room at all hours."
The obscenities Clappe hears on account of the camp's cramped
living conditions rupture her eastern notions of decorum, yet she
cannot help admitting to a subterranean admiration for their verbal inventiveness. "Some of these expressions," she says, "were they
not so fearfully blasphemous, would be grotesquely sublime."
While not forsaking her own standard of judgment – blasphemy
still stands for her as a serious charge – Clappe nevertheless dis-
plays an instinctive responsiveness to camp life and speech, and she
is wary of being too easily indignant. When she sees a parade of
drunken miners from Chile, Clappe says, "[I suppose] I ought to
have been shocked and horrified – to have shed salt tears, and have

uttered melancholy Jeremiads over their miserable degradation. But the world is so full of platitudes, my dear, that I think you will easily forgive me for not boring you with a temperance lecture, and will good-naturedly let me have my laugh, and not think me *very* wicked after all." When the Chileans are joined by carousing groups of different nationalities, Clappe declares, with a smile, "It was impossible to tell which nation was the most gloriously drunk."

Garlanded throughout Clappe's letters are innumerable quotations from the Bible and from European novelists, poets, and artists, which serve as a cultural backdrop against which to foreground various quoted bits of frontier California – whether snippets of speech, mining terminology, Spanish place-names, or her neighbors' nicknames (Yank, Little John, Chock, Big Bill, and Paganini Ned). Clappe's literary quotations form a kind of cultural buffer for her verbal sensibility that allows for animated, belletristic satire. "I *like* this wild and barbarous life," she writes in her final letter, and throughout *The Shirley Letters* Clappe finds her surroundings "delightfully primitive." She relishes the miners' frontier brags and mispronunciations (as when a Frenchman refers to "Shorge Washingtone"). The wit and incongruity of colloquial speech provide her with a constant source of amusement:

> If [the men of the Rich Bar camp] wish to borrow anything of you, they will mildly inquire if you have it "about your clothes." As an illustration; a man asked F. [her husband, Fayette] the other day, "If he had a spare pick-axe about his clothes." And F. himself gravely inquired of me this evening at the dinner table, if I had "a *pickle* about my clothes."

Clappe's amateur ethnography can verge at times on the precious and the socially complacent, as she tends to make the conventional equation between verbal sophistication (as she understands it) and moral character. She is quick to castigate churlishness and bigotry when she hears it, adverting on one occasion to "that vulgar 'I'm as good as you are,' spirit, which is, it must be confessed, peculiar to the lower classes of our people." The context for this remark is important, however, as it is prompted by an impending Fourth of July race riot between Mexican and American miners, precipitated by "vulgar Yankees" "drunk with whisky and patriotism." The riot is the inevitable outcome of the American miners' prejudice against the Mexicans, which is exemplified, Clappe notes, in their verbal behavior.

> Nothing is more amusing than to observe the different styles, in which the generality of the Americans talk *at* the unfortu-

nate Spaniard. In the first place, many of them really believe, that when they have learned *sabe* and *vamos,* (two words which they seldom use in the right place,) *poco tiempo, si* and *bueno,* (the last they *will* persist in pronouncing *whayno,*) they have the whole of the glorious Castilian at their tongue's end. . . . [Some] make the most excruciatingly grotesque gestures, and think that *that* is speaking Spanish. The majority, however, place a most beautiful and touching faith in *broken English,* and when they murder it, with the few words of Castilian quoted above, are firmly convinced, that it is nothing but their "ugly dispositions" which makes the Spaniards pretend not to understand them.

Clappe sympathizes with the Hispanic miners (at least those with winning manners), so it is little surprise to hear her defending them here from the racial biases of the American miners. It is unclear how much Spanish Clappe herself knows but she seems confident in satirizing the miners' demand that others speak a language they themselves do not speak correctly. But once again Clappe escapes the platitudes "the world is so full of" by referring to idiomatic speech. She concerns herself here less with a stuffy complaint that the miners murder English than with the manner in which they justify their own presumptuous nationalism. Because she empathizes with the Mexicans, she gains a distance on the American miners similar to that which allows her to refer to them at points not as men but as "bipeds." Their prejudices here are "touching" not because Clappe approves of their xenophobia but because their self-justifications prompt an inventive local usage: their grumbling about "ugly dispositions."

Clappe alternates between sympathy and distance in her view of mining-camp life. Take, for example, her description of a three-week holiday rampage the miners go on at Christmas. She wishes to reassure her sister about her own safety and firmly asserts that the men of Rich Bar are "generous, hospitable, intelligent and industrious people" and that only cultural deprivations, bad weather, and ("unkindest cut of all!") a lack of "pretty girls" have conspired to promote the present bacchanalia. Such reassurances, however, do not keep her from overlooking the "drunken heaps" in the barroom, the "reckless mania for pouring down liquor," and the "unearthly howling" of intoxicated miners that issues from the bar: "some barked like dogs, some roared like bulls, and others hissed like serpents and geese. Many were too far gone to imitate anything but their own animalized selves."

Yet rather than moralizing upon the degenerative effects of

frontier life, Clappe goes on to tell the fate of the few men who attempted to stay sober during the celebration:

> The revelers formed themselves into a mock vigilance committee, and when one of these [sober] unfortunates appeared outside, a constable, followed by those who were able to keep their legs, brought him before the Court, where he was tried on some amusing charge, and *invariably* sentenced to "treat the crowd." The prisoners had generally the good sense to submit cheerfully to their fate.

Clappe herself considers it "good sense" to submit cheerfully to her own situation as a woman in a remote California mining camp. Her appreciation of this mock vigilance committee does not at all disable her moral indignation or her sense of cultural propriety. But she is both too genial and too attentive a writer to ignore how the carnivalesque antics of the revelers are encapsulated in the mock injunction to "treat the crowd." Absorbing the quick-witted expedience and exuberance of California frontier life in her own responses to it, Clappe enjoyed what Bret Harte once called the "true humorist's capacity to be content with the enjoyment of his own fun." Her whimsical sensitivity to western idioms exemplifies a fascinated ambivalence about life in gold-rush California. Her letters (to borrow a term from Margery Sabin's excellent study of the English realist novel, *The Dialect of the Tribe*) establish a complex bilingualism, one that attempts to include both the language of eastern convention and the expressive possibilities of western wit and idiom.

* * * * * *

Isabella Bird shared Clappe's view of western speech as a measure of cultural redeemability, but she was more self-conscious than Clappe about how she herself might be sized up in the West. Witness her encounter, in an "irregular wooden inn" at Lake Tahoe, with "a San Francisco lady, much 'got up' in paint, emerald green velvet, Brussels lace, and diamonds."

> [She] rattled continuously for the amusement of the company, giving descriptions of persons and scenes in a racy Western twang, without the slightest scruple as to what she said. . . . I sustained the reputation which our country-women bear in America by looking a 'perfect guy'; and feeling that I was a salient point for the speaker's next sally, I was relieved when the landlady, a ladylike Englishwoman, asked me to join herself and her family in the bar-room, where we had much talk about the neighborhood and its wild beasts, especially bears.

This is a fine example of Bird's sensitiveness about her Englishness and her own appearance. (A male companion once described her, Janet Robinson says, as "wearing bloomers, riding cowboy fashion, with a face and figure not corresponding to our ideals.") Bird feels no qualms in stating her dislike for this gaudily bedecked woman, but she also realizes she is a satiric target for westerners like her, who are quick to judge others by their physical appearance and their nationality (though Bird was "nearly always taken for a Dane or a Swede" and thus often heard "a good deal of outspoken criticism" of the English).

A Lady's Life in the Rocky Mountains is based on Bird's letters to her sister Henrietta during her travels in the West in 1873. The book's best-selling popularity (seven editions in the first three years alone) was undoubtedly due in part to moments of self-dramatization like this one. But it was also and perhaps primarily due to the zestful appetite of this single, forty-one-year-old woman for adventure travel and for searching out picturesque scenery. Bird suffers numerous mishaps and constantly endures trying circumstances in her travels. She sleeps in "hot and airless" cabins "papered with the *Phrenological Journal*," rides in stuffy railroad cars "full of chewing, spitting Yankees," and eats in boarding-houses swarming with locusts and black flies. Her bedsheet freezes to her lip in her Estes Park abode, her foot freezes to her wooden stirrup at nine degrees below zero near Colorado Springs, and she suffers from nausea, altitude sickness, and snow blindness. She suffers innumerable equestrian falls (through broken ice into mountain streams, into snowdrifts up to her shoulders). On one occasion her horse is repeatedly charged by a vicious steer, on another her mount plunges to avoid a bear in the Sierras, and she is left to carry a heavy saddle for "nearly an hour" in "deep dust." She kills a rattlesnake near a cabin in the Rockies and takes its rattle, "which had eleven joints." She is forced at one point to eat the kernels of cherrystones she finds in a dead bear's stomach; at another point she rides for fourteen hours eating nothing but raisins. One of the first women to climb Long's Peak (the "American Matterhorn" at 14,255 feet), she suffers numerous hardships during the ascent, including a severe thirst brought on by oxygen debt: "our mouths and tongues [were] so dry that articulation was difficult, and the speech of all unnatural."

Yet nothing is more typical of Bird's travels than her invincible optimism and what she calls "my spirit for overcoming difficulties." Describing her ride through a particularly rough ravine, she remains almost comically resilient.

Ah! it was a wild place. My horse fell first, rolling over twice, and breaking off a part of the saddle, in his second roll knocking me over a shelf of three feet of descent. Then Mrs. C.'s horse and the mule fell on the top of each other, and on recovering themselves bit each other savagely. . . . I was cut and bruised, scratched and torn. A spine of a cactus penetrated my foot, and some vicious thing cut the back of my neck. Poor Mrs. C. was much bruised, and I pitied her, for she got no fun out of it as I did. It was an awful climb.

Bird characteristically turns a hardship to good – that is, to entertaining or picturesque – account. Mishaps are instantly forgotten as she listens appreciatively to "the night cries of beasts in the aromatic forests" or thrills to the spectacle of Rocky Mountain scenery: "an ocean of glistening peaks" that stretches "almost from the Arctic Circle to the Straits of Magellan." "This is another world," she marvels. "This scenery satisfies my soul."

For all her appreciation of alpine scenery in the West, however, Bird takes an unsentimental view of the society she encounters there, and this helps explain the rapid fluctuations between hardship and happiness, independence and vulnerability, euphoria and depression in her letters. "This region of hard greed," she says, "is not Arcadia." Cheyenne, Wyoming, strikes her as "an ill-arranged set of frame houses and shanties, and rubbish heaps" where "the offal of deer and antelope produce the foulest smells I have smelt for a long time." The town "abounds in slouching bar-room-looking characters, and looks a place of low, mean lives." "On one of the dreary spaces of the settlement," she adds, "six white-tilted wagons, each with twelve oxen, are standing on their way to a distant part. Everything suggests a beyond." New settlements like Fort Collins are "entirely utilitarian, . . . with coarse speech, coarse food, coarse everything, [and] nothing wherewith to satisfy the higher cravings if they exist."

The hard utilitarianism of the West was often exemplified for Bird in "coarse speech." Her appearance as a "perfect guy," for instance, does not protect her from ridicule when she is allowed to stay in a ragged, unhospitable mountain boarding house only on the condition, as the landlady puts it, that she make herself "agreeable":

having finished my own work, I offered to wash up the plates, but Mrs. C., with a look which conveyed more than words, a curl of her nose, and a sneer in her twang, said "Guess you'll make more work nor you'll do. Those hands of yours" (very brown and coarse they were) "ain't no good; never done nothing, I guess." Then to her awkward daughter: "This woman

says she'll wash up! Ha! ha! look at her arms and hands!" . . .
Since then I have risen in their estimation by . . . means of the
shell-pattern quilt I am knitting for you [Henrietta]. There
has been a tendency towards approving of it, and a few days
since the girl snatched it out of my hand, saying, "I want this,"
and apparently took it to the camp. This has resulted in my
having a knitting class, with the woman, her married daughter, and a woman from the camp, as pupils.

Bird knows the landlady's rebuke is unjustified, but it is clear that
her comments sting. Mrs. Chalmers "looks like one of the English
poor women of our childhood," Bird says, "lean, clean, toothless,
and [she] speaks like some of them, in a piping, discontented voice,
which seems to convey a personal reproach."

It would be a mistake, I think, to read this kind of comment only
along the lines of class conflict, just as the connection Bird draws
here between Mrs. Chalmers and surly Englishwomen keeps her
dislike of the former from being simply a matter of nationalistic
bias. Though Bird is touchy about unjustified denigration of the
English, she generally avoids cultural chauvinism, and she directs
her criticism at all levels of the social spectrum. At a remote mountain lodging, she immediately recognizes an English gentleman,
despite "his rough hunter's or miner's dress," because of his "Lord
Dundreary drawl and [his] general execration of everything." "I sat
in the chimney corner," she says, "speculating on the reason why
many of the upper class of my countrymen – 'High Toners,' as they
are called out here – make themselves so ludicrously absurd."

Bird's judgmental presence in this book, while never absent, is
less stridently self-assured and ironic than that in earlier travel
narratives by English visitors such as Frances Trollope's *Domestic
Manners of the Americans* (1832) or Charles Dickens's *American Notes*
(1842). She does not make a point of dramatizing her offended
sensibilities. While she does not find the Rocky Mountain scenery
"lovable," she says "it has an intense fascination." The same holds
true for her attitude toward western society and its rough speech.
"'There's a stranger! Heave arf a brick at him!' is said by many
travelers to express the feeling of the new settlers in these Territories," Bird says. "This is not my experience in my cheery mountain
home." She is quick to commend the free-hearted hospitality of
many western families, and in Estes Park she says a "true democratic equality prevails, not its counterfeit": "though various grades of
society are represented, . . . there is neither forwardness on one
side nor condescension on the other."

Bird's most memorable occasion for displaying her agile appreciation of western life is her portrait of Mountain Jim. Jim, whom she insists upon calling "Mr. Nugent," is a one-eyed "desperado" who lives with his collie "Ring" in a "rude black log cabin" surrounded by antlers, old horseshoes, the offal of wild animals, and beaver paws pinned to the beams. When she first arrives,

> His first impulse was to swear at the dog, but on seeing a lady he contented himself with kicking him, and coming to me he raised his cap, showing as he did so a magnificently-formed brow and head, and in a cultured tone of voice asked if there were anything he could do for me? I asked for some water, and he brought some in a battered tin, gracefully apologizing for not having anything more presentable. We entered into conversation, and as he spoke I forgot both his reputation and appearance, for his manner was that of a chivalrous gentleman, his accent refined, and his language easy and elegant. I inquired about some beavers' paws which were drying, and in a moment they hung on the horn of my saddle. . . . Of his genius and chivalry to women there does not appear to be any doubt; but he is a desperate character, and is subject to "ugly fits," when people think it best to avoid him.

Robertson notes that Bird edited the letters that make up *A Lady's Life in the Rocky Mountains* and did not mention the fact that Jim became "attached" to her. As she wrote to Henrietta but did not mention in the book, he was "a man whom any woman might love but who no sane woman would marry." The same compelling mix of affection and distaste characterizes her published portrayal of him. Jim serves as Bird's guide up Long's Peak and she is awakened during the climb to watch a "lemon colored" high-altitude dawn break over the gray plains with him. When the sun appears, Jim "involuntarily and reverently uncovered his head, and exclaimed, 'I believe there is a God.'" Later, after the climb, at a moonlit campfire, he weeps as he tells her of "a great sorrow which had led him on a lawless and desperate life." Bird cannot tell whether this is "semi-conscious acting" or whether "his dark soul [had] really [been] stirred to its depths by the silence, the beauty, and the memories of youth."

Apart from "a certain dazzle," Bird says, Jim's life "is a ruined and wasted one," and she answers her own question – "what of good can the future have in store for one who has for so long chosen evil?" – with a somber footnote added to the text: "September of the next year answered the question by laying him down in a dishonored grave, with a rifle bullet in his brain." Yet Bird continues to relish Jim's "breezy mountain recklessness" and she reaches for the western vernacular to pay him the highest compliment. "Mr. Nugent," she says, "is what is called 'splendid company.'"

Bird's delicately poised responsiveness to Jim and to the western society she encounters in *A Lady's Life* is emblematic of the way the most engaging western writers have been attracted to what Whitman called "the rich flashes of humor and genius and poetry" in western vernacular speech. To appreciate those qualities, these authors do not blind themselves to the mean-spirited or duplicitous dimensions of colloquial idioms. ("'Smartness,' which consists in over-reaching your neighbor in every fashion which is not illegal, is the quality which is held in the greatest repute" in the West, Bird notes dryly: "The boy who 'gets on' by cheating at his lessons is praised for being a 'smart boy,' and his satisfied parents foretell that he will make a 'smart man.'") But they balance that awareness with an understanding that the solitude and isolation of the West have shaped western speech. Behind the laconic shorthand of spoken speech Gretel Ehrlich encounters in Wyoming, for instance, "is shyness." "Not a hangdog shyness, or anything coy," she says in *The Solace of Open Spaces* (1985), for there is always "a robust spirit in evidence behind the restraint." It is the kind of quality that puts a mischievous sparkle in the speech of Cliff, "a small, skin-and-bones" auctioneer who once ran a lambing shed:

> He'd center a cigarette between his chapped lips, then roll it from one side of his mouth to the other, humming country tunes as he gave shots and suckled weak lambs. Fancying himself a songwriter, he read *Billboard* during coffee breaks and every morning when I arrived at the sheds he'd look me squarely in the eyes and say, "Gretel, when you're looking at me you're looking at country." The next year he quit the sheep business to raise pigs.

Cliff's sense of humor and his confidence that he'll make it do not, obviously, change the economic conditions that force him to change jobs so quickly. But neither, Ehrlich quietly suggests, does his vagrant drollery simply pale to insignificance in the light of such matters. Cliff might show up in another kind of western text as one more down-on-his-luck, self-deluded dreamer drifting through Wyoming. What makes a difference here is Ehrlich's ear for western idioms. Her ability to hear a wit and poignancy that outlast the circumstances which called them forth aligns her with a long and complicated tradition of other writers intrigued by colloquial western talk. She is willing – as were Clappe, Twain, and Bird in a different register – to immerse herself in the western vernacular and then listen to how much of her own mind the West has invented.

Works Cited

Bird, Isabella L. *A Lady's Life in the Rocky Mountains.* 1879. Rpt. Sausalito, CA: Comstock Editions, 1987.

Bridgman, Richard. *The Colloquial Style in America.* New York: Oxford UP, 1966.

Clappe, Louise. *The Shirley Letters.* 1854–55. Rpt. Salt Lake City: Peregrine Smith, 1985.

Ehrlich, Gretel. *The Solace of Open Spaces.* New York: Penguin, 1985.

Emerson, Ralph Waldo. "The American Scholar." *Ralph Waldo Emerson: Essays and Lectures.* Ed. Joel Porte. New York: Library of America, 1983, 53–71.

Fender, Stephen. *Plotting the Golden West: American Literature and the Rhetoric of the California Trail.* New York: Cambridge UP, 1981.

Harte, Bret. "Tennessee's Partner." In *The Outcasts of Poker Flat and Other Stories.* New York: Signet, 1961, 124–33.

Marx, Leo. "The Vernacular Tradition in American Literature." In *The Pilot and the Passenger: Essays on Literature, Technology, and Culture in the United States.* New York: Oxford UP, 1988, 3–17.

Mitchell, Lee Clark. "Verbally *Roughing It:* The West of Words." *Nineteenth-Century Literature,* 44, No. 1 (June 1989): 67–92.

Poirier, Richard. *Robert Frost: The Work of Knowing.* New York: Oxford UP, 1977.

Robertson, Janet. *The Magnificent Mountain Women: Adventures in the Colorado Rockies.* Lincoln: U of Nebraska P, 1990.

Sabin, Margery. *The Dialect of the Tribe: Speech and Community in Modern Fiction.* New York: Oxford UP, 1987.

Sewell, David R. *Mark Twain's Languages: Discourse, Dialogue, and Linguistic Variety.* Berkeley: U of California P, 1987.

Stegner, Wallace. "Introduction." Bret Harte, *The Outcasts of Poker Flat and Other Tales.* New York: Signet, 1961, vii–xvi.

Twain, Mark. *Roughing It. Mark Twain: The Innocents Abroad, Roughing It.* Ed. Guy Cardwell. New York: Library of America, 1984, 525–986.

Whitman, Walt. "Slang in America." In *Walt Whitman: Complete Poetry and Collected Prose.* Ed. Justin Kaplan. New York: Library of America, 1982, 1165–70.

Williams, Raymond. *The Country and the City.* New York: Oxford UP, 1973.

BIERSTADT'S SETTINGS, HARTE'S PLOTS

LEE MITCHELL

—————

In the mid-1860s, a painter and a writer burst into fame as the premier artists of America's Far West. Unlike anyone before, Albert Bierstadt (1830–1902) and Bret Harte (1836–1902) took the nation by storm, and yet in less than a decade, few Americans glanced at Bierstadt's grandiose landscapes or leafed through Harte's sentimental stories. Images that had recently captivated the imagination had come to seem either grossly inflated or baldly inaccurate, cloyingly mawkish, or simply banal. The fact that both painter and writer experienced such a meteoric rise and fall in reputation, at nearly the same time, raises the question of what contributed to such brief fame – especially given the notable influence both men continued to have on other artists of the Far West. Across the boundaries that separate painting from writing, is there a shared technique, or theme, or perspective that might explain their appeal to contemporaries? And what might that evanescent appeal reveal about the 1860s, about the people who responded so fully to such similarly extravagant visions?

One answer to this conundrum of lost popularity yet abiding effect may lie in the peculiar treatment both artists give to the West as a "direction of thought" rather than as a definite geographical region. They envision, whether in paint or in words, a psychological terrain far less local or specific than the Sierra Nevadas or Rocky Mountains. And in doing so, they first mapped a realm that subsequent artists could likewise transform into distinct emotional regions and yet nonetheless label "western." Moreover, the closer one looks at each man's career in terms of the other's, the easier it is to grasp how overnight fame and nearly instant neglect may in each case have stemmed from an inability to match the other artist's central vision: Bierstadt at his best created paradoxical landscapes that demanded strong narrative plots; Harte created paradoxical

99

characters who emerge from overly vague landscapes. Each artist aroused expectations for a West that neither alone could satisfy.

* * * * * *

When Albert Bierstadt returned from America to his birthplace in Germany in 1853, it was as a self-confident teenage painter, eager to master techniques at the famous Düsseldorf academy. By the time he returned across the Atlantic at the age of twenty-seven, he had become a well-respected artist, with career ambitions as grand as his new painterly style. Realizing the West would offer "my subject," he accompanied General Frederick W. Lander's 1859 survey to the Rocky Mountains, and excitedly began to paint what he found. Returning the following year, he won almost immediate acclaim in New York with his landscapes. And only three years later, he garnered international fame with *The Rocky Mountains* (1863), the wall-sized canvas that sold for an unprecedented $25,000 and secured his reputation as the heir to Turner. "On this American more than any other," London's *Art Journal* solemnly averred, "does the mantle of our greatest painter appear to have fallen." Within the decade, however, Bierstadt found the mantle slipping, and by 1885, he had fallen so far in esteem as to be rejected for an international show. Long before he died in New York, in 1902, he had grown accustomed to being ignored by his contemporaries.

If less convinced of his own artistic talent at so early an age, Bret Harte's career nonetheless offers parallels to Bierstadt's. Born in New York, the son of a schoolteacher, Harte moved to California at eighteen, where he took a number of odd jobs and began in a desultory way to write. By his late twenties, his poems and parodies had made him well-known on the San Francisco literary scene, but no one could have anticipated the response to his first story, "The Luck of Roaring Camp" (1868), which made his name a household word across the country. Two years later, riding a wave of popular acclaim, he signed a one-year contract to supply *The Atlantic Monthly* with a story per month for the unheard-of sum of $10,000. Within two years, however, his star had fallen; his contract was not renewed, his works were neglected, and by 1878 he had sailed to Europe, having accepted the position of consul in Rhenish Prussia. Reversing Bierstadt's move, Harte stayed abroad for the rest of his life, vainly attempting to attract the writing public that had turned so abruptly away from him. Long forgotten in America, he finally died in London the very year of Bierstadt's death.

Accounts of Bierstadt's and Harte's careers tend to devolve into either reductive or overdetermined interpretations. Too often,

popular enthusiasm for their work is simply equated with the images themselves, as if viewers' and readers' complex responses
could be measured in terms of the simple appeal of western scenes,
characters, and icons. More strictly historical explanations tend to
reduce delight in odd stories and extravagant paintings to a diffuse
public fascination with the unknown. An alleged national ignorance about details of landscape and life in the Far West was largely
rectified by the early 1870s, with the appearance of government
reports and the photographs of J. C. Hillers, Timothy O'Sullivan,
and William Henry Jackson. According to this explanation, the
turn away from Bierstadt and Harte is more or less directly attrib-
utable to an increasing familiarity with their actual subject. Western
facts, that is, finally caught up with their extravagant visions.

More distinctly formalist critics tend to attribute the sudden
popularity of Bierstadt and Harte to a momentary lapse in public
taste. It is easy, in both cases, to itemize assorted flaws in artistic
technique that contribute to an overall effect of excess, confusion,
or simple incompetence. Bierstadt's obvious problem in maintaining a consistent point of view is reflected in incompatible centers of
interest, while the mixed influence of photography on his art, his
awkward representation of figures, and his generally poor use of
painterly formulas all are adduced to explain why the viewing public finally turned away. Likewise, Harte's indulgence of the pathetic
fallacy, his resort to purple prose, his sentimental plot turns, and
his patronizing narrative tone all wore thin very rapidly, and readers simply found his later stories lacking in interest.

Biographers unable to account for either artist's sudden acclaim
often interpret their equally sudden loss of popularity to the sheer
weight of each man's reputation, which collapsed from nothing
more than being overinflated in the first place. Cultural analysts
identify the way both painter and writer fortuitously put their finger on the pulse of the nation, citing Bierstadt's enthusiasm for the
West as consumable empire, a grand spectacle for Americans newly
enabled by developing railroads to visit a region still exotic and
dangerous. That danger is, of course, never presented as either
actual or imminent, and in its overaestheticization suggests a theat-
ricalizing of experience, transforming the West into a safe stage set,
and thereby assuaging the viewer's potential uneasiness about the
unknown. Somewhat more economically, a similar end is achieved
by Harte through fictional evocations of a distant mining frontier
represented as a region already essentially civilized. Familiar civic
virtues appear in exotic circumstances, and strange wilderness garb
only serves to mask a conservative social order.

Apparently, a nation caught in the painful process of Civil War,

then Reconstruction, was eager to embrace the pastoral and uto-
pian fantasies purveyed by Bierstadt and Harte. But not for long,
as each of these interpretive perspectives helps to explain. Before
pressing such perspectives further in order to address the altering
relationship between artist and public, popular art and reception,
we might simply ask what it was that each man thought he was
doing. More specifically, beginning with Bierstadt, to what effect
does he seem to aspire in his painting, and what did he actually
succeed in producing?

* * * * * *

Perhaps the best place to begin is with Bierstadt's most celebrated
canvas, the painting that first made him famous: *The Rocky Mountains* (Figure 1). Exhibited in 1864, the six- by ten-foot canvas overwhelmed all but one of six hundred-odd other canvases at New
York's Sanitary Fair (a government-sponsored exhibition to raise
money for Civil War wounded). And not even Frederick Edwin
Church's equally grand, equally grandiose *Heart of the Andes* (which
hung directly opposite) could vie with the *tableau vivant* arranged
by Bierstadt in front of his canvas: nineteen Indians mutely standing among an array of a hundred-odd artifacts. Stripped of this
dramatic "frame," the painting still overpowers the viewer through
a deft combination of vast scale and exacting detail – the way it
celebrates the panoramic sweep of mountain peaks and peaceful
valley even as it renders exact features of rocks and trees, animals
and humans. The painting, in fact, compels attention not despite
its contradictory demands but *because* of them, by deliberately not
resolving pictorial elements into a balanced whole. The starkness
of the lighting itself compounds this effect by cleaving sunlight
from shade, while the luminous peaks hanging over dark trees are
accentuated through their central repetition in the mirroring lake
below.

   Indeed, the contrast of Alpine majesty with the domestic scenes
in the valley points to a larger division between the painting's separate modes – of landscape description and genre detail that divide
its top from bottom halves. Partially alleviating this disjunction are
the mountainous shape of the tepees that appear at the border of
these regions. Even so, the perspective is foreshortened to such a
radical degree that peaks appear to loom somehow on top of the
valley rather than in the distance behind. More generally, the painting's topography is broken into discrete *mise en scènes*, each with a
physical integrity that seems convincing only in terms of itself.
Attempts to coordinate them are stymied, most obviously in the

Figure 1. Albert Bierstadt, *The Rocky Mountains* (1863), oil on canvas, $73\frac{1}{4} \times 120\frac{3}{4}$ inches. The Metropolitan Museum of Art, Rogers Fund.

case of the ominous band of shadows broken by light on the water-fall, which are rendered unaccountable by the delicate cumulus clouds that Bierstadt depicts.

Far from a liability, however, these contrasts attest to the painting's achievement, as multiple centers of interest compete for the attention they never quite command. The group of Bannock Indians spread among the shadows of an evening encampment serves in muted tones merely to lend perspective to the scene, to humanize a landscape that is the site of such disparate efforts. The preparation of the mountain goat to the right; the white dog bounding across the valley floor; the tripod erected to keep food safe, depicted at lower left; the inquisitive prairie dog watching the whole even further to the left: among a series of other activities, each of these fosters a separate perspective that threatens but never succeeds in disrupting the overall scene. The artful conjunctions of the painting succeed by effecting a set of visual tensions, deliberately compelling the eye through a disparate mix of realistic detail, unfolding narrative enactments, and a powerfully melodramatic sweep of landscape.

As early as 1864, one of the most prominent critics of the period was provoked by just this artful conjunction, and offered a trenchant observation about Bierstadt's and Church's paintings at the Sanitary Fair: "With singular inconsistency of mind," so James Jackson Jarves wrote, "they idealize in composition and materialize in execution, so that, although the details of the scenery are substantially correct, the scene as a whole often is false." Accurate as this seems at first glance, the question that lingers is what it might mean for "the scene as whole" to be "false" – and false, in particular, when its details are said to be "substantially correct"? It is this sense of the false that lies at the heart of so much of the criticism directed at Bierstadt – of someone whose larger vision is unconvincing even though his realistic detail is unimpeachable.

This sense of "falseness" depends, of course, on viewers' expectations, expectations always hard on their own to identify, once removed from painterly contexts. But consider a shrewd insight expressed only seven years before Jarves wrote, about the kind of audience soon to be drawn to Bierstadt's art. "There is another class" of reader, so Herman Melville observed:

> who sit down to a work of amusement tolerantly as they sit at a play, and with much the same expectations and feelings. They look that fancy shall invoke scenes different from those of the same old crowd round the customhouse counter. . . . They

look not only for more entertainment, but, at bottom, even
for more reality than real life itself can show. Thus, though
they want novelty, they want nature, too; but nature unfettered, exhilarated, in effect transformed. . . . It is with fiction
as with religion: it should present another world, and yet one
to which we feel the tie.

Part of what critics have persistently thought of as the "problem" of
Bierstadt derives from this curiously transgressive, otherwise tran-
scendental yearning – the unappeased craving "for more reality
than real life itself can show." Like the fiction Melville describes,
Bierstadt's paintings represent "another world, and yet one to
which we feel the tie."

Bierstadt does this in part through the very profusion of authentic details in his paintings – the surfeit of realistic tableaux that
makes the eye pan for so long, over so many things rendered with
such extraordinary care. Like a documentary film, they force the
viewer to linger over every detail, every crag, tree, and windover, in
the effort to reveal how much more the painterly perspective (or
camera eye) can encompass than any actual eye could ever register.
That comprehensiveness is itself a sign of the surreal in Bierstadt's
imagination, of the "more reality than real life itself can show" that
prevails throughout his paintings. Yet he succeeded not only because he perfected such stylistic tricks as a crowded visual field, but
because of a more general enthusiasm developing in the postbellum period for what was termed the "secular sublime." Bierstadt
appeared at the right moment, displaying a series of non-sacred,
self-transforming aesthetic tableaux that redefined the West in
terms that religion was no longer capable of doing.

This possibility of "nature unfettered, exhilarated, in effect transformed" is exemplified as clearly as anywhere in *A Storm in the Rocky
Mountains, Mount Rosalie,* completed in 1866 (Figure 2). It is an
extravagant painting, complex and crowded, with dark, towering
mountains on the right sliding us into the frame, into the foreground pool, then into a series of further pools that lead to the
larger lakes in the middle and far distance. Over it all hang Bierstadt's signature clouds that just miss hiding the gleaming peak of
the title. Half a dozen centers of interest compete for the viewer's
attention, as if in a kind of cinematic competition (before the fact)
for the plot: from the startled ptarmigans winging into flight; to a
dead deer abandoned near the foreground pool; to Indians chasing a frightened horse; to the encampment of tepees near the river
that flows through the left middle distance – a river in which

Figure 2. Albert Bierstadt, *A Storm in the Rocky Mountains, Mount Rosalie* (1866), oil on canvas, 83 × 142¼ inches. The Brooklyn Museum, B. Woodward Memorial Fund, Bequest of Mark Finley.

mounted Indians ride three horses; on to deer quietly grazing beyond the chasing Indians; and so on, depending on how closely one looks. The point is that there is a surplus of stories, unrelated, unconflicting, randomly disposed, with figures afar as clear as the birds nearby. Unrealistic as such a foreshortening of perspective may be, it has the effect of allowing potential narratives to emanate from many points. And that effect is reinforced by our slight confusion over the source of the picture's light – confusion fostered by the rococo shadows, the darkened pines, and the distant thunderstorm.

One of the first viewers of the painting, in fact, angrily indicted it for doing just that – for flagrantly violating what he assumed was the "truth of nature." "The whole science of geology cries out against him," this critic charged:

> The law of gravitation leagues itself with geological law against the artist. Away up, above the clouds, near the top of the picture, the observer will perceive two pyramidal shapes. By further consultation of the index-sheet, the observer will ascertain that these things are the two "spurs" of Mount Rosalie. Now, let him work out a problem in arithmetic: The hills over which he looks, as we are told, are 3000 feet high; right over the hills tower huge masses of cloud which certainly carry the eye up to 10 or 12,000 feet higher; above these . . . the two "spurs"; what is the height of Mt. Rosalie? Answer: approximately, 10,000 miles or so. Impossible.

Clearly, Bierstadt has met his match, even if the attack reminds us of the Devil's mirror of rationality in Hans Christian Andersen's story, "The Snow Queen": science once again reducing art to a handful of preposterous images.

But in fact, if Melville is right in describing "nature unfettered, exhilarated, in effect transformed," then it was science itself that Bierstadt meant to oppose, as if he were actually leaguing himself against geological law. Repeatedly, even when paintings are named for actual sites, they *seem* fictitious, "wondrous inventions" that depend upon mélanges of topographical features – organized far more for theatrical effect than referential accuracy. He altered actual sites as he wished, working (as suggested above) much like a stage designer assembling some fantastic set. Moreover, the dramatic excess indulged *in* his paintings extended notoriously to their public display: the Indians posed in front of *The Rocky Mountains* clearly testify to this intended effect, leading one viewer supposedly to wonder when "the thing was going to move." Likewise, the draped, darkened, gas-lit chambers in which *Storm in the Rocky Mountains* was hung resembled a theatrical backdrop, compelling the viewer to imagine him- or herself walking into the landscape. "Seen as a whole," Nancy Anderson has observed, "the composition pulls the viewer into the landscape through dueling passages of bright sunlight and deep shadow. . . . For even without a darkened room and orchestrated lights, stepping close to the canvas was akin to stepping into the scene."

What is "false," then, is also a certain lawless world that evokes too much emotional fervor, too much astonishment at the "sensational," or the "lurid," or the otherwise extravagant. The alleged "falseness" of Bierstadt's West lies in its bleaching out of science and history, which is precisely the point: His finest, most compelling landscapes reflect not a coherent world, but a crowding together of contextual fragments, a melding of scenic materials whose very excess generates a sense of psychic and moral drama. More to the point, that excess challenges the viewer into a kind of scenic unpacking, an unfolding of the paintings' mixed descriptive moments into more or less straightforward temporal sequences that resemble nothing so much as the unreeling of film. Scenes that appear simultaneous on canvas are altered by their unusual perspective and conjunction, almost as if transformed into a cinematic succession that suggests the temporality of narrative.

Bierstadt, in short, imagines less a particular place than a singular process – or rather, a place waiting for the process of personal transformation. The Far West he memorialized was a region of psychological transfiguration that itself remains strangely untransformed – a frontier dividing emotional states, a liminal zone invented long before Frederick Jackson Turner described how the American wilderness "masters the colonist." And although countless other painters and illustrators ventured interpretations of America's Far West long before Bierstadt transferred his monumental images onto canvas, it was his striking vision of landscape that caught the nation's attention.

* * * * * *

Bierstadt's landscapes resonate with a powerful semantic excess, and even though frequently unpeopled, they embody a strangely dramatic character. Indeed, the very absence of human figures in so many of his canvases has the curious effect of investing his settings *as* settings with a disproportionate significance. His canvases seem to beg for the characters and plots that would later emerge in the paintings of Frederick Remington and Charles

Russell, and in the stories of Harte and of Owen Wister. This sense of a setting somehow waiting for plot has been described by the historian, Ray Allen Billington, in terms not of visual arts but of popular literature of the nineteenth century:

> Something more than a monotonous landscape was needed by the novelists; they must have oases where adventurers could find haven from desert heat, caves to shelter them from marauding Apaches, towering cliffs where hero and villain could battle with bowie knives, raging rivers where bad men could be swept to their deaths. Hence writers performed feats of geographic legerdemain remarkable to behold as they transformed the Southwest to suit their needs.

Bierstadt helped to invent this expectant terrain in a purely visual mode, by revealing the ways in which water, rock, trees, clouds, sunlight itself could create a cosmic drama always on the verge of becoming both moral and social.

Of course, despite certain apt analogies between the arts of painting and fiction, each remains a distinct medium, with different means of rendering setting and depicting the natural world. What lends to Bierstadt's paintings such an original power is precisely their conflicting perspectives, requiring a viewer's moving eye, creating a prototemporal sensation in the process of having their surfaces nervously scanned. In that sense, Bierstadt's landscapes seem to aspire not just to the condition of film, but to the condition of novelistic description itself, where only one thing can be read at a time with an effect achieved through the gradual accumulation of natural details. And if painting is finally not to be confused with either film or literature, it is nonetheless true that Bierstadt comes as close to the cinematic and novelistic as the painterly ever can.

More than any painter before, Bierstadt revealed those generative narrative possibilities that emerged from seeing the American landscape in a particular way. This angle of vision involved a peculiar psychologizing of the landscape, confirmed as early as 1869 by Ambrose Bierce (if unintentionally) when he denounced Bierstadt's influence on countless imitators. "We have had Yosemite in oils," he thundered, "in watercolor, in crayon, in chalk and charcoal until in our very dreams we imagine ourselves falling from the summit of El Capitan or descending in spray from the Bridal Veil cataract." Thus, the unpeopled vistas of Bierstadt's California were magically transformed by viewers themselves – vistas now no longer unpeopled, but become the setting for selves in motion, for nefarious plots and hot pursuits, if only "in our dreams."

At this point, it comes as less of a surprise that Bret Harte should have emerged at this historical moment to accomplish for the Far West in literature something like what Bierstadt was attempting in paint, and in a style equally extravagant. Compare, for instance, a landscape description from "The Outcasts of Poker Flat" with *Sunset in the Yosemite Valley* (Figure 3), painted in 1868, only a year before the story appeared:

> The spot was singularly wild and impressive. A wooded amphitheatre, surrounded on three sides by precipitous cliffs of naked granite, sloped gently toward the crest of another precipice that overlooked the valley. It was, undoubtedly, the most suitable spot for a camp, had camping been advisable. . . . [John Oakhurst] looked at the gloomy walls that rose a thousand feet sheer above the circling pines around him, at the sky ominously clouded, at the valley below, already deepening into shadow; and doing so, suddenly he heard his own name called.

Harte might almost be said to have had Bierstadt's landscape in mind – or rather, Harte seems to be describing a scene that is already an acknowledged visual fiction, a representation that needs re-presenting through blindingly golden clouds, bright cliffs, and gleaming water surfaces fused in a moment that (like so many of Bierstadt's) announces itself as one of dramatic, expectant transition. In addition, Harte creates the landscape as a scene of surprised self-identification, transforming description into the narrative of one's name emerging from the scene, a self elicited from the setting much as Bierstadt's spectacular landscapes do more generally in the guise of psychic dramas.

Other writers would later recreate the landscape in their own mental image – an emotional identification as old as landscape description itself (whether in paint or in words). But it was given a peculiarly western twist in the 1860s by Harte, whose descriptive prose seems to overtake narrative enactment itself by coming mysteriously alive. Even in his earliest stories, Harte toyed with this descriptive technique, as in the curiously ironic passage of murder from "M'Liss: An Idyl of Red Mountain" (1863):

> For some hours after a darkness thick and heavy brooded over the settlement. The somber pines encompassing the village seemed to close threateningly about it as if to reclaim the

Figure 3. Albert Bierstadt, *Sunset in the Yosemite Valley* (1868), oil on canvas, $35\frac{3}{4} \times 52$ inches. The Haggin Museum, Stockton, California.

wilderness that had been wrested from them. A low rustling as of dead leaves, and the damp breath of forest odors filled the lonely street. Emboldened by the darkness other shadows slipped by, leaving strange footprints in the moist ditches for people to point at next day, until the moon, round and full, was lifted above the crest of the opposite hill, and all was magically changed.

The shadows shrank away, leaving the straggling street sleeping in a beauty it never knew by day. All that was unlovely, harsh, and repulsive in its jagged outlines was subdued and softened by that uncertain light. It smoothed the rough furrows and unsightly chasms of the mountain with an ineffable love and tenderness. It fell upon the face of the sleeping M'liss, and left a tear glittering on her black lashes and a smile on her lip, which would have been rare to her at any other time; and fell also on the white upturned face of "Old Smith," with a pistol in his hand and a bullet in his heart, lying dead beside the empty pocket.

The corpse – a father shot by his daughter in this conclusion to the story's first chapter – is at once the central figure in a strangely articulated Memento Mori, and at the same time the most easily dispensable. Meanwhile, the landscape is strangely animated in the conditional tense of the narrative, "as if" the death of M'Liss's father "magically changed" the very environment in which she could exist. Or rather, the brooding, threatening, "emboldened," shrinking, slipping milieu has itself become the transformative agent, now revealed as the emotional cause of the human drama in its midst. The narrative inverts the usual placement of active figure and descriptive ground, making the landscape come alive against the passive forms of her and her victim, both with "white upturned face[s]." Character is revealed as an animistic force, transcribed from a supposedly intentional (adolescent) subject onto a magical western terrain.

Harte's recurrent indulgence of the pathetic fallacy only confirms how fully the natural world is for him not simply animate or active, but an actual vital character in whatever drama he narrates. This helps explain why silence in this natural world is never simply silence alone, but a revelation of the landscape's emotional constraint, indeed, of its psychological arrest – as in the "miraculous" birth that inspires the drama of "The Luck of Roaring Camp" (1868): "The pines stopped moaning, the river ceased to rush, and the fire to crackle. It seemed as if Nature had stopped to listen too."

The same occurs in the precisely converse situation, when the last two outcasts of "The Outcasts of Poker Flat" finally succumb to the snowstorm: "The wind lulled as if it feared to waken them. Feathery drifts of snow, shaken from the long pine boughs, flew like white winged birds, and settled about them as they slept. The moon through the rifted clouds looked down upon what had been the camp." The apparent restraint of the natural world suggests an even more fully configured emotional power recumbent in the landscape.

What critics usually have in mind when they disparage Harte's "purple prose" is the seemingly casual ubiquitousness of the pathetic fallacy throughout his stories. Yet simply to identify Harte's anthropomorphizing as a regretable stylistic tic overlooks the special resonances of the relationship otherwise everywhere identified between individuals and the western landscape. In "The Idyl of Red Gulch" (1869), the evening light "flickered, and faded, and went out" just as Miss Mary's defiant will also finally expires. "A momentary shadow" crosses the hero's path in "A Protégée of Jack Hamlin's" (1893) at the very moment a dark thought of murder happens to occur to him. "Mrs. Skaggs's Husbands" (1872) opens with "a dissipated looking hanging lamp, which was evidently the worse for having been up all night," that lights "a faded reveler of Angel's, who even then sputtered and flickered in *his* socket in an armchair below it." In each of these as well as many other passages, a symbiosis emerges between the human and the inanimate – a symbiosis that Harte significantly locates in the West.

For earlier writers, landscape had been a basic test of character, a touchstone by which individuals can be readily distinguished as moral agents: men from women, Indians from whites, good men from bad, and humans more generally from "the lower orders." Harte transformed this logic of landscape by erasing such invidious distinctions, establishing all characters as essentially the same, fundamentally good, living in a natural world revealed as likewise radically egalitarian. His identification of drunkenness as a form of sleep, for instance, becomes less a psychological observation than a metaphysical one, since sleep is also elsewhere identified as a kind of death (and vice versa). Harte's Far West everywhere elides the customary distinctions of person and place (and not only those, but distinctions as well between good and bad persons, good and bad places), with a strangely disorienting effect on the reader unaccustomed to his melodramatic style.

This readerly disorientation results from a flattening of moral distinctions that had earlier been reflected in terms of the landscape. For not only are all of Harte's landscapes rendered more or less equivalent, each of the elements within a given view likewise appears to be valued alike. The best analogy to this striking moral monochromaticism in Harte lies, strange as it seems, in Bierstadt's equally melodramatic, equally disorienting landscapes. The deft combinations of light and shadow in his paintings prevent the viewer from readily locating the sources of light, compelling the eye to flit back and forth indiscriminately across the canvas. The general effect is akin, in other words, to Harte's lack of moral distinctions.

In *Sunset in the Yosemite Valley* (1868) light emerges from the center of the painting, hot enough to be molten lava, burning an apparent hole through the cosmos as well as the canvas. And yet without the title, the time of day could seem almost indeterminate, anticipating the kind of day-for-night shots produced through filters by modern cinematographers. The sun, that is, appears too high and bright for actual sunset, or for the valley to be so dark, even with the low-lying wisps of clouds. The granite mountains rise out of the blinding brightness to tower, once again, over the sides of the canvas in what would be Bierstadt's signature mode. The ox-bowing river has been transformed from any realistic association with Thomas Cole in its intensely melodramatic reflection of a western sky. All told, the painting's stunning effect derives from its capacity to at once solicit yet evade our gaze, compelling us thereby into "another world," unreal, excessive, overdone. Like Harte's equally surreal landscapes, Bierstadt's gives the impression that it is more a depiction of another representation than of an actual site itself – as if he were likewise borrowing from a tradition of aesthetic conventions worn thin before he began. And like Harte as well, he repeatedly invests his scenes with a certain magical power, indulging in similar animistic fantasies that make his unpeopled landscapes seem to come preternaturally alive.

* * * * * *

The extraordinary popularity of Bierstadt and Harte, unlike anything before it in American art, defies either a strictly verbal or a painterly explanation. Instead, it was the compound of phantasmagoria, emotional heightening, narrative indirection, and a mixing of descriptive materials that defines their appeal – elements suggestive of melodrama, at least as Peter Brooks defines the mode:

> Melodrama handles its feelings and ideas virtually as plastic entities, visual and tactile models held out for all to see and to

handle. Emotions are given a full acting-out, a full representation before our eyes. . . . Nothing is *under*stood, all is *over*stated. Such moments provide us with the joy of a full emotional indulgence, the pleasures of an unadulterated exploitation of what we recognize from our psychic lives as one possible way to be, the victory of one integral inner force.

If this seems too inflated a description for Harte, it may be even less apparent how a painter might fit such a seemingly "narrative" mode, even when emphasis is placed so heavily on the "visual and tactile." But a glance at Bierstadt's *Storm in the Mountains* (c. 1866) suggests a number of answers (Figure 4). The painting, highly praised at the time, offers an apparently western scene that functions much as do so many of Bierstadt's more heroic landscapes. Once again, the magnitude of the panorama requires a distance in order to comprehend the whole, even as it draws the viewer closer to the canvas to discern the carefully arranged details. Tiny red farm buildings are posed against an overwhelming confluence of natural forces, while swirling clouds highlight the mountain peak hanging down over the valley. The entire painting forces us to shift our focus between mountain and fields beneath, defined respectively as bands of white and yellow paired in a kind of painterly tension. If this confluence of elements seems once again like something of a "false" combination, it is only because everything seems to be put on the table for us to "handle," and then invested with almost a surfeit of individual presence that creates the melodrama defined by Brooks.

The larger question of why some types of "overstatement" and "emotional indulgence" succeeded when they did, and specifically in terms of the Far West, is hardly apparent on the historical surface. Both Bierstadt and Harte caught the same public's attention, and their loss of popularity was similarly swift, which makes their "melodramatic" treatments of the Far West more than a matter of simple interest. It is almost as if their postbellum American audience craved the fantastic images they offered, and − soon embarrassed by that craving − repressed its expression as quickly as it could. That should not be too surprising, since repression is usually the fate of melodrama, a mode that arouses critical resistance precisely by its refusal to be moderate, restrained, commonsensical.

The melodrama in Harte can hardly be denied, even if it was repressed: Few major writers are more embarrassingly excessive, or rely less in their plots on narrative indirection and emotional restraint. Indeed, at the level of diction and style, he might well be

Figure 4. Albert Bierstadt, *Storm in the Mountains* (undated), oil on canvas, 38 × 60 inches. Museum of Fine Arts, Boston. M. and M. Koralik Collection.

said to exemplify the concept of "purple prose," which derives from a visual analogy with the idea of regal excess, of costumed brilliance, ornateness, a gorgeous, lurid show. Sharing with Bierstadt a propensity to grand overstatement, Harte constantly strains to dress up familiar clichés, draining them in the process of whatever life they have left. Cherokee Sal, in "The Luck of Roaring Camp," is only among the first victims of his overstated prose: "Dissolute, abandoned, and irreclaimable, she was yet suffering a martyrdom hard enough to bear even when veiled by sympathizing womanhood, but now terrible in her loneliness. The primal curse had come to her in that original isolation which must have made the punishment of the first transgression so dreadful." Tightening descriptive adjectives and plot circumstances to a dramatic pitch, the narrator succeeds at last in getting all Nature to succumb:

> Above the swaying and moaning of the pines, the swift rush of the river, and the crackling of the fire rose a sharp, querulous cry − a cry unlike anything heard before in the camp. The pines stopped moaning, the river ceased to rush, and the fire to crackle. It seemed as if Nature had stopped to listen too.

Harte operates much as Bierstadt does, welding local particulars to grandiose claims, alternating perspectives in what otherwise seems like a series of stark oppositions. And here, his imperturbable impulse to overstate − to find the most extreme expression of local, subjective knowledge − results in a scene of unsurpassed bathos.

Elsewhere, Harte inverts the process, building on vaguely sentimental expectations that are punctured by an explosion of immediate action. The very title of "How Santa Claus Came to Simpson's Bar" belies the possibility of a realistic plot, and the story's opening scenes increase the emotional pressure for a soothing conclusion to a boy's Christmas expectations. Yet Harte strikes through grandly inflated abstractions with a moment of visual extravagance.

> There was a leap, a scrambling struggle, a bound, a wild retreat of the crowd, a circle of flying hoofs, two springless leaps that jarred the earth, a rapid play and jingle of spurs, a plunge, and then the voice of Dick somewhere in the darkness. "All right."

And so, Santa Claus appears in a melodramatic swirl, with (in Brooks' words) "a full representation before our eyes" of expectant emotion.

One of the advantages of the melodramatic mode, for painter as well as for writer, is that it consists of a kind of "sign language" by which values are supposedly arrayed outside an immediate social context. In Bierstadt, this is achieved through a nervously floating eye that can never establish a priority of perspectives; in Harte, through plots that collapse moral distinctions as simply effects of equal distinction, like colorful beads on a string. "In a universe of such pure signs," Brooks adds, "we are freed of a concern with their reference . . . and enabled to attend to their interrelationship and hierarchy." Brooks might almost be speaking of music, with its interplay of pure structure. Yet the individual "signs" agglomerated in Harte's stories or Bierstadt's canvases are also "pure" – their "purity" as signs guaranteed by their very extravagance, their flagrancy, their dramatic élan, their "falseness." For Brooks, this is the meaning of melodrama, which he calls the "mode of excess." Whether a verbal realm, in which events are represented sententiously, or a visual sphere in which depictions are cosmically inflated, the effect of melodrama is always the same: to press against realistic conventions in order to evoke that other fancifully charged "world . . . to which we feel the tie."

This melodramatic logic is at work in much of Bierstadt, but achieves a special clarity in *Night at Valley View* (Figure 5), completed in 1884. The cliffs interrupt each other, breaking through their respective picture planes; the moonlit surface of water and mountains compete with the bright reflection of the campfire. Obviously indebted to the pictorial Gothic, the scene focuses on blasted trees, shaggy cliffs, distant mountains enveloped in glowing mist, and even a rushing cataract – all in the apparent effort to isolate them as pure painterly "signs." Bierstadt confirms this isolation through a self-conscious representation of space, in his sharply perpendicular cliffs and powerful vertical shifts of paint. Normal topographical expectations are once again subverted, as a middle distance evaporates in the overall flattening of perspective. And light itself is obscured, emerging mysteriously from lake, sky, campfire, even from the mountains themselves.

Yet the result of this semiotic self-consciousness – of painterly gestures, flourishes, conventions, and habits that seem somehow greater than themselves, and thereby draw attention to their inadequacy as signifiers – is rarely in Bierstadt allowed to remain merely at the level of conventional painterly reference. Rather, the viewer comes to recognize something beyond the everyday, in which (Brooks again) "the ordinary and humble and quotidian [reveals] itself full of excitement, suspense, and peripety, conferred by the play of cosmic moral relations and forces." This effect is achieved

Figure 5. Albert Bierstadt, *Night at Valley View* (1884), oil on canvas, 34 × 27⅛ inches. Yosemite National Park Museum, Yosemite, California, Robert Woolard.

in Harte through the use of narrative voice itself, which consistently transgresses against the conventional muted voice of third-person consciousness. "And here I must pause," the narrator claims, or interrupts himself with "I stay my hand with difficulty," or hurries on with "I shall not stop to inquire." Interjecting anxiety, he often adds "I regret to say" or "grieve to say" or "fear": all a part of the obsessively recurrent self-consciousness of these narratives that draws our attention to their actively fictive power. Indeed,

Harte's stories (much like Bierstadt's paintings) actively embrace the very qualities that so alarm critics, for whom both artists have so often been scorned as victims of the "mode of excess."

Harte's stories and Bierstadt's landscapes revealed as nothing more than melodrama: the observation is a commonplace in the mouths of angry critics, even if the term need hardly be denigratory. Indeed, their most successful works appeal not as coherent depictions of actual scenes, but as self-conscious occasions for the exhibition of people and settings – of gamblers, prostitutes, stage-coach drivers, or of clouds, mountains, pools, and trees – regardless in either case of actual or historical referents. While critics predictably dismiss such treatments as realistic liabilities, they can in fact be seen conversely as assets. Indeed, the energy with which both artists mix their "signs," compelling oppositions that seem exaggerated or simply confused, attests to imaginative possibilities in which melodramatic surfaces are asked to bear a fuller weight of meaning, of either significant settings or relevant plots. In the case of Bierstadt, we are put in the presence of stark abysses, brilliant ascents, gigantic trees, blazing reflections, impassable (and impossible) terrains that remind us of nothing so much as our dreams – even if dreams with us as the dreamers removed, and therefore with narratives yet to be plotted. In the case of Harte, we are put in the presence of kind-hearted prostitutes, noble gamblers, ruthless housewives, and amiably drunken stage drivers who supply our dreams with figures somehow larger than life, waiting for plotted landscapes to be drawn. In both cases, the "plot" that is called for can only be supplied by the reader/viewer.

* * * * * *

Parallels in the careers of Bierstadt and Harte may seem at first like a coincidence in the post–Civil War period – intriguing, but in the end an historical by-blow. Both men maintained surprisingly similar styles and standards; both achieved the artistic fame they aspired to early and easily; and both were drawn as if magnetically to lives of affluence and high social standing, enough so that critics accused them both of selling out their art to line their purses. The widespread esteem that each enjoyed from the mid-1860s through the early 1870s, and the wholly unprecedented sums they received for their separate efforts, attests to the enthusiasm with which their striking visions of the Far West were received. By the same token, their sudden fall from the limelight into frustrating years of neglect – of diminished fees, mounting critical attacks, and letters of flat rejection – attests to an abrupt transition in popular opinion.

Certainly, the fault was not theirs, as even a brief formal review of their art confirms; they altered little in either subject matter or technique, from early years of acclaim to long, productive years of neglect. As Bret Harte confessed, somewhat forlornly, in an 1879 letter: "I grind out the old tunes on the old organ and gather up the coppers, but I never know whether my audience behind the window blinds are wishing me to 'move on' or not." In fact, both artists' audiences simply melted away, unwilling in the 1870s to countenance what, a bare decade before, could hardly satisfy demand.

The issue of artistic reception is invariably a difficult one to resolve, so overdetermined is it by considerations far from the realm of formal aesthetics that no simple answer could emerge to explain the careers of Bierstadt and Harte. Their closely parallel experiences in the period following the Civil War, however, prompt us to speculate about what it was that audiences required of them. Both artists were such singular beneficiaries – then such prominent victims – of public appeal, and their treatments were so similarly melodramatic in a period of sharply changing views of the West, that they seem to offer a key into American popular psychology at the time.

An explanation adumbrated all along lies in the considerable expectations both men aroused – expectations both for their own art, and for each other's. Each was perceived upon his debut as something of a genius, the best practitioner of his chosen medium and someone promising greater things to come. Bierstadt was named the successor of Turner, while Harte was praised as a possible rival of both Dickens and Cooper. That very overinflation of reputations led in turn (by the predictable process of self-correction) to their collapse. Neither artist, in short, was able to live up to admirers' expectations, and the fact that Harte's stories and Bierstadt's paintings remained essentially the same only proved that neither was the great American artist so many had anticipated.

Yet as well, the expectations both men aroused may have contributed to a corresponding dissatisfaction with the other's art. That is, Bierstadt's grand landscapes and Harte's distinctive characters represent two halves of a larger imaginative enterprise, and their very success independently entailed some growing disappointment in the absence of that larger whole. Bierstadt's canvases, in other words, were waiting for Harte's characters to people them, while Harte's narratives needed a more distinctively western setting. The expectation left so clearly unfulfilled in Bierstadt's paintings is the promise of dramatic renewal, of personal transformation, of transcendence beyond the physical facts of topography itself. He presents a series of dramatic scenarios that offer the assurance of individual redemption – unnatural landscapes that celebrate the prospect of personal transformation, self-conscious backdrops imbued with a power both melodramatic and morally resurgent. Yet that promise cannot be redeemed until the western narrative itself is invented. Bierstadt, in other words, excites a melodramatic imagination that he cannot possibly fulfill, although the recognition of that impossibility took some years for his public to realize. His spectacular paintings first captured the popular imagination, therefore, in a way that, say, the more subdued, more straightforwardly realistic achievements of Thomas Moran never did. And unlike Frederick Edwin Church's equally spectacular monuments to the South American Andes, Bierstadt claims a transformative power for a distinctly national landscape identified with the Far West.

Harte, conversely, proclaims that a set of rough-hewn western characters need no such personal transformation to become upright, middle-class Americans. They already are what they have yet supposedly to become, essentially civilized beings under the wild and wooly costumes, morally abiding citizens hidden by the exotic customs and outlandish behavior. In the largely unpeopled California frontier – a landscape, as Harte presented it, frequently hard to distinguish from parts of New England, the Midwest, the South, or (for that matter) even England's Lake Country – Americans were playing out a national drama of acculturation, self-sacrifice, and moral regeneration that matched sentimental dramas closer to home. The new cast of characters that Harte introduced caught the public's imagination, but only long enough to make readers realize how their fantasies needed more elaborate, more detailed, firmer placement in a Far Western landscape.

We need to remind ourselves how resistant we are to the lures of melodrama, whose hold on our imaginations remains nonetheless quite powerful. Its stark oppositions and aesthetic incoherence invariably seem excessive, which explains why we so regularly resist it in either verbal or visual forms. No better evidence of this resistance exists than the persistent attacks on Bierstadt and Harte, which testify as well to the continuing power that makes both artists seem so worth attacking. The scenes that Bierstadt fixed in paint, and that Harte memorably set in prose, established how convincingly the Far West could be seen as a magical land that was also America writ small – a place where deeply troubling issues of jus-

tice, manhood, and social control might be safely and surely resolved. Turning to Peter Brooks a last time:

> For melodrama has the distinct value of being about recogni-
> tion and clarification, about how to be clear what the stakes
> are and what their representative signs mean, and how to face
> them. Melodrama substitutes for the rite of sacrifice an urg-
> ing toward combat in life, an active, lucid confrontation of
> evil. It works to steel man for resistance, it keeps him going in
> the face of threat. Even if we cannot believe in the easier
> forms of reward that melodrama traditionally offers, there is
> virtue in clarity of recognition of what is being fought for and
> against.

Bierstadt and Harte established the kinds of scenes (whether in
California's Sierra Nevadas or Colorado's high Rockies) where this
stark, combative recognition might be expected to occur and then
obsessively reoccur in response to our deepest desires. By mapping
out the regional plots of ground wherein narrative plot can unfold,
Bierstadt figuratively cleared the ground for Harte's distinctive set
of characters, enabling their reinvention by hundreds of writers
over the next century. No longer would conventional claims of
either geology or sociology stand warrant against the collective
challenge separately mounted by both men, who reshaped both the
landscape and American history into a logic conducive to our most
powerful dreams.

Works Cited

Anderson, Nancy K. "'Wondrously Full of Invention': The Western Land-
    scapes of Albert Bierstadt." In *Albert Bierstadt: Art and Enterprise*. Eds.
    Nancy K. Anderson and Linda S. Ferber. New York: The Brooklyn
    Museum, 1990, 69–106.
Anonymous Critic. *The Art Journal* (London), October 1859. Qtd. in Gor-
    don Hendricks: *Albert Bierstadt: Painter of the American West*. New York:
    Harry N. Abrams, 1972.
Anonymous Critic [on Bierstadt's *A Storm in the Rocky Mountains, Mount
    Rosalie*]. *Watson's Weekly Art Journal*, 3 March 1866. Qtd. in Hendricks.
Bierce, Ambrose. *San Francisco News Letter and California Advertiser*, 4 Sep-
    tember 1869. Qtd. in Anderson.
Billington, Ray Allen. *Land of Savagery, Land of Promise: The European Image
    of the American Frontier in the Nineteenth Century*. New York: W. W.
    Norton, 1981.

Brooks, Peter. *The Melodramatic Imagination: Balzac, Henry James, Melodrama, and the Mode of Excess*. New Haven: Yale UP, 1976.

Harte, Bret. Letter (1879). Qtd. in Wallace Stegner, "Introduction." *The Outcasts of Poker Flat and Other Stories*. Ed. Wallace Stegner. New York: New American Library, 1961, vii–xvi.

————. "How Santa Claus Came to Simpson's Bar." In *The Outcasts of Poker Flat and Other Stories*, 165–81.

————. "The Idyl of Red Gulch." In *The Outcasts of Poker Flat and Other Stories*, 134–43.

————. "The Luck of Roaring Camp." In *The Outcasts of Poker Flat and Other Stories*, 100–11.

————. "M'Liss: An Idyl of Red Mountain." In *The Outcasts of Poker Flat and Other Stories*, 25–100.

————. "Mrs. Skagg's Husbands." In *The Outcasts of Poker Flat and Other Stories*, 182–213.

————. "The Outcasts of Poker Flat." In *The Outcasts of Poker Flat and Other Stories*, 112–23.

————. "A Protégée of Jack Hamlin's." In *The Outcasts of Poker Flat and Other Stories*, 270–99.

Jarves, James Jackson. *The Art Idea*. New York: Hurd & Houghton, 1864. Qtd. in Hendricks.

Melville, Herman. *The Confidence-Man*. 1857. Rpt. New York: W. W. Norton & Co., 1971.

Turner, Frederick Jackson. "The Significance of the Frontier in American History." 1893. Rpt. in *The Frontier in American History*. New York: Henry Holt and Co., 1940, 1–38.

MODERN WESTERN REVISIONS

SENTIMENTALISM IN THE AMERICAN SOUTHWEST: JOHN C. VAN DYKE, MARY AUSTIN, AND EDWARD ABBEY

PETER WILD

Up on his emotional tiptoes, the writer invites his audience to follow him "beyond the wire fence of civilization to those places . . . where the trail is unbroken." A reader's reward will be exhilaration and transport to "glory" in a new and pristine world of nature. First published in 1901, John C. Van Dyke's *The Desert* occupies a strategic position in the literary history of the American Southwest. The little volume was the first in the now popular genre of desert writing. Up until the year of its publication, the nation's South-western deserts were often scorned as wastelands, as the "Devil's Domain." Practically speaking, this was true. Hardscrabble home-steaders searching for welcoming lands of rich greenery and abun-dant water considered the expanses of sand and thorns largely useless.

Van Dyke's work, however, was the first book to take the opposite view. Van Dyke rejected the pioneers' utilitarianism and replaced it with an airy estheticism. Though widely accepted today, the stance was a radical change for the time. Van Dyke turned the common wisdom upside down. Surveying the region's unique qualities, he praised the Southwestern desert in terms of the chromatic imagery of indigo lizards and peaks glowing like heated garnets in the dra-matic desert sunsets. He thrilled his readers, most of them on the overcrowded East Coast, with prospects of a wild land of stark and seemingly endless mountain ranges and of sudden sandstorms whirling up huge, golden clouds that turn the sun red. To Van Dyke, the region was not only "the most decorative landscape in the world," it was, he said, "a dream landscape." With the help of his new view, one emphasizing mystery and awe, the scales began fall-ing from the nation's eyes. The public started to see the desert in terms of Van Dyke's colorful vision. With his little volume – still the best and among the most popular on the subject – Van Dyke became the grandfather of a tribe of desert writers which continues to echo his enthusiasm for arid spaces as beautiful, as restful places for the longing soul. That one man's book – helped by Mary Austin's *The Land of Little Rain,* which appeared two years later – could turn the head of a country and continue to shape our attitudes toward desert landscape is certainly to Van Dyke's credit. But far more is operating here than the efficacy of two western pens. Complex ironies lie in the conversions the books effected, and even in the books themselves, ironies that present-day desert lovers, enjoying these works' sublimity, often miss or prefer not to test.

To consider the larger picture before returning to the American Southwest, it is notable that almost everyone today, from politicians to presidents of corporations to schoolchildren – whatever their motives or knowledge – mouth favorable sentiments about nature. It seems helpful, in this regard, to consider one of the rare dissenting voices. Writing a few years ago in *Antaeus,* Joyce Carol Oates observed of nature: "It inspires a painfully limited set of responses in 'nature-writers' – REVERENCE, AWE, PIETY, MYSTICAL ONENESS. It eludes us even as it prepares to swallow us up, books and all."

Her essay, boldly titled "Against Nature," appeared among pieces by other writers rendering heartfelt applause of nature. Oates was not on a tantrum of nature-bashing. In fact, she showed far more humility than many of her fellow writers, who variously contorted themselves in praise of their subject. Oates did not condemn nature but writers' simplistic fawning before it, an obeisance which too often becomes, ironically, an act of self-glorification. Quoting Oscar Wilde, she asserted that "Nature is no great mother who has borne us. She is our creation." Her point is well-taken. Many nature writers fall into the category of the self-made man who worships his creator. Scott Slovic begins the first chapter of his book, *Seeking Awareness in American Nature Writing,* with a comment on four current icons in the field: "Such writers as Annie Dillard, Edward Abbey, Wendell Berry, and Barry Lopez are not merely, or even primarily, analysts of nature or appreciators of nature – rather, they are students of the human mind, literary psychologists." Each has the goal of using nature to discover his own "awareness of self." In other words, though Slovic does not put a negative cast on the point, much of what is passing as "nature writing" today represents a drift away from nature and into self-absorption.

The intellectual prelude to this position has a long history, much of which involves far more than the desire to seek personal enlightenment and balm for our battered psyches in nature. People, wherever they are and of whatever culture, yearn for what they do not have and then spin a rich mythology about that yearning. In the case of Europe, the ancient Greeks imagined a happy land lying westward beyond the Mediterranean in the unexplored Atlantic Ocean. The impulse took on various fanciful guises – Isles of Angels and Isles of Witches – depending on where one was in Europe, but the upshot was that centuries later when the New World was discovered, Europeans largely perceived the vast and strange lands in terms of their previous imaginings, as a fulfillment of fantasy that Howard Mumford Jones details in *O Strange New World*. Into this category fall such examples as the Seven Cities of Gold and the Fountain of Youth that lured on Spanish explorers and seemed to be confirmed by the dazzling wealth found in Aztecan Mexico.

A powerful set of intellectual concerns motivated and accompanied such European enthusiasms. Englishmen yearned across the Atlantic and envisioned themselves walking down streets of gold in Virginia. They also saw wealth of a different kind, in the form of a second chance. If, as the seventeenth-century philosopher John Locke observed, "in the beginning all the world was *America*" – that is, a pristine place of natural harmony and abundance – it took no great mind to realize that the original earthly paradise had badly degenerated into Europe's unhappy condition. The pinched circumstances resulting from frequent warfare, landless peasants, overcrowding, disease, and starvation all amply testified to that. In contrast, the New World represented a great hope on the horizon, an opportunity for civilization to start over again, to do it right this time. With a new start, settlers might enjoy physical abundance from nature's untapped resources as well as the freedom to find their full potential as rational, caring human beings. The very language of our Declaration of Independence, about "Life, Liberty, and the Pursuit of Happiness," reflects this urge, a shucking off of the old, unworkable ways in favor of a far brighter future. Because of these historical yearnings, the optimism which took root in America exemplified a romantic efflorescence, one pointing toward economic prosperity, wider opportunity for all, and what has collectively become known as "self-fulfillment" and an improved "quality of life" – changes most people in the nation understandably applaud. Yet there is no sense in pretending that these accomplishments have not occurred without a set of romantic delusions many people continue to grasp with enthusiasm.

John M. Ellis reminds us that, in the first century A.D., the Roman historian Tacitus fancied that the "uncivilized" tribes living to the north in the wilderness of Germany enjoyed an enviable state of primitive innocence. To him these forest dwellers lived "close to nature," as we would say today. They were democratic, sweet-souled, and without greed, noble to their fingertips. They stood in happy contrast, in other words, to the corrupt and oppressive society Tacitus felt he was forced to endure in his own "overcivilized" Rome. The sweet-souled people a naive Tacitus admired, however, were also the same tribes which some years later came roaring out of the woods to sack the Roman Empire. In our country, at least as far back as James Fenimore Cooper's novels we see a wilderness lover turning his back on a noxious civilization and fulfilling his psychic needs in wild nature. Today, thoroughly urbanized as we are, Americans nonetheless cling to a romantic notion confirmed and reconfirmed through the decades, from Natty Bumppo to Nick Adams to Edward Abbey. Nature heals us, and if we can't get away for a backpacking trip now and then to recharge our spiritual batteries, or if we are too lazy to get up the gumption to hit the trail, reading about nature might do.

Nature, of course, *can* heal, at certain times and with certain individuals. The problem arises when people try to substitute an idea (as Tacitus did) for everyday reality or when a concept is accepted out of hand, without analysis, and without acknowledging that nature, too, demands a price in return. Then we have not an enriching concept as presented by Aldo Leopold and others in our long tradition of wilderness lovers but a shallow substitute – one, furthermore, in which nature is not honored but is instead distorted and forced to serve our own limited ends. Annie Dillard is an example in this regard. As Elaine Tietjen puts it, Dillard uses the woods about her in her popular *Pilgrim at Tinker Creek* (1974) not to investigate nature but to explore her "own idiosyncratic life" in hopes of resolving "her own unresolved experiences." Similarly self-absorbed writers often, as Peter Reyner Banham says, tell us less about nature than "about their own delicate little egos."

This is not to say that Dillard is not a writer of admirable wit and sophistication. But her position, no matter how sophisticated the words spun from it, undercuts the natural world by relegating it to second-class status. Nature as a grand, overpowering system – both wondrous and scientifically fascinating – in which human beings and their petty gripes are as nothing, ends up being conveniently overlooked. Thus we lose the power found in such a book as, say, Ann Zwinger's *Wind in the Rock* (1978), a work that keeps nature insistently in focus, much to readers' lasting delight as along with Zwinger they explore the wild, labyrinthine canyons of south-

eastern Utah. What Zwinger finds there is not herself but a treasure far more important, the "massive dignity about sandstone
beds that tell of a past long before human breathing, that bear the
patterns of ancient winds and water in their crossbeddings."

Using Dillard and Zwinger as contrasting writers, what we have
in contemporary nature writing, then, is the old tug between romanticism and classicism – with the romantics presently holding
most of the rope. Much of this boils down to a fairly simple pattern
in human nature. People fear the unknown and they tend to appreciate what they are losing. Roderick Nash admirably documents
this syndrome in *Wilderness and the American Mind.* To the helpless,
starving settlers in Plymouth Colony the New England forest was a
forbidding place, a "howling wilderness" full of wild beasts and
savage Indians. To civilize such a place involved a challenging, if
not holy, obligation – as well as an immensely profitable one – and
off the growing nation went, leveling the forests, killing the animals
with abandon, and slaughtering the Indians who stood in the way.
Yet remorse eventually set in. What was thought of as the boldness
and physicality of the American character depended upon having
wilderness to conquer. Around the turn of the century, people
began to realize that their wild lands were fast disappearing, and
fear of a different sort began to trouble the nation: the fear that
without wilderness we would become an overcivilized, etiolated society of pantywaists. Urban folk, as T. J. Jackson Lears points out,
went looking for "authentic experiences" as antidotes for their
supposedly artificial lives in the cities. In the past, wild nature had
been one of the remedies, so a romantic age supposed, but where
could people go, now that the land was fenced and under the plow?
"To the desert!" cried Van Dyke.

Until then, the Southwest had been a huge chunk of overlooked
real estate, ignored by almost everyone except miners and ranchers. Van Dyke and others after him found it a lodestone for their
romantic searchings for mystery and awe, an exotic and wild place
far different than any other region in the United States. Its dry
climate was healthful, a cure for the very real respiratory problems
widespread in the country. In the Southwest wolves still howled at
the moon and one could ride for days, wandering through landscapes of strange plants and animals. Ancient artifacts appeared at
nearly every hand – and better yet, ancient people still danced to
bring rain and appease the gods. The Southwest offered the promise of mystery, excitement, and self-fulfillment, a cure for the real
or imagined ills of civilization.

In the rush to be awed, almost no one wrote about the ironies.

To begin with, the Southwest was not as wild as Van Dyke had made out. By his time, the Indians had been bludgeoned and safely packed off to reservations. Wolves were being shot on sight, soon to disappear entirely. Yes, the land was vast, but it was also fenced. Travelers could whizz across the formerly forbidding desert in Pullman-car comfort, dazzled by the strange sights – if they had the price of a ticket. The supreme irony of all was that, far from "living off the land," the ample financial means of Van Dyke and many of his followers made them more long-term tourists than settlers. They could enjoy the desert because they could *afford* to enjoy it, without the very real dangers endured by the generations before them. Such writers could pay for their self-fulfillment, while less-fortunate settlers were ditching and grubbing. With the coming of general prosperity, the attitudes engendered by well-off romantic searchers spread throughout the society. What began with aristocratic Easterner Van Dyke now permeates the American population. Loving nature has become democratized.

Van Dyke stands as one of the heroes in the mainstream of American sentimentalism. Many right-thinking people see him as embodying their values and have turned him into a wilderness saint of the arid lands. In this view, not only was Van Dyke the first to proclaim the desert a lovely place, his complaints about the encroaching developments of his time foreshadow what present-day desert lovers decry each year as American ticky-tacky expands ever farther around such cities as Phoenix and Las Vegas. Some modern readers wistfully picture Van Dyke riding his horse out beyond the wire fence of civilization, where he had the desert to himself, pristine and better than anyone can have it today, and this causes no end of pining for the lost, good old days: the very same pang that had our ancestors of a hundred years ago swooning for lost nature. Not only was Van Dyke a manly loner, savvy in the ways of wilderness survival, knowledgeable about desert plants and animals – as manly and savvy and as knowledgeable as contemporary backpackers would like to be – he also possessed a delicate soul, which made him a prototype of the "sensitive male" of the desert. As he pictures his relationship with the scorned vastness of thorn trees and Gila monsters: "The desert has gone a-begging for a word of praise these many years. It never had a sacred poet; it has in me only a lover."

Van Dyke was what people should be in their approach to treasured but assaulted nature (or so the common wisdom goes), a man capable of ecstatic flights at her beauty and emotional slumps over her destruction. This has inspired a nearly endless stream of encomiums which place Van Dyke on a pedestal, both as a superb outdoorsman and, in Lawrence Clark Powell's words, a superb "indoorsman," a man "who truly saw it first and said it best." Even Van Dyke's rare critics, such as Peter Reyner Banham, accept his image as a stalwart and eccentric adventurer and inadvertently lend support to it by seeing Van Dyke as a forerunner of the "desert maniacs of the [present] ecological generation."

The problem with this happy portrait is that it is largely false, and the widespread acceptance of the falseness is testimony to the power of an American sentimentalism which tends to see not what is there but what it dearly wants to find. Van Dyke calls himself a "lover" in his preface, and the little he says about himself thereafter hints at the appealing image of the rugged frontiersman combined with that of the high-minded romantic. After the short preface and the first chapter, however, one finds little to support this bold self-portrait. Indeed, a close reading of *The Desert* and his other writings, combined with what we have recently learned about Van Dyke's life, shows that quite the opposite appears to be true.

As I have argued elsewhere (with Neil Carmony), there is every reason to believe that Van Dyke never traveled across the desert in the manner he implies. Van Dyke was a cultured professor of art history at Rutgers University and concurrently the librarian at the prestigious New Brunswick Theological Seminary, still perched on what is called "Holy Hill." Certainly, his refined professional circumstances do not in themselves rule out a parallel life of derring-do in the wild. But when Van Dyke in his autobiography and his other books describes his exploits in the outdoors – his encounters with threatening wolves and grizzly bears, and his romps about the Wild West with Indians – his accounts are, by turns, so vague, colorful, and downright impossible as to throw the possibility of a lone trek for hundreds of miles across arid, hostile country into the category of the tall tale.

More than likely, the refined Van Dyke, who regularly put up in the best hotels when traveling in Europe, probably followed suit in the desert. He saw much of what he wrote about from the porch of his brother's ranch house in the Mojave desert and from the windows of Pullman cars. In other words, Van Dyke's adventures in *The Desert* and elsewhere often present the airy imaginings of a romantic fabulist. Modern readers tend to seize on the hints planted in *The Desert* and embroider them according to their own fancies until they have created their desired image of an heroic nature writer.

Further statements by Van Dyke outside *The Desert* strengthen

the case. Far from being an expansive, large-souled person who
wished to lead his fellow man to salving nature, as his preface to *The
Desert* suggests, Van Dyke did not relish the thought of the general
public overrunning his esthetic domain. Powell quotes a sarcastic
letter by Van Dyke to his editor at Scribner's, W. C. Brownell, about
his forthcoming book: "[*The Desert*] is a whole lot better than the
swash which today is being turned out as 'literature.'" He adds,
"and it will sell too, but not up in the hundreds of thousands. It is
not so bad as that. My audience is only a few thousand, thank God."
If Van Dyke had a low opinion of Das Volk, he does not always
seem to care much for the desert either. Looking back decades later
on the desert travel that resulted in his most famous book, he writes
– in chapter twenty of his autobiography – about returning to
New Jersey: "Strange to say, the civilized agreed with me where the
wild had not. I had always believed that 'back to nature' was a
panacea for all ills, but, lo!, it was not. I had overdone everything,
walked myself to a shadow like a town postman, chased nature up a
tree, and worn 'out of doors' to a frazzle."

How offhanded Van Dyke could be about natural phenomena
can also be seen in the pages of *The Desert* itself. In not a few
passages he gets his natural history badly tangled. He describes the
showy flower of the saguaro cactus as purple, whereas it is white.
He also informs his readers that the coyote, famous for pursuing
rabbits and other fleet-footed game, "seldom runs after things,"
and he boldly declares the rattlesnake is "in fact sluggish," a dangerous supposition about that poisonous viper. These and many
other examples add up to far more than understandable human
errors. Some of Van Dyke's information is so out of whack that one
wonders if he ever actually spent a night sleeping out on the hard
ground. Yet his reputation as a nature lover is so valued that, with
the exception of Banham, no writer – naturalist, nature writer, or
otherwise – has bothered to challenge Van Dyke in print on the
matter in the nearly hundred years since the publication of *The
Desert*. Such is the power of what certain people want to believe.

And yet, though Van Dyke violated many of the tenets of what
would now be considered proper thinking about nature, we are
faced with one incontrovertible and overriding fact. He wrote the
best book we have on the Southwestern deserts. Though ignoring
the points detailed above, scholars have at least touched on the
driving force behind Van Dyke's prose: his unique way of seeing.
Van Dyke's theories about art schooled him to see the desert with
an art critic's eye and made him, in Banham's words, "a connoisseur
of views, a skilled savorer of lights and colors." A devotee of Art for

Art's Sake and impressionism, Van Dyke held appreciation of the beauty of form and color as among life's highest pleasures – and this regardless of their human context, use, or meaning. Related to this was the devotion of many aesthetes of Van Dyke's class and persuasion to wild nature as a vast canvas of visual delights. Hence, when Van Dyke viewed the desert, he saw not noxious wastelands scorned by the practically minded but new and pleasing blendings of form and color.

Students of Van Dyke tend to let it go at that, however, and to miss the larger implications of his esthetic attitudes. A measure of the still unexplored complexities of those attitudes and of Van Dyke's evasiveness and low regard for the mass of readers occurs in the easily overlooked dedicatee of *The Desert*'s preface, the unidentified "A. M. C." This person, as I have proposed with Zita Ingham, was none other than Van Dyke's close friend, steel magnate Andrew Carnegie. That the nation's greatest advocate of desert preservation dedicated his book to one of the age's avid captains of industry – the richest man in America and hardly a conservationist – is less a contradiction than one might expect. It was at least one Van Dyke himself rationalized with ease. He uses his dedicatee as a code word, for he knew his inner circle of readers would recognize Carnegie, a man sympathetic to Van Dyke's esthetic views, behind the initials. Furthermore, the "you" of Van Dyke's preface is not the generalized "you" of his readership, as might be naturally supposed. It refers instead to Carnegie himself. Thus when Van Dyke hopes in his preface that "you, and the nature-loving public you represent, will accept this record," he is addressing an exclusive circle of cognoscenti, mostly wealthy friends who sympathized with his esthetic approach to nature. Only they, it is implied, have the intelligence and sensitivity to appreciate what the following pages will reveal.

The ironies surrounding Van Dyke multiply and turn on themselves. A crustily conservative man who was a revolutionary in terms of changing the nation's view of the desert, Van Dyke actually disdained his adoring public. Along with others of his persuasion, he remained convinced that both society and individuals were pretty much beyond redemption. He also did not delude himself that he could discover self-awareness in nature. Rather, he viewed the loveliness of nature as an escape both from society and from his own, sometimes morbid self. In their place he wanted the exhilaration of "the boundless and the fathomless." He wanted nothing less than "the sublime that we feel in immensity and mystery," and that the forms and colors of nature freely offered. Van Dyke keeps

nature, not himself, tightly in focus, and in this sense the grandfather of most desert writing rejects, rather than confirms, current
trends in nature writing.

If Van Dyke is misperceived as a desert Houyhnhnm largely
because the desert-loving public insists on having an idol according
to its desires, both the life and writing of Mary Austin would seem to
match reality with public wish-fulfillment. As self-described in her
autobiography, *Earth Horizon* (1932), Austin was a victim who tri-
umphed. She was a woman of humble origins who, disappointed
with her husband, overcame personal hardships, striking out on her
own in a day when the independence of women was not encouraged,
and by sheer strength of will and her own talents achieved success. In
the process, she lost none of her sensitivity, either toward her fellow
humans or toward the land. To the contrary, she developed into a
social reformer, advocating the rights of women, children, Indians,
and the poor. She was a pioneer in what have become the popular
causes of today, and all this occurred while Austin developed into
one of the most influential writers of her time and wrote one book,
The Land of Little Rain (1903), that rivals Van Dyke's work in its
celebration of the desert. Austin would seem to be the all-around
model for the modern woman. Yet certain ironies and disjunctions
in her work tend to qualify this image.

It is striking how closely the desert books by Van Dyke and
Austin echo one another, given the fact that in all their extensive
publications there is not a single reference of one writer to the
other. (Van Dyke's *The Desert* appeared in 1901, Austin's *The Land of
Little Rain* two years later. Both authors were in the desert portion
of Southern California at the same time. Both were widely read
individuals with access to the literary circles of the day. It is thus
difficult to imagine that Austin was not familiar with Van Dyke's
desert book when she wrote hers, but the silence prevails.) Although generalizations do not always hold true for the two volumes, Van Dyke often aims for the grand sweep and the large
scene – for "the majesty" and "fierceness" of the desert. For her
part, Austin draws readers more to the detail. Hiding by a spring at
night to observe the mice and other small creatures coming in to
drink, for instance, she describes elf owls hunting through the
darkness as "speckled fluffs of greediness."

It is on the geographical score that further differences between
the two authors begin to emerge. In the concluding paragraphs of
their prefaces, each writer refers to himself as a "lover," yet the two
writers turn out to be lovers of rather different sorts, each with a
distinctive awareness: in traditional terms, one manly, the other

feminine. As a part of his grand rhetorical approach, Van Dyke takes in the whole arid Southwest, treating its features generically in such chapters as "Desert Animals" and "Winged Life." Only rarely do we know exactly where he is. Austin, on the other hand, stays close to her stomping grounds in Southern California's Owens Valley and its environs. Neither writer denies that nature is red in tooth and claw, but Van Dyke celebrates the Darwinian workings of a vast and incomprehensible universe in which all men are ultimately lost and helpless, while Austin wishes to show us her home ground with the gentleness and warmth of a private pleasure. Whereas Van Dyke remains personally aloof from his subject, Austin encourages her readers' intimacy with the land, urging them to tap the nurturing correspondence between the things of the earth and the things of the heart. Van Dyke invites us to ride off manfully into the wild unknown; Austin invites us to knock "at the door of the brown house under the willow-tree at the end of the village street" so we can visit her familiar haunts and hear her "news of the land."

The chief difference between the two authors centers around the relationship between people and the land. For esthetic reasons, there are no human beings in *The Desert*. Man, after all, is nature's enemy, her destroyer, as the opening sentences of Van Dyke's preface illustrate clearly: "After the making of Eden came a serpent, and after the gorgeous furnishing of the world, a human being. Why the existence of the destroyers? What monstrous folly, think you, ever led Nature to creature her one great enemy – man!" Austin's *The Land of Little Rain,* on the other hand, is full of people – but of a particular sort and for a particular reason. Austin is enamored of Indians, Mexicans, and poor whites. Such people, her book leads one to believe, live "in harmony with the land," as the current expression goes, in contrast to the prosperous white males who are abusing nature. (Van Dyke also wanted to preserve the wildness of nature but for esthetic rather than social reasons. Urban development, as Banham notes, would have obscured and interrupted Van Dyke's "committed enjoyment of the visual wonders" of the desert.)

Austin's version of a rural idyll in which the downtrodden live in balance with nature has immense romantic appeal. Her handling of episodes such as that in which a prospector has a near-mystical encounter with wild sheep in a snowstorm is often compelling in literary terms, especially for city-bound readers yearning to believe such experiences are possible. Yet her fetching anecdotes about the desert and its people also tend toward delusion. She sees her desert people through rose-colored glasses, and one must stretch to believe that all of them lived in a difficult land with the joyous harmony she describes. She celebrates the virtues of people victimized by society, but the logic of her presentation of them dictates that they can keep their virtues only by continuing to suffer. Such is the implication of her portrait of an old, blind Indian woman in a Paiute camp:

> And in time she paid the toll of the smoky huts and became blind. This is a thing so long expected by the Paiutes that when it comes they find it neither bitter nor sweet, but tolerable because common. There were three other blind women in the campoodie, withered fruit on a bough, but they had memory and speech. By noon of the sun there were never any left in the campoodie but these or some mother of weanlings, and they sat to keep the ashes warm upon the hearth. If it were cold, they burrowed in the blankets of the hut; if it were warm, they followed the shadow of the wickiup around. Stir much out of their places they hardly dared, since one might not help another; but they called, in high, old cracked voices, gossip and reminder across the ash heaps.

Austin can also be condescending as she fosters stereotypes. Her Mexican village in the concluding chapter of the book is populated by guitar-strumming country folk who sing and dance at the drop of a hat:

> At Las Uvas they keep up all the good customs brought out of Old Mexico or bred in a lotus-eating land; drink, and are merry and look out for something to eat afterward; have children, nine or ten to a family, have cock-fights, keep the siesta, smoke cigarettes and wait for the sun to go down. And always they dance; at dusk on the smooth adobe floors, afternoons under the trellises where the earth is damp and has a fruity smell. A betrothal, a wedding, or a christening, or the mere proximity of a guitar is sufficient occasion; and if the occasion lacks, send for the guitar and dance anyway.

According to Austin, then, these simple people have few of the conflicts and tensions that test and sometimes strengthen people elsewhere. In idealizing the Mexicans according to her own romantic lights, in other words, she denigrates them, stereotyping them and robbing them of their individualism and their humanity.

The Mexican village becomes Austin's heaven on earth, just as Van Dyke looked to the wild desert for a kind of secular salvation.

The difference lies in this. Aesthetician Van Dyke distinguished between illusion and delusion, for he insisted in *The Desert* that "The reality is one thing, the appearance quite another." In a way his reverential public still rarely understands as it turns him into a figure he was not, he accepted his lovely and sustaining views of nature for what they were, beautiful illusions that had little or nothing to do with the realities of everyday life. As an American sentimentalist of the sort more and more holding sway in contemporary life, Austin on the other hand presents illusion and reality as one and the same. In this she comes full circle, being far more in the tradition of Western civilization than she realized or would have wished to admit. Had she been born in Europe centuries earlier, she too might have imagined Isles of Flowers and Isles of Angels existing out there in the gauzy haze beyond the Gates of Hercules.

Though Van Dyke was misinterpreted for his hidden intent, both he and Mary Austin embodied the romantic longings of their day for nature and set the direction for the Southwestern writers who have continued in their footsteps into contemporary times. Edwin Corle, Joseph Wood Krutch, John Nichols, and a growing number of other desert writers have dazzled readers with the variety of their talents while alerting the larger public to the exotic enticements of the nation's desert heritage. Because of the welcome diversity of their approaches, it is difficult to generalize about what has become a genre, except to point out two common features: almost all such writers celebrate the Southwest as a heady antidote for the flagging spirits of what they perceive as the overindustrialized and repressive twentieth century and, as a corollary of this urge, they promote the preservation of what remains wild in the region.

Because of the happy variety, it is also risky to pull out any one figure as typical or representative of the others. Failing in that, we *can* point to one who has been among the most influential, both in rousing the public and in setting the tone for younger writers.

From his days spent as a ranger in Utah's Arches National Monument, Edward Abbey distilled a desert paean that at first all but befuddles with its wild swings and inconsistencies. In *Desert Solitaire* (1968), Abbey by turns delights in the adolescent mischief of rolling old automobile tires into the Grand Canyon, then damns the tourist lobby that won't rest until it has pushed roads into every inaccessible cranny of the desert wilderness. At one moment he celebrates liberated women, then in the next we find him simpering at the feet of some sex object. As an expansive democrat who sees nature as the public's salvation, he chastises tourists to get out of their cars, to abandon their "motorized wheelchairs" and "walk – *walk* – WALK upon our sweet and blessed land!" Then, turning churlish, he scourges the noxious herd dribbling Coke bottles and paper cups across what should be *his* private wilderness domain. In short, Abbey seems an *enfant terrible* of inconsistency.

Scott Slovic sees Abbey's bombardment of readers' emotions as a tool calculated to jar people out of their "secure mental ruts" so that they will consider nature anew. There may be some truth in this – certainly it can be one effect of Abbey's style – though something quite different and less calculated is at work here. A natural-born rebel, Abbey caught the spirit of the youth culture of the 1960s and applied it to nature writing. If anything, such times were a romantic spinoff sanctioning rebellion against authority and the necessity of immediate gratification. As Emerson taught us long before, consistency is not the issue. The issue is the celebration of self, to do what one wills (in Abbey's case using nature as the vehicle) while at the same time giving at least lip service to the right of others to do likewise.

In this, Abbey is the curious offspring of Van Dyke and Austin, the quite different parents of the Southwest's literature. The short list of desert books Abbey recommends to his readers includes both Van Dyke and Austin. Taking his cue from an elitist and sharp-tongued Van Dyke railing against mankind as nature's enemy, Abbey verbally bludgeons tourists whose first query upon entering the desert glories of Arches National Monument is "Where's the Coke machine?" He, like Van Dyke, is fixated on nature as life's highest good, as an escape from the oppression of irredeemable humanity. He echos the Van Dyke who shouted against development by declaring that "The deserts should never be reclaimed. They are the breathing-spaces of the west and should be preserved forever," Abbey wants to keep the riffraff from trampling across his wilderness and marring his pleasure.

As the child of both Van Dyke and Austin, Abbey, as sometimes happens with children, is a nice blend of opposites in at least one respect. Both Van Dyke and Austin pine for "lost worlds," though for different lost worlds and for different reasons: Van Dyke, as noted, because he cannot possibly rid his garden of the intruder; Austin because her admired common folk, as is true of her Paiutes, are anachronisms in an industrial society. Abbey also indulges in the literary luxury of celebrating a romantic land that has just slipped though his fingers: "most of what I write about in this book is already gone or going under fast."

As often happens in families, one of the parents inevitably influences the child more than the other, and in Abbey's case it is clearly Austin. Abbey, with a master's degree in philosophy and well-read outside his field is, like Van Dyke, a sophisticated writer, able to draw on the ironies of modern life to enliven his prose. But beneath the lively surface beats the heart of a sentimentalist. Austin features old, blind Indian women and guitar-strumming Mexicans, ready figures to call onto the stage and win the sympathies of a sentimentally disposed audience. For all his skill as a writer who can deftly manipulate his readers up and down emotional scales, easy sentiment also lies at Abbey's core. As he makes clear in his introduction to *Desert Solitaire:*

> For my part I am pleased enough with surfaces – in fact they alone seem to me to be of much importance. Such things for example as the grasp of a child's hand in your own, the flavor of an apple, the embrace of friend or lover, the silk of a girl's thigh, the sunlight on rock and leaves, the feel of music. . . , the plunge of clear water into a pool, the face of the wind – what else is there? What else do we need?

The question smacks of cliché. Some people may be satisfied with a steady dose of "the silk of a girl's thigh" and "the feel of music." Yet the truth is that however pleasurable such things indeed are, nature also has a great deal more to offer, complexities beyond the sensations of the moment and the gauzy prospects of sentimentalists, though admittedly such a stance as Abbey's currently prevails in Southwestern nature writing.

Scratching through the surface of works by the three nature writers discussed here reveals a collective mass of hidden intentions, wrongheaded concepts, and outright deceptions, along with other negative qualities often easily accepted by the authors' enthusiastic audience. This should come as little surprise, for such conditions often obtain for much lasting literature. Aesthetically, the situation should not bother us. Van Dyke's powerful words as Baboquivari Peak progresses through heated colors in a fierce desert sunset until the towerlike shaft glows like "a clouded garnet" in the growing darkness leave us with a pleasurable *frisson*. And this effect is achieved regardless of whether he was camping out in the wilds of northern Mexico as he implies or was on a gentleman's tour of the region.

One can argue, however, that nature writing is not only a more persuasive genre than others – it is also more immediate and more influential for good or ill in our everyday lives. As does not hold with most readers of sea tales or detective stories, practically all of us are familiar in one degree or another with nature, and even urban readers are aware of the larger expanses surrounding their cities as a reality, a presence they have visited and remember. In nature writing, then, the subject and its literature, if not the same, are assumed to be very close. In turn, our attitudes toward nature shaped by books about it influence our treatment of the very earth that gives us sustenance. In this sense, nature writing has a palpable bearing on how we and our children live with the earth. And here, we can get into deep trouble when the illusions of literature become the delusions by which we wish to live.

Little harm – and perhaps much good – was caused by Van Dyke's *The Desert*. Full of inaccuracies and based on a literary scam, the book's power nonetheless roused the public to demand that the government set aside large desert sweeps now forming magnificent natural legacies in the Southwest. So, too, Edward Abbey's appeal to the rebel child in us all helps keep up the pressure for continued preservation.

Yet such easy sentimentalization can also be troubling. One questions the long-term good generated by the self-pleasing "Bambi" concept of nature in which many people luxuriate. Just as Austin's rosy estimate of native peoples can lead to dehumanizing stereotypes, our failure to recognize the often harsh complexities of nature can lead to an imagined Disneyland that is immediately attractive but false. As in other aspects of our national life, the shift is from the subject to our feelings about it, from nature to self-absorption, from substance to an appealing but shallow symbolism. Even today, as the nation gives lip service to caring for nature more than it ever has, the Southwest's natural legacies are being overwhelmed by overpopulation and pollution. This in part because we will or cannot look beyond self-absorption to address the very real problems afflicting the region, one of the country's most romantic but also most vulnerable landscapes.

Works Cited

Abbey, Edward. *Desert Solitaire: A Season in the Wilderness*. New York: McGraw-Hill, 1968.

Austin, Mary. *The Land of Little Rain*. Boston: Houghton Mifflin, 1903.

Banham, Peter Reyner. *Scenes in America Deserta*. Salt Lake City: Peregrine Smith, 1982.

Ellis, John M. "The Western Tradition of Political Correctness." *Academic Questions* 5, no. 2 (1992): 24–31.

Ingham, Zita, and Peter Wild. "The Preface as Illumination: The Curious

(If not Tricky) Case of John C. Van Dyke's *The Desert.*" *Rhetoric Review* 9, no. 2 (1991): 328–39.

Lears, T. J. Jackson. *No Place of Grace: Antimodernism and the Transformation of American Culture, 1880–1920.* New York: Pantheon, 1981.

Locke, John. *Two Treatises of Government* (1690). Ed. Peter Laslett. Cambridge: Cambridge UP, 1960.

Oates, Joyce Carol. "Against Nature." *Antaeus* 57 (1986): 236–43.

Powell, Lawrence Clark. "John C. Van Dyke: *The Desert.*" In *Southwest Classics: The Creative Literature of the Arid Lands.* 1974. Rpt. Tucson: U of Arizona P, 1982, 314–28.

Slovic, Scott. *Seeking Awareness in American Nature Writing: Henry Thoreau, Annie Dillard, Edward Abbey, Wendell Berry, Barry Lopez.* Salt Lake City: U of Utah P, 1992.

Tietjen, Elaine. "Perceptions of Nature: Annie Dillard's *Pilgrim at Tinker Creek.*" *North Dakota Quarterly* 56, no. 3 (1988): 101–13.

Van Dyke, John C. *The Autobiography of John C. Van Dyke: A Personal Narrative of American Life from 1861–1931.* Ed. Peter Wild. Salt Lake City: U of Utah P, 1993.

———. *The Desert: Further Studies in Natural Appearances.* New York: Charles Scribner's, 1901.

Wild, Peter, and Neil Carmony. "The Trip Not Taken." *Journal of Arizona History* 34, no. 1 (1993): 65–80.

Zwinger, Ann. *Wind in the Rock: The Canyonlands of Southeastern Utah.* 1978. Rpt. Tucson: U of Arizona P, 1988.

REVISIONIST WESTERN CLASSICS

THOMAS J. LYON

The first generation of "serious" or "literary" western poetry and fiction writers, beginning with Robinson Jeffers (b. 1887) and including Harvey Fergusson (1890–1971), Vardis Fisher (1895–1968), A. B. Guthrie, Jr. (1901–1990), and Frank Waters (1902–), were sharply aware of the received mythology of the West. Each strove for a realist's stance vis-à-vis his own personal history, and attempted to view larger historical matters with similar objectivity. With the exception of Vardis Fisher's occasional lapses into romantic projection, these writers did not view the West as an endless frontier; they did not make one-dimensional heroes of explorers, trappers, cowboys, gunfighters, and so forth; and they did not share the arrogance of Manifest Destiny. In short, their works are not simple-minded. Their writings' complexity anticipates by several decades the analytic position of the current "New Historicism." In some cases – particularly in the philosophies of Robinson Jeffers and Frank Waters – these classic writers have mapped territory that remains untraveled by most contemporary critics of the West.

Jeffers's home in Carmel, the famous "Tor House," which was anchored to bedrock on a grassy hill only a few yards from the Pacific, aptly symbolized the poet's philosophical position. Whole eras of expansion and migration lay behind him, in effect, filling the continent; he stood at the edge of the ocean, looking outward, absorbed in the untamed, elemental power and transcendent beauty he saw daily. He made the wild wholeness of the universe his reference, and became a critic of partial, anthropocentric views. When he helped build Tor House, he did not provide for electricity, a significant decision. His standard seems not to have been convenience; the omission of wiring, indeed, may not have been influenced much by any of the usual human desires or contexts. In "Night," published in 1925, some years after Tor House was finished, Jeffers wrote apostrophically to the Night – that is, the dark, the unknown, the ultimate wildness – and asked it to "pardon . . . the lamp in my tower," along with "the fretfulness/ Of cities, the cressets of the planets, the pride of the/ stars." Clearly his stance transcends the ordinary viewpoint of our species. "Something utterly wild had crept into his mind and marked his features," Loren Eiseley wrote in 1965. What is "revisionist" about Jeffers is that he attempted to go beyond the standpoint of anthropocentric thought. His paradigm, as we would say, was not set solely by speciesist rules. "Something utterly wild had crept into his mind."

Jeffers's first extended examination of what it might mean to "go beyond" in this fashion is found in "The Tower Beyond Tragedy," published in 1925. In this long poem, which is Jeffers's version of the Aeschylean story of Orestes, the protagonist kills his mother Clytemnestra to avenge her murder of his father Agamemnon, leaves Mycenae in apparent madness (so far Jeffers's and the classic plot are the same), but then returns mysteriously transformed, to announce to his sister Electra that he has "outgrown the city a little." Electra cannot understand him. She begs Orestes, and tries to tempt him sexually, to stay in the city and take over the kingship of their murdered father. But Orestes is not tempted. (Incest here has the symbolic meaning, common in Jeffers's work, of a turning inward – a very great error.) He is now "suddenly awakened" and says that he will no longer "waste inward/ Upon humanity, having found a fairer object."

He explains what this "fairer object" is, and how he came to know it. He has, he tells Electra, "entered the life of the brown forest," and "felt the changes in the veins/ In the throat of the mountain." Orestes's new position seems to have saved his sanity. (In Aeschylus's version, mental balance is lost.) His newfound power to intuit the processes of wild nature has widened and deepened his entire frame of reference. From the new perspective, mankind appears naturalistically as "a moving lichen/ On the cheek of the round stone." Humanity is thus part of the totality, albeit much reduced from its usual self-image. This adjusted sense of things is what Jeffers's body of poetry moves toward and suggests as curative. The wise, in Jeffers, leave behind the "city" and the "ancient house" (figures for the world we build, building on our self-centeredness), and come to a position like that of the speaker in "Nova":

We can, by force and self-discipline, by many refusals and a
    few assertions, in the teeth of fortune assure ourselves

Freedom and integrity in life or integrity in death. And
  we know that the enormous invulnerable beauty of things
Is the face of God, to live gladly in its presence, and die
  without grief or fear knowing it survives us.

Jeffers's stance is panhuman, and of course supraregional; it
does not seem right or complete, somehow, to refer to him as a
western poet. But when we look at the particular circumstances of
his coming into his own as a writer, we find him occupying a piece
of western turf, both literally and symbolically. Carmel sits almost
as far west as it is possible to go in the forty-eight contiguous states.
Although it had been a writer's colony of sorts for some time, its
main street was yet unpaved when the Jefferses arrived in 1913,
and in the hills south of town toward Point Sur, isolated ranchers
lived lives that seemed to Jeffers, as he said in the introduction to
his 1938 *Selected Poetry,* little changed from those of back-country
people "in the Idyls or the Sagas, or in Homer's Ithaca. Men were
riding after cattle, or plowing the headland, hovered by white sea-
gulls, as they have done for thousands of years, and will for thousands of years to come." Thus he was on a kind of frontier, where
what he termed the "permanent life" of nonmodern culture could
be observed, and where the sheer magnificence and vastness of the
coastal environment – an epitome of the true wildness of this world
– stood as a reminder that all human life is a mere flicker within
something unimaginably greater. The setting was sanative, and
perhaps this is expectably western. But whereas Zane Grey, for
example, described a redemptive power in the western landscape,
his descriptions remained on a personal and somewhat sentimental
level. Jeffers's western wilderness was a key to perceiving the essential wildness of the universe as a whole, in which human personality
is only something like a lichen on a rock. No tall heroics for Jeffers.

It is interesting to guess at the possible ways, and the influencing
factors, by which Jeffers came to this wild point of view. He had
had a childhood discipline toward serious matters, he had early
developed solitary habits, and he was accustomed to long walks in
natural surroundings, and no doubt all of this worked in concert
with the splendidly beautiful California coast. But his first book
from his new life in Carmel (*Californians,* 1916) was rather conventional; indeed, there is as much of a mysterious gap between that
book and Jeffers's next (*Tamar,* 1924), as there is between Walt
Whitman's utterances of the 1840s and the incandescent *Leaves of
Grass* of 1855.

The one new discipline Jeffers engaged in during those eight
years was housebuilding. In this work, the first manual labor he
had ever engaged in, he handled natural materials in an intimate
way, a way that counted. In "Tor House," published in 1928, Jeffers
wrote that his "fingers/ had the art/ To make stone love stone," but
in the beginning, according to his wife Una, he "hadn't any skill of
any kind, so he did the hardest and plainest job (at $4.00 a day, I
think), mixed mortar and carried the hod to the master mason." He
apprenticed himself, in effect, and this represented a major commitment. He began to learn through his hands, slowly developing
an artisan's confidence. This humble mixing and lugging and fit-
ting was to become revelatory work.

The experience came soon after World War I – an important
circumstance. The war had illuminated for Jeffers, as for so many
others, a hollowness underneath the deceptively self-confident surface of modern civilization. But in practical and immediate terms,
he had been torn, during the war, over what his own role in it
should be. Twin sons had been born to Una and him in 1916, and
as America became more involved in the Great War, Jeffers felt
caught between his life in place and family on the one hand, and an
assumed duty to enlist on the other. He agonized in indecision.
Finally, after "suffering considerable disturbance of mind," in
Una's description, Jeffers tried to enlist, and eventually was accepted into the balloon corps. He was awaiting assignment when
the war ended. Some nine months after that sudden release,
Jeffers began his work with stone. Now, after such a cathartic time,
circumstances appeared to work to profound effect. In Una's account, "As he helped the masons shift and place the wind and wave-
worn granite I think he realized some kinship with it, and became
aware of strengths within himself unknown before. Thus at the age
of thirty-one there came to him a kind of awakening such as adoles-
cents and religious converts are said to experience." Concurrently,
Jeffers began to feel sure of his vocation as a poet. By 1922, when
he wrote an explanatory preface for the book he was then prepar-
ing, he had come to believe that the function of poetry was to
express profound philosophical ultimates, to show man under the
aspect of the wild – that is, the universal. "Poetry is more primitive
than prose," he said. "It existed before prose and will exist after-
ward, it is not domesticated, it is wilder and more natural. It be-
longs out-of-doors, it has tides as nature has; while prose is a cultured interior thing, prose is of the house, where lamplight
abolishes even the tides of day and night, and human caprice

rules." This is the voice of the mature Jeffers, solidly rooted in place, sure of the bases of his thought. Again, what is revisionist about this thought is that it has not just exchanged certain ideas about history for others, but has adopted a wholly different frame of reference from the anthropocentrism and partial-mindedness that create history.

In the case of the novels of Harvey Fergusson, a more easily accessible dualism is transcended: where Jeffers concerns himself almost cosmically with the ultimate polarity of humanity and nature, Fergusson deals with the opposition of romance and realism, on a contemporary or near-historical stage. Much of his attention, novelistically, is focused on the nineteenth-century West, and what seems to interest him most is the struggle between nostalgia and static allegiances on the one hand, and realistic adaptation on the other. His characters who can change with changing circumstances are viewed favorably, in general, and those who become stuck in a past, or in habit, are not.

Fergusson's own life choices may be instructive, because although he considered himself at heart a "rebellious, individualistic loner," in the words of his biographer Robert Gish, and although he was greatly drawn to the back country of New Mexico (where he worked as a timber cruiser for a brief time), he spent most of his adult life in cities on the east and west coasts, a friendly and reasonably social man. He did not lose himself in nostalgia for New Mexico, where he had grown up as a member of a prominent family, and where, as it happens, many critics have located the essence of the magnetic, western mystique, but simply moved on, first to Washington, D.C., then New York, Hollywood, and finally, Berkeley, California. "Fergusson's need for wilderness and solitude was countered by an equal need for the stimulus and challenge of urban living," writes Gish. In his fiction, there is a cool, assessing quality in Fergusson's depictions of the tug of the old West on people's spirits. He had no special brief, apparently, for the romanticism of the frontier, and this freedom is the precondition of a postfrontier or revisionist view.

Nowhere is Fergusson's balance better demonstrated than in his remarkable novel, *Wolf Song*, published in 1927. In this treatment of the "mountain-man" era, there was full opportunity for the author to revel in the two stock, early-western conditions: wilderness surroundings and freedom from nearly all restraint and conventional responsibility. His protagonist, Sam Lash, is a fully heroic type, on first glance; the language by which he and his two trapping partners are introduced onto the stage of the novel is grand, epical: "Up from the edge of the prairie and over the range rode three." Shortly, we learn that Sam, a free spirit, "could stay nowhere." The life of the mountains was dangerous, passionate, and restless. Sam had become one with the wilderness in a practical fashion: "He knew all the great game of the Rockies – buffalo and antelope that winter in the lower valleys, elk that run over the high ridges in black-necked herds, deer and bear, black and grizzly, and the wild sheep that range to the tops of the highest peaks. He had killed and eaten them all. He was flesh of their flesh – a man nourished on wildness."

Fergusson depicts the wilderness with sharp, memorable images, honoring it by his precision: "Great blue fool-hens boomed up beside the trail and perched tame in tall dark spruce trees silver-tipped with the new year's growth"; "Badgers threw up fresh dirt from their underground hunting and stuck out grizzled noses stained with clay and blood." But *Wolf Song* doesn't rest on the romantic side, the wild side. Sam Lash may be a "man's man," and the wilderness may be glorious, but, as it turns out, there is also town (Taos), and there are also women – in particular, there is Lola Salazar. She is the pampered daughter of a *rico,* and as depicted by Fergusson appears to be the very quintessence of effete living, but she captures Sam Lash's affections quickly and almost completely. Nevertheless, not quite: after taking her for his own in a dramatic horseback elopement, Sam removes her to Bent's Fort, where they are married and begin to lead a kind of middle life, not quite Taos, and not quite wilderness. When it comes time for Sam to go on a trapping expedition ("He felt like a squaw-man hanging around when everyone else had gone"), Lola pleads with him to stay. He is classically torn now: "He felt as though he were trapped and tangled in her long black hair." After much dithering, he goes to the mountains. "A real world began to claim him. He lived again in his eyes. . . . Scattered antelope were pale dots over the prairie."

For a time, the solitude and wildness are tonic, and Sam feels a whole man again. But he begins to learn that Lola is more to him than just another woman, and soon enough Sam is divided again: "While he rode one way his mind kept going back the other." Eventually, we see Sam Lash returning to Taos (where Lola has gone during his absence from Bent's Fort), and being told by the Salazars' padre that if he will join the church, and be married again under its aegis, the family will consider him "one of us." He will, the padre reveals, be given land; he will become a Mexican citizen. Sam reflects irresolutely. "Everything that binds a man down goes with a woman," he thinks, and imagines the house he will presumably build and occupy as a trap, the woman he loves as a trap. But he accedes. Lola, for her part, has been through an ordeal, too, and when the couple are finally reunited at the close of the novel, the scene is complex and unresolved. The last words of *Wolf Song* are, "Antagonists who could neither triumph, they struggled in a grip neither could break. . . ."

What this ambiguous, realistic ending reveals is Harvey Fergusson's postfrontier habit of mind. The frontier mind is forthrightly dualistic: here is wilderness, there is civilization; here is solitude, there is responsibility. But Fergusson is neither progressivist nor primitivist. His novelistic truth refuses the dualistic gambit, as it were; he shows the utter attractiveness of both sides of our national polarity. In later novels, the West is built up – the grant of kingdom is developed, and eventually we move into the modern, urban period – but the essential human dilemmas remain roughly the same, and Fergusson continues to dramatize what might be called the wavering at the core of the American personality. His novels transcend romance, where the choices are clear-cut and the characters are types. He honors the past, which is always wilder, freer; but just *here* is where we are now.

Vardis Fisher presents a curious case. Certain of his novels, *Mountain Man* (1965) for instance, lean heavily toward romance, perhaps even fantasy. This is quite western in the prerevisionist sense. But an equally strong drive, apparently his original impulse as an autobiographical writer, in fact, was to get at the truth of his own life – a life he considered representative – whatever chagrin, guilt, and embarrassment the search might reveal. *Orphans in Gethsemane*, Fisher's 1960 version of an autobiographical tetralogy published in the 1930s, is marked by an amazingly frank self-criticism and is replete with references to the author's quest for truth in historical sources. Fisher claimed to have read 2,500 books in the course of his research for the tetralogy and its successors (a remarkable series of historical novels beginning in pre-"cave-man" days), and it is clear that he took extensive notes. The end product is a skeptical view of Western civilization, in the sense that when we come to the end of the capstone work, *Orphans*, the autobiographical protagonist no longer believes in the traditional means by which members of our civilization justify their lives and their choices. He comes to view himself and his culture more objectively. He refers frequently to the "evasions" of western civilization, the illusions passed on from generation to generation, forming a pattern which eventually produces, in Idaho, a young man so unreal in his values and so skewed in his perceptions that he knows neither himself nor, when he marries and moves out into the greater world of Salt Lake City and then Chicago, his young wife. When she commits suicide (an event that in real life took place on September 8, 1924), Vridar Hunter at first wishes only to take his own life. Slowly, though, helped by his psychologist brother, he decides to go on, and within a few years has embarked upon an ambitious self-examination that will eventually result in the novels mentioned above. In the 1930s novels and in *Orphans*, Fisher damns Vridar for a fool, and gives a good deal of evidence, and then attempts to look beyond his protagonist for the sources of his tragic unconsciousness. His analysis of Western culture proceeds according to the highest standards of scholarship and the free mind, he tells his readers.

Yet one major pillar of his civilization stayed unshaken and apparently unquestioned – its philosophically and psychologically dualistic basis. Fisher saw the world most characteristically in terms of contest and opposition. Even the titles of some of his books suggest his habit of perception: *God or Caesar?; Murder or Suicide?* (a study of the mysterious death of Meriwether Lewis); *Love and Death.* In the tetralogy, *Orphans*, and the late novel *Mountain Man*, a dualistically framed emotional extremism is common. Nature is either wondrously benign or the opposite, freezing cold and heavy with the threat of death. *Mountain Man* is told in terms of extravagant polarities: sunshine and storm, wholeness and terrible wounding, boundless love and soul-chilling loss. Not much is middle-of-the-road. In *Idaho: A Guide in Word and Picture* (1950), a volume Fisher researched while directing the Idaho WPA Writers Project, the chapter titled "Fauna" is perhaps as revealing as the novels. "Of hawks, Idaho has too few of the right kind and too many of the wrong. To the latter belong most of the falcons," Fisher wrote. This strongly dichotomized and judgmental sense of the world conflicted with Fisher's truth-seeking; it limited his revisionist propensities, directing him toward political extremism in his notorious newspaper columns, and restricting, so I believe, some of the insights into character in his fiction. In *Mountain Man*, for example, Fisher reveres his hero Sam Minard so thoroughly that he fails to notice what is historically true, that the beaver trappers ("mountain men") were themselves involved in the opening up – thus eventual transformation – of the pristine, fetterless landscapes they reveled in. They "killed the thing they loved," as the common phrase has it. But Fisher's mountain man (and thus Fisher?) does not see this tragic knot: at the close of the novel, he looks down upon a wagon train of emigrants and records his disgust at the thought of the cropped fields, fences, and cities he knows they will bring to the once-glorious West. He turns his horse and rides toward the north (Canada, presumably) where there will still be some free wilderness for a while.

In *The Big Sky* (1947), A. B. Guthrie, Jr., conveys his heartfelt allegiance to the wild, beautiful West that was, but his "mountain man" novel goes much further than Fisher's in both characterization and historical recognition. The two dimensions are intimately related. Guthrie's novel is built upon the fact that the mountain man was complicit in the loss of the world he relished, so his protagonist, the perhaps symbolically named Boone Caudill, is not depicted as a heroic, simple figure. Guthrie shows him to be a victim of certain unfairnesses in civilization, a lover of the wild with a primitive but keen aesthetic sense, and on the other hand a fiercely self-centered and violent boor. The character portrait does not sort out neatly and surely. We see the world through Boone's eyes for most of the novel, and are led thus to an inward sense of his life. We sympathize with him in his mistreatment by his "Pap" in Kentucky and by a sadistic sheriff, and we glory in his release into the wide open spaces and his slowly earned competence as a wilderness man. At the same time, we are given good evidence that Boone is a very limited man, intellectually and socially. When he marries into the Blackfeet, we enjoy his idyll at the tipi door but soon see that he has not accepted – in fact has arrogantly denied – any sense of memberlike responsibility. When his father-in-law asks him not to guide a white entrepreneur through tribal lands (the man is looking for a railroad route), Boone answers curtly, "I reckon I'll do as I please." One could ask for no better demonstration of underdevelopment of personality. Later, when Boone rather paranoically (and incorrectly) suspects his longtime companion of cuckolding him, he does not bother to ask questions, but simply kills his friend. All questions and answers are contained within his own solipsistic universe. But he has now ruined the idyll.

At the close of the novel, Boone, having fled the "big sky" country, stops at his former trapping partner Dick Summers's farm in Missouri. The two men drink whiskey together, and eventually Boone's tongue loosens and he speaks of the West they had known: "It's all sp'iled, I reckon, Dick. The whole caboodle." Summers's answer subsumes Guthrie's wisdom of retrospect: "'I don't guess we could help it,' Summers answered, nodding. 'There was beaver for us and free country and a big way of livin', and everything we done it looks like we done against ourselves and couldn't do different if we'd knowed. . . . We ain't seen the end of it yet, Boone, not to what the mountain man does against hisself.'" Summers is a reflective man, clearly, and throughout the novel the contrast with the less intelligent, impulsive Boone makes for depth of characterization. Now, slowly, Boone comes to a realization about himself that Summers, with his perspicacity and outward look, would never have needed to make:

> "This here hand done it," Boone said, holding the hand before him. . . . "I kilt Jim."
> "Kilt Jim!"
> "I been tellin' myself I done right, Dick. But I don't know. I don't know for sure. Maybe I ain't honest."

This is the first apparently self-analytical remark Boone has made, but it is immediately followed by "It's like it's all sp'iled for me now, Dick," showing that the essential self-centeredness remains in place. We last see Boone stumbling off into the darkness. The final lines of the story are written from Summers's point of view, and in Guthrie's next western novel, *The Way West* (1949), Summers is present but not Boone. Clearly, the latter is a dead end as a character. He does "come back" in *Fair Land, Fair Land* (1980), but only as a murderous frontier type of the lowest order. In *Fair Land, Fair Land* the central character is again Dick Summers, and his essential moral goodness is set forth as a kind of standard against which western history – particularly the unconscionable treatment of the Indians – is measured. Guthrie's revisionist concept of western history, his transcending of the myth of progress in particular, is again seen in *Big Sky, Fair Land: The Environmental Essays of A. B. Guthrie, Jr.* (1988), edited by David Petersen. The author's stance toward the West, made up of equal parts of love of the land and disgust with its spoilers, and seasoned by the important, Summers-like reflection that we are all involved in the despoliation, remained the consistent core of his writing.

The last of the classic western revisionists I wish to treat here is Frank Waters, saved for last because his vision, I believe, comprehends those of the others mentioned, and because it may be the most complex and profound of the group. Waters's work includes the historical critique of someone like Guthrie, the quest for personal insight and truth of someone like Fisher, the recognition of the polar attractiveness of both wilderness and civilization that is found in Fergusson, and the sense for ultimates that distinguishes the poetry of Robinson Jeffers.

In his coverage of western history, a major interest of Waters's is what was done to the Indians, and what this might reveal about ourselves. *The Colorado* (1946) states the position: "History in the long perspective . . . is immune to propaganda, to the lie that might makes right." If we denounce Hitler, we must denounce such American frontier characters as J. M. Chivington, a Methodist minister who led the Sand Creek Massacre in 1864, in Colorado.

> What manner of men were these whose crime parallels the worst of the Nazis? Good, average Americans, city dwellers not menaced by peaceful Indians. The most prosperous and respected banker of my home town [Colorado Springs] was one; I well remember his pompous speeches on the subject to us school children. He was always proud of his participation, and because of it was given signal prominence in the town's *Pioneer Reminiscences* so tidily published a few years back. He had helped to "Win the West." As for Chivington, he even ran for the legislature afterward.

The personal response has an earned provenance in this aspect of Waters's work, because his father was part Indian. Ever since his father's death in 1914, it might fairly be said, Waters has been looking to understand him, looking to know the whole of the relationship between whites and Indians, looking to integrate or make sense of the Indian element in himself. His view of western history is, I would argue, deeply informed, not simply because he has gone beyond self-justifying mythology, but because he has attempted positively to understand the inward elements, the differences in psyche and culture between Indians and whites. He has attempted to understand history as a working out of what might be called cultural personality. There are an enormous number of factors involved in mapping the polarity of the "white" and the "red," of course, from religious beliefs to political life to aesthetic and ceremonial activities. Waters has become an autodidact of impressive range.

Perhaps his most ambitious attempt to describe the historical polarity he believes in is *The Woman at Otowi Crossing*, a novel published in 1966 and offered again in a revised version in 1987. This work of fiction is based on the true-life story of a New Mexico woman, Edith Warner, who ran a small café at a bridge over the Rio Grande River near the San Ildefonso Pueblo. According to an historical account (see *The House at Otowi Bridge*, by Peggy Pond Church [1959]), Warner developed a profound awareness of her chosen place and its native people. In Waters's hands, the woman at Otowi Crossing stands between and bridges two entire worlds, realms of the human spirit. On the one side is the Pueblo, with its kiva and its yearlong series of ceremonies intended (as Waters had shown in *Masked Gods,* in 1950) to dramatize the essential oneness of existence and the constant need for humanity to remind itself of this unity and stay in harmony with it. On the other side, during most of the time period covered by the novel, is the secret "atomic city" of Los Alamos, built on a plateau above Otowi Crossing, and dedicated to a major, technical manipulation of nature. Waters's woman, Helen Chalmers, meets these two worlds. Her life takes place in the "crucible of conflict," as the author terms the Four Corners area, where the fundamental dualities of human nature are writ large and plain. Helen is humanity, then, at the modern crossroads. Her inward life, which in Waters's view forms a microcosm of the historical world, represents the essence of this novel. She undergoes an emergence into a unified, enlightened outlook. As a result of certain powerful, epiphanic experiences, she gradually leaves behind the alienated, ego-concerned life that most of us lead. She now has no need for power, in the "power-over" sense. In her new breadth and depth of view, she sees into relationships with a calm and penetrating objectivity; she dreams and intuits the inner significance of much that is going on around her; and perhaps most instructively of all, she takes a profound joy in the simplest details of her life and her location. By the close of the novel it has become clear that Waters means to outline, in his character's transcendence, a possible and desirable outcome of the human road of life. Such a thing is within our capacities; Helen writes to her former lover, Jack Turner,

> *How many thousands of obscure people like me all the world over are having the same experience right now? And for no apparent reason, like me. Keeping quiet about it, too, because they can't quite understand it at first or their friends might believe them mentally unbalanced. That's why someday you'll get this Dime-Store ledger. To reassure you it's a normal, natural experience that eventually comes to every one of us. So when your turn comes, Jack, don't be afraid. Be glad! It's our greatest experience, our mysterious voyage of discovery into the last unknown, man's only true adventure . . .*

Frank Waters's revisionist view of the West is not limited to a topical analysis of history. His work obviously contains that aspect, but what gives his sense of history its energy and what grounds his analysis is more personal. It is a "Woman"-like, Indian-like, sense of the whole. Where the "frontier mind" projects a needful, egoistic, separate identity, Waters proceeds from a systemic or totalistic assumption. This transcending of fragmentation is his original revision, the source for all the rest. Back in 1942, in *The Man Who Killed the Deer,* Waters depicted the progress of his protagonist, a Pueblo Indian named Martiniano, toward just such a unified view. Despite all his efforts toward individual self-sufficiency, and despite a latterly-taken-on wish to be heroic in the eyes of his tribe, Martiniano began to learn that action taken from an egoistic point of view only makes trouble and causes further unenlightened action to have to be taken. (This is History, Waters implies, in both its sum and its particulars.) Finally, after a particularly ignominious failure, Martiniano begins to be a bit more open to things, less actively manipulative. Waters signals his progress with a beautifully realized, deceptively simple sentence: "So little by little the richness and the wonder and the mystery of life stole in upon him." Within that sentence, embodied in its syntax alone, resides a critique of an entire civilization. Revision, it would seem, can go little further.

Works Cited

Eiseley, Loren. "Foreword." *Not Man Apart.* Ed. David Brower. San Francisco: Sierra Club, 1965, 23–24.

Fergusson, Harvey. *Wolf Song.* 1927. Rpt. Lincoln: U of Nebraska P, 1981.

Fisher, Vardis. *Idaho: A Guide in Word and Picture.* New York: Oxford UP, 1950.

Gish, Robert. *Frontier's End: The Life and Literature of Harvey Fergusson.* Lincoln: U of Nebraska P, 1988.

Guthrie, A. B., Jr. *The Big Sky.* New York: Sloane, 1947.

Jeffers, Robinson. "Preface" (1922). Qtd. in Alberts, S. S. *A Bibliography of the Works of Robinson Jeffers.* 1932. Rpt. New York: Burt Franklin, 1968.

———. *The Selected Poetry of Robinson Jeffers.* New York: Random House, 1938.

Jeffers, Una. Qtd. in Frederic I. Carpenter, *Robinson Jeffers.* New York: Twayne, 1962.

Waters, Frank. *The Colorado.* New York: Rinehart, 1946.

———. *The Man Who Killed the Deer.* New York: Farrar, Rinehart, 1942.

MOLLY'S TRUTHTELLING, OR JEAN STAFFORD REWRITES THE WESTERN

SUSAN J. ROSOWSKI

Like it or not, reading the West means acknowledging the formula western. It is indisputably the cultural form with which the region is most identified and arguably the one that bears its most elevated claims. Robert Warshow, for example, looks to the western for its "serious orientation to the problem of violence which can be found almost nowhere else in our culture"; John Cawelti in *Adventure, Mystery, and Romance* (1976) reads it as the product of an "epic moment" in our history; and Jane Tompkins turns to it in "an attempt to understand why men act the way they do and to come to terms with it emotionally."

What *is* the formula about which such claims are made? Critics agree that its setting is a geographical region transformed into an imaginative landscape, then give it their personal spins. Cawelti argues that its basic situation develops from the moment when society is balanced against wilderness, civilization against violence, and savages against townspeople. By its formulaic action of chase and pursuit, the hero mediates between those forces. For Warshow, the point of the western is "a certain image of man, a style, which expresses itself most clearly in violence" – that of the lonely hero defending the purity of his honor. And Leslie Fiedler, in *Love and Death in the American Novel* (1960), drawing upon Freud's theories in *Civilization and Its Discontents,* reads the hero's destruction of the savage (native or outlaw) as a modern society's repression of spontaneous sexuality.

But what of women and the western? As characters, we are told, they are scarce, appearing (when they do) as children (Warshow), symbols of civilization (Cawelti), or superegos that disrupt the relationship between hero and savage (Fiedler). As readers, they are sorely underrepresented among the critics, for with the welcome exception of Jane Tompkins, this is territory claimed by men. Indeed, Tompkins's point in *West of Everything* (1992) is precisely that. Conceding the western formula as it is written by Owen Wister, Zane Grey, and Louis L'Amour, Tompkins offers a woman's reading of a male formula, provocative in its gendered point of view as much as in its substance. Any number of critics could have written that "the Western is secular, materialist, and antifeminist; it focuses on conflict in the public space, is obsessed by death, and worships the phallus." But hearing Jane's rather than John's voice breathe life into these words gives them new meaning.

If gender makes a difference in *reading* the West, it makes an even greater difference in *writing* it. In *The Mountain Lion* (1947), Jean Stafford uses her pen as a divining rod to reveal sources of the psychosexual violence so thinly veiled in formula western fiction. The setting of a cattle ranch, the plot of male bonding, the action of the hunt: these familiar ingredients of the formula western are laid bare in Stafford's novel. The cattle ranch is a breeding business, at the heart of male bonding is sexual anxiety, and the hunt represents undisguised aggression against women. Exposed, too, is the experience of women, given voice in the character of a girl who, finding herself in a world structured by the western formula, is inevitably the victim of its action. But *The Mountain Lion* extends as well as exposes the literary West, for it is also Stafford's *künstlerroman* and, as such, the novel in which she treats directly the theme running as an undercurrent throughout her oeuvre: the story of a girl destined to be a writer who is born into a literary tradition that, as Jane Tompkins has argued, sprang from hostility toward precisely that destiny. As such it is one of the most radical explorations of gender, creativity, and the significance of the West in American literature, and it offers a paradigm for feminist criticism.

Stafford's double protagonists, brother and sister Ralph and Molly Fawcett, dramatize venerated gender divisions in the formula western, with its rigid separation between male and female cultures. Growing up, Ralph and Molly do basically the same things in a presexual (and prewestern) state of innocence. Their presexual (and prewestern) relationship is one of friendship and exchange, each complementing and completing the other. Molly repeats Ralph's jokes and tells his dreams, "pretending that they were her own," and Ralph tells her story of eating nitrate fertilizer as if it had happened to him. Yet even in childhood there is an awareness that beneath it all, gender makes a primary and fundamental difference: "There was only one thing about Molly he did not like, Ralph decided, and that was the way she copied him. It was natural for her to want to be a boy (who *wouldn't*) but he knew for a fact that she couldn't be." As a boy, Ralph recognizes that gender signifies privilege (he long believes that the words in the song "America" were "For spacious guys"). To grow up male, Ralph feels, is to grow up celebrated by the national anthem. To grow up male is also to go west.

Two trips west structure the novel, dividing it almost exactly in half. The first part tells of Ralph and Molly's loss of childhood innocence when confronted with the mystery of death. Ralph is ten and Molly eight when their Grandfather Kenyon dies while visiting them; as a result of his death, they meet their uncle Claude, who comes for his father's funeral, and they spend the summer at Claude's Colorado ranch. In the second part of the novel, set four years later, both children are initiated into another mystery, that of sex. In order to take her older daughters around the world, their mother sends Ralph and Molly to their uncle's ranch for a year. There Ralph joins Claude in hunting a female mountain lion while Molly devotes herself to becoming a writer. The action reaches its violent conclusion when, unknown to one another, hunter and hunted meet, Claude and Ralph firing simultaneously at the lion, the man killing the cat and the boy killing Molly.

As Stafford exposes the sexism inherent in the action of the formula western, she plumbs the implications of its symbolism. "The symbolic landscape of the western formula is a field of action that centers upon the point of encounter between civilization and wilderness, East and West, settled society and lawless openness," John Cawelti says in *Adventure, Mystery, and Romance*, a tradition Stafford incorporates in *The Mountain Lion*. James Fenimore Cooper's nature versus civilization and Owen Wister's East versus West are echoed in Stafford's contrasting settings: her story opens in California – a manufactured landscape detached from place; it moves to a cattle ranch in Colorado, the West of literary legend; and it anticipates a future in Connecticut, an East emptied of meaning – civilized or otherwise. For Stafford the point of encounter is between formula and fantasy, literary convention and cultural desire; and the symbolism of her settings is self-reflexively critical of the very formulas that they evoke.

California, in the novel, is located on the other side of the West, inhabited by sojourners vaguely on their way elsewhere who in the meantime construct a pastiche of exotic imported scenes: an orange grove sometimes inhabited by bright birds resting on their flight from the South Seas to Japan, a neat dairy run by a fat German, a yard populated by a postmistress with cartoonlike animal characters. California doesn't qualify as a place, their Grandpa

Kenyon explains to Ralph and Molly. Then, as if defining "place" for them, he tells them a story of divining water on his ranch in the Panhandle. There wasn't a drop of water on his forty-five thousand acres when he bought it, but he chose a spot where he meant to build his house, took a holly wand, "holding a fork of it in either hand. By and by, the rod bent down: where she showed him, there was a deep clear spring that had never yet gone dry."

The landscape that Ralph and Molly claim for their own is not California but the West, which they identify with a dry creekbed where they play, "a deep, dry arroyo called 'the Wash.'" Near their home yet out of time and place, the Wash offers magical possibilities: "On the floor of the Wash, Ralph and Molly could find bright-colored stones, pink and green and yellow and blue. After a heavy rain, there was sometimes fool's gold in the puddles. Strange harsh shallow-rooted flowers grew all over the steep slopes and clumps of mallow that yielded bitter milk. . . . All mystery and evil came from the Wash." The Wash, as their Grandpa Kenyon recognized, made a person "think of a place that is a place"; that is, it made him think of his ranch. Once their Grandpa Kenyon christened the Wash with his story of divining, it became an occasion for Molly's and Ralph's yearnings. "Golly *Moses*, I'd like to go out West," Ralph sighs as they pass it, for the Wash reminds them of the West, which is clearly the promised land.

From the Wash come other stories – as rich and endless as the spring their grandfather had divined – family ones of their father's heroism in rescuing a woman from a flood that swept through the Wash, and stories of their own imagining, by which "those smooth colored stones they gathered were really stolen jewels and the thief was a coal-black Skalawag who slept in the daytime in Mr. Vogelman's cornbin but kept watch at night." Why was he so watchful? The Skalawag "feared someone might come with a divining rod and once water was found, all his gems would be washed away."

The parable of the Skalawag introduces the symbolism that will inform *The Mountain Lion*, by which the West is a source of storytelling. The West, like the Wash, was occupied by a thief who claimed its storytelling for himself and who feared that someone with inspiration, by divining what lay at its heart, would write truthfully, for truthful writing would disprove his rhetoric as surely as water would wash away the Skalawag's gems. Informed by this parable, *The Mountain Lion* announces that the desire behind its narrative is to divine its own source.

When Ralph and Molly go to Colorado, they enter a West codified by the formula western, readily recognizable as such. There are the familiar ingredients, such as the setting – a cattle ranch (the Bar K) with a spacious, rambling house facing a stream (the Caribou), pastures opening onto foothills leading to the summer range, and beyond them, mountains, remote yet confining, that "wore peril conspicuously on their horny faces." The characters at the ranch are as familiar as the setting – cowboys we have met in film and fiction:

> The men were skillful, good-humored, living with the present time and on a large scale. When they got drunk on a Saturday night, they did so with abandon, behaving exactly as drunk people in the movies did. Their lawlessness seemed natural. It seemed altogether reasonable that they hunted at all times except during the open season when, as Uncle Claude said, "there was too much danger of getting shot at by them dudes from Denver."

Like its setting, the action of *The Mountain Lion* is codified by the formula. Cooper announced the theme of initiation into heroic identity structured by a hunt, by which, as Cawelti observes in *Adventure, Mystery, and Romance*, a man "kills . . . , receives the name of hunter and warrior, . . . shows his capacity for adult leadership, . . . demonstrates his ability to abide by the wilderness code of honor, and . . . rejects the worldly [woman's] advances in favor of the violent masculine life of the wilderness." These elements remain the important themes of the western formula, and these are the elements Stafford draws upon. Once at the ranch, ten-year-old Ralph begins the lessons necessary to be accepted in the company of men: to ride, shoot, butcher, and drink.

These are still important themes of the formula – so familiar, indeed, that they have become cliché today, made seductively familiar by their repetition in a myriad of forms – advertising's Marlboro man, Hollywood's Clint Eastwood, politics' Ronald Reagan and George Bush – all merge as a product that is unmistakably American. By so self-consciously drawing upon the formula, Stafford instills self-consciousness about the formula itself. Few would object to Cawelti's argument that formulas become "collective cultural products because they successfully articulate a pattern of fantasy that is at least acceptable to if not preferred by . . . cultural groups." The interesting question is not *what* that pattern is – but what lies at its source. It is a question that calls for a psychology of the formula, and one to which Stafford responded.

While the traditional western works by disguising fantasies of sex and violence in a formulaic chase or hunt, *The Mountain Lion*

works by removing the disguise to reveal the desire behind the
fantasy. Ralph's mentor in the masculine code is Uncle Claude,
whose appearance identifies him with the animals he tends, destined for breeding and butchering: the man's "shoulders were massive, bullish, and his arms hung forward from them in an animal
heaviness, terminating in the biggest hands the boy had ever seen
. . . scarcely like hands at all but slabs of meat with the rind still on."
Molly's contrasting mentors similarly symbolize the desire behind
the formula: the housekeeper Mrs. Brotherman, sad and mild-
mannered, about whom clings the odor of apples as if in temptation to join a female culture of passive kindness; and Magdalene,
the black cook who speaks of sex and violence, and offers not
kindness but wisdom. Molly imagines Magdalene to be the wife of
the Skalawag, and she imagines herself to be Magdalene's child.

As for the plot, Stafford there, too, removes the disguise behind
the familiar initiation story to reveal its source in sexuality. While
Ralph and Molly remain good friends in Covina, they are estranged at the ranch, an estrangement that begins late in the August of their first summer there, when Ralph becomes conscious of
the sexuality he had only dimly sensed before in awful comments
made by neighbor children while cutting open a watermelon or in
his uncle's solitary nighttime trips to a particular street in town
whose business Ralph will not let himself imagine. In the last days
of their first summer at the ranch Ralph witnesses birth:

> Uncle Claude took him one day to a deep wet-weather branch
> where a cow was calving and at the moment he saw the horri-
> ble little hoof appear, he felt a painful exultation. . . . He was
> not in the least embarrassed, only filled with wonder at the
> bewildered wet calf that was finally born and immediately
> stood up although it was so small and weak it swayed piteously
> under its mother's big rosy tongue.

The experience creates a yearning in Ralph for the language to
articulate what he has witnessed: "he tried to remember what Mais-
ol and Maisaka had said that day in the watermelon patch," and he
tries to tell Molly about the calving, but words elude him and Molly
refuses to hear. Fearful and defensive, Molly "stuck her fingers in
her ears and screamed at him, 'You're a dirty liar!' and her nose
began to bleed."

When he returns to the West at fourteen, Ralph becomes conscious of his personal sexuality in the biological changes that are
inexorably transforming him into a man. Approaching his uncle's
ranch, the train on which Ralph is riding passes through fourteen

tunnels marking the fourteen years moving him toward manhood. As he passes through each, Ralph's sexual thoughts intensify, culminating in the last, longest tunnel in which he sees "as an apotheosis of his own black, sinful mind" that he has coveted the half-cousin he will see at the ranch and the woman with children in the train with him. Feeling himself on the precipice of a Fall and seeking redemption (Stafford writes with a fine comic sympathy here), Ralph thinks of his sister beside him, imagining that she might save him and saying "in the lowest voice, 'Molly, tell me all the dirty words you know.'"

In describing Ralph's awareness of sexuality as an apotheosis, Stafford describes desire seeking form, awareness longing for articulation. Here as elsewhere, beneath Ralph's initiation into a manhood suspicious of talk runs Ralph's desire to talk. At times it takes the form of a compulsion that leads him to ask inane questions, at other times an invitation to which others respond. Ralph's request for "dirty words" from Molly signals the breech between them made by gender and age, for his younger sister has as yet fiercely refused to admit to the fact of sexuality. Back at the ranch, Molly wraps herself in incommunicability until, in furious retreat, Uncle Claude calls Ralph to a window, from which he points to a bull pastured near the house. Denied language, Claude and Ralph mutely observe the animal suffering from displaced sexuality, "bellowing with pain and fury" from a "great tumor" (a hairball in his jaw) that he is seeking to relieve by "faunching" and "rubbing" against a tree.

Male bonding – a "companionship . . . so complete that it almost frightened Ralph" – occurs in "this brief time of their brutal preoccupation" with the bull, who "seemed to stare directly into their eyes with hatred as if they were responsible for his torment." The experience is for Ralph an epiphany: a sudden, clarifying insight into the masculinity that underlies the code of the West:

> it was as though he had set forth on an adventure whose terms were so inexorable that he could not possibly change his mind and go back, as if they were in the middle of a boat in the middle of a landless sea. He looked at the heavy, small-chinned face [of his uncle] in which, as the dark clear eyes studied the sick bull, there was a certain ponderous stupidity, a sort of virile opacity, an undeviating dedication to the sickness and health and the breeding of animals. The bull, by acquiring this infirmity, had temporarily become a nothing since he could not perform his function as a sire. It was al-

most as if he had made a fool of himself, for surely the smile that came and went in Uncle Claude's face was a mocking one. While this discovery appalled him, he was determined never to be degraded in the man's eyes as the bull had degraded himself, as Molly had done, simply by being the kind of person she was, bookish and unhealthy. Even so, he was mixed in his feeling about Uncle Claude and his resolution was the result not of a refreshed admiration but of the desire to go unnoticed by having no shortcomings. Because his own masculinity was, in its articulation, so ugly, and he could therefore take no pleasure in himself, neither could he respect it in anyone else.

Again, Stafford relentlessly probes the fantasy of a male hero at the heart of the formula western, revealing its source in anxiety over an articulation of masculinity. Beneath the bravado is a fear of becoming "a nothing" if "he could not perform his function as a sire," fear of impotence made comically clear by word play. The name of the bull is Advance Anxiety; elsewhere, upon seeing Winifred and her beau, Ralph is afraid he is "going to become too limp to stand up straight."

Negation is the threatened result of such fear. Aware of his uncle Claude's gaze, Ralph refrains from comforting Molly and from lying amongst flowers lest his manliness be questioned. Obeying his uncle's suggestion that he leave his glasses off, Ralph at first suffers headaches so severe he vomits, then gradually (as Stafford writes with great irony, for eventually Ralph will shoot his sister, mistaking her for a lion), he "was able to see almost as well as he had done with his glasses." Most painfully, Ralph must renounce language as a part of a female culture held suspect by a man's man. In California men use language to dominate, whether under the guise of Ralph's Grandfather Bonney's "art of conversation," effete allusions to classical literature delivered as is if by "a professional forum leader," or of the Reverend Follansbe's speeches that, because he "was a rhetorician and cared little for give and take," were delivered "as if he were in the pulpit." The masculine use of language is similarly repressive at his uncle's western ranch, where among the hands "the talk was endless but it seemed to be made up almost altogether of non sequiturs. The men did not interrupt one another, but they did not listen."

Forbidden the language of love, Stafford's western men give voice to inchoate longings when they talk of hunting, the one subject they can speak of freely. Describing the prey they are tracking,

Claude displaces onto the yellow mountain lion the image of the golden girl of cultural myth: Ingrid Bergman and Carole Lombard – today we would add Marilyn Monroe and Madonna. "He thought about her so much that he had given her a name," Claude tells Ralph; "he called her Goldilocks because, running the way she had in the sunlight, she had been as blonde as a movie star." By deciding to let Ralph hunt her too, Claude formalizes their bond; by resolving "that it would be *he*, not the man, who got the lion," Ralph defines the bond as competitive. The hunt as displaced sexuality, driven by fear of its articulation, emerges in the violence of its language as well as in the violence of its action. The men name their prey "Goldilocks" because she reminds them of a movie star. They determine to "have her," swear to "blast the yellow bitch," identify the housekeeper's daughter with a cat, and tell stories with double entendres about hunting beavers.

Given such a code, it is inevitable, perhaps, that Molly is sacrificed, for as Blanche Gelfant has written, the male initiation story demands the exclusion of the female. It *is*, after all, a female mountain lion that the men hunt, its femaleness intensified by Ralph's fantasy of finding her in her den with her cubs and killing them all. Ralph comes to resent Molly's intrusion into the "pure masculinity" of his friendship with their uncle. But such an explanation acknowledges only half of Stafford's story, that concerning male initiation. By means of her double protagonist, Stafford presents a second story of initiation: Molly's. As a girl/woman Molly simply represented the "other" in the male script, but she is the *subject* of her own female script, a transference that demands a rereading – this time from Molly's point of view.

On one level, Molly tells the female version of the male initiation story of the hunt. Like Ralph, Molly is coming of age sexually, and her dawning awareness is as complex – as enticing and foreboding – as is his. Beneath Molly's social awkwardness is her secret femininity revealed in her fantasy of herself as beautiful. In a "bag which she kept locked and hidden away on the topmost shelf of her closet," Molly has assembled products designed to transport and transfigure her: bathsalts that give off "a sweet scent" and with which she can "imagine that she was in a garden," soap "in the form of a yellow rose, Armand's talcum powder, a bottle of Hind's Honey and Almond, a jar of Daggett and Ramsdell vanishing cream, a bottle of Glostora shampoo, a jar of Dr. Scholl's foot balm, a jar of freckle remover." Were these salts, soaps, powders, and creams to work as their advertising promises, they would transform Molly into a golden girl. And here, chillingly, Molly's fantasy joins with

that of the male hunt, from the perspective of the hunted rather
than that of the hunter. The fundamental lesson of growing up
female, Stafford suggests, is that to be beautiful is to be desired,
and to be desired is to be pursued. When Molly finally sees the
mountain lion and identifies with it, wishing to be golden, small,
and beautiful, she articulates her role in the masculine myth. When
she dies because she is mistaken for the lion, she fulfills that role.

Yet while her fantasy may be one of being beautiful, Molly is
actually becoming a writer. Whereas Ralph's initiation into manhood proceeds inevitably from a gendered culture, Molly's initiation into writing proceeds inevitably from her character. The central fact about Molly (and about *The Mountain Lion*) is that she is
truly defined not by her appearance but by her sensitivity to language. Though she plans "to be a salesman for the *Book of Knowledge,* a grocer, a government walnut inspector, a trolley conductor
in Tia Juana; . . . her real vocation was writing and these were to be
only sidelines."

By giving to Molly the vocation of writing, Stafford announces a
second initiation story for which she appropriates the symbolic forms
of the literary West. Claiming the metaphor of the hunt, Stafford
describes the vocation of the writer as a "hunt for the proper words."
The quotation is from a talk Stafford gave the year that *The Mountain
Lion* appeared; she could be describing Molly's story.

The competing claims on the metaphor of the hunt appear in
the narrative's structure, for Molly's initiation into a writer's life
runs in counterpoint to Ralph's initiation into manhood. While
Ralph learns to ride, Molly stays "at home to . . . write"; rather than
learning to shoot, she writes of Ralph's doing so; and when Ralph is
out on the range, Molly remains at the ranch composing an article
for *Good Housekeeping* called "My Summer at the Bar K." As Ralph's
initiation is attested to by his developing skill with a gun, Molly's is
told through her developing skill with words. For Molly as for
Ralph, independence signals success – for Molly, measured by uses
of language. When young, she and Ralph share the humor of
verbal puns, echoing each other or together repeating a joke, and
speaking "as a dialogue." Yet just as Ralph's childhood awareness of
gender separated Ralph from Molly, so Molly's childhood sensitivity to language separates her from him. Molly's poem, "Gravel,"
illustrates the difference:

Gravel, gravel on the ground
Lying there so safe and sound,
Why is it you look so dead?
Is it because you have no head?

"It doesn't make any sense," Ralph replies, for gravel does not have a head. "That's what I said. 'Is it because you have no *head?*'" Molly replies – her words a repetition of the poem as well as an indictment of Ralph for not understanding. The poem becomes a touchstone, repeated by both Molly and Ralph, though he is never able to understand it.

At the ranch the breach between them widens, for as Molly is entering a writer's realm of words, Ralph remains imprisoned within the literal:

> He liked her when they were alone, but she embarrassed him in public because she said such peculiar things. For instance, she said to Mrs. Brotherman this afternoon, "Do you have any opinion on the false Armistice?" and when Mrs. Brotherman said no, she really had not, Molly had said, "Oh, of course you don't live in California so you wouldn't have seen the Los Angeles *Gazette.*" What she was talking about was the old newspaper they had with the one word PEACE printed in letters four inches high on the front page, but how was Mrs. Brotherman to know?

Like Ralph's hunt for the mountain lion, Molly's hunt for words has its stages of preparation and tests of worthiness. As if an exercise for the imagination, Molly keeps a diary, recording everything Ralph says and does, inflated by imagination and rhetoric so that the pack rat he shoots becomes in Molly's diary "three Rocky Mountain laughing hyenas." As if a testimony to her patience in her "hunt for the proper words themselves," she writes a long humorous ballad called "The Fierce Mexican," then tears it up with loathing when "the imperfection of the rhyme of 'Mexican' and 'Mohican' stuck to her mind like paste"; and as if an exercise in narrative logic, she begins a detective novel, fantastic in its intricate plot. Measured by Stafford's criterion of a writer's finding the language that is adequate to convey exactly what she has seen and what she has deduced from it, Molly's progress is steady. Gradually, puns give way to wit, and rhetoric to the clarity of truthtelling.

Gradually, too, Molly's training moves from the ranch into the mountains, for as with the western hero generally, nature provides the setting for her apotheosis. Again, the effect is of appropriating the western tradition. Like countless western figures before her, Molly enters the wilderness in search of solitude, but the solitude she seeks is for writing; the materials she carries in her knapsack are pen and paper, rather than gun and trap. Similarly, Molly's nature echoes a heroic tradition when she selects as her lookout Garland Peak, because "from the summit she commanded a view of the entire valley, of the range as far as the eye could see." But whereas a mountain man would use the vista as a lookout for enemies, Molly is perfecting the observation she will need to write; and whereas the mountain man feels at home in the forest by taking part in the eternal action of the hunt, Molly does so by finding "an ideal glade for her study." A western equivalent of the room of her own that Virginia Woolf said the woman writer needed, the glade that Molly claims is "very small and surrounded so densely by trees and chokecherry that they were almost like walls, and right in the middle as if planned for her, was a big flat rock."

Molly's version of training herself in the ways of the wild consists of observing closely and recording exactly. Gradually, rhetoric drops away and her observations become clear – as when Stafford describes Molly's view from Garland Peak with such precise prose that the effect is of "getting" the experience as surely as any hunter "gets" his quarry: "On a clear day it was possible to see the men on the ricks on the pastures, pitching down feed to the herd which appeared to be hundreds of small red blocks on the glaring snow, as small as her ladybugs. The Caribou was frozen solid and all the trees on either side of it were bare."

Armed with an arsenal of words, Molly engages in confrontations familiar to the western hero: she is "fearless and level-headed" in facing down Uncle Claude; she maintains "a vigilant silence" in defending herself against the tyranny of a group; and when her mother says she wants to talk with her, Molly replies, "Go ahead. Shoot." Her scenes are structured not by physical battles, but as verbal ones providing her with occasions to defend truth – that is, by a right use of language against mistreatments of it by the ignorant, dishonest, and uxorious. When a horse thief comes onto the ranch, for example, it is Molly who defeats him in a verbal shootout: the stranger is stopped short in the middle of one of his stories when, her voice coming out of the darkness, Molly says, "'I doubt that.' . . . Her voice was firm and clear and its effect upon the stranger was so prompt that sweat came out on his forehead, glittering in the firelight, and his hand trembled."

The overwhelming effect is that Molly establishes words as powerful in ways that others perceive as dangerous. Molly's mother "at times was really afraid" of Molly, "and the things she said!" And once Molly is in possession of the words Ralph spoke to her while on the train passing through the tunnel, she terrorizes him by inserting the word "tunnel" into conversations, and he feels panic lest she "She has *told*!" Ralph fears their mother's return and their move to Connecticut, where he would be separated from Uncle

Claude, and where, "always at hand, would be Molly who could ruin him, blow up his world if she chose." He knows she will do nothing against him as long as they are at their uncle's ranch, "but in that bare wasteland where they were to live under the shadow of the trinity of fat men, he must guard himself against her weapon." In ceasing to echo Ralph, Molly appropriates the stance of the western hero by becoming the straight-talking, farsighted, and fearless outsider.

The two initiation stories come together in three successive versions of the hunt, each set on Garland Peak. The name announces its symbolic significance – to reach the peak, the formula promises, is to receive the garland. Garland for *what,* however, is the question evoked by competing claims upon its symbolism: the mountain lion lives there; Claude follows her there on his hunt; Ralph follows Claude there in his initiation into masculinity; and Molly goes there to find the solitude to write.

The first hunt is told from Molly's point of view. Uncle Claude and Ralph have accompanied Molly to Garland, where the mountain lion first reveals herself to them. Molly's response involves a moment of artistic possession. Her sensitivity, clarity of vision, and precision of language all capture the mountain lion in art, so that she flashes into life on the page:

> She was honey-colored all over save for her face which was darker, a sort of yellow-brown. They had a perfect view of her, for the mesa there was bare of anything and the sun illuminated her so clearly that it was as if they saw her close up. She allowed them to look at her for only a few seconds and then she bounded across the place where the columbines grew in summer and disappeared among the trees.

Molly feels the freedom of self-forgetfulness: The lion's "wastless grace and her speed did not make Molly think immediately of her fear but of her power," Stafford writes, and the antecedent of "her" remains tellingly ambiguous. The lion and Molly momentarily merge as one, for in seeing and translating this moment into language, Molly experiences an artist's "wastless grace" and "power."

The writer must be "patient in waiting for . . . observations to mature," Stafford counseled in "The Psychological Novel," in order that they may "lose their confused immediacy." On this first hunt Molly is still young, and her artistic impulse toward truth ends in confusion. Immediately following her "perfect view" of the lion, Molly becomes aware of her uncle's anger and her brother's secret smile, and the cat grows "to huge proportions in her reflection. She imagined its claws, its teeth, the way it would hiss." Betraying her own observation in adopting the jargon of pulp fiction, Molly imagines a creature that would corroborate a male script, then casts herself in the formulaic role of a helpless female, fearful of entering the wilderness until the men have made it safe by killing the ferocious animals lurking there. She then betrays herself further in thinking, "if only she had yellow hair . . . she would be an entirely different kind of person." But the confusion promises to be temporary, for the first version of the hunt ends with Molly's requesting a typewriter. Just as Ralph and Claude arm themselves with a gun, Molly will arm herself with her own weapon.

For her second version of the hunt, Stafford shifts to Ralph's point of view to describe an impulse of love that is displaced into violence. Remembering the household cat he had loved as a child, Ralph dreams of the mountain lion by seeing himself "taking perfect aim, shooting her through her proud head with its wary eyes, and then running across the mesa to stroke her soft saffron flanks and paws." Love and violence interweave, one obscenely justifying the other. Ralph resolves that "if he got her" he would not skin her, but "would have her stuffed and keep her in his room all his life." Ralph's image of the animal skinned, stuffed, and caged within his room is grotesquely at odds with Molly's image of her, flashing with movement and the color of life. Similarly, Ralph's justification of his desire to "have her" is grotesquely at odds with the exchange of Molly's encounter. Ralph feels that "somehow . . . he had more right to Goldilocks" than his uncle "because he loved her, but Uncle Claude wanted her only because she was something rare." In Molly's scene, love occurred as a reciprocity by which the cat "allowed [her] to look at her."

Molly's version of the hunt ends in her confrontation with gender expectations; Ralph's version of the hunt ends with a similar confrontation. Ralph and his uncle Claude come upon the mountain lion feeding, and she leaps away before they can raise their rifles. Left with the remnant of the hunt, Ralph finds interlocked antlered skulls of stags. Taking them to Molly and mutely giving them to her, he avoids language when "they exchanged, at last, after these months, a look of understanding and Molly said, 'Thanks, Ralph. I'll shoot them with my Brownie.'" It is a painfully brief moment of exchange, but it provides a temporary respite from the relentlessly formulaic hunt in which they are both caught.

In the third hunt, the characters are separated by the distraction of sex and the encumbrance of violence. Because Uncle Claude is taking a mare to stud, he leaves before the others, to join them later; and because Ralph is carrying a gun, he can't climb up the face of the mountain but must separate from Winifred and Molly. Most important, because each of them holds memories that distort their experience, they quarrel and separate. Seeking to escape his confusion and Molly's anger, Ralph goes alone to "a little glade he knew of with a flat rock in the center of it like a table," where he hears a sound, sees "Goldilocks feeding upon a jackrabbit," hears another sound, then shoots. Contrary emotions rush together in Ralph's mind: exultation over shooting the lion, tenderness upon turning her over ("She's so little. . . . Why, she isn't any bigger than a dog. She isn't as *big*"), and manly anger that it was his uncle's, not his bullet that killed the lion.

Immediately upon Uncle Claude's proposal that they call themselves "a corporation" (that is, they band as partners in killing the lion), they hear another sound, one "that could come only from a human throat." It is Molly's truthtelling, articulated as "a bubbling of blood." They "stood up and looked at one another in an agony of terror." When they find Molly, "her glasses lay in fragments on her cheeks and the frame, torn from one ear, stuck up at a raffish angle. The elastic had come out of one leg of her gym bloomers and it hung down to her shin." The violence of the hunt reaches its apotheosis in an image of rape which extends not only to the female body but also to Molly's head, where there is "a wound like a burst fruit in her forehead."

Stafford ends *The Mountain Lion* by returning to the parable with which she began. Magdalene, the black cook whom Molly had imagined as "the wife of the Skalawag at the Wash," says upon seeing Molly, "Lord Jesus. The pore little old piece of white trash." Her words, which are dramatically and radically at variance with the image of a manly hunt basic to the western formula driving the action, signal Ralph's collapse. Screaming and throwing himself on the ground, Ralph invites the question most commonly asked by critics: Why did Molly have to die?

The critical consensus is that Molly is sacrificed in order to reestablish the status quo. Mary Ellen Williams Walsh says that Molly "must die" because she "does not cope and is unable to accept the limited life open to her as a female. Consequently . . . she is accidentally shot to death by Ralph, who thus frees himself so that he can reach his full masculine possibilities." William Pilkington writes that "she and the mountain lion must both die because both are misfits who somehow threaten to disrupt the delicately balanced social arrangements that encircle them." Blanche Gelfant argues that "Her death is demanded by the great masculine myth of the

West," for as a female, Molly's "constant presence reminds [Ralph] of a part of himself he can no longer endure as he grows up, and indeed must kill: the feminine side of his nature." Each assumes that with Molly's death there will be a resumption of masculine possibilities (Walsh), social arrangements (Pilkington), or a timeless male initiation into adulthood (Gelfant). Yet the status quo means a return to the formula that would equate the hunt with initiation into manhood, and Stafford has irreparably broken with that formula. She has appropriated the hunt for her writer, and in the process she has redefined the territory of its action as language and recast the terms of its struggle into who has possession of storytelling.

The Mountain Lion depicts the West as a place for a reversion to primitive modes of communication. There, the formula promises, people may relate directly to an elemental reality, without the intervention of language. At their uncle's ranch, Molly and Ralph could "*look directly* at the ledge from which a packhorse had slipped and fallen to her dreadful, screaming death," and "They *knew the place* where a bold dude had frozen in midsummer" (my emphases). The descriptions recall the conventions of the formula western, whereby a ledge automatically signals danger and a dude helplessness. They also illustrate the principle of communication most closely identified with the West, that of substituting thing for word. Uncomfortable discussing sex with her daughter, Mrs. Fawcett decides the breeding ranch would be "good" for Molly "at her age"; frustrated over a conversation turned hostile, Claude mutely takes Ralph to see a bull in pain; unable to talk about growing up male, Ralph silently gives to Molly the skulls of stags with their antlers interlocked.

It is a method akin to pantomime, and it is the method fundamental to the ritual most celebrated by the western, that of the hunt, by which men go together into the woods and point to objects by which they express emotions, indicate their desires, control one another, and gather trophies. Yet primitive modes of communication satisfy only the most primitive of desires. The acts of pointing to an object or gesturing in pantomime are woefully inadequate to the human desire to transform experience into concepts, to formulate and express ideas. And this is the desire that runs as a subtext through *The Mountain Lion*. To understand sex, Molly desperately needs not the example of a breeding ranch but the complex association of sense and feeling that language might offer. To assuage his loneliness, Claude just as desperately needs to articulate the threatening masculinity that he and Ralph share. So too, the interlocked skulls of stags offer a poor substitute for Ralph's and Molly's desire to communicate their experience of growing up.

Into a West that has traditionally been defined as profoundly hostile to language, Stafford sends Molly, whose primary reality is verbal rather than physical. In creating Molly as a girl whose true vocation is writing, Stafford casts her development in terms of language. Within a year after completing *The Mountain Lion* and speaking as if she were describing Molly, Stafford explained in "The Psychological Novel" what it means to be a writer:

> probably the reason writing is the most backbreaking of all professions is that it is so very difficult to tell the truth. Even though we may know certainly that our perceptions are accurate and that only one set of conclusions can be drawn from them, we are still faced with how to communicate the findings perceptively and conclusively. The language seems at times inadequate to convey exactly what we have seen and what we have deduced from it and much too often writers shirk their responsibility and take refuge in rhetoric – as the preaching novelists do – or in snobbish, esoteric reference, as Henry Miller and his followers do, in samples of language other than their own and in jargon, and in elaborate approximations that almost but do not quite say what they mean. But the language is quite able to take care of any of our needs if we are only affectionate and respectful toward it and, above all, patient with ourselves: patient, not only in our hunt for the proper words themselves, but patient in waiting for our observations to mature in us, to lose their confused immediacy so that their timelessness will emerge and their meaning will become available to our reader and applicable to him as well as to ourselves.

Almost thirty years later, Stafford remained firm in her allegiance to language. As she declared in "Miss McKeehan's Pocketbook" (and as Molly might have said), "language is and has always been my principal interest, my principal concern, and my principal delight. I'd rather read a dictionary than go to the moon." For Molly as for her creator, the dictionary offers possibility and power that far exceeds that of science. It offers the potential not only to express, but to create reality.

Childhood play in *The Mountain Lion* is play with the possibilities of words – puns that display language's capacity to move from the literal to the figurative, symbolic, and metaphoric. Molly and Ralph enjoy their greatest joy and communion through their shared delight in words. Together they recite a joke that turns upon the word "hide," one moment meaning a thing (the skin of a cow) and the next an act (that of concealing from sight). What distinguishes Molly from Ralph and from the western literary tradition that he represents is the fact that she understands that language is thoroughly symbolic, while Ralph objects that "gravel doesn't have any head."

Conception, generation, and creativity are, according to Stafford, made possible through language. In structuring Molly's story as an appropriation of metaphor, Stafford invests Molly with a power of which her young writer is as yet unaware. Metaphor is to language what myth is to culture – the point at which words take on the power of revolution. Metaphor, as Susanne Langer says in *Philosophy in a New Key*, is the force that makes language "essentially *relational*, intellectual, forever showing up new, abstractable *forms* in reality, forever laying down a deposit of old, abstracted concepts in an increasing treasure of general words." Metaphor in *The Mountain Lion* works in precisely this way. Stafford begins with the metaphor of the hunt as it has appeared in the formula western, then gives it new life by making Molly both hunted and hunter.

Stafford gives to Molly the writer's task of hunting the words to tell the truth. Had she lived (a question far more interesting, I believe, than why she died), what is the truth she would have told? It is that the western myth is not only profoundly hostile to women, but that it is hostile to language, and that the result is a violence of silencing. This is the challenge Stafford faced as Molly's creator: how could she tell the story of growing up in the West as a girl destined to write, when the truth was that such a girl would be silenced? Stafford responded by infusing her character with her own life, and by doing so she extended her story beyond the confines of the novel. "Gradually I became Molly," Stafford recalled of writing her story, according to biographer Charlotte Goodman; "'I was so much Molly that finally I had to write her book." Indeed, Stafford was so much Molly that to read *The Mountain Lion* means reading not only the words on the page but also the life that lies behind them.

It is a fusion of fiction with fact, creator with created, that Stafford invited the reader to recognize when she infused her story with autobiography. She gave to Molly her childhood home in Covina, complete with the dried-up creek called the Wash and the cat named Budge. Jean's brother Dick, though renamed Ralph, is recognizable in innumerable details (Dick's reprimand of Jean for wearing his Boy Scout shirt, for example, appears as Ralph's reprimand of Molly). Stafford's gift to Molly of her own precocity with language came complete with "Gravel," a poem Stafford herself composed when she was a child. By embedding into her story a series of personal puns, Stafford also extended Molly's story into the adult life of the author. Stafford's nickname of "Eanbeaner," which biographer David Roberts says "she proudly wore in its many variations, including Ean, Bean, and Beaner," appears in Molly's pun upon herself as "stringbean," and the fictional reference to Goldilocks echoes the "bears" that she and Robert ("Cal") Lowell chose as their literary persona when, young and newly married, they were learning their craft.

To read Stafford's life is to read a story of continuing silencing, for critics have remained as watchful over their West as Molly's and Ralph's Scalawags over the Wash. Despite the fact that Stafford is a Pulitzer Prize-winning writer who came from and wrote of the West, she is ignored in major anthologies and bibliographies of western writing: there is no mention of her by J. Golden Taylor (himself from Stafford's Colorado) in *The Literature of the American West* (1971), no mention by John R. Milton in *The Novel of the American West* (1980), no mention by Fred Erisman and Richard W. Etulain in *Fifty Western Writers: A Biobibliographical Sourcebook* (1982), and no mention by James C. Work in *Prose and Poetry of the American West* (1990).

What happens when Stafford is included in the western canon? She invites her reader to reread western literature more generally, using *The Mountain Lion* as a divining rod to reveal the desire beneath a fantasy as it is revealed in language. The most popular modern westerns provide a ground for such rereadings: Owen Wister's *The Virginian* (1902), Zane Grey's *Riders of the Purple Sage* (1912), and Jack Schaefer's *Shane* (1949). The plot of each falls into the pattern familiar to the western, its action concerning a male outsider who enters a community, defends the townspeople/settlers/farmers against the Indians/wilderness/ranchers and, after restoring order, departs. He departs, but only after having changed the mode of communication from language to pantomime, for the western celebrates a reversion to the primitive, savage, and elemental. A man comes into a situation unsatisfactorily structured by language and establishes himself as the Word – as the Virginian, Lassiter, or Shane.

"Historically, the western represents a moment when the forces of civilization and wilderness are in balance," Cawelti writes in *Adventure, Mystery, and Romance*, "the epic moment at which the old life and the new confront each other, and individual actions may tip the balance one way or another, thus shaping the future history of the whole settlement." Jean Stafford rewrites the western so that it represents a moment when the forces of truth versus falsehood, art versus formula, are in balance, and the future being shaped concerns the settlement that occurs with language. For it is by our language that we claim a country, settle it by certain principles, and make it habitable for ourselves and others. And it is by language, too, that we may commit, then justify, the cruelest violence.

Works Cited

Cawelti, John G. *Adventure, Mystery, and Romance: Formula Stories as Art and Popular Culture*. Chicago: U of Chicago P, 1976.

Gelfant, Blanche H. "Revolutionary Turnings: *The Mountain Lion* Reread." *The Massachusetts Review* 20, no. 1 (Spring 1979): 117–25.

Goodman, Charlotte Margolis. *Jean Stafford: The Savage Heart*. Austin: U of Texas P, 1990.

Langer, Susanne K. *Philosophy in a New Key: A Study in the Symbolism of Reason, Rite, and Art*. Cambridge, MA: Harvard UP, 1967.

Pilkington, William T. "On Jean Stafford's *The Mountain Lion*." In *Critical Essays on the Western American Novel*. Ed. William T. Pilkington. Boston: G. K. Hall, 1980, 182–86.

Roberts, David. *Jean Stafford*. Boston: Little, Brown, 1988.

Stafford, Jean. "The Psychological Novel." *The Kenyon Review* 10, no. 2 (Spring 1948): 214–27.

———. *The Mountain Lion*. 1947; Rpt. New York: Farrar, Straus & Giroux, 1972.

———. "Miss McKeehan's Pocketbook." *Colorado Quarterly* 24 (1976): 407–11.

Tompkins, Jane. *West of Everything: The Inner Life of Westerns*. New York: Oxford UP, 1992.

Walsh, Mary Ellen Williams. *Jean Stafford*. Boston: Twayne, 1985.

Warshow, Robert. "Movie Chronicle: The Westerner." In *The Immediate Experience: Movies, Comics, Theatre and Other Aspects of Popular Culture*. Garden City, NY: Doubleday, 1962, 135–54.

BORDERS, FRONTIERS, AND MOUNTAINS: MAPPING THE HISTORY OF "U.S. HISPANIC LITERATURE"

MARGARET GARCÍA DAVIDSON

When the general reader thinks of the literature of the American West, he does not first think of Latino/Latina writers as representative voices of the region. Instead, the romanticized vision of the West which captured the collective imagination of the United States during the nineteenth century lingers still in the country's consciousness – the West of the Gold Rush, of Indian raids, of cattle barons, cowboys, and outlaws, of gamblers, saloon-hall dancers and the building of the railroad to link East with West. The tenacity of that image in the American psyche continues to be evidenced by the recent resurgence of Hollywood westerns such as *Unforgiven* (1992), *Tombstone* (1993), *Geronimo* (1993), and most recently in 1994, *Bad Girls, Maverick,* and *Wyatt Earp.* While some of the new films have attempted to deglamorize the romantic myth of the West (e.g., *Unforgiven*) or to recast the story by enlarging the roles of women or Native Americans (e.g., *Bad Girls, Geronimo*), the current films generally succeed only in reinscribing the myth, despite some effort to acknowledge revisionist histories.

Tombstone opens with the unprovoked and violent massacre of an entire wedding party – guests, bride, groom, and priest – outside an adobe mission church in a small bordertown by the Texas outlaw gang, "the Cowboys." The scene, complete with the priest quoting from *Revelations* just before he is shot, serves more as a symbol of the absolute evil riding the frontier rather than any direct acknowledgment of cultural conflict along the border. The film appears intentionally vague about whether the town is north or south of the border. While the wedding party and townspeople appear to be Mexican by their dress and use of Spanish, they also clearly understand English and these American outlaws. The Mexican briefly appears here as the silent and passive victim of American individualism and entrepreneurship gone fatally awry.

After the massacre, the movie then segues into Tombstone, with Wyatt Earp, his brothers, and the main conflict of the plot – law and order versus the violent anarchy of "the Cowboys." Although Tombstone is a mining town in southern Arizona, geographically inhabiting a border space, the film focuses on the American presence, the American legend of Wyatt Earp, the romanticized West of popular culture. Except for the wedding massacre in which they are victims, there is no Mexican-American presence in the film. *Tombstone* demonstrates the continued national desire to elaborate upon and reinscribe this fictional image of the nineteenth-century West. Despite changing scripts which subtly suggest cultural conflict ("the Cowboys" are Texans and the deeply ingrained feud between Texans and Mexicans is obliquely hinted at in *Tombstone*), current films do not fundamentally alter the myth of the western frontier but rather provide a reflection of how deeply embedded it remains.

Despite popular culture's limited vision of the West as a place where loose women, fast horses, and smoking guns define entrepreneurship and individual success, another picture of the land and its history from Texas to California is currently evolving as scholars of Latina/Latino studies work to recover and restore the U.S. Hispanic contribution to American literature. The uniquely American metaphor of the frontier as a wild, unsettled expanse of land with unlimited opportunity has been transformed into an academic discourse about borders, where multiple intersecting cultures engage in complex interactions of resistance and accommodation, conflict and assimilation. The questions about race and gender addressed by contemporary historians of the West are the same questions American literary critics are also beginning to address. Both literal and metaphorical relationships with the land play an important role in this evaluation of the literature, just as in the history of this geographic region. And, just as the history of the West has a past longer than the history of the United States and its Puritan roots, so too does the literature.

The 1990s have seen a virtual explosion in the publication of texts – both literary and critical – written and edited by Latino/Latina scholars and writers. The range in works seems unlimited, from historical recuperation and translation of Spanish colonial texts from the West and Southwest to anthologies containing previously out of print (or never before published) selections from nineteenth-century texts, Spanish language newspapers, oral stories, *corridos*, as well as poems and short stories by contemporary Latina/Latino writers. The variety is based not only on history and genre, but includes distinctions between the various nationalities which compose the Latino population, such as Mexicano/Chicano, Cuban, and Puerto Rican.

The burst in Latina/Latino publications is fueled partly by the general increased interest in multiethnic literature and partly by the efforts of the Recovering the U.S. Hispanic Literary Heritage project, directed by Nicolás Kanellos from the Center for U.S. Hispanic Literature at the University of Houston. The project initially came together in November 1990 at a conference where scholars of varying disciplines – American Literature, Spanish, History, Latin American Studies, and Ethnic Studies – converged to bring together their work and to plan this extensive program to fill what Kanellos calls the "large gap which exists in American literature: the Hispanic contribution." Considering the centuries-long Spanish/Mexican influence upon the history, culture, and literature of the West and Southwest, the inception of this project is long overdue, most welcome, and an exciting opportunity for scholarship and research. Such a project could potentially reshape our concept of American literature in general, and American literature of the West and multiethnic literature in particular.

As the project of recovering an Hispanic literary heritage proceeds, another image of the West evolves. Again, however, this image of the West is very much rooted in historical and imaginative recreations of the nineteenth century. There is a clear consensus among Chicana/Chicano literary critics of the pivotal nature of the nineteenth century for Mexican-American writers – as a point of rupture and disjunction. The events leading up to and immediately following the war between the United States and Mexico in 1846–48 profoundly affect Mexican-American literature and provide a stark contrast to the more popular romanticized image of the West. The stereotypical conflict of the West is between American settlers and Indians; the conflict is about civilization moving westward, occupying "empty" land, and taming the "wilderness."

In this commonly held image of the frontier West, little note is made of the complex tensions between Mexicans and Americans which led to war and the eventual surrender of half of Mexico's territory (and a large number of citizens) to the United States under the Treaty of Guadalupe-Hidalgo. "With the stroke of a pen" a large group of Mexican citizens become citizens of the United States, automatically acquiring a hyphenated identity as Mexican-Americans. Thus, the nineteenth century signals a major shift in national borders and citizenship which leads to a dramatic, often vexed, confusion regarding ethnic identity for Mexican-American writers. In this chaotic reordering of allegiances, the only stable element is the land itself, which provides a constant reassurance of history and community, even while ownership of the land is in flux.

With 1848 establishing an exact point of disjuncture, the project of recovering a literary tradition inherits a volatile political memory that continues to influence the present. The Mexican–American War not only marks a shift in national identity and language in the West, it also marks the existence of a mixed resistance to that transformation from Mexican to American, from Spanish to English. Such resistance, ranging from the subtle to the overt, from the passive to the violent, has carried forward into the twentieth century. In fact, contemporary Chicana/Chicano literature is often defined as a literature of resistance, reflecting the continuing cultural conflict evident in daily life at multiple levels.

While the war with Mexico provides concrete historical reasons for focusing on resistance as an important feature of the post-1848 literature, positing resistance as the defining element of these texts is problematic. The literature of the late nineteenth and early twentieth centuries often reveals a complex and tangled duality of politics rather than an unambiguous statement of resistance. Despite the fact of the war, the nineteenth century offers a study in contradictions in U.S.–Mexican relations. Mexico initially encouraged American settlers to its northern frontier; a brisk trade along the Santa Fe Trail up to St. Louis was profitable for both Americans and Mexicans; Mexican families sent their children to private schools in the Midwest as well as in the East; and mixed marriages between Mexicans and the American settlers were not uncommon. The war between the United States and Mexico was as divisive for Mexican families on the border as the Civil War would later be for southern families in the United States. Mexicans were divided between welcoming the Americans because of longstanding economic, marital, and educational ties and resisting the Americans because of increasing cultural conflicts and power struggles over land use and ownership. The war merely acknowledged rather than resolved the border tensions in the West. One might even argue that the legal dispossession of Mexican-Americans in the decades following the Treaty of Guadalupe-Hidalgo led to considerably more resistance to American hegemony than the conflict which initiated the war.

Because the nineteenth century is continually evoked as the critical moment in defining Mexican-American resistance to American domination, the rhetoric of resistance and border tension has attained a certain mythmaking status for Latina/Latino writers and literary scholars. This re-visioning of the West as continual cultural conflict is often no less narrow than the persistent vision of the West as a wild, untamed expanse of unlimited opportunity. The critical emphasis on reading resistance as the defining feature of these texts ultimately overshadows other complex and important elements of the literature, such as the ways in which intersecting cultures result in syncretic mixtures, racial and cultural *mestizaje* (the mixing of cultures and races), and the use of the land as both a literal and metaphorical reflection of ethnic identity.

The issue of resistance stands out as a lightning rod in negotiating the political and ideological implications inherent in an effort to recover an Hispanic literary tradition within American literature. If Chicana/Chicano literature is defined primarily as a literature of resistance and the resistance itself is defined (simplistically) as the cultural conflict between Mexican-American and American, then how do we define the literature written prior to 1848? What place do the earlier Spanish colonial narratives of the Southwest hold in the larger scope of a literary heritage? These first narratives from Spain's northern frontier clearly reflect an exercise of power and domination – not resistance; they involve the Spanish explorers, settlers, and Catholic missionaries – not the Americans; it is the native Indian populations who have been colonized, not the Mexican-American.

One of the debates affecting any answer to these questions revolves around semantics and the problem of labeling, as "U.S. Hispanic" and "Chicana/Chicano" are not necessarily interchangeable terms when applied to literature. Ramón Gutiérrez and Genaro Padilla define the term "U.S. Hispanic" as a "broad cultural term that most succinctly captures the history of the diaspora of Spain's peoples, institutions, and language throughout the American hemisphere." While readily admitting the limitations and often negative response the term can elicit, Gutiérrez and Padilla argue for the historical inclusiveness the term provides in explaining its usage in *Recovering the U.S. Hispanic Literary Heritage* (1993).

Although the term "U.S. Hispanic" provides an all-encompassing label for the literature (albeit with political connotations no less troublesome than those surrounding the term "Chicana/Chicano"), the project to recover a U.S. Hispanic literary heritage is strongly influenced by the issues and debates defining Chicana/Chicano literature. Often the terms are conflated and broadly used to mean the same thing, but just as often Chicana/Chicano literature refers to a much more narrow and specific time period of contemporary literature, beginning with José Antonio Villarreal's *Pocho* in 1959 and dealing with specific issues of ethnic identity, resistance to American hegemony, and a cultural tension resulting from the mixed interplay of cultures – American, Mexican, Spanish, and Indian. Any discussion, analysis, or evaluation of literature written before 1960, including the pre-1848 literature, inevitably engages the question of resistance. While the label "Hispanic" is used in an effort to broaden the field, the critical emphasis remains on how a particular text reveals resistance and cultural conflict. Such an emphasis is especially problematic with some nineteenth- and early twentieth-century texts, such as volumes one and two of Miguel Antonio Otero's *My Life on the Frontier* (1935; 1939) and Nina Otero-Warren's *Old Spain in Our Southwest* (1936).

While critics often acknowledge such factors as the varied regional histories and the inevitable process of *mestizaje* along the border, they frequently minimize their importance in an effort to demonstrate a unilateral and determined resistance within these texts. Regional historical experience is, however, a strong factor in constructions of ethnic identity and to some extent it literally defines the ways in which resistance is written into a text. The individual experiences of the Californio, the Tejano, and the Nuevo Mexicano reveal a wide range of cultural intersections. The rapid influx of U.S. citizens first to Texas for land and cattle, then later to California during the Gold Rush often led to an immediate, frequently violent clash of cultures. New Mexico was more isolated and slower to become Americanized – a fact which contributed to its delay in achieving statehood. New Mexico was the last southwestern territory to shed its territorial status. The regional histories are complex and while some degree of social resistance to American hegemony is shared from Texas to California, the influence of regional histories upon constructions of ethnic identity cannot be reduced to unilateral resistance.

Such an emphasis upon the many ways in which resistance is encoded in these early texts can only yield mixed results. As the project to recover a literary heritage progresses, the critical evaluation and analysis of this literature are also in a state of rapid evolution. These earlier texts stimulate provocative questions about the ways in which resistance yields to assimilation and accommodation, as well as about the ways in which intersecting cultures result in something that is neither Mexican nor American but some mixture unique to a border geography. Early texts, as a rule, do not comfortably fit an exclusivist reading of resistance. Because of this, many scholars have found them to be problematic, often marginalizing them within a literature which itself is struggling against marginalization.

Historically, the two most obvious connections between pre- and post-1848 Hispanic literature are the emphasis on place (regional history and relationship to the land) and the exercise of power (Spanish colonial domination of native people and American colonial domination of native people, including Native Americans and Spanish or Mexican settlers). Discussing Spanish colonial narratives and the early formation of Mexican–American autobiography, Genaro Padilla points out that beginning with the Spanish explorers and missionaries, the Hispanic narrative in the West has focused on place, on translating the land into text, on mapping the terrain – geographically by naming and marking specific areas explored, as well as culturally by settling on the land and establishing communities. The cartographic impulse of the diaries, letters, and reports reinforces the Spanish colonial domination of the land by topographically naming and charting the region as well as physically emphasizing the presence of the Spanish.

The shift in national borders because of the Mexican–American War did not, however, lessen the intense narrative preoccupation with the land for Mexican-American writers. According to Padilla, the difference "is that whereas the colonial cartographic narrative is a discourse of power, a discourse in which the Spanish subject is a figure of domination, the post-1848 narrative is a discourse in which figurations, or self-conceits, of power are cracking at the seams." While Padilla continues this argument about power/powerlessness to build a strong case for reading the post-1848 texts as "narratives of resistance to the American hegemony," the differences he notes in narrative strategy can also be read another way. The preoccupation with recreating a specific place, with the nostalgic remembering of the land, occurs much less as an effort to map, name, or dominate the landscape than as an effort to stabilize an ethnic and cultural identity inextricably linked to or reflected by the land itself. While it is true that power relationships may be read as a critical factor in stabilizing an ethnic identity, the tension between expressions of power and powerlessness does not necessarily explain all the complexities inherent in a writer's imaginative reconstruction of ethnicity.

As the work of recovering a U.S. Hispanic literary tradition continues, the nineteenth century maintains a vivid imaginative space: not so much the persistent vision of loose women, fast horses, and smoking guns deeply embedded in the public consciousness, but another vision of the West in which borders, frontiers, and mountains metaphorically and literally reveal the complex construction of ethnic identity. During the first half of the twentieth century, Mexican-American writers are especially engaged in recalling the past, often evoking a romanticized history of the West from individual and communal memories. Miguel Antonio Otero and Nina Otero-Warren provide examples of this impulse to recreate some Edenic version of nineteenth-century life on the border.

In separate narratives, both writers demonstrate the connection between the land and ethnic identity from strikingly different perspectives, made more significant because of gender and generational differences, because of their close familial ties, and also because the texts were written within a few years of each other. The Oteros reflect in microcosm the multiple ways in which geographical location and intersecting cultures determine the relationship between regional and ethnic identity for Mexican-American writers. While the Oteros are somewhat representative of Padilla's post-1848 narratives of resistance, they more particularly reflect a narrative preoccupation with the land and the "cartographic impulse" implied by naming, describing, and establishing a firm connection between imagined ethnicity and the landscape.

Borders, frontiers, and mountains serve as markers for the complex connection between the land and ethnic identity in *Old Spain in Our Southwest* and in *My Life on the Frontier*. The "Border" of my title refers implicitly to that particular border separating the United States and Mexico, but also to the metaphorical use of borders to mark both physical and cultural landscapes. By definition, borders appear to separate. But in fact, as Renato Rosaldo points out in *Culture and Truth,* borders are permeable and porous. Rather than simply separating and keeping out they also allow for exchange, for crossing back and forth, for mixing. Borders suggest a complex space that contains both the tensions maintaining separateness between distinct entities (nations, people, and cultures) and the inevitable blurring of distinct entities due to proximity and the process of *mestizaje.*

The dual and sometimes contradictory nature of the frontier as both an international border and as an unsettled, open expanse of land clearly complicates the project to recover a U.S. Hispanic literary heritage. Both the literature itself and evaluations of that literature reflect conflicting geographical/cultural perspectives: looking south and west does not provide the same view of the border as looking north and east. Mountains literally and figuratively combine to provide yet another definition of borders. As a physical feature of the land, a rock-solid object, mountains serve as physical boundaries between places – tangible borders more real than the lines of black ink on a map. For the Oteros, mountains are particularly important because of their physical ability to isolate as well as to be an obstacle. As a visual marker, mountains become signifiers for both the border and the frontier as the Oteros write ethnicity onto the landscape. For Otero-Warren, the mountains reflect a certain spirituality, both a oneness with nature as well as a religious echo of her Roman Catholic faith. For Otero, the mountains simply reflect the wild ruggedness of the "unsettled frontier" – a place lush in game and fish, and rich in prospects for valuable mineral ore. The mountains represent material largesse for the taking and a luxury retreat associated with the wealthy. Borders, frontiers, and mountains literally provide the landscape and the setting, as well as the point of view, for both Oteros.

The Oteros' texts demonstrate the varied historical experience and strong regional identification of Mexican-American writers that provide the basis for establishing a firm identification with the land as they imagine ethnicity. U.S. Hispanic literature is profoundly concerned with place, with the varied ways in which ethnic identity is written into regional landscapes. The Oteros provide a small example of the widely differing visions of the West among Mexican-American writers. By evoking the nineteenth century from a twentieth-century vantage, the Oteros also demonstrate its significance in the tangled connections between the landscape and the ways in which ethnic identity is imagined.

What these two writers share in common is that they are both writing about roughly the same geographic region, the New Mexico territory before it achieved statehood, and both are writing during the 1930s, attempting to recall a way of life rapidly disappearing from memory. The similarities between texts ends there. Otero's perspective of the frontier is shaped to parallel his own coming of age and his sense of ethnic identity, while Otero-Warren's much more tightly focused narrative reveals the complexity of the relationship between land and ethnic identity in the West. Otero-Warren covers a seemingly eclectic variety of topics (flowers, place names, the history of education, folklore), but she loosely holds them together with the common purpose of illuminating the title of her book: *Old Spain in Our Southwest*. Indeed, the purpose of *Old Spain in Our Southwest* is to show the ways in which "Old Spain," as a marker of Spanish/Mexican ethnic identity, has been literally written into the landscape itself, "Our Southwest."

In the first two volumes of his autobiography, *My Life on the*

Frontier: 1864–1882 (1935) and *My Life on the Frontier: 1882–1897* (1939), Otero obviously considers himself a firsthand observer/participant in "blazing the way across the plains" and in "the early settlement and development of the New West." As the observer/participant he feels a public obligation to record his experience. His autobiography consists of personal history and a coming-of-age story – moving from boyhood to manhood, from protected son to patriarch, protector of family, and governor of territory. The autobiography is also meant as a public history, the story of a particular region's coming of age as the community develops order out of lawlessness, and moves from a rural, communal economy to capitalism with the building of the railroad, telephones, banking, mining, increased commerce, and trade.

This parallel development of frontier and self reveals a strong identification of self with the land and subsequent vexed notions of ethnic identity. A closer look at the subtitle of the first volume of Otero's autobiography – *Incidents and Characters of the Period when Kansas, Colorado, and New Mexico were passing through the last of their Wild and Romantic Years* – reveals the casual conflation of a coming-of-age story for both the writer and for the frontier landscape. Both pass "through the last of their Wild and Romantic years" via the building of the railroad across the West. The progress of the railroad provides a marker for Otero's own growth, just as the changes in the landscape can be measured by the arrival of the railroad from state to state. Chapter one opens suggestively with the railroad as metaphor and memorable event: "As the railway lines pushed their way westward through Kansas, I migrated from one rough and sporadic terminal town to another, scraping acquaintance with Westport Landing, Leavenworth, Ellsworth, Hays City, Sheridan and Fort Wallace in quick succession during my boyhood." Otero's adventures and his knowledge of the frontier as an open expanse of land, largely unsettled and rich in possibilities, parallel the movement of the railroad westward. He is intimately involved, even as a young boy, with the settlement of a long series of towns which inevitably followed the laying of railroad tracks.

Otero's father, Don Miguel, had been instrumental in bringing the railroad into New Mexico and, as Otero traces the building of the railroad through Kansas and Colorado into New Mexico, it becomes clear that the family investment in the railroad is much more than economic – it is also emotional. The railroad meant economic prosperity for those in its path, but more important than the material wealth is the literal connection it will provide between the New Mexico territory and the rest of the United States.

The Oteros engaged in a strong effort to Americanize the Mexican-American population of the territory in a preparatory effort toward statehood. Although politically controversial even then, their effort was twofold. Not only did they encourage the economic development and Americanization of New Mexico, they also tried to acquaint the rest of the nation with New Mexico in an effort to dispel many misperceptions and negative stereotypes. To many Americans at the time, New Mexico was too closely aligned with Mexico – it bordered Mexico, the natives were "Mexicans" moreso than "Americans," they spoke Spanish rather than English. In fact, even the name contributed to the confusion: the difference between "New" and "Old" Mexico remained unclear to many. (The confusion continues today. Every so often the New Mexico Bureau of Tourism receives inquiries about whether or not a passport is necessary for a visit and questions about the safety of the water for drinking.) While Otero's autobiography seems to read as assimilationist, or at the very least extremely accommodating to American culture and interests, he is primarily recording the consequences of a daily intersection between two very different cultures, Mexican/Spanish and American. Negotiating such conflicting terrain often resulted in a complex mixing of both cultures.

Because Otero's interest in the railroad lies in its ability to connect New Mexico (as the frontier/border) with the Midwest and the East, once the railroad reaches Las Vegas, New Mexico, its progress is less important to Otero's story. The boy has become a young man and the story moves forward to reflect his education in business and public life, as well as his initiation into politics. As an adult, Otero maintains a strong connection with the railroad but now the railroad signifies a strong link to the larger U.S. cities. References to the railroad continue in the context of travel eastward to New York or Washington, D.C., sometimes north to St. Louis and Chicago. The westward impetus of the railroad continues – but, off the pages of the text. The movement of the railroad across the West and into New Mexico is the means by which Otero comes to know the frontier as well as the means by which "the Wild and Romantic" years of the frontier will end. Once settled in the West, however, the railroad and Otero turn their attention East, reinforcing the continual exchange, both political and commercial, between East and West.

As the subtitle to volume one indicates, Otero's description of the frontier is infused with the myth-making rhetoric of the nineteenth-century West, the West of popular culture, the wild romance of an imagined frontier. Although the general tone of the book appears to cast a familiar image of the West, Otero is very much aware that the public vision of the frontier has been sensationalized far beyond his actual experience of it. He intends his autobiography as a corrective vision of the West. He explains in the introduction to his second volume that he limits his "writing to actual facts . . . adher[ing] strictly to the truth," regardless of consequences. As an elder statesman with years of political service in the public interest behind him, Otero knows that his reconstruction of the frontier will be controversial in many quarters.

Although attempting to desensationalize the West, Otero cannot avoid evoking it as a place that emphasizes entrepreneurship and individual success. There is a distinct narrative preoccupation with every colorful (Anglo-American) character who crossed the western frontier between 1867 and 1907. Otero's approach in relating his acquaintanceship with such legends as Buffalo Bill Cody, Wild Bill Hickock, Kit Carson, Calamity Jane, Billy the Kid, Clay Allison, Doc Holliday, and others is to humanize them rather than indulge in idle star-gazing. He emphasizes the ordinary nature of these larger-than-life figures, their individual quirks, personality flaws, and virtues.

Women have a very small role in this autobiography of a boy's transformation to a young man and an untamed country into a civilized community. While Otero briefly sketches out some family history early in the first volume, he emphasizes his father's influence and gives minimal acknowledgment to his maternal background and his mother. Other female family members are mainly relegated to footnotes or asides. In chapter two of the first volume he mentions Calamity Jane and addresses the role of women on the frontier during this period. In his effort to dispel some of the romantic notions about the West, however, his discussion of the hard life women faced is limited to the saloons and dance-hall girls.

Otero has little to say about mothers, sisters, or wives and much to say about the "wholesale trafficking in female human flesh." Unfortunately, his emphasis on "loose women" reinforces all the myths and stereotypes about frontier women: the notion that the frontier woman often ended up as a dance-hall girl or a prostitute with "a heart of gold" who after a short, hard life of degradation ended her "unhappy existence by first stupefying her mind with large quantities of poor whiskey, and then topping it off with a dose of poison sufficient to kill fifty grey wolves." The only success stories, Otero notes, are of those women with a sharp business acumen, saloon keepers such as Delores "Steamboat" Martinez and Chata Baca. In his discussion of frontier women there is a subtle tension regarding issues of class and ethnic identity. In the lower and working-class group, it is the "native" women who succeed, at least financially, during this transition period with the railroad's arrival, and the women from the East – American girls – who fall into disrepute. In the middle and upper classes, American women traveling west, as well as the women from the older established Mexican/Spanish families, are almost entirely omitted from Otero's description of women on the frontier except when included as part of a larger social event.

Similarly, when Otero evokes the vision of fast horses and smoking guns, it is in the well-worn images of outlaws, shoot-outs, and vigilante committees. Horses and guns seem inextricably bound to each other, ubiquitous on the frontier, and the final arbiter in settling any and all disputes. Nearly every chapter finds Otero describing some incident involving the law as determined by the quickest draw. While Otero is clearly caught in the rhetoric of this violent image of the West, he also manages to convey disquieting ways in which race complicates the picture. Most of the outlaws he profiles are famous American figures of the West such as Billy the Kid, and he often portrays them in a sympathetic light. (In fact, his fascination with Billy the Kid led to his writing a biography of the young outlaw, *The Real Billy the Kid; With New Light on the Lincoln County War* [1936], between volumes one and two of his own autobiography.) Conversely, he profiles few Mexican-American outlaws, and they are uniformly cast in a more negative light. In his short sketch of Vicente Silva and his gang, Otero can find no redeeming characteristics, labeling Silva a "notorious killer." Las Gorras Blancas (the White Caps) provide another example of an outlaw gang which Otero portrays with unilateral condemnation. This is in sharp contrast to contemporary historians who now find the violence of these Mexican-American outlaws complicated by issues of cultural conflict and social resistance.

Such a negative and judgmental portrayal of Mexican-Americans directly challenges Otero's envisioning of ethnic identity and his self-identification as a "native" New Mexican. The wild and romantic American vision of the West allows a certain respectability for the outlaw and any reckless violence which accompanies him – unless the outlaw is Mexican-American. However, Otero must also come to terms with another vision of the West, one which he inherits from his father's family. As the son of a Spanish/Mexican Don, he has spent enough time in New Mexico to experience a strong sense of established community. Despite his fascination with the outlaws of the West, Otero is also at pains to detail a cosmopolitan air of gracious entertaining, appreciation for the arts and world travel, highly stylized manners, and rules of reciprocity regarding hospitality specific to Mexican-American culture. He describes the many social occasions such as dances and parties that move from one home to another, continuing for a week at a time. The guests at such parties include a broad mix of the middle- and upper-class citizens of the area, as well as any visiting royalty from Europe or political dignitaries passing through. This image of the frontier contradicts the notion of a wild, unsettled land with the image of a community with a long history of Spanish traditions and cosmopolitan manners, a community that traditionally has conceived of the frontier as a border settlement.

The importance of place frames the autobiography with all the conflicting definitions of the frontier. For Miguel Otero, the story of self is also the story of "frontier." While suggesting unlimited space and freedom, Otero's use of the frontier is actually quite limited – restricted to western Kansas, southern Colorado, and northern New Mexico. Otero's description of the frontier clearly employs an American sensibility with subtle undertones of ethnic identity which contradict that notion of the frontier. While the frontier symbolizes unlimited adventure and a certain lawlessness, it also represents home; it is civilized and sophisticated with gracious hospitality and entertainment, and contains a long history with his father's family as a part of a stable community. Otero appears to maintain conflicting images of the land as both lawless frontier and settled community as he negotiates the varying intersections of an American present and a Spanish/Mexican past. That same ambiguity and conflict reflects itself in the indirect ways in which he acknowledges the complexity of his own ethnic identity and mixed heritage as the son of a Spanish/Mexican Don and the grandson of a southern plantation owner.

The complex connection between the land and ethnic identity is approached in a very different manner by Nina Otero-Warren. Tey Diana Rebolledo uses *Old Spain in Our Southwest* as an example of the early ways in which Hispanic writers conceived of the southwestern landscape as bound in family and cultural traditions. Otero-Warren writes a communal autobiography quite different from Miguel Otero's coming-of-age story. She uses the landscape as both a literal and metaphorical representation of the culture she wishes to preserve in a complex combination of autobiography and ethnography. Rebolledo explains this perception of landscape as an attempt to transmit a special sense of identity: "one that is female, Chicana, and deeply connected to the land, myth, and self."

That Otero-Warren felt an affinity between her own "interior landscape" and the world outside is evident in the extended description of the violent nighttime storm and the subsequent quiet of the following sunrise in the chapter that opens *Old Spain*. Alone, in her one-room adobe house at sunset, she describes the land, the setting sun, the approaching storm, and her temporary neighbors – a shepherd and an Indian. The description continues through the storm and the night, ending with the rising sun and each individual's response to the new day and contrasting her own reactions with those of the shepherd and the Indian. The chapter opens with the approaching storm:

> A storm was coming over the country around Santa Fé, the ancient City of the Holy Faith. This southwestern country, explored and settled nearly four hundred years ago by a people who loved nature, worshiped God and feared no evil, is still a region of struggles.
>
> I spent this night on my homestead in a small adobe house in the midst of cedars on the top of a hill. We face the great *Sangre de Cristo* range as we look to the rising sun: a beauty too great for human beings to have had a hand in creating. Cedars and piñones, twisted, knotted, dwarfed by the wind, were all around me. Arroyos were cut in the ground, innocent looking in dry weather, but terrible in storms, for the water rushing through them can fell trees and roll bowlders as easily as children roll marbles.

What is most evident in these first two paragraphs is the presence of the autobiographical self and the relationship of this self to the land. As the description of the landscape unfolds in the chapter, the land becomes ethnicized through the repeated use of Spanish place names across centuries, as well as through the use of history and religion to demonstrate a firm connection to the land. In effect, the land subtly begins to mirror and reinforce a sense of ethnic identity introduced by the juxtaposition of history, religion, and the linguistic play between Spanish and English. Identifying "Santa Fé" as "the ancient City of the Holy Faith" not only establishes a geographic location for the book, it also evokes a sense of history with the descriptive phrase "the ancient City." Religion is cast as an important facet inextricable from place and time with Santa Fé explicitly translated as the "City of the Holy Faith."

Otero-Warren subtly reminds her audience that Santa Fé is a Spanish name with a specific English translation, the "City of the Holy Faith." She often italicizes Spanish words, such as when discussing the "Sangre de Cristo" mountain range. But Santa Fé is not italicized and the only suggestion of its Spanish origin is found in its spelling, the use of the accent mark, and the casual translation which immediately follows. The introduction of this translation slips unobtrusively into the text, to be read in quite different ways by a mixed audience. An audience clearly familiar with Santa Fé as a place in New Mexico but not familiar with Spanish could easily miss the act of translation and consider the title "City of the Holy Faith" simply another nickname, a slogan for the town, or a romantic exaggeration of its Spanish Catholic heritage. A more practiced eye, familiar with Spanish and some history of the town, would immediately note the usage of the accent mark over Santa Fé as a deliberate acknowledgment of the correct Spanish spelling. Furthermore, the abbreviated English translation faintly echoes the grandeur of Santa Fé's full name, La Villa Real de la Santa Fé de San Francisco de Asis. The ambiguous play between Spanish place names and English translations occurs throughout the text with a wide range of results and effects. Always Otero-Warren remains quietly insistent on the proper Spanish identification which exists prior to the English translation or the American appropriation (and alteration) of Spanish words and place names.

By identifying the land as "still a region of struggles," Otero-Warren clearly proposes conflict as an ongoing or constant force in New Mexico. A sense of historical, as well as immediate, struggles permeates this particular place: a struggle to explore and settle the land four hundred years ago but nevertheless a struggle that continues into the present, "still." As the land and the people are identified historically, they are also identified religiously. The translation, "City of the Holy Faith," conveys a lived Catholicism exemplified in Otero-Warren's description of a "people who loved nature, worshiped God and feared no evil." The historical impulse to explore and settle is linked to the expression of religion and becomes an integral part of her effort to describe the community, the intersection of cultures, and the land. The importance of this religious identification of the land is further strengthened by the line's clear allusion to the Twenty-third Psalm.

The opening chapter provides a significant foundation for reading *Old Spain* as autobiography. Clearly the "I" of this chapter positions the writer as both an integral element of the landscape and the narrative, yet apart, separate from the community she attempts to describe. She writes herself into the text as a point of comparison between her fears and the fearlessness of a shepherd and an Indian. She begins by setting herself in sharp contrast to the scene she is describing – the vast mountain range of the Sangre de Cristo, the arroyos, the trees shaped and beaten by wind and fierce rains. She describes the scene outside from the safety of her small adobe homestead. She is separate from and "not in complete tune" with the landscape in the way the Indian and the shepherd are "accustomed" to each other and "closer to nature." Yet despite this separateness, the use of autobiographical fact finally connects the narrator to the land and to the culture Otero-Warren is describing.

The problem of language as a mediating factor between cultures is apparent in the slippage between English and Spanish that continues throughout the text. While Spanish is often acknowledged, italicized, or translated, just as often it is used automatically without translation, certain words seeming to function equally in both languages. The only indication that these words might not be English, or might require some further explanation, is the occasional mark emphasizing pronunciation – the tilde over the "n" or an accent mark – and the glossary at the back of the book. How much of the glossary and translations should be credited to the author is unclear, but the glossary's very existence supports the linguistic complexity of *Old Spain*. Otero-Warren cannot describe the landscape without employing Spanish to name the familiar, which cannot be named as easily in English. She repeatedly suggests the importance of a dual language in writing about a place that is geographically and culturally a borderland.

Both *Old Spain* and *My Life on the Frontier* exemplify the importance of the past and specific geographic ties in defining ethnic identity. By mixing genres – combining history, autobiography, ethnography, and folklore – Nina Otero-Warren recreates a way of life that has sometimes been criticized as "romantic nostalgia." Miguel Otero's emphasis on the passing of the "Wild and Romantic years" of the frontier is no less nostalgic in its preoccupation with larger-than-life outlaws and the transformation of a territory into statehood. Certainly, there are other problems with both writers for Chicano scholars: Nina Otero-Warren's ethnic identification as "Spanish American" privileges an upper-class status and a European heritage, erasing a long historical connection with Mexico.

Her continual reference to the Spanish conquistadors is often offensive and the issue of class arises in the condescending tone she uses to describe the very culture she is attempting to preserve. Miguel Otero's autobiography is no less problematic, as he is often criticized for his assimilationist politics. These problems aside, the striking feature of both texts is that the Oteros connect writing history, religion, and language (the shift between English and Spanish) with the land itself, with a particular geographic region.

Having maintained active political careers and public lives in various positions of community service for most of their lives, both Miguel Otero and Nina Otero-Warren show an acute awareness of and responsibility for the very public nature of their role as representatives of the Spanish/Mexican–American community and New Mexico in general. Both Oteros self-consciously negotiate the duality of being both Spanish/Mexican and American in their autobiographies. The intense sociocultural focus of Americanization and nationalism during the early twentieth century further complicates their efforts to relate the multiple stories of intersecting cultures. As public figures, their ethnic identities become complex subtexts written against negative stereotypes of the Mexican and the Spanish. For the Oteros, culture and ethnicity become an unspoken private element of a written public self: The tension between public and private shapes the ways in which culture and ethnicity are inscribed when writing the self.

Both Oteros are part of a small group of known Mexican-American writers who published in English during the late nineteenth and early twentieth century. During this period, these writers and others who published in Spanish, as well as those who wrote personal narratives (such as diaries, memoirs, and letters just now beginning to see publication), share a similar sensibility about the historical importance of their narrative efforts. Critics such as Padilla and Rebolledo have shown how early writers like Mariano Vallejo, Rafael Chacón, Cleofas Jaramillo, and Fabiola Cabeza de Baca often weave subtle and occasionally direct threads of social resistance into their texts. While definitions of cultural resistance are anchored in the historical fact of conflict, what is often missing from any discussion of these writers and the Oteros is a broader conception of the ways in which the historical impulse of their narratives reveals an ethnic identity entangled with the landscape as much as with cultural conflict. Thus, Vallejo attempts through personal memoir to write the history of California from the perspective of the Mexican-American after American colonization. María Amparo Ruiz de Burton uses historical romance to highlight the struggle over land ownership between the Californios and the American settlers in *The Squatter and the Don* (1885).

Like Otero-Warren, Jaramillo in *Sombras del Pasado/Shadows of the Past* (1941) and Cabeza de Baca in *We Fed Them Cactus* (1954) attempt to describe a way of life more in tune with the rhythms of the New Mexican landscape – the high desert and the mountains – before Americanization. María Cristina Mena in various short stories such as "The Education of Popo," "The Vine Leaf," and "The Birth of the War God," published from 1913–1915 in *Century Magazine,* and Josephina Niggli in *Mexican Village* (1945) also write about a border landscape often set south of the border but just as complicated by vexed intersections with American culture. (Mena, Jaramillo, and Cabeza de Baca, as well as many other early Latina/Latino writers are currently being reprinted in various anthologies such as *North of the Rio Grande: The Mexican-American Experience in Short Fiction* (1992) and *Infinite Divisions: An Anthology of Chicana Literature* (1993). The Oteros, as well as these other writers, clearly write from a sense of responsibility to history, a need to record not only a struggle between American and Spanish/Mexican culture but a need to voice a presence and identity shaped by various encounters with the land across centuries.

Miguel Antonio Otero and Nina Otero-Warren are representative of these early writers in their impulse to inscribe history through their autobiographical texts. *My Life on the Frontier* was written to allow the "coming generation . . . to hear the development of the New West," according to someone who experienced it and actually helped shape it. *Old Spain* was written to preserve (and recapture) a rapidly disappearing culture for both native New Mexicans and those unfamiliar with the Southwest. Both books could be said to have been addressed to a dual audience. They are designed to explain New Mexico and New Mexicans to the rest of the United States as well as to preserve a Mexican-American history for their own ethnic group.

While inscribing the history of a particular region, New Mexico, through the narratives of their own lives, the Oteros are now themselves being inscribed within a particular historical tradition in the recovery of a U.S. Hispanic literary heritage. As the project to recover that heritage continues, the contribution of these writers will enlarge and add another facet to our vision of the West as a complex multicultural landscape rather than as the one-dimensional, ubiquitous, and romanticized myth persistently reflected by Hollywood westerns and embedded in the American psyche.

Works Cited

Gutiérrez, Ramón and Genaro Padilla, eds. "Introduction." *Recovering the U.S. Hispanic Literary Heritage.* Houston: Arte Público, 1993, 17–25.

Kanellos, Nicolás. "Foreword." *Recovering the U.S. Hispanic Literary Heritage.* Eds. Ramón Gutiérrez and Genaro Padilla. Houston: Arte Público, 1993, 13–15.

Otero, Miguel Antonio. *My Life on the Frontier: 1864–1882.* New York: The Press of the Pioneers, 1935.

———. *My Life on the Frontier: 1882–1897.* Albuquerque: U of New Mexico P, 1939.

Otero-Warren, Nina. *Old Spain in Our Southwest.* New York: Harcourt, Brace and Company, 1936.

Padilla, Genaro. "Discontinuous Continuities: Remapping the Terrain of Spanish Colonial Narrative." In *Reconstructing a Chicano/a Literary Heritage: Hispanic Colonial Literature of the Southwest.* Ed. María Herrera-Sobek. Tucson: U of Arizona P, 1993, 24–36.

Rebolledo, Tey Diana. "Tradition and Mythology: Signatures of Landscape in Chicano Literature." In *The Desert Is No Lady: Southwestern Landscapes in Women's Writing and Art.* Eds. Vera Norwood and Janice Monk. New Haven: Yale UP, 1987, 96–124.

CONTEMPORARY WESTERN
WRITING: A MOSAIC

THE RETURN OF THE NATIVE:
THE POLITICS OF IDENTITY
IN AMERICAN INDIAN FICTION
OF THE WEST

PHILIP BURNHAM

> They were like any other people in this respect – that individuals
> varied exceedingly; some you admired and some you detested on
> sight. . . . Even the first thing you thought of, color, had almost as
> many variations as there were single Indians. There were all shades
> of brown, some almost black ones, and a good many were as olive-
> skinned as a Spaniard.
>
> — D'Arcy McNickle, *The Surrounded*

East or West, the Indian is the romantic heavy in the story of
America. For early historians, the native could choose between the
role of scoundrel or reluctant accomplice in the spectacle of westward Progress. In Frederick Jackson Turner's "frontier thesis" of
1893, the Indian – bless him – was even said to have played a
critical role in forging the nation's character. Turner described the
western frontier as the crucible of American values, the melding
point of savage and civilized where the self-reliant principles of
democracy matured. Radically qualified, if not rejected, by revisionist historians today, the Turner theory still has a hold on the
public imagination. From supermarket fiction to big-budget Hollywood westerns, Indian people seem tied to the West of buffalo,
wide open plains, and the obligatory setting sun.

Later critics borrowed Turner's dualistic landscape, if not his
ideology. In 1968, Leslie Fiedler defined the genre of the western
as the "encounter with the Indian," noting of the mythical West
that "only the Indian survives, however ghettoized, debased, de-
bauched, to remind us with his alien stare of the new kind of space
in which the baffled refugees from Europe first found him."

Fiedler's *The Return of the Vanishing American* is one of the first sympathetic treatments of native peoples in American fiction. But it hardly comes as a surprise that his argument is awash in the moral rhetoric of the sixties as much as Turner's was imbued with the cant of turn-of-the-century progressivism. On the dedication page the critic goes so far as to thank "the Blackfoot tribe who adopted me." A white boy from Newark in revisionist buckskin, Fiedler had been "born again."

In fact, the turbulent sixties saw a revival in the image of the "white shaman," the non-Indian who captures the essence of the native spirit through an extended stay in Indian country. Later discredited, the "white shamanism" movement fascinated Fiedler for what it said about the old wish to combine the native and immigrant souls of America, a theme proposed by D. H. Lawrence in the twenties. In its broadest sense the western portrayed, for Fiedler, the fraternal bonding of white and Indian, told from the white point of view – from James Fenimore Cooper's Natty Bumppo and Chingachgook to Ken Kesey's Chief Bromden and Randle Patrick McMurphy. It was a form of wish fulfillment, the myth of Tonto and the Lone Ranger riding off arm in arm into a glorious sunset. It was also – added Fiedler – a lie. The myth of the blood brother was a pittance of compensation for the real failure of the races to get along.

The tradition of white-told tales about North American Indians is alive and well, if with higher standards of verisimilitude than Cooper was held to. The Navajo whodunits of Tony Hillerman and the reservation stories of W. P. Kinsella both bear out that the white writer is still compelled to describe the encounter with the aboriginal world of the West. But Fiedler wrote his book just before the surge in Indian fiction erupted in 1968 with the publication of N. Scott Momaday's *House Made of Dawn*. Today there is no dearth of Indian writers to revise the Turner thesis and Fiedler's ironic variation of it – a native perspective on the mythical place of the West in American history.

The West in the work of current Indian writers such as James Welch, Leslie Silko, Scott Momaday, Louise Erdrich, and Linda Hogan is – as it long was for whites – a wide-open terrain. In contemporary Indian fiction the West represents, as it once did for Turner, a cutting edge of identity. But now the frontier resides, if anywhere, within the individual, not without: The forces of "civilization" and "savagery" are not so easily separated as they were a century ago. The war between red and white has become the subject of, in Gerald Vizenor's phrase, "crossblood stories" in the hands of contemporary native writers. As Fiedler foresaw twenty-five years ago, the vanishing American has returned.

Indian literature about the West isn't new. From John Rollin Ridge to D'Arcy McNickle, from Luther Standing Bear to Will Rogers and Black Elk, Indian voices during the past century and a half have portrayed an experience of the trans-Mississippi West vastly different than that described by mountain men, government agents, salvage anthropologists, and educated tourists crashing the Cumberland Gap with a literary reputation to make. If indeed the natives have "returned," it is clear that, in the literary world, they never actually left in the first place.

But what Fiedler called the "Western" (the "encounter with the Indian") was at odds with the typical Indian pilgrimage to the east. One of the ironies of the literary West has been the journey of the Indian writer eastward – to be brow-beaten, educated, inspired, or displayed as the traveling specimen of a mythical region called "the Wild West." Ridge (*The Life and Adventures of Joaquin Murieta, the Celebrated California Bandit,* 1854) went to boarding school in New England at the age of fourteen; Charles Eastman (*From the Deep Woods to Civilization,* 1916) graduated from Dartmouth College and Boston University Medical School; Luther Standing Bear (*My People the Sioux,* 1938) went to the infamous Carlisle School in Pennsylvania; John Joseph Mathews (*Wah'Kon-Tah,* 1932) and D'Arcy McNickle attended Oxford. Black Elk (*Black Elk Speaks,* 1932) toured with Buffalo Bill and came back to tell about a meeting in a world across the water with "Grandmother England" – otherwise known as Queen Victoria.

For the early Indian writer, the motto of Horace Greeley might just as well have been "Go east, young man." But the eastern journey could be a painful one. As Luther Standing Bear remembered of his experience at Carlisle, "Now, after having had my hair cut, a new thought came into my head. I felt that I was no more Indian, but would be an imitation of a white man." The humiliating rite of passage for the tribal child sent to boarding school was an echo of other Indian journeys that crossed the country eastward – the renegade Apache leaders deported to Florida; various chiefs gone to Washington to parley with the Great White Father; and later, World War I volunteers whose bravery would eventually earn, in 1924, the right for all Indians to vote. "For Indians from the remoter West the invitation of delegations served another significant purpose" writes historian Francis Paul Prucha, "to impress upon the Indians the size, population, strength, and accomplishments of the United States." The nineteenth-century journey of assimilation went against the grain of "westward the course of empire," against the direction of the railroads, the Homestead Act, and the unfolding of Manifest Destiny. Since contact with whites, going east has tended to be an act of submission; going west an act of destiny – however tragic – that at least gave hope for escape from the strictures of the white world.

In the late twentieth century, much has changed. Most of the best-known current writers, for example, were born in the West, educated there, and continue to live in the region. Silko, Welch, Hogan, Momaday, Craig Lesley, and Simon Ortiz have more truck with Albuquerque, Denver, and Portland than with Boston and the nation's capital. Others, such as Louise Erdrich and Michael Dorris, hail from the West even if their careers have been forged in traditional eastern havens for Indian education like Dartmouth College. To a degree, the locus of power for Indian writers has changed.

The preponderance of western roots among contemporary Indian writers is also the reflection of a demographic fact. According to the 1990 census, 75 percent of Native Americans live in the West; there are more Indians in Oklahoma and California together than in all the states east of the Mississippi. Numbers can be misleading, but for American Indians demography speaks volumes. Whether by early colonial rivalries, pressure from neighboring tribes, or outright government fiat, many Indian peoples were pushed westward across the continent beginning as early as the sixteenth century. The western Cherokee and the Sioux seem anchored on the Plains today, but it is only within recent historical memory – the Sioux crossing the Missouri River in the late eighteenth century, the Cherokee forcibly removed from Georgia in 1830 – that they came to be there. Their descendants, some of them writers, have grappled with that migration – the conditions imposed by removal, war, and the federal reservation system. Due to patterns of historical movement, the Indian – in recent history, in particular – seems tied to the West as a place of tribal "emergence."

There's another reason for the literary importance of the West. Since the creation of reservations in the mid-nineteenth century, the West is where the vast majority of Indian trust land resides. Land is seminal to our understanding of Indian history, and in recognition of the claims that remain to be settled in U.S. courts, of the future of Indian Country as well. The land – by implication, the West – is not a settled thing. Indian novel after novel shows the reservation return of sons and daughters in crisis, a testament to the tenuous

political existence of people with a shrinking land base. Most Indian land is in the West; thus, by extension, so is Indian destiny.

For the contemporary Indian writer, however, "Go East, Young
Man" has a certain resonance still. With some exceptions, stories
and novels of Indian life are brought to us by the conglomerate
publishers in New York. Though significant books have appeared
from university presses in the West, it is the East Coast publishing
clique on which contemporary Indian literature largely depends.
Eastern "do-gooders," "reformists," and "Indian lovers" are notorious in American history for their well-meaning plans to "save the
Indian." The persistence of this trend today plays itself out in the
big-stakes poker game of publishing – the tribal writer must sell a
paperback option in New York just as surely as the land-claims
lobbyist has to camp out in a hallway on Capitol Hill.

Even if the novels are published back East, we can take comfort
that they are largely told by Indians, not just about them. Meanwhile, the race to mythologize the Indian continues apace on the
other end of the continent. The archetypal Hollywood shtick that
gives us a white-directed version of the native world – the mythical
brand described so well by Fiedler – in *Dances With Wolves* (1990),
The Last of the Mohicans (1992), or *Son of the Morning Star* (1991)
offers a vision far less groundbreaking and authentic by comparison.

The native has literally "returned." Indian peoples were, after
all, the first to see the West – many of them on their way somewhere else – in the prehistorical migration that traversed the
Americas thousands of years ago. Within historical memory, only
the West has been deemed large enough to hold what remains of
aboriginal America. Indian peoples have long written about their
conflict with the white world – it is only in the last generation that a
significant portion of America has begun to listen.

Categories like "Indian literature" often leave traditional songs,
chants, and legends to the more established realm of anthropology.
Owing to problems of transcription and translation, older genres
have conventionally been the province of "salvage ethnography"
more often than literary criticism. But earlier Indian accounts of
the West dating back several centuries are many and varied. It is
the work of anthropologists (native and white) who have enhanced
the experience of these forms for the general public. Dennis Tedlock's *Finding the Center* (1972), a transcription of Zuni Pueblo tales,
emphasizes the dimension of oral performance in rendering traditional stories. Alfonso Ortiz and Richard Erdoes give a continental

perspective on creation stories, trickster tales, and other indigenous narratives in their collection, *American Indian Myths and Legends* (1984). Anthropologists are revising the way we see "tribal
genres" once thought to be static and unchanging.

Still, native literature about the West is also in keeping with
contemporary forms and styles. Vine Deloria Jr.'s biting essays on
subjects ranging from pending Indian land claims to racial stereotypes and native religion are an important part of Indian "literature." The poetry of Joy Harjo, James Welch, Simon Ortiz, Duane
Niatum, and many others offers an insight into the American West
from a native perspective that – in its sheer volume – is unprecedented in the history of American publishing.

Notwithstanding the claims of native poets, playwrights, essay-
ists, and ethnologists, the most celebrated surge in western writing
has come in fiction, particularly the novel. At least this is how the
majority culture has promoted it, judging by the account books of
the big publishers, the literary prizes and MacArthur "genius
grants" awarded, or the media acclaim accorded novelists in the
rush to publish and promote American minorities. Of course,
there is tension in the phrase "Indian novel" – the words connote
distant tribal origins as well as the most international of literary
forms. With a few exceptions – notably D'Arcy McNickle in the
thirties – it was only in the late 1960s that native writers began to
employ the novel with a far different notion of the West than
Turner's "frontier" or even what Fiedler meant by the "encounter
with the Indian."

One reason for the popularity of fiction among native writers
may be the plasticity of the novel, its flexible shape in holding
traditional forms within it while still answering the usual demands
of the genre. Through cinematic cross-cutting, the novel can establish a structural dialogue between past and present, native and
non-native, and negotiate the sometimes invisible line between secular and sacred. In *The Surrounded* (1936), McNickle incorporates
the Salish tale "The Thing That Will Make Life Easy" as an ironic
commentary on the disintegration of tribal life. McNickle's natural
and straightforward use of narrative tradition (in a local storytelling session) provides an effective parenthesis to the encroaching
presence of white culture. In the late sixties, the use of traditional
forms in the "Indian western" became bolder. In *House Made of
Dawn* (1968), Scott Momaday uses the Navajo Night Chant as a
redeeming ritual for a fallen protagonist. A decade later Silko
would weave traditional tales through the texture of a fragmented
prose narrative in *Ceremony* (1977); fifteen years later, in *Almanac of*

the Dead (1991), she employs – even invents – the pieces of a "lost" Mayan book of prophecy. The novel has by no means displaced traditional forms in the hands of Indian writers, for in a larger sense, it carries them within. From a critical point of view, the subject of "cross-blood stories" announced by Gerald Vizenor has been paralleled by a creative use of cross-blood forms in fictional structure.

Indeed, the notion of the mixed-blood or hybrid has long been a part of Indian literature about the West. The mixed-blood character balancing on the edge of two worlds has even become something of a generic stereotype. Early Indian fiction such as *The Surrounded* (McNickle); *Co-g-we-a, the Half-Blood* (1927) by Mourning Dove; *Brothers Three* (1935) by John Oskison; and *Sundown* (1934) by John Joseph Mathews spoke of the conflict between cultures. It is a theme so persistent that conflict between worlds has become thoroughly internalized in the typical narrator who, like Abel in *House Made of Dawn,* is forced to come to terms with the prospect of being "homogenized" in the great American Melting Pot. Indian writers have long sought a fictional antidote to assimilation, a character alloy stronger and more resistant than the "mixed blood" or "half breed" of conventional narrative.

The struggle between worlds is underlined by a device noted by many critics. Native American novels are often marked at the outset by a "homecoming." The protagonist returns to the western reservation drunk (Abel in *House Made of Dawn*), to attend a funeral (Albertine Johnson in Erdrich's *Love Medicine* [1984]), as a confused veteran (Tayo in *Ceremony*), or simply for a farewell visit (Archilde in *The Surrounded*). Thomas Wolfe's adage that "you can't go home again" seems, in the context of Indian fiction, a cliché in the unmaking. In light of many Indian novels of the West, "you have to go home again": to be healed, to pay family dues, to make amends to the ancestors. In these books the protagonists are "recreated" by a return to the reservation, whether or not in the final act they are also destroyed.

The new Indian novel might be called a "re-creation" story. This fiction is a kind of modern reworking of the traditional creation tale, best explained by Momaday's memoir *The Way to Rainy Mountain* (1969), where he compares his own mission to the migratory journey that his people – the Kiowa – made centuries ago: "The journey herein recalled continues to be made anew each time the miracle comes to mind, for that is peculiarly the right and responsibility of the imagination." Like many traditional stories, the new novel seeks to explain origins – the name of a grandfather, recon-

ciliation with a parent, a recovering of lost knowledge. The return
to the reservation isn't just nomadic, but part of a deliberate quest.
If in Genesis the act of creation is sudden and unyielding, in many
Indian tales migration from one world to another is a necessary act
of emergence. Human re-creation is a struggle.

The mixed-blood character in Indian fiction is oddly in keeping
with a common motif from these creation stories. For many tribes,
a set of twins – one good, one evil – plays an active role in creating
the world. Their presence not only accounts for good and evil, but
light and darkness, birth and death, happiness and misery. The
cross-blood character so familiar in these novels is a cultural "hero"
with a memory of two worlds as he searches for a place to resolve
the mystery of origins. In creation tales from the Southwest –
where Silko and Momaday hail from – the notion is widespread
that there are plural worlds within this one, an echo not only of the
migration theme, but an assertion that identity can have myriad
phases. In its most literal sense, then, the Indian novel is a "re-
creation" story. Modern fiction is a secular (re-creational) form
rather than a sacred one as posed in the original tribal stories.

Indian writing – of creation or re-creation – has been a response to the "extinction myth" propagated about Indian people
by friend and foe alike. D. H. Lawrence wrote in 1923 that "within
the present generation the surviving Red Indians are due to merge
in the great white swamp." Anyone who has spent time on a reservation knows that that has not entirely happened. The idea that
Native Americans are vanishing has proven to be a demographic
falsehood. To paraphrase Mark Twain (no mean Indianhater himself), accounts of the demise of Native Americans have been greatly
exaggerated. So it is that Indian peoples have started to reinvent
their identity in the paradigm popularly known as the "American
mosaic." This reinvention occurs most often under western skies,
and much of it with the conviction that "Indianness" is a state of
existence (as opposed to a state of mind) worthy of America's
attention.

Literary critics can illuminate nooks and crannies. But what we
identify as "Indian literature" is not as easy a task as it would seem.
In the contemporary politics of cultural identity, it has become chic
to be "Indian," whether in the government census rolls or the
world of New York publishing. Many presses now actively seek
Native American "voices," a change in attitude – mostly for the
better – that has spawned the publication of much worthy writing
in recent years. In the rarified climate of the literary world, being

"native" can be a distinct advantage; being poor and Indian on a reservation is, of course, another thing.

All the same, our categories create problems. If it is wrong to think that Indians are going to vanish anytime soon, it is equally mistaken to believe that there exists an "Indian fiction" distinctly separate from the mainstream. Many critics flex their muscles to give Indian writing a separate identity in the American mosaic – as though they were doing it a favor. Native novelists and white critics often exalt some of the common characteristics of the new Indian literature: e.g., gallows humor, bitter cultural conflict, the presence of a mediating trickster figure, the ritual use of language. The presence of "sacred" texts in Silko and Momaday, for example, parallels the role of naming as an act of invention in native creation tales – a magical moment when saying a word aloud can bring the very thing it designated into existence.

Yet for all these common features, critics must be careful how they characterize Indian fiction. Granted, certain themes may be present in Indian fiction, but they also occur in novels that belong to different traditions altogether, some not even from the West. Ralph Ellison's *Invisible Man* contains thematic features such as a trickster figure and cultural conflict, but they appear in a novel that derives ultimately from African roots and the later popular improvisations of jazz. One of the dangers in identifying literary trends is isolating writers too much, equating origins with destiny, and placing writers in a confining school. The Cult of the Minority has in some respects replaced Bloomsbury and the Algonquin Round Table. As with African American literature, the success of Indian fiction may one day be measured by the extent to which its practitioners object to being defined by an ethnic tag on a book jacket.

Cultures are more codependent than autonomous in the American grain. To imagine Momaday without the language of the Elizabethans or Erdrich without Faulkner's experiments in multiple perspective is not only difficult but impoverishing. Yet it is similarly futile to talk about Gary Snyder without the native concept of Turtle Island or Kesey's *One Flew Over the Cuckoo's Nest* (1962) without the tradition of first-person Indian narrative. Arnold Krupat has argued, in the context of autobiography, that "there simply were no Native American texts until whites decided to collaborate with Indians and make them." He is right. The public would know less about Black Elk without John Neihardt, or even the nineteenth-century Cheyenne without the fictional romp of Thomas Berger's *Little Big Man* (1964). But like the twins of traditional myths, such an admission is a half-truth if we forget that writers from Oliver LaFarge to Frank Cushing and Mary Austin have interpreted native peoples for the further enrichment of white culture – and secured formidable personal reputations in doing so.

The question of identity is crucial for "Indian writers." For most of this century, they have been people of mixed-blood parentage who have chosen – at various times in their careers – to emphasize the native side of their heritage. Given the marginalized social conditions of most Indian people, it was understandable for them to emphasize "exotic" parentage in a context where that had more value than mundane European origins. But in the current rage over "minority" writers, important questions need to be asked about the relative weight of nature and nurture, the competing influences of ethnicity and class, and the continuing temptation to "choose one's ancestors" according to the literary flavor of the day. How should we best categorize a writer – according to where she spent her formative years; whether she enrolled with a scholarship in a creative writing program; or by how the Bureau of the Census classified the racial status of her parents?

What should not be surprising is that the identity of Indian writers embraces a whole spectrum of backgrounds. One might well ask if Louise Erdrich (of German and Ojibway descent) could just as logically open Oktoberfest as a traditional pow-wow? Could Leslie Silko conceivably be seen as a "white writer" because part of her heritage is such? What keeps Acoma poet and short-story writer Simon Ortiz from being classified as "Hispanic"? Questions of ethnicity depend on context as much as blood quantum. Jamake Highwater, that renegade ethnic who claims Blackfoot/Cherokee heritage and authored a number of books and video programs about Native Americans, has already raised the issue of literary persona – much as the fabled Jewish "Chicano" of Los Angeles, Danny Santiago, did several years ago – and some in the Indian community have indignantly disowned him as a fake. But Indian is Indian, at least in the imagination of greater America. What, then, are we to do with the Ermineskin Reserve of W. P. Kinsella, a Canadian writer whose stories tell us much about reservation life north or south of the international border – and who, for the record, is "white"? As the term "Indian" becomes more difficult to define, the debate over its meaning becomes more heated.

Even the literary reputation of great chiefs from the past doesn't seem safe. In a recent controversy, the celebrated 1854 speech of Chief Seattle (Suquamish tribe) – a by now classic piece of Indian oratory – was shown to be, in part, the concoction of a writer who scripted an environmental film made in 1971. Seattle, a baptized Roman Catholic, was certainly Indian, but how many of the words we know him by he really uttered himself is something open to question. Upon closer examination, literary reputations may themselves be "cross-blood stories." From translated speeches to "as told to" autobiographies to the multicultural authors of contemporary fiction, the "Indian voice" has many facets. If American natives have "returned" at all, it is with a lot of baggage they did not seem to be carrying before they disappeared.

So the common theme encountered in the Indian western (looking for roots, seeking parents) is not simply a literary conceit. Many Indian writers of mixed ethnic background have been "born again" – with the aid of a publishing industry playing the willing midwife – to meet the new American creed of ethnic "origins." Like most publishing trends, this one is guided by a hidden ideological agenda. In the context of Indian–white relations, Momaday spoke out in the early sixties about the relative disadvantages of both "the morality of intolerance" and the "morality of pity." A good question today is how much current publishing fads derive from the impetus of white guilt. Are native people who assimilate to the majority culture as marketable as those who don't? Is the publishing world likely to represent the process of acculturation – successful military service or strong Christian belief – in its array of outspoken voices? The playful sorties of Vizenor have, in fact, been begging this question for years.

Vizenor's impish crusade has been to ask which modes of behavior are truly "Indian" and which are simply imagined as such. In early books like *Wordarrows* (1978), he confronts the dilemma of Indian identity on what he calls the "urban reservation." In one story a tribal "advocate" advises an alcoholic Indian that if she really wants to keep drinking, she should learn how to do it without feeling guilty, adopting a trickster ruse to redeem her from the web of the white social service network. In *Griever: An American Monkey King in China* (1987) Vizenor foregoes not only the rural reservation but America itself, taking his tribal trickster to the People's Republic of China, a kind of comic revenge on the Bering Strait theory that has long had Indian people moving in a one-way exodus from Asia to the Americas with nary a thought of return.

The problem of just what "Indian literature" really means has another side. If "Indian" – a collective misnomer owing to Columbus – is inadequate as a name, so is the conception of "Indian" writers as a coherent category. Much has been written in recent years about the failure of the non-Indian world to acknowledge the diversity of native peoples. Paula Gunn Allen has argued that the solution found by the eponymous hero in James Welch's *The Death of Jim Loney* (1979) is a Plains-like response that differs in kind from that of Abel in Momaday's *House Made of Dawn,* set in the Southwest. Indian literature is, she acknowledges, "multiethnic." It may be that what ties much of this writing together is a link to the land, to the wide open West and places rural. But as poet Wendy Rose has suggested, it could also be that the urban native will have the greatest claim to being "pan-Indian" in the future. Indian demographics have changed in the last generation, owing in part to the government relocation program aimed at resettling tribal peoples in urban areas and so making them more "independent." In cities like Los Angeles, Minneapolis, and Chicago, native peoples have mixed in a way that the tribal reservation system precluded. In short, the notion of "Indian" is changing.

Finally, how do national boundaries reflect contemporary ideas of ethnicity? Perhaps the hardest task will be to broaden our concept of America to include the Americas. If there is hope for a pan-Indianism – even in the literary world – it may, after looking westward, veer sharply to the south, ignoring the international border. Mexico, at least in our history, is a part of the West. If any discernible degree of Indian blood makes one "Indian," are Mexicans Juan Rulfo and Carlos Fuentes "Indian writers"? Has an "Indian" (Octavio Paz) already won the Nobel Prize for literature? Within our own borders, how are we to classify a conservative "Hispanic" writer like Richard Rodriguez – who acknowledges more than just a drop of Aztec blood? National pride aside, the Great American Indian western may ultimately come from the "south." Leslie Silko's *Almanac of the Dead,* an effort of galloping ambition inextricably tied to the West, may have been simply the first stab north of the border. As always, literary disputes reflect political ones. Maybe Navajo kids should start learning how to speak Spanish now that the North American Free Trade Agreement is in effect.

In the end, the danger is that Indianness may become, to use a phrase from Rodriguez, a "bureaucratic integer" in the calculations of the new ethnic math. It's not that the terms "Native American" – or "white" – are empty of meaning. But as terms of identity they are not as definitive as we once thought. If we are to believe the projections for the next century, AmerIndians will become, in the United States, a tiny minority dominated by other minorities – not to mention the amorphous majority called "white." Alliances of convenience (if for no other reason) may be the order of tomorrow in fashioning American political and literary success.

Ethnic arguments revolve around questions of identity and, by extension, ownership. The West is the playing ground for much of the controversy over who, exactly, owns what and who is what. There is the battle over whose history we should memorialize – why celebrate the Custer "massacre" and not the one at Wounded Knee? There is the fight over the authenticity of Indian medicine people – the followers of Harley "Swiftdeer" Reagan who practice "traditional" ways do so without proof of tribal identity. And there is the question of who owns the Black Hills – the Sioux, who had them stolen by white interlopers, or those whom they displaced only a century before – a legal battle with great ramifications for federal Indian policy and private development. "What is Indian?" and "Who is Indian?" are questions of continuing debate that ring far beyond the literary world.

Demographic trends suggest that more and more Americans of the future will perceive their place of origin in the West. In an odd twist of fate, Indian removal and migration were a foreshadowing of things to come for the white world, including the flow of electoral votes and congressional power westward, the replacing of New York by Los Angeles as the national center for immigration, and the rise of the Pacific Rim at the end of the "American Century." The rebellion of the West against eastern "convention" is an echo of the earlier American revolt against Europe. This time we can be sure that Indian writers – however they decide who they are – will have something to say about the battle.

Works Cited

Allen, Paula Gunn. "Paula Gunn Allen" (Interview). In Laura Coltelli, *Winged Words: American Indian Writers Speak*. Lincoln: U of Nebraska P, 1990, 11–39.

Black Elk. *Black Elk Speaks*. As told to John Niehardt. New York: William Morrow & Co., 1932.

Fiedler, Leslie. *The Return of the Vanishing American*. New York: Stein & Day, 1968.

Krupat, Arnold. *For Those Who Come After: A Study of Native American Autobiography*. Berkeley: U of California P, 1985.

Lawrence, D. H. *Studies in Classic American Literature*. 1923. Rpt. Baltimore: Penguin, 1971.

McNickle, D'Arcy. *The Surrounded*. 1936. Rpt. Albuquerque: U of New Mexico P, 1978.

Momaday, N. Scott. "N. Scott Momaday" (Interview). In *Winged Words*, 89–100.

————. *The Way to Rainy Mountain*. Albuquerque: U of New Mexico P, 1969.

Prucha, Francis Paul. "Presents and Delegations." In *Handbook of North American Indians*. Vol. 4. Ed. Wilcomb Washburn. Washington, D.C.: Smithsonian Institution, 1988, 238–45.

Rodriguez, Richard. "Mexico's Children." In *Days of Obligation: An Argument with My Mexican Father*. New York: Viking, 1992, 48–79.

Rose, Wendy. "Wendy Rose" (Interview). In *Winged Words*, 121–33.

Standing Bear, Luther. *My People the Sioux*. 1938. Rpt. Lincoln: U of Nebraska P, 1975.

Vizenor, Gerald. *Landfill Meditation: Crossblood Stories*. Hanover, NH: U P of New England, 1991.

————. *Wordarrows: Indians and Whites in the New Fur Trade*. Minneapolis: U of Minnesota P, 1978.

REGIONALISM MAKES GOOD:
THE SAN FRANCISCO RENAISSANCE

LINDA HAMALIAN

Not long after the Louisiana Purchase of 1803, the inexorable tide of American civilization rolled westward. Within decades countless settlements, carved from mountain and timberland, grew up and became major centers of industry and commerce. The powerful notion of manifest destiny convinced nineteenth-century Americans that the conquest of the continent was inevitable. The felling of the forest, the slaughter of indigenous wildlife, the gradual liquidation of Native Americans were all viewed as signs of progress, the triumph of civilization over savages and wilderness.

More specifically, the West became the place for some individuals to assert their freedom – artistic, political, personal, and otherwise. The city favored by these pioneers was San Francisco, both for its natural, spectacular landscape and for its newborn identity as a rough and tough place, populated by immigrants, gold diggers, hearty sailors, independent women, and more conventional types who could appreciate adventure wherever they found it. The region also attracted its fair share of writers.

However, the poets who first gravitated to the city did not shuck their allegiance to the western European traditions that had nurtured them, and drawn as they were to the natural splendor of the region, they satirized or sentimentalized it, imposing a provincial gloss that undercut the freshness of their vista. As Michael Davidson has pointed out in *The San Francisco Renaissance: Poetics and Community at Mid-Century* (1989), poets like Joaquin Miller, Ina Coolbirth, George Sterling, and Edwin Markham imported their aestheticism. Another half century passed before a regional poetry could develop, in part because it took time for Americans to comprehend the social injustice that helped the West get settled, and to develop a rebellious spirit that did not feed on destruction. The

213

future generations of poets sought to assimilate into the region rather than take it over.

An early indication of this new relationship to the region can be seen in a small publishing venture during the 1930s sponsored by the northern California branch of the Federal Writers Project. A number of writers collected essays and poems for a projected magazine, entitled *Material Gathered on the Federal Writers Project*. Its guiding principle was that the WPA should offer writers more regional journals that would not be subject to the whim of skittish advertisers. Kenneth Rexroth, who had moved to San Francisco from Chicago in 1927, was one of its moving spirits.

Under the pseudonym of J. Rand Talbot, Rexroth wrote an essay for this magazine entitled "The Possibilities of an Intelligent Regionalism in California," which argued that creative writing magazines of a regional nature would tap a large source of potential readers who were "too poor or too illiterate" to spend time and money on glossy national publications filled with stories and poems that had little to do with them. Under his own name he contributed a few poems, among them "Hiking on the Coast Range," written to commemorate the maritime General Strike of July 16, 1934, and to deplore institutionalized violence, represented here by police brutality. In "Hiking on the Coast Range," Rexroth composed lines of vivid imagery and contemplative lyricism, combining an acute observation of the natural environment with a radical social conscience.

> The skirl of the kingfisher was never
> more clear than now, nor the scream of the jay
> as the deer shifts her cover at a footfall,
> nor the wild rose-poppy ever brighter
> in the white spent wheat, nor the pain
> of a wasp stab ever an omen more sure,
> the blood alternately dark and brilliant,
> on the blue and white bandana pattern.

The poem continues in this vein, gently asserting that our moral sense cannot remain intact when we feel and see the shock of violence (thereby anticipating some contemporary psychological theories about the origin of violence). When the poem later reappeared in Rexroth's first published volume of poetry, he changed the "wild rose-poppy ever brighter/ in the white spent wheat" to a "butterfly tulip," saving the color red to emphasize bloodshed only.

In November 1936 The League of American Writers sponsored a three-day Western Writers Conference. More than 250 West Coast writers listened to papers and speeches by Upton Sinclair,

Mike Gold, John Steinbeck, William Saroyan, Budd Schulberg, Irwin Shaw, Nathanael West, and also Harry Bridges, leader of the longshoremen's union. Lectures were devoted to "The Writers in a Changing World," "Fascist Trends," "Writing and Propaganda," "Makers of Mass Neuroses," and the importance of regionalism. Writers were encouraged to identify with the region where they lived; it was agreed by many in attendance that a strong sense of place constituted one of the writer's essential tools.

These writers understood the pitfalls of promoting regional writing. In a speech delivered earlier that year at a conference of midwestern writers in Chicago, Meridel LeSueur spoke about how establishing roots to a particular geographical section of the country created confident writers and receptive audiences, but she expressed a fear of what she called "reactionary regionalism," her term for the kind of work that co-opts a region as fodder. Rexroth took this issue further in a paper he delivered at the Western Writers Conference entitled "The Function of the Poet in Society." He addressed the question of regionalism in terms of supporting artists and writers not only with money but also by providing them with local outlets for distributing their work, giving both writer and reader the opportunity to celebrate the landscape to which they were immediately connected and from which they drew their sustenance.

Rexroth longed for a system where all people would have the opportunity to appreciate the arts if they so chose. He did not want to write with what he called a divided personality enjoyed by modernist writers like Yeats and Eliot, whose poetry though "truly revolutionary in its final implications" was, in his opinion, socially ineffective. Yeats and Eliot had evolved for themselves, not necessarily for anyone else, systems of theosophy and Anglocatholicism deeply critical of middle-class values which Rexroth also held in contempt. But Rexroth believed that the way for poets to reach their audience was to stimulate a responsive literary sensibility in potential readers. If the United States was going to become truly civilized, he and his colleagues had to reach out to "all producing classes of the west," the workers and the farmers whom the country depended on, using language associated with factories, farms, and trades.

Rexroth was ultimately pleading for the recognition of regional literary magazines committed to good writing. More basically, he was stating that in order for people to tap into their creative energy, and to respect, seek, and support the art and poetry of others, they had to feel deeply connected to their own environment, neither above nor beneath it but *of* it. He tried as best he could to express this position without condescension. In a sense Rexroth was defining democracy in dynamic terms by asserting that a free country was one that nurtured and validated an artistic sensibility in all people irrespective of race, region, or class, a position that Walt Whitman had articulated more than fifty years earlier in *Democratic Vistas* but which had not been taken up by his contemporaries.

Early signs of this perspective surfaced in California's Bay Area where poetry workshops and readings became part of its quiet cultural life, giving ordinary citizens the opportunity to test their talent. As early as 1919, Witter Bynner, poet and translator of Chinese poetry, conducted classes in the Extension Division of the University of California, Berkeley. James Hart, who would become director of the Bancroft Library, also led workshops in 1936. As many as one hundred students attended James Caldwell's weekly poetry readings, which began in 1936, also on the Berkeley campus. Still, there were no major bookstores in San Francisco that could serve as meeting places for writers and their readers, and the few local publishers had little interest in poetry. In nearby Carmel, Robinson Jeffers was the sole West Coast poet with a national reputation, an isolated case, both in terms of his reputation and his relationship to the potential literary community. No local literary magazines existed. Whatever momentum had developed was dissipated temporarily with the onset of World War II.

The war, ironically enough, played a substantial role in helping to establish the Bay Area as an important literary region. Many conscientious objectors were living at the Civilian Public Service Camp at Waldport, Oregon, one of several camps established through the efforts of various churches to ensure humane treatment for conscientious objectors. Special schools were established in each of these camps and conscientious objectors could request assignment according to their particular interests. Waldport became a fine-arts center, with workshops for printers, writers, painters, musicians, and actors. Several artists from other camps transferred to Waldport, including Adrian Wilson, who became one of the foremost book designers in the country, and Martin Ponch, who brought the literary/pacifist journal *The Compass* with him from the East Coast. Fresno-born poet William Everson was there, printing *Untide,* an arts and anarchist/pacifist newsletter that served as an alternative to the official newsletter of the camp, *The Tide.* On their furloughs, the men caught the slow bus to San Francisco, where many of them would call on Rexroth, who had been there since 1927, and by the midforties had established himself as a man of letters with a volume of lyrical and political poems, *In What Hour* (1940), to his credit. When the war was over, many of the conscientious objectors settled in San Francisco and Berkeley, bringing with them the little magazines and printing presses that would help create new outlets for linking the life of the imagination with a pacifist/anarchist consciousness.

Rexroth was "at home" on Potrero Hill Friday evenings. Started as a literary soiree of sorts, this occasion turned into a regular gathering for poetry readings, philosophical discussions, and storytelling, as well as gossip and social banter. Overall, these sessions provided what Berkeley poet, professor, and scholar Thomas Parkinson described as "genuinely intellectual discussions" as well as a sense of community for Bay Area poets and philosophical anarchists. Several of the poets who attended these gatherings – among them Rexroth, Muriel Rukeyser, William Everson, Jack Spicer, Thomas Parkinson, and Robert Duncan – also attended meetings of the Libertarian Circle, a group of philosophical anarchists who met on the top floor of a house on Steiner Street. Duncan organized additional poetry readings and discussions at a rundown rooming house on Telegraph Avenue in Berkeley called Throckmorton Manor. On the Berkeley campus, Josephine Miles coordinated poetry readings and classes, some of which were conducted by her own graduate students, poets such as Jack Spicer, Robin Blaser, and Robert Duncan. In San Francisco, Madeline Gleason arranged a series of poetry readings that many Berkeley poets attended. In 1954 Ruth Witt-Diamant founded the Poetry Center at San Francisco State College; she made sure that it was funded in part with private funds so that she could schedule readings off campus for audiences disinclined to hear poetry in an academic setting. Yvor Winters attracted high-powered graduate students to his Stanford classroom, among them Thom Gunn, J. V. Cunningham, and Herbert Blau, who would become the codirector of the Actors Workshop. More informally, the literary scene could be observed in coffeehouses and clubs like the Black Cat, the Cellar, Cafe Trieste, The Place, Gino & Carlo's, and Vesuvio's.

Among the new magazines that offered a forum for postwar West Coast literary energy, *Circle* was the earliest and perhaps the best known. It was antiwar, antiauthoritarian, and committed to new art forms. Its editor, George Leite, also owned a bookstore called Daliel's, which served as another literary center, celebrating with book parties and readings the works sold there by Bay Area poets. The artwork and design were done by assistant editor Bern Porter, future publisher of Robert Duncan, Philip Lamantia, and Henry Miller. In its first issue, which was mimeographed, Leite published a prefatory statement that reflected its international scope. He declared that the journal would look particularly to Eu-

rope and the French surrealists, but he also made it clear that West
Coast writers would be fully represented on its pages. It also expressed the growing suspicion that the East Coast literary establishment would never take West Coast writers as seriously as their own,
a feeling that was confirmed as years passed. West Coast poets in
the ten published issues of the magazine included Rexroth, Lamantia, Everson, Duncan, Miles, and Kenneth Patchen. Other magazines that would contribute to the Bay Area's growing avant-garde,
politically hip reputation were *Ark, City Lights, Goad, Inferno, Golden
Goose,* and *Beatitude.*

Adding to the furor created by the new movement was an article
that appeared in the April 1947 issue of *Harper's,* "The New Cult of
Sex and Anarchy," by Mildred Edie Brady, an economist and freelance writer living in Berkeley. Claiming that her observations were
made at close range, she denigrated both the art and intellectual
activity that had emerged in the Bay Area, dividing these new
Bohemians into two camps: the Henry Millers and the Kenneth
Rexroths. Those who gravitated toward Miller did so because of his
pacifist booklet *Murder the Murderers* (1944), which he dared to
publish during the war, and because they admired his uncensored
books such as *The Colossus of Maroussi* (1941), *Sunday After the War*
(1944), and *The Air-Conditioned Nightmare* (1945), from which they
"imbibed an engaging potpourri of mysticism, egoism, sexualism,
surrealism and anarchism." This group emulated Miller's lifestyle,
living in ramshackle cabins along the coast near Monterey, about
sixty miles south of San Francisco. The members of Rexroth's
group were more bookish: they liked to discuss English anarchists
and Kropotkin, "leavening the politics liberally with psychoanalytic
interpretations from [Wilhelm] Reich," the inventor of orgone
therapy. She insisted that their poetry was incomprehensible, and
was convinced that both groups placed their faith in the irrational,
and measured their spiritual and psychological health by the number of orgasms they were capable of having. Brady's remarks
stirred a storm in the Bay Area, although not every member of the
community took her seriously. More than one suspected that now
that they had been attacked in a respectable East Coast magazine
like *Harper's,* they were sure to succeed.

For many Bay Area poets, the life of the imagination became
inextricably intertwined with political consciousness, establishing
what William Everson described in *Archetype West: The Pacific Coast
as a Literary Region* (1976) as a "distinct West Coast literary situation" where the "poet's role as *vates* was affirmed, [and] his prophetic stance as refresher and invigorator of stultified literary so-

cial forms was asserted." No attempt was made to separate poetry and politics, nor did these poets think it important to create personae to speak their poems. Significantly, many of them wanted the West Coast landscape to play a more vital role in their work than it had in the poetry of the previous generations, with the exception of Robinson Jeffers.

The dramatic setting of the West Coast infiltrated the sensibility and perception of these poets, creating a palpable background against which they could articulate philosophical and political concerns as well as highly charged emotions. They slipped into the spell of the California spaces, of its mountains, its forests, its wild terrain, and of the Pacific Ocean itself. The place created a pervasive, even comforting conviction that no artistic accomplishment could compete with the magic of this landscape. This aroused in several of these poets – particularly Rexroth, Everson, and later Gary Snyder – a sense of sacramental presence in all things, reminiscent of Walt Whitman's discovery that each particle of matter contains an immensity. Many of their poems bear the stamp of that discovery, as in the first section of Rexroth's "Toward an Organic Philosophy," entitled "Spring, Coast Range" in *In What Hour:*

> The glow of my campfire is dark red and flameless,
> The circle of white ash widens around it.
> I get up and walk off in the moonlight and each time
> I look back the red is deeper and the light smaller.
> Scorpio rises late with Mars caught in his claw;
> The moon has come before them, the light
> Like a choir of children in the young laurel trees.
> It is April; the shad, the hot headed fish,
> Climbs the rivers; there is trillium in the damp canyons;
> The foetid adder's tongue lolls by the waterfall.

Poems like this focus sharply on flora and fauna, human anatomy, and geological measurements. The settings and details serve as texts for observations about social issues, romantic love, family relationships, and personal revelations. The authenticity of these settings and details is often the bedrock of the poems themselves.

What needs to be emphasized here is that a poem like "Spring, Coast Range" ran against the grain of modernist poets and New Critics who believed that poetry should be written in an impersonal voice and should suggest layers of meaning for national discourse. Poets were not supposed to write in a personal voice, directly from their own experience. Moreover, modernists regarded regionalism as a problem: they felt that somehow poetry had to rise above what they saw as ingenuous provincialism. William Everson would argue in *Archetype West* that poets who had been relegated to minor status because they were regarded as provincial or regional, were in actuality positioned to write about cosmic reality because they had merged with their own particular world. Rexroth reiterated this position frequently: in his essay on *Leaves of Grass* in *Classics Revisited* (1968), he writes that Whitman "found his cosmogony under his heel, all about him in the most believable details of mundane existence. So his endless lists of the facts of life, which we expect to be tedious, are instead exhilarating, especially if read aloud."

This is the background for what came to be known as the San Francisco Renaissance, the literary movement that the media would have had us believe burst upon the American scene in the 1950s like a tempest. Some would argue that the more appropriate title for it would be "The Berkeley Renaissance" since so much of the activity revolved around such poets as Robin Blaser, Jack Spicer, and Robert Duncan who were graduate students and instructors at the university. As Edward Foster points out in *Jack Spicer* (1991), the movement was not really a renaissance since nothing was reborn, yet "the name seemed to call for manifestos and revolution, and indeed the poems and theories . . . changed the direction of American poetry dramatically." It represented new definitions for poetry with the hope that it might become a more egalitarian art form as well as a more experimental one.

The literature and philosophy of Japan, China, and American Indians became equal in importance to that of Europe; the natural beauty of the West Coast inspired poets and instilled within them a commitment to promote ecological sanity. Before long in this atmosphere of public concern, the concept of poetry as performance was revived and poetry/jazz became popular. Soon a Berkeley radio station, KPFA, the first listener-sponsored station in the country, was founded. It created still another outlet for poetry readings and book reviews, and enabled poets to register protest against the Korean War and the terror of McCarthyism that swept across the country in the fifties. The poets associated with this West Coast phenomenon were dearly trying to mesh their art with their lifestyle, doing their best to build a vibrant community that nurtured and supported all its inhabitants, no matter what their vocation. Since they were not a homogeneous group, tensions and ideological differences often surfaced. Nevertheless, the poets who made the Renaissance happen were extreme embodiments of the romantic spirit in their desire and determination to create a new sense of community and a pluralistic social order.

Robert Duncan, one of the true stars of this group, resisted the idea that it was an issue of regionalism that bound him to the other poets who happened to be writing in the Bay Area. For him, the word "renaissance" connoted Renaissance literature. During the mid-fifties, he was more closely associated with the Black Mountain College poets. According to Michael Davidson, Duncan felt it was coincidental that he was grouped with the San Francisco poets. For Duncan place was "an imaginative construct, the boundaries of which are constantly under revision." He felt bound less by region and more by "coterie," the particular group of poets with whom he associated, many of whom were homosexual. He would tell Ekbert Fass in an interview in *Towards a New American Poetics* (1978) that his ties were to Pound, Stein, and surrealist writers, whom he perceived as part of the Romantic continuum.

That he disclaimed ties to modernism, however, put him at home with his San Francisco colleagues, as did his interest in non-western cultures. The heterosexual Bay Area community – at least the literary community – did not think less of Duncan because he was homosexual. Moreover, Duncan assumed a similar non-hierarchical stance to his environment as a source of inspiration. In his essay "Towards an Open Universe," Duncan states that "the imagination of this cosmos is as immediate to me as the imagination of my household or my self, for I have taken my being in what I know of the sun and of the magnitude of the cosmos, as I have taken my being in what I know of domestic things." Despite his disclaimer, his poems of mystical personal quest were occasionally grounded in the western landscape, as these lines from "Apprehensions" illustrate:

To survive we conquer life or must find
dream or vision, the grandfathers' fathers' trail.
    But it was my grandfather who made that trek
after the war into the Oregon Territory
and my grandmother who entered the dragon West
    enacting what is now a map
where we crawl on hands and knees along the edge
    of the rug
to the house of the Bear Chiefs.

* * * * * *

This general optimism of the San Francisco Renaissance carried on through the mid-sixties as the city received a whole new generation of writers who wanted to write poetry of hope and responsibility –

earth poetry, so to speak, that articulated the human experience in fresh terms. Their strong sense of place became "the ground of numinous presence," as Michael Davidson describes it, a vehicle for participating "directly in ecological orders." Their intentions, however, were distorted and misunderstood for some years by the inordinate attention East Coast media gave to the Renaissance, largely in the form of sensational accounts of their frequent public readings, especially those in smoke-filled jazz clubs. The most well known of these readings took place on October 13, 1955, at the Six Gallery, an auto-repair garage on Fillmore Street below Union that had been converted into a space for displaying the work of young Bay Area artists.

The Six Gallery Reading became one of the most celebrated events in San Francisco literary history. Painter Wally Hedrick proposed that a group poetry reading be held there, and Rexroth passed on the idea to Allen Ginsberg who had been living in the Bay Area since 1953. Through Rexroth he had met many local poets including Gary Snyder, who had recently returned from a summer working on a trail crew at Yosemite National Park and resumed studying Asian languages at Berkeley. Snyder brought in Philip Whalen. Ginsberg rounded up Michael McClure and Philip Lamantia and the event was set, with Rexroth to serve as master of ceremonies. (Robert Duncan was in Majorca at the time.) Ginsberg left announcements in all the North Beach bars and sent out one hundred postcard invitations. The space – about twenty-five feet deep and twenty-feet wide with a small stage at one end – was packed that evening with an audience poets dream of.

Working the group, Jack Kerouac collected money for jugs of wine. He had been visiting Ginsberg, who was eager to show him that the cultural and political revolution about which they had rhapsodized back east was taking shape. Ginsberg read *Howl,* electrifying the audience, and stamping the occasion as a literary landmark. Between lines and verses, Kerouac and his friend Neal Cassady led cheers of appreciation. Lamantia read the poems of his late friend John Hoffman. Philip Whalen read among other poems "Plus ça Change," which Michael McClure has described as "metamorphic" because its plain language not only celebrated the ordinariness of the everyday world but helped to change that world by making poetry out of it. McClure read his elegy "For the Death of 100 Whales," deploring "the murder" of these sea mammals. McClure says that he called on D. H. Lawrence at the end to be "the tutelary figure of the past" because he admired his poignant description of whales copulating, and "his imaginings of the angels moving from body to body in the mammoth act."

For many of the San Francisco poets, first reading Lawrence was like discovering a talented contemporary. Rexroth had been an admirer of Lawrence's neglected poetry as he reveals in his introduction to Lawrence's *Selected Poems,* entitled "Poetry, Regeneration, and D. H. Lawrence." This critical manifesto was one factor that drew such poets as Duncan and Everson into Lawrence's orbit early in their careers. Rexroth articulated for them the strategies by which Lawrence entered the natural world, identified with it, and wrote about it from the inside out. Lawrence also validated for them their commitment to write erotic poetry if they so chose. Furthermore, Lawrence had been among the first English writers to explore the irrational component in the human psyche, an area that both Duncan and Everson found important for the sexual imagery of their own poetry. Lawrence had also become fascinated by the culture of the American Indian that would figure in their work. It is interesting to note here that Lawrence, of course, was not held in such high esteem by more urbanized East Coast literati.

The last poet to read at the Six Gallery was Gary Snyder, who delighted everyone with "A Berry Feast," a poem that he had written during his stay on the Warm Springs Reservation in the summer of 1950, and that was specifically inspired by a Warm Springs Indian tribal celebration called "A Berry Feast." This poem may be responsible for the label of "bearshit on the trail" poetry that sometimes gets attached to California poetry: a wilderness setting, a lone observer-speaker, a reference to a star that orients the speaker and the reader, a picturesque locale – near a creek, at the foot of a snow-capped mountain, with precise observations of the surrounding natural life, the birds, beasts, and flowers.

As Bob Stueding points out in his study of Snyder, the reader is given a "sense of the beauty, relative permanence, and superiority of the wilderness in contrast to the machinations of men." Snyder would soon leave the United States to study Buddhism in a monastery in Japan, a spiritual quest that his fellow poet and friend Philip Whalen would also undertake. Snyder returned to the United States and the West Coast (Nevada City, California) where he worked out a life for himself in which his poetry, politics, and lifestyle could merge. From the beginning, he understood and wrote lyrically about the absolute and final beauty of the mundane real. Embedding and locating his poems in particular places in western America, and taking in them an equally sensuous and chaste delight, he is explicit and detailed in recreating in himself and his readers the wonder of first knowledge. The usual, in his lyrics, is seen as the unique, the common and the human as rare. His observations are guided by the principle that it is presumptuous for human beings to regard themselves as separate from the other creatures of the universe. As an advocate in the past decade for bioregionalism, he has promoted the idea that communities should be defined by the natural boundaries of the land, not by arbitrary borders created by national treaties and city legislators.

After the Six Gallery reading, the media announced that the Beat Generation had arrived. *Howl* was the poem that got the greatest attention, and while the poem can claim San Francisco as only part of its location, its evocative, incantatory qualities, its politics, its blatantly personal style, and its openness put it at home in the Bay Area. But it is important to remember that the Beat poets did not make the San Francisco Renaissance. They were part of it, nurtured by it, in praise of it – see Kerouac's fictional account of the period, *The Dharma Bums* (1958) – but they were not all of it. With time, the label "beat poets" lost its efficacy. Rexroth's early defense of their work, his essay "Disengagement and the Art of the Beat Generation" (1957), helped define their important place in literary history, and at the same time reiterated the mission of Bay Area poets. He described these younger poets as people for whom the creative act was an effective defense against despair and hopelessness, but people who also realized that they could not keep their integrity if they also yearned for acceptance from the literary establishment. Their heroes of European civilization were not the ones sanctioned by the East Coast literary culture, but William Blake, Walt Whitman, D. H. Lawrence, and William Carlos Williams. Like those of their mentors, their own poems grew out of personal vision and everyday experience.

It is also worth noting here that the first publisher of *Howl* was Lawrence Ferlinghetti's City Lights Books. With Peter Martin, Ferlinghetti had opened the City Lights Pocket Book Shop on San Francisco's Columbus Avenue in 1953, and the store had become a popular gathering place for local writers. After Martin returned to New York City, Ferlinghetti started to implement his idea of publishing small, inexpensive editions of avant-garde poetry with the bookstore acting as a major outlet for publicity and distribution. In the United States, there was no bookstore or publisher like this that would serve people who were interested in reading serious literature but who could not afford the stiff prices attached to hardcover editions. Nor was anyone particularly concerned about finding ways to lower the cost of publication so that more poets would have a chance at getting published. Ferlinghetti managed to bring this off, and City Lights Press started publishing its Pocket Poets series in 1955, the idea behind the name being that people could carry these small volumes in their back pockets, reaching for them whenever and wherever they wanted to. This egalitarian perspective towards literature, this belief that appreciative audiences for poetry existed locally, of course, was very much in the spirit of the San Francisco Renaissance.

The first volume in the series was Ferlinghetti's *Pictures of the Gone World* (1955). In this volume, and the others that would follow, Ferlinghetti would demonstrate his interest in and talent for writing populist or street poetry that was political, dramatic, idiomatic, and meant to be read aloud to jazz accompaniment if possible. "One Thousand Fearful Words for Fidel Castro" is one that he performed particularly well at The Cellar. The opening lines illustrate his ability to disclose his politics in lines that appear to be spontaneous, down to earth, humorous and deadly serious at the same time:

> I am sitting in Mike's place trying to figure out
> what's going to happen
> without Fidel Castro
> Among the salami sandwiches and spittoons
> I see no solution
> It's going to be a tragedy
> I see no way out.

Thirty years later, the poem's concerns are eerily prescient of Cuba's current political crisis. The poem also shows that all San Francisco poets did not feel compelled to ground their work in nature. Living in western spaces where there was a recognizable audience for new kinds of poetry was enough for some to explore new boundaries of composition, whether in form or content.

The second volume in the Pocket Poets series was Rexroth's *Thirty Spanish Poems of Love and Exile* (1956); the third, Kenneth Patchen's *Poems of Humor and Protest* (1956). After the Six Gallery reading, Ferlinghetti asked Ginsberg for permission to publish *Howl*, and *Howl and Other Poems* (1956) became the fourth in the series. The book did well from the start, though at first far better in San Francisco than New York City, where several literary critics who had been Ginsberg's teachers at Columbia did not approve of his latest work. For the first edition, Ferlinghetti used an English printer, Villiers, because he respected his work and fair pricing. The second printing was seized by U.S. Customs officials in March 1957 on charges of obscenity. In the meantime, City Lights had printed a new edition, which removed it from the jurisdiction of Customs officials. In retaliation, the San Francisco Police arrested

Ferlinghetti and Shig Murao, the bookstore's manager, for selling obscene literature. After a trial that lasted nearly the entire summer, Judge Clayton Horn ruled that the book had redeeming social value and was not obscene. Many San Francisco professors and poets had testified on behalf of the defense, including Kenneth Patchen, Robert Duncan, Kenneth Rexroth, Mark Schorer (the biographer of Sinclair Lewis and a Berkeley professor), and Herbert Blau. Here was further evidence that the Bay Area had developed a strong sense of community and allegiance to its writers, even the ones in only temporary residence, and to the people who worked to disseminate art to the people.

City Lights also published four volumes of work by the now legendary Bob Kaufman, one of the original Beat poets who sometimes hung out at the Co-Existence Bagel Shop on Grant Avenue and Green Street. Essentially improvisational, his style owes something to the Surrealists' automatic writing. His poems were visionary lyrics but they were also satirical and full of social protest. Both Amiri Baraka and Ed Bullins, who spent time in the Bay Area, were influenced by Kaufman's extemporaneous technique, best seen in *Golden Sardine* (1967).

From the perspective of this last decade of the twentieth century, the writers of this period look innocent. They thought that their poetry would make the world a better place. Although these poets took the risk of sounding polemical, they often succeeded in articulating their pacifist, antiimperialist politics because they approached their writing organically, as part of a larger creative act outside of themselves. They were guided by the natural rhythms of the pulse of life, by the movement of sea and sky and stars around them, by the space created by the mountains and forests, by their region. In other words, for all the confidence they had in their political positions and determined as they were to be poets, they were humble about language and vision, aware that words and the world around them were not commodities and required respectful handling. Moreover, their willingness to experiment with ways of perception and coherence encouraged younger generations of writers to trust their fresh visions of the world.

The San Francisco Renaissance seems to have been a literary movement comprised mostly of white men. Women poets were on the scene but they did not draw the same kinds of audiences as the men, or experience the sometimes groupie-like following that the men enjoyed or endured. (The exception is Lenore Kandel, whose sensational *Howl*-like poem, "First They Slaughtered the Angels," made her briefly a cult figure in North Beach.) Helen Adam, who studied with Robert Duncan in the early fifties, revived the ballad tradition, redefined classic images of witches and shining knights in white armor with a female-identified perspective. She contributed to the growing interest in poetry as performance by singing her songs, which often had a political, anti-bourgeois edge to them. By Michael Davidson's account, her male colleagues accepted her because "she was neither poetic innovator nor sexual threat." Joanne Kyger, too, was closely associated with the Renaissance in the late fifties, and with the exception of four years in Japan in the sixties, she has made California her home. She was apparently as comfortable with Robert Duncan's circle as she was with the Beat writers. Her poetry is personal, conversational, and grounded in her everyday experiences. She did not hesitate to transform the domestic scenes of her life into poetry. She creates a poignant and tender lyric, for example, in "Of all things for you to go away mad" out of an argument she has with her companion and lover because she asked him to change his shirt after wearing it for three days. Feeling conciliatory, she prepares dinner:

> We'll sit at the table, and don't put me on, the room in my heart
> gets nourished, by your friendly handsome looks. You read a lot of books.

Muriel Rukeyser's experience had been somewhat different. She had first come to San Francisco in 1937 to celebrate the opening of the Golden Gate Bridge, and returned in the mid-forties to teach poetry at the California Labor School, where she could escape what she called the "wit writing" that was being promoted on East Coast campuses. She participated in Kenneth Rexroth's literary evenings, and became friends with Robert Duncan, poets Marie de L. Welch and Octavio Paz, and Donnan Jeffers, a son of Robinson Jeffers. Although she would return to New York in 1954, her decade in California was productive. She wrote *Orpheus* (1949), *The Green Wave* (1948), and sections of *Body of Waking* (1958).

In San Francisco, she felt encouraged to write poetry that Louise Kertesz describes as "open and direct." An excerpt from "This Place in the Ways" exemplifies her poetry of personal statement, which was passionate and idealistic and brimming with what many San Francisco poets believed was faith in their mission as poets.

> Having failed in all things
> I enter a new age
> seeing the old ways as toys,

the houses of a stage
painted and long forgot;
and I find love and rage.

Although she was very much on the scene in San Francisco during the forties, and in tune with left-wing politics and the antimodernist ethos, she believed that her ties to the San Francisco Renaissance went unrecognized because she was not, as Kertesz says, a "group person" and because, as Rukeyser acknowledged, she was a single parent at the time, always "pushing a baby carriage." But clearly she was part of it, there in the forties when all the momentum was growing.

Have the poets of the San Francisco Renaissance influenced succeeding generations? Diane Wakoski, who as an undergraduate at Berkeley studied with Thomas Parkinson, believes that this literary movement made it possible for the influence of Walt Whitman to assert itself after lying dormant under the era of the New Critics. In an essay entitled "The Birth of the San Francisco Renaissance: Something Now Called the Whitman Tradition," Wakoski points out that contemporary American poets have been able to use the autobiographical voice because this West Coast literary movement encouraged such writing. Furthermore, the onus of the term "regionalism" has now been lifted. An autobiographical poet herself, she supports her observation by citing the example of Robert Frost, whose poetry is so closely connected to New England.

> What the great success and popularity of Frost's poetry meant in the 1940s was not that he was seen as a truly American poet, a poet in the Whitman tradition, but that he was seen as a poet whose verse was so good that it transcended the things that made it American, the regional commonality of a popular language and culture.

This "regional commonality" is just what these West Coast poets hung onto, turning precise observations of the world around them into both lyrical and metaphysical verse, and allowing their poems to contain outright statements about love, politics, and their search for community and meaningful lives. Frost's poetry, also centered on nature, was of a different stripe. Properly distanced, his gnomic observations of New England life were controlled and abstracted.

Moreover, the identity of the United States was linked with the New England region; for many people, in fact, they were one and the same. With the San Francisco Renaissance, the looming homogenization of the United States was suspended. With the emergence of the West Coast as a literary center, a kind of "multiregionalism" took over, which perhaps formed a prototype for the current multiculturalism (with the old boys network short-circuited). Certainly, the flowering of countless poetry journals and small quality private presses on the West Coast, and throughout the country for that matter, has offered evidence of that. So many of the writers whose work appears on their pages anchor their work in political conscience, personal vision, and experience lived at home. They want to move into interpersonal communication, to create acts of imaginative identification between themselves and the men and women who live nearby and afar. They believe that poets are indispensable to the rediscovery of a world community and a common literary sensibility.

Works Cited

Brady, Mildred Edie. "The New Cult of Sex and Anarchy." *Harper's* (April 1947), 312–22.

Davidson, Michael. *The San Francisco Renaissance: Poetics and Community at Mid-century.* New York: Cambridge UP, 1989.

Duncan, Robert. *Roots and Branches.* New York: New Directions, 1964.

———. "Towards an Open Universe." In *Poets on Poetry.* Ed., Howard Nemerov. New York: Basic Books, 1966, 133–46.

Everson, William. *Archetype West: The Pacific Coast as Literary Region.* Berkeley: Oyez, 1976.

Ferlinghetti, Lawrence. *Starting from San Francisco.* New York: New Directions, 1961.

Foster, Edward Halsey. *Jack Spicer.* Boise, Idaho: Boise State UP, 1991.

Kertesz, Louise. *The Poetic Vision of Muriel Rukeyser.* Baton Rouge: Louisiana State UP, 1980.

Kyger, Joanne. *All This Every Day.* Bolinas, CA: Big Sky Books, 1975.

LeSueur, Meridel. *Pacific Weekly,* 16 November 1936. Qtd. in Daniel Aaron. *Writers on the Left: Episodes in American Literary Communism.* New York: Octagon Books, 1974.

McClure, Michael. *Scratching the Beat Surface.* San Francisco: North Point P, 1982.

Parkinson, Thomas. "The Poets Take Over: New Forums for Literature in the Bay Area." *The Literary Review,* 32, no. 1 (Fall 1988), 16–20.

Rexroth, Kenneth. "Walt Whitman: *Leaves of Grass.*" In *Classics Revisited.* 1968. Rpt. New York: New Directions, 1986, 249–53.

———. "The Function of the Poet in Society." In *World Outside the Window: The Selected Essays of Kenneth Rexroth.* Ed. Bradford Morrow. New York: New Directions, 1987, 1–7.

———. *In What Hour.* New York: Macmillan, 1940.

Rukeyser, Muriel. *The Green Wave.* New York: Doubleday, 1948.

Steuding, Bob. *Gary Snyder*. Boston: G. K. Hall, 1976.

Talbot, J. Rand [Kenneth Rexroth]. "The Possibility of an Intelligent Regionalism in California" (1936). Qtd. in Linda Hamalian. *A Life of Kenneth Rexroth*. New York: Norton, 1991.

Wakoski, Diane. "The Birth of the San Francisco Renaissance: Something Now Called the Whitman Tradition." *The Literary Review*, 32, no. 1 (Fall 1988), 36–41.

"THE CIRCLE ALMOST CIRCLED": SOME NOTES ON CALIFORNIA'S FICTION

JAMES D. HOUSTON

I'm going to California
Where they sleep out every night.

I'm leaving you, mama,
cause you know you don't treat me right.
  – Jimmie Rodgers, "California Blues"
       (1928)

California began as a novelist's invention. Long before it existed as a place on the map, it had a place in the mind. The idea of a legendary land glittering out there at the farthest edge of the known world was planted some two-and-a-half centuries before this coast was explored overland by Europeans. *The Adventures of Esplandian* (1510) by Garcia Ordoñez de Montalvo is a romance, a tale of chivalry and preposterous exploits carried out by a bold Spanish knight. Few people now living have read this book from start to finish, or care to. It has survived into postmodern times only because one of Esplandian's adventures takes him to a curious and exotic island ruled by a queen named Calafia. Montalvo's description seems eerily prophetic:

> Know then, that on the right hand of the Indies, there is an island called California, very close to the side of the Terrestrial Paradise, and it was peopled by black women, without any man among them, for they lived in the fashion of Amazons. They were of strong and hardy bodies, of ardent courage and great force. Their island was the strongest in all the world, with its steep cliffs and rocky shores. Their armaments

were all of gold, and so was the harness of the wild beasts which they tamed and rode. For, in the whole island, there was no metal but gold.

The book was published in Madrid in 1510, twenty-five years before Hernando Cortez sighted and named what is now the tip of lower or Baja California. The name is not Spanish. It is a Spanish-sounding word that etymologists tried for quite some time to unravel. (Could *Cali*, like *calor*, refer to heat? Could *fornia* have come from *fornax*, the Latin root for furnace?) The fact is, it's a fantastical name, much like those dreamed up by science fictionists today, for oceans and continents a million light years from earth. In all likelihood Cortez had read Montalvo's novel, since it is the only known source for the name. Even so, why would a conquistador on a mission to claim land for God and Spain depart from the Christian habit of naming newfound places for saints and holy days? John Steinbeck provides one possible explanation. In 1940 he sailed the Baja coast with his biologist mentor Ed Ricketts. In *The Log from "The Sea of Cortez"* Steinbeck describes the look of the lower peninsula:

> As we moved up the Gulf the mirage we had heard about began to distort the land. . . . As you pass a headland it suddenly splits off and becomes an island and then the water seems to stretch inward and pinch it to a mushroom-shaped cliff, and finally to liberate it from the earth entirely so that it hangs in the air.

Perhaps Cortez, sailing north from Acapulco, thought he had reached a place as strange and improbable as the island Montalvo had invented. When Juan Rodriguez Cabrillo moved the Spanish exploration farther north, pushing past what is now the Mexican border, in 1542, the name came with him.

What then does it prophesy, this vision of Montalvo's? It tells us that California is an island. It tells us it is filled with gold. It also tells us the dream came first. The place came later. His novel was a concoction that actually fed the hopes of the region's earliest explorers. And this sequence, the dream preceding the reality, has shaped the life of this region and the ways it has been perceived ever since.

California was not the first place to get this type of advance billing. Explorations of every kind have been fueled by heady visions and inflated hopes. An essential feature of the region's history is the extent to which its array of natural endowments – climate and landscape and bountiful resources – has lived up to some of the visions and fleshed out the hopes for a blessed and promised land. Fray Juan Crespi was chaplain and diarist with Gaspar de Portolá's expedition, and thus the first to write at length about the fauna and the flora and the look of the land. His diary is sprinkled with observations such as this one, from August 20, 1769, while encamped near Santa Barbara: "These heathen seem to be very well supplied with everything, especially with plenty of fish of all kinds; in fact they brought to the camp so much that it was necessary to tell them not to bring any more, for it would eventually have to spoil."

When gold was discovered in 1848, when this distant frontier actually delivered up pockets and seams of the fabled ore so many adventurers had dreamed about, the imagination of the entire world had a new touchstone. There *was* an El Dorado, after all – and the Gold Rush was to become California's formative event, politically, economically, symbolically, mythologically.

For every success story, of course, there were two or three or four stories of disillusionment, loss, or disaster, none more notorious than that of the Donner Party, a parallel event from the 1840s, or perhaps a kind of prologue, from the same mountain range. Starting too late from Missouri the expedition fell prey to squabbling along the trail, entered the Sierras well past the season when it was considered safe to cross, and found themselves caught in the early winter of 1846. It is a story not only of seekers pushed past their limits, who devour human flesh in order to survive. It is a cautionary tale from a place where the weather can turn on you in an hour, where landscape is no longer an ally or bountiful provider and where nature is an adversary, or a mentor you can never afford to take for granted.

Together these twin legends from the early years of settlement tell us that The Land of Promise is really a Land of Two Promises, where abundant possibilities and the potential for disaster coexist in the elements themselves. But that is not how the myth of California has come down to us. Even now, 150 years later, the Donner Party saga tends to get bleached out by the blinding light of the boom time so many have preferred to remember, the great example of the dream coming true. It continues to be news when things go wrong in the golden state, for a great many who live here, as well as for many who regard it from afar. The dream has come first. A grasp of the place, its habits and its hazards, tends to come later. This gap, this chasm, between expectation and reality, has provided an ongoing theme in the literature.

The California dream has seldom been promoted by serious fiction. Chambers of Commerce have done this along with popular songs, quick-draw journalism, and ad campaigns for real estate, railroads, and sports cars. One of the most influential nineteenth-century books about the West Coast was *California: For Health, Pleasure, and Residence* by Charles Nordhoff (grandfather of a later Charles Nordhoff who co-authored *Mutiny on the Bounty*). Published by Harper Brothers in 1872, this book was financed by the Southern Pacific Railroad Company, hoping to sell some of its land and pay for the new transcontinental track, and is said to have attracted more people west than any other volume of its day.

What fiction has provided time and time again is counterpoint, playing under or against the promotional copy, to explore the ironies, to look around the edges of the dream, where so many Donner Passes have lurked, right beside the seams of gold. One of the first to do so was Bret Harte, who came west from New York in 1854 and launched his career from San Francisco, writing stories about the gold country. Together with Mark Twain, Ambrose Bierce, and a few others, he helped to establish San Francisco as the first literary town west of the Mississippi. From there he edited *The Overland Monthly*, where several of his own stories first appeared, among them, in 1869, "The Outcasts of Poker Flat." This tale recounts the fate of several people forced out of a mining camp to meet their death in a snowstorm they are not at all prepared for. Reputed to be a realm of mineral wealth and rich opportunity, the high country is deceptively hostile. Harte describes the sun's look after a storm.

> It was one of the peculiarities of that mountain climate that its rays diffused a kindly warmth over the wintry landscape, as if in regretful commiseration of the past. But it revealed drift upon drift of snow piled high around the hut – a hopeless, uncharted, trackless sea of white lying below the rocky shores to which the castaways still clung.

"The Outcasts of Poker Flat" signaled many stories to come. For one thing it is an immigrant story. None of its characters have been in California more than a year or two. They are vulnerable travelers who have headed west in search of new possibilities or the second chance or to play the final card. It foreshadows the kind of story John Steinbeck would be writing a couple of generations later, a much larger and more ambitious tale of immigrants moving across the continent toward what they hope will be better times. One of America's most territorial writers, Steinbeck continues to be the most widely read novelist to emerge from California. *The Grapes of Wrath* is his masterpiece, and it is still regarded by many as the classic California novel. Since it first appeared in 1939, it has never gone out of print. In 1989 Viking Press reissued a fiftieth-anniversary hardbound edition, which was reviewed widely as a work that still speaks to us half a century later.

The first half of the novel brims with hope, as the Joads, in their pilgrimage from dustbowl Oklahoma, become the archetypal seekers. Their anticipation builds toward a radiant view of the land of promise, exactly as they have imagined it. At Tehachapi Pass Al Joad pulls off the highway and they all gaze into the lower San Joaquin Valley:

> Ruthie and Winfield scrambled down from the car, and then they stood, silent and awestruck, embarrassed before the great valley. The distance was thinned with haze, and the land grew softer and softer in the distance. A windmill flashed in the sun, and its turning blades were like a little heliograph, far away. Ruthie and Winfield looked at it, and Ruthie whispered, "It's California."

From that point onward, just about everything goes wrong. What appears to be a pastoral wonderland is in fact a world of labor battles and short housing, peopled by thousands of roaming and desperate migrant workers like themselves. By the end of the novel the Joad family is sleeping in a boxcar, watching floodwaters rise. Today we would number them among the homeless. They have no money, no food, no connections, and few prospects. If anything remains for them, it is the inextinguishable flame of the spirit. Much of this novel's holding power can be found right there, in the way Steinbeck honors the tenacity of the human spirit and the will to survive. But the region and its high promise have failed the Joads. The western earth itself has turned against them, as they watch the orchards turn to mud.

The Grapes of Wrath was published in the same year as *The Day of the Locust*, another definitive California work, which depicts another version of the embattled dream. The place is Los Angeles rather than the Central Valley; the promise betrayed is not in the fertile soil, but lodged somewhere in the mythologies of filmland. Nathanael West was in the first wave of literary writers lured to the coast by the prices being paid for scripts. Some of these writers were then lured, by the nature of the bizarre and contradictory world they had entered, to explore it in fiction, in works such as Horace McCoy's *They Shoot Horses, Don't They?* (1935), Aldous Huxley's *After Many a Summer Dies the Swan* (1939), F. Scott Fitzgerald's *The Last Tycoon* (1940), and Budd Schulberg's *What Makes Sammy Run?* (1941). In these novels, as well as in dozens that have followed, the movies merge with a titillating but doomed southern California mix of fantasy, self-delusion, excess, and eccentricity. *The Day of the Locust* was among the earliest, and many still consider it the best of the genre. Short and brutally satiric, it is peopled with tragicomic immigrants from the South and Midwest who "have come to California to die." Movie sets mirror hollow lives, while L.A./Hollywood becomes a place where the worst possibilities of the Far West find their most grotesque expression.

Throughout the novel the central character, a set designer from the East Coast named Todd Hackett, is working on a huge painting he calls "The Burning of Los Angeles." It is an apocalyptic crowd scene that shows the city in flames, a final rebellion by the frustrated and dissatisfied multitudes. In light of what erupted in South Central Los Angeles in the spring of 1992, West's book suggests that even fifty years ago some sort of volatile tension was already in the air above the city. Written in the midst of the Great Depression, it provides an eerie foreshadowing of the explosive night of fire and fury the whole world was witness to decades later. Set at the outermost edge of the continent, *The Day of the Locust* is a book about the underside of the American Dream, what happens when the dream turns sour, and how disappointment runs that much deeper when the place itself has seemed to promise opportunities that have somehow passed us by.

These two novels represent two very broad but by no means all-inclusive groupings of works that have emerged from California in this century, one urban, the other more earthy, or more closely tied to physical features the Far West has been famous for.

The cities have given us the fiction of filmland. They have also given us the hard-boiled private eye, a character type developed by Raymond Chandler in the south, and Dashiell Hammett in the north. Hammett's Continental Op and Sam Spade and Chandler's Philip Marlowe inhabit a world much different from the world that produced Sherlock Holmes or Hercule Poirot. In the detective tradition they departed from, crime was an aberration, murder will out, justice will be done, and order will probably be restored in a more or less reasonable society. In the stories of Hammett and Chandler, crime is the norm, justice is not expected, and any order is temporary because their heroes live, as Chandler writes in an introduction to a collection of his stories, "in a world gone wrong," where "the law was something to manipulate for profit and power."

A cynical, unflappable, world-weary survivor, the hard-boiled detective might have been spawned in just about any American city of the 1920s and '30s. But San Francisco and Los Angeles served as well as, if not better than, most. Both cities have baroque histories of violence and corruption inseparable from the politics and plunderings of the wide open West. And this seems to be the way Spade viewed it in 1929. "Most things in San Francisco," he remarks in *The Maltese Falcon*, "can be bought, or taken."

Among the numerous detectives who have continued prowling some of these streets there is Ross MacDonald's Lew Archer, hero of several films and some nineteen novels, such as *The Goodbye Look* (1969), *The Underground Man* (1971), and *The Blue Hammer* (1976). There is Moses Wine, hero of half a dozen books by Roger Simon, among them *The Big Fix* (1978) and *California Roll* (1985). Wine quotes Spinoza and Gail Sheehy and roams the coast from East L.A. to Silicon Valley. In James Ellroy's *White Jazz* (1992) there is police lieutenant David Klein. The hardest of the hard, he out-Spades Spade and out-Marlowes Marlowe. In these fictional cities of the West, survivors have to be toughly plated, like another L.A. police officer, Lieutenant Tom Spellacy, in John Gregory Dunne's *True Confessions* (1977), who outlives his priest-brother not because he is better or has tried harder, but because he is meaner and trusts no one. In *The Last Days of Louisiana Red* (1974), Ishmael Reed's kaleidoscopic morality play and detective-novel parody, the city is Berkeley, and it is afflicted with a malady called Louisiana Red. The symptoms are malice, bitterness, and hypocrisy. At the end the one who comes out smiling is private eye La Bas, the worldly veteran and voodoo investigator.

Meanwhile, the undefended and the vulnerable are liable to get consumed or seriously damaged. At the end of *The Day of the Locust* Todd Hackett is driven away in a police car, screaming, unable to face the mob violence outside a film premiere. And at the end of Joan Didion's *Play It As It Lays* (1971), Maria Wyeth finds herself in a sanitarium where "nothing applies." Didion's novel presents an equally harrowing view of the sun-drenched danger zone. A sometime actress, Maria does not know where films end and she begins. The book is composed of short cuts and takes, like the movies she usually thinks she's living through. She is addicted to freeways and finds there some solace in the midst of her tormented life:

She drove it as a riverman runs a river, every day more attuned to its currents, its deceptions. . . . Again and again she returned to the intricate stretch just south of the interchange where successful passage from the Hollywood onto the Harbor required a diagonal move across four lanes of traffic. On the afternoon she finally did it without once braking or once losing the beat on the radio she was exhilarated, and that night she slept dreamlessly.

Nowadays over half of California's thirty-one million people can be found in its two freeway-girded metropolitan regions, the San Francisco Bay Area and Los Angeles County. But the state is a great deal larger than that. Laid across a map of the eastern seaboard it would encompass everything from Boston to Cape Hatteras. It would include the Adirondacks and parts of Appalachia. Most of it still presents the kinds of terrain that have influenced and inspired so much of the best writing from all parts of the American West – broad fertile valleys, open desert, high wilderness, and the astonishing scale of the Coast Range, the Cascades, and the Sierras. These natural gifts have stirred writers as various as Frank Norris (*The Octopus*, 1901), Mary Austin (*The Land of Little Rain*, 1903), Jack Kerouac (*The Dharma Bums*, 1958), Wallace Stegner (*Angle of Repose*, 1971), and Ursula K. Le Guin (*Always Coming Home*, 1985). Brutal struggles for control of the land and shares of its produce have been acted out in the verdant and seductive lowlands, while the mountains rise up to test the prowess or to be endowed with deep, transformative power, sometimes sacred power.

If any single feature of the natural world has provided a distinctive theme or thrust for narrative from California, it has been the western shoreline. Much more than a thousand-mile scenic wonder, it has acquired the high symbolic role of Outer Limit and Farthest Edge, where the land ends and where dreams are put to some final test. This fateful presence has loomed in the minds of writer after writer. In "The Railroad Earth" (1957), Kerouac talks about "old Frisco with end-of-land sadness." In Steinbeck's *The Red Pony* (1937), a Salinas Valley rancher who once led a wagon train across the plains tells his grandson, "There's no place to go. There's the ocean to stop you. There's a line of old men along the shore hating the ocean because it stopped them." In *Slouching Toward Bethlehem* (1968), Joan Didion notes, "the mind is troubled by some buried but ineradicable suspicion that things had better work here, because here, beneath that immense bleached sky, is where we run out of continent."

No writer voiced this theme more passionately and deliberately than Robinson Jeffers. For him the meeting of shore and sea was a scene of wild and holy magnificence. It was also the cultural edge, where cross-continental destinies are somehow completed. He himself moved west to California from Pennsylvania in 1903, eventually settled in Carmel, and laid such powerful claim to the wind-torn Big Sur coastline that it is still referred to as Jeffers Country. His perception of it was announced in his famous early poem, "Continent's End" (1924),

> I gazing at the boundaries of granite and spray,
>   the established sea-marks, felt behind me
> Mountain and plain, the immense breadth of the continent,
>   before me the mass and doubled stretch of water.

This title helped many readers begin to grasp not only the work of Jeffers but an essential feature of this region's literature. Twenty years later the image was used by San Francisco critic and bookman Joseph Henry Jackson, to title the first significant West Coast anthology, *Continent's End: A Collection of California Writing* (including works by Jeffers, Steinbeck, Saroyan, M.F.K. Fisher, Gertrude Atherton, John Fante, and James M. Cain, among others), which Jackson edited for McGraw-Hill in 1944.

Jeffers, of course, is remembered as a poet, not a novelist. But his most ambitious work took the form of long narratives in long lines of verse: *Tamar* (1924), *Roan Stallion* (1925), *Cawdor* (1928), *Thurso's Landing* (1932), and *Give Your Heart to the Hawks* (1933). These are plotted stories, sometimes one hundred pages or more, with the weight of novellas, and with an overpowering sense of place. Like Steinbeck and Stegner, Jeffers was a regional writer in the richest sense of that word, one who manages to dig through the surface and plumb a region's deeper implications, tapping into the profound matter of how a place or a piece of territory, whatever its terms may be, can shape character, can bear upon one's sense of history and one's sense of self.

Jeffers's place happened to reverse the traditional view of western landscape. For him, at the Far West's outer edge, there were no wide open spaces. In a typical Jeffers drama the time is 1912, and there is a family inhabiting a ranch halfway up one of the steep coastal canyons that mark the long shoreline. There are horses and wagons, rifles and dogs, and some kind of trouble between the husband and the wife, or between the sons and the father. The pot of emotion and old blood feuds is stewing, and there is no escape, no way anyone can "light out for the territory." To the east, behind them, is the unforgiving wilderness of the Santa Lucia Range; to the west the surf rolls in from a boundless sea to crash at the foot of monumental headlands; the roads south and north to Monterey

are muddy and rutted and probably washed out. The landscape
then is not expansive and liberating. The coves and canyons make
enclosures that force the action. For good or for ill, the family
drama has to work itself out. Midway through *Cawdor* we see Big
Sur from overhead:

> The rain increased all night. At dawn a high sea-bird,
> If any had risen so high, watching the hoary light
> Creep down to sea, under the cloud-streams, down
> The many canyons the great sea-wall of coast
> Is notched with like a murderer's gun-stock, would have seen
> Each canyon's creek-mouth smoke its mud-brown torrent
> Into the shoring gray; and as the light gained
> Have seen the whole wall gleam with a glaze of water.

As it stands against the sea, this shoreline is a wall both glorious and
threatening. It inspires the writer to celebrate its loveliness, while it
traps his characters, physically and emblematically shaping their
fate.

This picture of the western shore has a place in the much broader picture of a continent settled from east to west, so that its meaning derives in large part from the long history of travel, migration,
and settlement that began in Europe five centuries ago. This is a
Eurocentric view that has been reinforced explicitly and implicitly
by the literature of the past 150 years or so, since until recently
most of the prominent writers associated with the West Coast have
arrived from that direction, or their ancestors did. What this large
picture tends to leave out are the waves of people who have arrived
from other directions.

For Asian American writers such as Maxine Hong Kingston,
Amy Tan, Gus Lee, David Wong Louie, Cynthia Kadohata, Hisaye
Yamamoto, and Chitra Divakaruni, history has been pushing toward this coastline eastward, from across the water. In the works of
Chicano writers such as Victor Villaseñor, Ana Castillo, Lucha Cor-
pi, Gary Soto, and José Antonio Villarreal, the coastline is not felt
much at all. For them history pushes northward, from the south,
across a border that oftentimes seems artificial, into a land some of
their forbears once held title to. In stories by American Indian
writers such as Janet Campbell Hale, Darryl Babe Wilson, Gerald
Vizenor, and Louis Owens, the ancestry pushes straight up from
the soil beneath their feet.

El Dorado was California's first large metaphor. Continent's End
was the second. In recent years a third has risen into view, as a way
of describing this region's place on the map and in the mind. Pacific

Rim suggests a circle. The term itself locates the western shoreline not at the outer edge of European expansion – or rather, not *only* there – but also on a great wheel of peoples who surround a basin, an ocean whose shores touch the South Pacific, Asia, and Latin America. The term is geographical. It also speaks to California's extraordinary cultural mix. For quite some time this has been a multicultural region, ever since 1769, when the Portolá expedition started up the coast from San Diego. But only in the past thirty years or so have we begun to have a literature that reflects the region's cultural diversity.

Maxine Hong Kingston was the first writer of Asian ancestry to appear on the front page of the *New York Times Book Review*. The occasion was *The Woman Warrior* (1976). Subtitled "A Memoir of a Girlhood Among Ghosts," this book floats between fiction and nonfiction, a compelling mix of personal memory, family history, myth, and magic. It is the story of a young woman coming of age in a valley town inland from San Francisco, much influenced by the tales and superstitions of her Chinese mother.

> After I grew up, I heard the chant of Fa Mu Lan, the girl who took her father's place in battle. Instantly I remembered that as a child I had followed my mother about the house, the two of us singing about how much Fa Mu Lan fought gloriously and returned alive from war to settle in the village. I had forgotten this chant that was once mine, given me by my mother, who may not have known its power to remind.

An old chant crosses the ocean, from a village near Canton, in south China, where the mother first heard it, to empower the daughter/writer growing up in Stockton, in the delta lands of the San Joaquin.

Later in this same book the mother goes to San Francisco to meet a sister she has not seen in thirty years. The sister's name is Moon Orchid. The mother's name is Brave Orchid. From the airport Brave Orchid is working a benevolent spell.

> She had begun this waiting at home, getting up a half-hour before Moon Orchid's plane took off in Hong Kong. Brave Orchid would add her will power to the forces that keep an airplane up. Her head hurt with concentration. The plane had to be light, so no matter how tired she felt, she dared not rest her spirit on a wing but continuously pushed up on the plane's belly. She had already been waiting at the airport for nine hours.

Brave Orchid has family lines that reach thousands of miles westward. In her mind she is reaching out across the water to keep the
plane aloft, to ensure a safe landing. For these sisters the western
shore is not the last stop, it is the first stop, the point of entry. In
their story San Francisco and south China are linked by air, by
water, and by blood.

In her third book, *Tripmaster Monkey* (1989), Kingston lays claim
to this Pacific world with a zany and visionary embrace. The central
character is a young would-be playwright/actor who lives in a small
Chinatown apartment. In the novel's early scenes he roams the
mid-1960s Bay Area, brooding, checking out landmarks and movies and parties, looking for women, and dreaming bizarre dramas
that keep his mind leaping across the ocean. His name, Wittman
Ah Sing, is one key to what this book is doing. He is named for Walt
Whitman, with a whimsical reference to "One's-Self I sing," the
exuberant opening to *Leaves of Grass*. *Tripmaster Monkey* is a book of
word-play and word playfulness, in both English and Chinese, full
of improvisation and runaway spontaneity. Wittman is also a very
literary fellow who quotes Beckett and Kerouac and some crucial
lines from Whitman's California poem, composed in 1860. From
the top of Telegraph Hill he looks north across the bay toward
Alcatraz and Angel Island, infamous holding zone for early immigrants from China.

> Wittman said a mantra for this place by the poet that
> his father had tried to name him after.
>> *Facing west from California's shores*
>> *Inquiring, tireless, seeking what is yet unfound,*
>> *I, a child, very old, over waves, toward the house*
>>   *of maternity, the land of migrations, look afar,*
>> *Look off the shores of my Western sea, the circle*
>>   *almost circled.*

This is where Kingston positions her wild-minded hero. Facing
west from California's shores, he mind-vaults across the water.

> Wittman Ah Sing wrote into the dark of the night, through
> dinner time and theater time and bar time. . . . He followed
> the music boat on courses of waterways – sailing the Long
> River across the Earth and guided by the River of Stars in the
> sky – to the mouth or the ass end of China – the Pearl River
> Delta, where American comes from.

It is a book about languages and ethnicity, and partly about
cross-cultural love, since Wittman has a white girl-friend, and they

get married, twice. He has an eccentric and affectionate family, aunties and a mother who jitterbugged their way through World War II. The novel is filled with soliloquies from the mind and the mouth and the scripts of Wittman, as he reinvents epic tales from Chinese mythology, based in large part upon classic legends of the Monkey King. At the same time he reads Rilke, and remembers popular song lyrics, and the plots of every movie he's seen. In his mandala imagination, Chinese warriors and Balinese Ranga masks lie side by side with the severed head of the famed bandido, Joaquin Murieta. In a 1988 interview Kingston said, "The Monkey King has seventy-two transformations, and of course he changes into an American, a Californian, a North Beach–Chinatown cat. He does stand-up comedy, and stand-up tragedy."

Tripmaster Monkey is not an immigrant's story, not a story of struggling to gain a foothold in the new land. Nor is it a story of being caught between cultures. Wittman's family has been here longer than most. He is a fifth-generation American of Chinese background, with a mind all his own, shaped by the assimilation of legends and lore, tastes and attitudes, details large and small from both sides of the water. His story is Kingston's attempt to give voice to a trans-Pacific consciousness, to declare the uniqueness of an ethnic identity and to do so by reveling in the originality of mind and bicultural inventions of the tripmaster/writer herself.

Is the Pacific then fiction's new frontier? Not necessarily. In the early days *frontier* was an accurate way to talk about the West. But those days are long gone. Maybe *border* is the word. The Pacific Coast is now a kind of borderland, where the continent still meets the sea, where Asia meets America, where cultures and subcultures touch, collide, and sometimes intermingle.

It is dangerous to generalize too much about this region of uncontainable variety. When Twain and Harte were writing California's first short stories, the total population was under half a million. By the early 1930s, when Steinbeck and William Saroyan began to publish, it was around six million. Sixty years later that number has increased more than fivefold, and like the life in California, literature nowadays is moving in all directions at once. This is due in part to the continuing influx of people from every background, in part to the so-called open society the Far West is noted for, and in part to the sheer multitude of writers. More writers live along the West Coast – roughly along the corridor between Mendocino and the Mexican border – than in any other part of the country, outside the similar corridor that includes Boston, New York, and Washington D.C. In and of itself this does not make the coast a worse or better, a poorer or a richer place. It does mean an abundance of fiction gets produced here, of every imaginable kind. From the Gold Rush onward, writers have been drawn to this coast-line by the action or by climate, or by the movies or a campus job. As often as not they have lived here and written about other climes, other countries, sometimes other planets and galaxies. But there continues to be a range of works that in one way or another bear upon the experiences of the West Coast, the lives lived, the dreams dreamed, the histories that have gathered here. A few more exam-ples from recent years can at least suggest some of the ways con-temporary writers have used familiar features of the literary ter-rain as points of departure, to explore the borderlands of what we see and how we see.

Al Young is a Palo Alto writer who was born in Mississippi, grew up in Detroit, and moved to the West Coast thirty years ago. In *Seduction by Light* (1988), he takes the Hollywood novel and turns it upside down, giving us a story that looks deception and betrayal in the eye, yet is free of doomsday cynicism. His heartful narrator, an African American housekeeper named Mamie Franklin, was once among the multitudes trying to make it in show business. Years earlier she came out from the South, a young singer with stars in her eyes. After marrying and leaving a fast-talking bandleader, she played in a few pictures. Now she is backstage, working for a studio producer for whom she is both cook and counselor, while her film-school son is trying to get started writing scripts.

This book is Mamie's life story, her free-wheeling view of the world and of tinseltown, a place she sees from the inside out. She knows its hazards as well as anyone, but she has not been chewed up or defeated. She has become a salty, seasoned wisdom figure. Psychic and sexy, she seduces a younger man. She reads auras. She can leave her body and return. She has long conversations with her dead husband, Burley. The first time his luminous figure appears, a week after he has been buried, she perceives a link between the spirit world and the flickering power of the silver screen that drew her and so many others out to filmland. Both are elusive and se-ductive, unreal and real. Her metaphor is light.

> I'll be doggoned if that thing didn't move up alongside the bed to where I was layin and reach out its hand and place it on my jaw. Well, anyway, I thought it was a hand and I thought it was my jaw, but somehow there really wasn't no connection. At least I didn't feel anything. The only way I can explain it would be to say it was quite a bit like bein touched by light

from a movie projector. And when you got right down to it, the whole experience was something like being in a theater that's set up to show off some newfangled, fancy, overwhelmin technical advance in motion pictures.

Carolyn See is a Southern California writer whose sixth and best novel has some things in common with the work of both Young and Kingston. In *Making History* (1991) she, too, is reaching farther westward. The story starts and ends on the outskirts of L.A., but the action touches Maui, Tokyo, Singapore, Jakarta, the Indonesian island of Komodo, and the top of Ayers Rock in central Australia. Jerry Bridges is a broker/developer, a financial wizard, who hopes to pull money in from various sources around the Rim and with it create on the beaches of New Guinea a new utopia, "Not just a resort, not just a workplace, but a new city – hotels, factories, affordable housing for the native work force, golf courses to lure Asian executives."

Jerry knows a lot about money. The trouble is, he has not been to New Guinea. See, the novelist, has an impressive sense for the feel and nuance of these many places. She knows her way around the Pacific. Jerry Bridges does not, though he travels widely. And that's part of the point. He is a well-financed American romantic whose glowing plans exceed his hands-on knowledge of the realm he hopes to package and transform.

The distance between his dream and the overseas cultural and geographical facts of life is symptomatic of how he lives. His quest for perfection is too much in his head and in his computer. His Pacific Rim vision is not shared by his family and does not include them. Even when he is home from his travels, Jerry is seldom there. Wynn Bridges married him for his money and position and the security she hoped this would bring to her two children from an earlier marriage. She is honest with herself about the very calculating way she went after him; she cannot complain too loudly about the emptiness at the center of their well-furnished Pacific Palisades life.

The female who appeals most to Jerry – though he never acts upon his desire – is his sixteen-year-old stepdaughter, Whitney. The family story centers on two gruesome highway collisions. Injured badly in the first, Whitney dies in the second. The car that kills her has come out of nowhere, an agent of death not exclusive to Southern California but in keeping with a story from car-culture headquarters. There is a lot of driving and time behind the wheel in this novel. In the larger and more openroaded West, cars and trucks still stand for freedom and release. For Didion's Maria Wyeth, the freeway provides an interval of mindless relief. For See's shattered family, the Pacific Coast Highway outside Santa Monica offers up the terrifying specter of pointless death and random chaos.

Wynn and Jerry can barely cope with this devastating loss. She withdraws, while he plunges back into his schedule. Though emotionally distant, he is not a villain. There are no villains. There are self-absorption, folly, and delusion, but these are not the culprits. See does not condemn her characters. She wants Wynn and Jerry to survive. The novelist has a kind of faith her mourning parents do not yet possess.

What saves them, and what lifts *Making History* past what it could have been – yet another version of urban overload in upscale Los Angeles – is located in a second narrative track that interweaves with the family drama. It is a track buzzing with intuitive knowledge, with uncanny synchronicities, glimpses into after-lives and prior lives, disembodied voices commenting on human blindness from the other side of death. See herself moves back and forth across the border between this life and the next, speaking through spirits that hover above the freeway. Three pages from the end, in a stunning scene, the heart of Jerry Bridges is literally opened. The spirit of his dead stepdaughter enters, to merge with his and thus revive his will to continue and to reach anew toward his grieving wife. This does not result from a moral choice or anything he has learned or done. It is presented as an act of grace.

The beguiling western landscape continues to play an essential role as habitat and as emblematic presence. Louis Owens grew up near the sources of the long Salinas River, and this foothill country is the main locale for his first novel, *The Sharpest Sight* (1992), which was selected by the University of Oklahoma Press to launch its American Indian Literature Series. In form it is a murder mystery, with skillful plotting and lots of suspects. But the place is as important as the mystery, and the true suspense is found in the lives and ancestry of the McCurtain family. Like Owens, they are mixed-blood, of Choctaw, Cherokee, and Irish descent.

The lower end of the Salinas river valley is not too far from where Steinbeck set *Of Mice and Men* (1937), *In Dubious Battle* (1936), and *East of Eden* (1952). Like Steinbeck, Owens sees tensions in the terrain that mirror those in the human drama. In the opening scenes a deputy sheriff named Mundo Morales stops on a bridge during a downpour and happens to see a body he thinks he recognizes, floating in the swollen waters. Before we see the body, we have seen what the river means to him.

It was an underground river, the largest one in California, the largest in the country, maybe the world. Most of the year it was nothing, like the people who had come to live along its banks, just a half-mile wide stretch of sand and brush and scattered trees. But in the winter and early spring, when the rains came pounding down out of the coastal mountains, the river rose out of its bed and became huge, taking everything in its path. Growing up on the edge of the river, he'd come to wait each year for the rising waters, grown to love with a kind of ache the seasonal violence when the river tried to destroy everything within reach.

The dead body is that of Attis McCurtain, who came home from Vietnam, killed a girl-friend in a fit of rage, and ended up in a state mental hospital. Morales played high-school ball with Attis and wants to know who killed him. So does Cole McCurtain, Attis's younger brother, who is soon called back to his father's homeland in Mississippi. The one who calls him is his Choctaw great-uncle Luther, a rascal and a philosopher who lives alone in a swamp-surrounded shack where panthers howl in the night. A man of many powers, he already knows about the death because the spirit-form of Attis has appeared to him. According to Luther the war was yet another symptom of a world out of synch with the laws of nature. It released something in Attis, who killed his girl and then was killed by someone else. From this, great-uncle Cole learns that his first task is not to find the killer but to find the bones of his dead brother and to bury them properly, so that his troubled spirit can be put to rest and this cycle can be stopped before another life is taken.

As the story moves back and forth between Mississippi and the coast, scenes from this classic central California community – with its oak-dotted hillsides, slow main street, sheriff's office, honky-tonk, and a lonesome woman living on a ranch outside of town – are interlaced with the spells and incantations and trickster pranks of a shaman working his powers to shape the outcome. The term "magic realism" is sometimes used to describe the stranger moments in such a story, and to separate them somehow from the everyday realism of the five agreed-upon senses. Applied here the term could be misleading. The writing in *The Sharpest Sight* suggests that Owens wants us to give equal credence to the powers of the

uncle, the poetry of the river bed, and the familiar realities of a
police procedural. At the end, Cole and his father have come to
terms with their mixed-blood heritage; they are leaving California,
heading east toward uncle Luther and the homeland. Other questions still hang in the air: How do we know the things we know?
And how wide is the range of what we call "real"?

For Ursula Le Guin the landscape of the Far West has a mythic
future, as well as a cataclysmic and legendary past. She lives in
Portland now. Born in California, she is one of those writers of
fantasy and science fiction who consistently transcend the genre.
In *Always Coming Home* (1985), she combines her skill as a futurist
with a reverent vision of the coast range five hundred years hence.
Toxic wastes and radioactivity have depleted populations. Metropolitan areas have dissolved. Computer data-banks are running in
regional Exchanges and in underground depots here and there,
storing and retrieving endless realms of information. But the Kesh
people don't access it much. They live very close to the earth, with
only a dim sense for the larger world or the rest of the continent.
They live a tribal life, and their place is called The Valley.

For Le Guin's purpose of creating a future fable with universal
resonance, this could be a valley anywhere. The accretion of detail,
the fauna and the flora, tell us very precisely where we are: red-
woods, manzanita, madrone, bluejays, geysers and hot springs,
morning fog. All the place names have changed, but from maps
included with the text we learn that their valley lies roughly north
of what is now Marin, up toward Lake county and Mendecino.

The Kesh do subsistence farming, they maintain vineyards and
trade wine for cotton grown in another valley farther south where
the people speak a different tongue. Languages are local again. All
the references, all the ways the Kesh measure and define themselves are localized. The word *Indian* is never mentioned, nor the
name of any tribe we would recognize now, but the Kesh have
somehow remembered or perhaps reinvented habits of life that tell
us they are in touch with some of the older forms of ecological
wisdom. They honor the cycles of the seasons. They are in dialogue
with the rocks, the trees, the other creatures with whom they share
this world. A generous-spirited people, for whom the words *wealth*
and *giving* are synonymous, they have worked out a low-tech style
of mutual coexistence. But this is no utopia. There is a warrior
class. Lifespans have been shortened by the after-effects of radioactivity. Repeated earthquakes have transformed major landmarks.
In-flowing waters from the Pacific have covered the end of the San

Francisco peninsula, and the central part of what used to be California is once again an inland sea.

Always Coming Home is part narrative, part ethnographic handbook, with entries on clothing, food, mating, arts and crafts, and burial rites. There are illustrations too, along with the maps, pages of ritual poetry, an alphabet, and a glossary. All these pieces combine to make the fully imagined tapestry of a postapocalyptic era. In her prologue Le Guin calls the book "An Archeology of the Future." In her long-range scenario we see how portions of the western earth have healed, or started to, while the human survivors have relearned how to be attentive to the habits of the land, which do not change that much from century to century. It is another cautionary tale, one that includes the magic of a fable, the cultural data of an anthropologist's report, and a luminous sense of place, the respect for place that has been a strong current in prose from this region since the days of John Muir.

Sense of place, of course, is a loaded term when the subject is California. It is now almost impossible to separate the places on the map from the places in the mind. Le Guin's novel is one example of how they interweave. Her affection for the terrain is projected upon an imagined landscape that may never exist; yet we somehow recognize it, while it tests our perceptions of the world we inhabit now.

California's literature has become so abundant and so various, it is ever more difficult to draw conclusions. But if there has been a defining touchpoint for the fictional imagination, it is most likely to be found somewhere in this ongoing dialogue between the regions of the earth – the bountiful endowments, from Mt. Shasta to Big Sur, from the soil of the wine country to the Kern County oil reserves – and the legend-making regions of the mind, from El Dorado onward. While the state has become a sociocultural borderland along the Pacific Rim, the California Promise continues to collide with its terrestrial realities. The famous Dream is still here, if only to be betrayed, as potent and as insistent as the coastline.

Works Cited

Chandler, Raymond. "The Simple Art of Murder." In *The Simple Art of Murder.* 1950. Rpt. New York: Ballantine, 1980, 1–21.

Crespi, Fray Juan. Diary Entry, 20 August 1769. In Herbert Eugene Bolton, *Fray Juan Crespi: Missionary Explorer of the Pacific Coast, 1769–1774.* 1927. Rpt. New York: AMS P, 1971.

Didion, Joan. "Notes from a Native Daughter." In *Slouching Towards Bethlehem.* 1968. Rpt. New York: Noonday P, 1991, 171–86.

———. *Play It As It Lays.* New York: Farrar, Straus and Giroux, 1970.

Hammett, Dashiell. *The Maltese Falcon.* New York: Knopf, 1929.

Harte, Bret. "The Outcasts of Poker Flat." In *The Outcasts of Poker Flat and Other Tales.* Ed. Wallace Stegner. New York: New American Library, 1961, 112–23.

Jeffers, Robinson. *Cawdor.* In *Cawdor and Other Poems.* 1928. Rpt. New York: Random House, 1934, 7–126.

———. "Continent's End." In *Robinson Jeffers: Selected Poems.* New York: Vintage Books, 1965.

Kerouac, Jack. "The Railroad Earth." In *Lonesome Traveler.* 1960. Rpt. New York: Grove P, 1970, 37–83.

Kingston, Maxine Hong. "Maxine Hong Kingston Introduces 'Tripmaster Monkey.'" *Humanities Network* 10, no. 4 (Spring 1988): 4.

———. *Tripmaster Monkey: His Fake Book.* New York: Knopf, 1989.

———. *The Woman Warrior: A Memoir of a Girlhood Among Ghosts.* New York: Knopf, 1976.

Le Guin, Ursula K. *Always Coming Home.* New York: Harper and Row, 1985.

Montalvo, Garcia Ordoñez de. *Las Sergas de Esplandian* (1510). Rpt. as *The Queen of California.* Trans. Edward Everett Hale. San Francisco: The Colt Press, 1945.

Owens, Louis. *The Sharpest Sight.* Norman: U of Oklahoma P, 1992.

See, Carolyn. *Making History.* Boston: Houghton Mifflin, 1991.

Steinbeck, John. *The Grapes of Wrath.* New York: Viking, 1939.

———. *The Log from the "Sea of Cortez".* New York: Viking, 1941.

———. *The Red Pony.* New York: Viking, 1945.

West, Nathanael. *The Day of the Locust. Miss Lonelyhearts & the Day of the Locust.* New York: New Directions, 1969, 59–185.

Young, Al. *Seduction By Light.* New York: Dell/Delta, 1988.

FIGHTING THE RELIGION OF THE PRESENT: WESTERN MOTIFS IN THE FIRST WAVE OF ASIAN AMERICAN PLAYS

MISHA BERSON

═══════

In 1848, the first cluster of Chinese immigrants to the United States docked in California, soon to be joined by tens of thousands more. In succeeding decades waves of newcomers from Japan, Korea, the Philippines, Hawaii, Samoa, and Southeast Asia would follow, planting new roots in American soil.

In 1989, the California-bred writer David Henry Hwang became the first Asian American playwright to win a Tony Award, the prestigious honor bestowed for achievements in Broadway theater. It was presented in honor of Hwang's hugely successful play, *M. Butterfly*, the first nonmusical drama by an Asian American author to reach Broadway.

Between 1848 and 1989 lie 150 years in which Asian immigrants, and American-born citizens of Asian ancestry, played crucial roles in the economy, culture, and social dynamic of the American West, where they predominately settled. In the literary realm, Asian Americans early on began to distinguish themselves as journalists, novelists, and poets, as well as authors of autobiographical and academic works.

Yet for a nexus of reasons, including an insidious and longstanding racism that allowed artists of color only marginal status in the national entertainment establishment, Asian American writers of Hwang's generation (he was born in 1957) and those a few years older were the first to dramatize this Asian American participation, and chart its reverberant implications.

The initial wave of important Asian American playwrights was swift and prolific, and in a sense making up for lost time. These authors seized on theater as a fruitful medium for personal and

251

political discourse. Hwang and some others also used it as a major conduit for information, insights, and questions about historical facets of the American West – facets long ignored in mainstream stage literature, but ripe for vivid dramatization. Essentially, Asian American play writing was born in the American West, and unsurprisingly, many of its recurring themes and motifs reflect dimensions of the western experience.

I will explore some of those motifs in detail later on. It is important first to build a framework for them. Within their own communities, Asian Americans had long participated in amateur theater and musical theater groups, and enthusiastically imported traditional performances from their ancestral homelands in Asia. But the early stirrings of a grassroots Asian American theater movement did not occur until the mid-1960s. It was, at the start, primarily a California phenomenon, growing stronger and more diverse as Asian Americans of differing backgrounds united to build political coalitions and express themselves collectively. During this initial phase of Asian American theater, few established mainstream drama companies were interested in producing Asian American plays, or even in casting Asian American actors in roles outside the narrow range of "Oriental" stereotypes. It was therefore left to Asian American stage artists to create their own venues: a constellation of small, nonprofit, ethnic-specific venues where they could develop plays and train actors.

The first of these grassroots institutions, the East West Players, opened in 1965 in Los Angeles – a city with a large, well-entrenched population of Asian Americans, as well as the highest concentration of actors in the country. Soon more troupes sprang up in other communities with strong Asian American components: the Asian American Theatre Workshop (later renamed the Asian American Theatre) in San Francisco, the Asian Exclusion Act (now known as the Northwest Asian American Theatre Company) in Seattle, the Kumu Kahuah in Hawaii, and the Pan Asian Repertory in New York City. These companies became alternative arenas for plays outside the dominant European American canon, and they drew an Asian American audience which had largely ignored the offerings of mainstream American theater – perhaps because it rarely spoke directly to or about them.

Asian American plays are still infrequently presented to a mass audience. However, some of the dramatists who found opportunity in these smaller venues have broken through cultural and economic barriers to get their work performed in mainstream West Coast regional theaters (the Mark Taper Forum in Los Angeles and the Berkeley Repertory Theatre in Northern California), in commercial Broadway and Off Broadway theaters, and on public television. This flowering of stage literature, in concert with the national emergence of such prominent Asian American novelists as Amy Tan and Maxine Hong Kingston, poets such as Garrett Hongo, and filmmakers such as Wayne Wang, reflects the increased visibility and volubility of a large, variegated minority group falsely stereotyped in earlier times as "passive," "quiet," and "clannish."

Japanese American playwright Philip Kan Gotanda has pointed out that the designation "Asian American" is largely an invented political term of solidarity, just as the all-purpose term "Asia" is actually a geopolitical rather than a cultural construct. Indeed, the cultures of East Asia to which first-, second-, third-, and fourth-generation Asian Americans are connected by ancestry are markedly disparate. The circumstances of immigration, too, have been strikingly various, from the sagas of the young men seeking work in California's gold fields, to the Vietnamese boat people fleeing the ravages of war in Southeast Asia, to the sons and daughters of affluent Hong Kong families seeking advanced educational and business opportunities. But the political clout that these 7.2 million individuals together can wield, as 2.9 percent of the total U.S. population (according to the 1990 census), is a binding fact. Their impact is intensified in the western states (California, Washington, and Hawaii in particular), where the percentage of Asian Americans is much higher than the national average and their relative socioeconomic and cultural effect more impressive.

But as David Henry Hwang has noted, the common ground for Asian Americans is their general reception by American society at large, which still tends to perceive people of Asian extraction as similar and interchangeable. Hwang remarked in an interview with the San Francisco Chronicle that his parents, well-educated and cosmopolitan Chinese immigrants who came to the United States from Shanghai and the Philippines, taught him to regard his Asian heritage "as a minor detail, like having red hair." But Hwang quickly learned that many of his fellow Americans saw him quite differently. He noted, "I feel very American and yet I'm often perceived as a foreigner."

For Hwang, a Southern Californian and Stanford University graduate, and for other notable Asian American playrights raised in the American West, uncovering pieces of buried or bypassed history has been a major project – a way to comprehend the racial and cultural underpinnings of the present more fully. And there has been a great deal of fascinating, revealing, and disturbing Asian American history for these writers to excavate.

In Hwang's view, examining the past is not simply a political proposition, but a spiritual imperative as well. "It seems there's a certain spiritual bankruptcy in this country which comes from an unwillingness to recognize the past," he remarks, in an interview for the book *In Their Own Words*. "Theatre throughout the world comes from ritual or a gathering of people to celebrate commonality. The fact that you get a group in one space looking at their own people doing things implies that. In this country, in this age, the way to create spiritually in the theatre is to forge a link to something further back. That's one way to deal with, to fight the religion of the present in America."

It is no accident, one might say, that the "religion of the present" is nowhere as devoutly practiced as in our final frontier, the American West.

Hwang, Gotanda, Frank Chin, Laurence Yep, Wakako Yamauchi, Genny Lim, and Velina Hasu Houston are among the better known, most widely produced and published West Coast Asian American playwrights whose work will be addressed in the remainder of this essay. Their plays, at one time or another, have considered several recurring, often intertwined, themes strongly associated with the American West: (1) the exploration, and in some instances revision, of aspects of western American history which had previously been romanticized, distorted, or ignored in mainstream accounts; (2) the deconstruction, reinterpretation, and fusion of Eastern and Western mythologies and stereotypes; and (3) the dramatization of the Asian wing of the American odyssey, as it pertains to immigrant and post-immigrant generations, individual identity, bigotry, assimilation, male-female relations, and nuclear family dynamics – themes which prominent American playwrights from numerous other ethnic backgrounds (Eugene O'Neill, Lorraine Hansberry, Clifford Odets, to name a few) have confronted in earlier stage literature, themes which appear to be central to cultural self-definition in our polyglot society.

The plays considered here are mostly (though not all) early works by these playwrights, composed primarily (but not exclusively) in the 1970s and 1980s. They display Japanese American and Chinese American, male and female, historical and contemporary perspectives on the western experience. Taken as a whole, one can find in them a composite view, a variegated and layered "reading" of the West that is in some ways markedly different, in others closely parallel, to the visions other American dramatists have given us.

* * * * * *

The anguished poetry scratched onto cell walls by Chinese newcomers who had been detained for weeks, sometimes months, by government officials on Angel Island near San Francisco, inspired Chinese American poet-playwright Genny Lim's *Paper Angels* (1980). This illuminating, heart-rending drama – premiered by the Asian American Theatre Company and later aired on public television's *American Playhouse* series – centers on a group of Chinese detainees in 1915. The detainees are men and women, young and elderly, coming to the United States from a variety of circumstances for a variety of reasons. Some of these characters do ultimately gain admittance to the society. Others are deported before ever reaching the mainland, because they fail to surmount the notoriously tough entry obstacles set forth in the "Asian Exclusion Act," a longstanding law which slowed Asian immigration to the United States to a trickle.

Asian American history is filled with such dramatically charged material. Other Chinese American playwrights have reached back farther than Lim, to the Gold Rush era of the mid-nineteenth century, when thousands of Chinese fled harsh economic conditions, drought, and political turmoil to seek work in booming pioneer California. Early on, the European American citizens of California welcomed the "Celestials," as the predominately male Chinese immigrants were called in the white press. They were branded as industrious and clannish, and prized for their willingness to do the thankless jobs many white men disdained, at wages lower than most whites would accept. Later, as economic conditions worsened in the West, distanced respect for the Chinese newcomers turned into economic resentment, and sometimes violent animosity – as witnessed and duly noted by a clear-eyed observer with the pen name Mark Twain.

In his acclaimed, Obie-winning 1981 play, *The Dance and the Railroad*, David Henry Hwang looks beyond the narrow stereotypes of early Chinese immigrants and into their multidimensional reality. He does so by imagining an evocative 1867 encounter between two "Chinamen" employed in building the transcontinental railroad lines that bisected the California Sierras.

The characters Ma and Lone (named for actors Tzi Ma and John Lone, stars of the original 1981 production of the play) function as agents of Chinese immigrant history, each with a different story to tell and embody. In China, Lone was a student of traditional Chinese Opera; in America, his regal bearing, artistic sensibility, and defiant attitude now set him apart from many of his fellow laborers. (The thrilling spectacle of Chinese opera, it should be noted, remained a popular entertainment among Chinese Americans well into the twentieth century. During the Gold Rush era, visiting troupes from Asia performed often in Chinatowns and around the California outback, appearing before predominately Chinese audiences but also a smattering of curious white viewers.)

When *The Dance and the Railroad* opens Lone is off by himself, practicing the heroic, acrobatic choreography he learned as a boy. Ma, an eager and seemingly naive colleague, seeks out Lone and begs him for acting lessons. He longs to someday play the commanding character of Gwan Gung, a legendary Chinese warrior who is a leading figure in Cantonese opera. The humorous and tense interactions between Ma and Lone, which form the crux of the play, unfold over a week's time, during a strike by Chinese railroad laborers in the Sierras for better pay and working conditions. (Such a strike actually did occur in 1861.)

In his early encounters with Ma, Lone contemptuously calls his Chinese peers undisciplined "dead men," and castigates them for toiling for white bosses and wasting their money gambling. Ma challenges that view:

> MA: They're on strike; dead men don't go on strike, Lone.
> The white devils – they try and stick us with a ten-hour day.
> We want a return to eight hours and also a fourteen-dollar-
> a-month raise. I learned the demon English – listen: "Eight
> hours a day good for white man, all same good for China-
> Man." These are the demands of live ChinaMen, Lone.
> Dead men don't complain.

Lone reluctantly agrees to coach Ma during the strike period, and their sessions take on a ritualistic, symbolic tone as the men impersonate locusts (recalling the infestations that caused famine in China) and reenact the stories of how they came to the Sierras – known to the Chinese as Gold Mountain. Lone tells of being sold by his parents to an opera company for ten years, after which his family forced him to leave for America to earn more money for his relations: "I went from a room with eighty boys to a ship with three hundred men. So you see it does not come easy playing Gwan Gung."

Later, the two men act out Ma's story of fleeing famine and chasing the dream of prosperity to California:

MA: Nothing would make my brothers angrier than seeing me rich.

LONE: Rich? After the bad crops of the last three years, even the fleas are thinking of moving south.

MA: I heard a white devil talk yesterday. . . . He said we can make our fortunes on the Gold Mountain, where work is play and the sun scares off snow.

Trading lines in a choral mode, the characters describe Ma's passage to America: 303 men pay an agent the then enormous sum of $125 for a brutal voyage. By the time they arrive 180 have died and "will not see – Our Gold Mountain dream."

The Dance and the Railroad affects audiences on numerous levels. Without a trace of the leaden exposition that afflicts many history plays, it imaginatively exposes a long-hidden aspect of pioneer California, striking chords reminiscent of other potent immigrant sagas. By invoking the strike, Hwang challenges the notion of "Chinaman" passivity. The deft mingling of historical materials with the artifice of stylized Asian theatrical movement, and of aphoristic, slightly surreal dialogue with a quasi-realistic dramatic structure (the juxtaposition of the latter two elements were influenced by the work of Sam Shepard and Irene Maria Fornes, playwrights Hwang admired and studied with) makes this an especially bracing excursion into the past.

The play's subtle reversal of the characters' attitudes about their status and mission as immigrants, and its ambiguous ending – the Chinese win their strike, but at what economic compromise and spiritual cost? – pose deep questions about personal identity as well as social equity. Embedded here as well is the image of artist as warrior, and an inquiry into what makes a hero: seeking one's own path of discipline and artistic expression? Or joining with others to take social action? It is to Hwang's credit that *The Dance and the Railroad* leaves behind more stimulating questions than firm answers.

A one-act play by Laurence Yep, *Pay the Chinaman*, employs a similar dramatic scheme to examine related concerns. It also pivots on a confrontation between two Chinese male immigrants in Northern California: an eager young greenhorn and a crusty older man. But the date is 1893, by which time the railroad was completed, California's economy had worsened, and white hostility toward the Chinese had escalated into brutal vigilante attacks, the formation of racist political parties, and the enactment of laws restricting Asian immigration.

Yep, an award-winning children's book author before he became a playwright, has noted that in the Sierras "the Chinese cooks would rent out card and board games to the lumberjacks for entertainments," and the attendant phrase "Pay the Chinaman" meant "pay up, pay the piper. I found that phrase symbolic of Chinese immigrants who managed to manipulate the American environment and come out ahead."

Though one would not guess it at first, both of the play's characters turn out to be wily cardsharps. (Yep says a major influence on the work was Herman Melville's novel, *The Confidence-Man* [1857].) The older con-man challenges the younger to a card game, and as the stakes grow increasingly higher the two reveal more about themselves – their pasts and their edgy condition as outsiders scrambling for an elusive slice of the American pie.

As in *The Dance and the Railroad*, there is a sense here of dreamers duped in the pursuit of a counterfeit dream, particularly in the older man's remembrance of how a Chinese shipping agent talked him into heading West:

> CON MAN: You'll get rich if you go. Why do you think they call it the land of the Golden Mountain? Nuggets big as your fists right there in the dirt. Just scoop 'em up. Hell, here's a tip just 'cause I like you. You find yourself a nice hill and lay down and the nuggets roll right in your palms.
>
> YOUNG MAN: Who said that?
>
> CON MAN: Last man I trusted.

The older character also expounds on his mistrust of "white demons" – white men in general, but in particular the bigoted, violent settlers of the unnamed California town where the play is set:

> CON MAN: This is the third Chinatown. First one used to be over there in the demon town. But a mob of demons burnt it down. So the Chinese built a new one on this side of the river. And the mob torched that one down. So the Chinese put up a third. Stubborn.

On the one hand *Pay the Chinaman* pays homage to the tenacity of the Chinese immigrants who persevered in such conditions. But on the other it points up the loss of self and solidarity the transition to the West exacted of these cagey survivors as the price of their survival:

YOUNG MAN: So don't ever let anyone know what you're thinking.

CON MAN: Or who you are. Or what you are. Give people a blank page and they draw their own picture.

YOUNG MAN: Do anything to hook the marks.

CON MAN: Even use your own pain.

As Yep has remarked, the toll this kind of "invisible man" endurance takes is immense: "One of the things that's almost monstrous about the young man . . . is that he denies his past and any sense of having roots. It's as if he wants to erase himself, and if you erase yourself totally there's nothing but a hole there."

* * * * * *

Dragonwings (1992), a Yep script based on his popular children's book of the same title, fills in another historical gap by reimagining the little-publicized experiments of a Chinese American airplane inventor in 1909, around the time of the Wright Brothers' early flights. This piece has elementary aims elaborately realized: to teach young audiences something about the challenges facing Chinese immigrants at the beginning of the century, and to show that there have been unsung Asian Americans worthy of admiration for their enterprise and vision. In the original Berkeley Repertory Theatre production, those points were enhanced by stagecraft that deftly melded Western realism with images and theatrical techniques from Chinese opera.

Asian American playwrights have also dramatized the oppression endured by early Chinese plantation workers in Hawaii (*Bitter Cane* [1989] by Genny Lim), the relations between Chinese immigrants and Yurok Indians in California (*Yin Chin Bow* [1986], by Cherylene Lee), the history of Filipino immigrants in the Northwest (*Oceans of Dreams* [1991] by Timoteo Cordova), and the phenomenon of popular Chinatown nightclubs in the 1940s (*Canton Jazz Club* [1991] by Tim Dang), among many documentary topics.

In the work of Japanese American dramatists, however, one historical event dwarfs all others: the U.S. government's callous 1942–45 internment of virtually every American citizen of Japanese ancestry, on the justification that they posed a security risk in the war against Japan. It took a shift of generations, and the militancy of the children and grandchildren of those interned, to reopen this dark chapter of American history forty years after the fact. But that does not mean it was forgotten or forgiven by those who lived through it. "You put 120,000 people in prison, lock them up for four years, and it's going to influence their mass psychology," suggests Philip Kan Gotanda. "Anytime I dip into the psyche of any Japanese-American character, I find the camps and the issue of racism there. Whether you deal with it explicitly or implicitly or don't talk about it at all, it's always there."

In his own plays, Gotanda has usually preferred to consider the subject obliquely. His *Song for a Nisei Fisherman*, an elegiac portrait of a Hawaiian-born doctor penned in 1980, suggests with some subtlety how the internment shattered the spirits of Japanese Americans who felt they had been punished after obeying all the rules. "It's about a man who, like my father, comes from Hawaii with an 'I can do it' attitude and puts himself through medical school," Gotanda has explained. "The American dream seems to work for him — until he reaches the camp. After that point he's never the same. He feels betrayed, and gets very confused about how he's supposed to negotiate the world."

The camp experience also serves as a subtext for the behavior of Nobu, the embittered patriarch in Gotanda's *The Wash*, a successful 1987 play filmed the following year for theatrical release and public television broadcast. A restrained, insightful look at Nobu and Masi, an estranged Stockton, California, couple in their sixties, the play uses the internment as a point of reference in their relationship. At one juncture, Nobu reminds Masi of their courtship: "Remember those dances they used to have in the Camps? You were a good dancer. You were. Best in the camps."

But Gotanda also implies that the lingering trauma of internment is at least partly responsible for Nobu's failure to accept his children's choices and understand his wife's frustration and estrangement. It also clearly has something to do with the psychological wall he retreats behind to shield himself from further pain and disappointment. At times, when trying to pull the newly independent Masi back under his control, Nobu only drives her farther away by reopening old wartime wounds. Take, for example, this exchange about the way a man named Shig is running a produce business owned originally by Masi's father:

NOBU: If I was running the store it woulda been different. Different. And your old man said he'd get me that store.

MASI: It wasn't his fault. He didn't plan on the war, Nobu.

NOBU: He promised he could set me . . .

MASI: (overlapping) It wasn't his fault.

NOBU: . . . up in business or anything else I wanted to do.

MASI: IT WASN'T HIS FAULT! (Silence.) Who wanted to be in the Relocation Camps? Did you? Do you think he wanted to be in there? It broke Papa's heart. He spent his entire life building up that farm. Papa was a proud man. A very proud man. It broke his heart when he lost it.

The play version of *The Wash* was a hit in Los Angeles, New York, and San Francisco, but it is interesting to note that some critics found the tone of the piece too understated, to the point of being dramatically monochromatic. That may be a culturally conditioned response. As Gotanda has suggested in interviews, the older Japanese American characters in the play have been socialized to suppress and hide their unpleasant feelings, a tendency the camp experience may have exacerbated.

Other writers have confronted the camp experience head-on. One notable example is *12-1-A* by Wakako Yamauchi, a California native who was interned with her Issei (first-generation Japanese American) parents at a bleak relocation camp in Poston, Arizona. The 1982 play is clearly drawn from the author's memories: It centers on the Tanaka family, including daughter Koko Tanaka – at seventeen, about the same age as Yamauchi when she was incarcerated.

12-1-A (the title refers to the address of the camp barracks to which the Tanakas are assigned) has the tone of a standard domestic melodrama. But it depicts with surprising humor and much candor a compelling and relatively untapped subject: the tensions, fears, and spirit of resistance among suddenly disempowered Japanese Americans faced with tough choices.

At one point in the story, Koko's brother Mitch (Michio) reacts to the pressure the government exerts on him and other young men in camp to join the Army. He understands that the Japanese Americans in combat units are being placed in the front lines of battle so they can "prove" their loyalty to America:

MITCH: The goddamn recruiters. It's a frame-up . . . it's a trap! They need cannon fodder! (slams his fist on the table) They got us again. . . . What does it take for us to wise up? (he grows stony) Well, I'm not falling for it. No. I'll stay right here. I'll stay here 'til I rot.

KOKO: But Mitch, if you don't say yes, they might put you in jail.

MRS. TANAKA: Jail!

MITCH: I don't care. If I say yes, they'll put me in the

frontline. They take away every right we have except the
right to be shot at. No. I'll rot here first. I'll rot.

Later the Tanakas decide to stand up against the government, in
the only way possible: by refusing to sign oaths swearing their sole
allegiance to the United States. For this courageous gesture of "No-
No" resistance (based on the real actions of numerous Japanese
Americans), they are banished to an even bleaker camp. But they
go with their heads held high and their dignity intact.

The family interdynamics of *12-1-A* place it in the abiding
American literary tradition of domestic drama. Like so many other
American playwrights of diverse ethnic origins, many Asian Amer-
ican authors have depicted the family as a microcosm, and used
intergenerational domestic conflict as a vehicle for probing over-
arching political and sociological as well as psychological concerns.
As these plays reveal the specific textures and strains of Asian
American family life, they often do so against a specifically western
American backdrop – a landscape rich in promise and
disappointment.

A relatively early, very striking example of this is Frank Chin's
brash, dark tragicomedy, *The Year of the Dragon,* which dates back to
1974. It was one of the first modern Asian American plays produced Off Broadway, as was an earlier Chin success, *Chickencoop
Chinaman* (1972). *The Year of the Dragon* was also videotaped for
public television and aired in 1975.

Set in San Francisco's Chinatown during the festive, tourist-
oriented Chinese New Year's celebration, *The Year of the Dragon*
focuses on a modern family pulling in several directions at once.
Fred Eng is a cynical, frustrated travel agent tired of putting on a
phoney pidgin accent and spouting self-deprecating Charlie Chan
jokes for his crowd-pleasing tours of Chinatown. His spiels to the
white customers he escorts alternate with scenes in the Eng home,
where Fred's elderly mother and cantankerous, dying father –
immigrants whose first language is Chinese – see the world very
differently than their children do. They want the family, and the
family travel business which has brought them respectability and
status within Chinatown, to endure.

But Fred's sister Mattie, a successful businesswoman visiting
from the East Coast with her Caucasian husband Ross, has already
broken away. She keeps some of the trappings of her Asian ancestry for commercial use (she markets Chinese food under the brand
name "Mama Fu Fu") but rejects further ethnic identification. "It
didn't matter where I was born or what color I was," she insists.

Johnny, the youngest Eng child, has taken another path entirely: He's a street kid in a tough, multiracial urban milieu, and he's beyond the control of his concerned siblings and his old world parents. He tells his brother Fred: "I got everything you ever said about Chinatown in my head. But out there is Chinatown and it's not what you talked . . . I feel like some freak of evolution here, man. I don't know what it feels like to be 'at home.'"

This is a family in disintegration, whose estranged members speak different languages, display clashing needs, and have a rough time getting through to one another. But just as disturbing as the domestic fragmentation Chin sketches is the image he paints of Chinatown as a kind of oppressive, freakish theme park. As Dorothy Ritsuko McDonald writes in her introduction to the published version of the play, "To Chin, Chinese America has lost its 'soul,' or integrity, along with its past. Chinatown is a Shangri-La, a Hollywood set, run by Christian converts. . . . Thus the Chinatown of 'The Year of the Dragon' is not what is seen by the thousands of tourists during the New Year's parade, but [a] psychological 'deathcamp.'"

In the end, the play zeroes in on Fred's struggle to define himself on his own terms apart from his father's assimilationist choices – a struggle that mirrors many another Oedipal father–son battle for power and approval played out in the American drama of O'Neill, Arthur Miller, August Wilson, Lillian Hellman, et al. But *The Year of the Dragon* makes some very specific points about the wrenching loss of a cohesive and positive ethnic identity – a bold, rugged, individualistic male identity Chin links to pioneer Chinese immigrants (railway laborers, gold miners), in a vividly romanticized Asian American Wild West. When, after a violent family confrontation, Pa Eng finally dies, Fred declares, "I woulda like to have picked him up into the Sierras and buried him by the railroad."

The phenomenon of interracial marriage, an increasingly common occurrence among Asian Americans, is a subtheme in *The Year of the Dragon* and an issue raised in numerous other Asian American family dramas. In Gotanda's *The Wash* the bitter father Nobu has a very difficult time accepting a mixed-race grandson born to his daughter Judy and her African American husband. Judy tries to explain the situation from her own perspective:

JUDY: Everyone marries out, OK? Sanseis [third-generation Japanese Americans] don't like sanseis.

NOBU: Tak's son married a Nihojin [Japanese], Shig's daughter did, your cousin Patsy . . .

JUDY: OK, OK, I didn't, I didn't, alright?

NOBU: . . . and Marsha's going to.

JUDY: But happa [multiracial kids] are the next generation, too.

NOBU: No. Japanese marry other Japanese, their kids are yonsei [fourth-generation Japanese American] – not these damn ainoko [multiracial]! (Silence.)

JUDY: You're gonna die out, you know that. You're gonna be extinct and nobody's gonna give a goddam.

Only when Nobu begins to realize that his attitudes are isolating him from human contact can he begin taking tentative steps to accept the grandchild and son-in-law he earlier spurned.

Velina Hasu Houston has considered intermarriage and family life from another angle, and in a different part of the American West, in her play *Tea*. This 1987 drama portrays five Japanese women who married American soldiers in the aftermath of World War II, and settled with their husbands in a small city in the prairie heartland of Kansas.

Wrote Houston in an introductory note to her script, "My passion for these Japanese international brides of World War II is both personal and political. An Amerasian born of America's first war with Asia, I am the daughter of one such Japanese 'war bride' and an American soldier who was half Native American Indian and half black."

To investigate the subject further, Houston interviewed 50 Japanese "war brides" still living in Kansas. She titled her play "Tea" as an evocation of the tea-drinking ritual that is such a venerable and meaningful tradition in Japan, and which has been transported to this country by the immigrant wives of the play. Houston notes that her script explores "the 'tea ceremony' of everyday life, especially for Japanese women of the prewar generation who have had to survive the barren, foreign cultural frontier of Kansas for the last 30 to 40 years."

Tea is structured as a kind of choral montage, a multilayered meditation with Himiko Hamilton's murder of her abusive husband and her subsequent suicide at the center. In the process of piecing together Himiko's story, the play also gives voice to the collective experience of four other Japanese "war brides." The actresses playing these women also assume the parts of the war brides' husbands and children.

Through a collage of voices and memories, soliloquies and exchanges, we learn that the women see themselves as double outcasts, not fully embraced by America yet ostracized as traitors by postwar Japan. They feel rejected not only by fellow Japanese and by non-Asian Americans, but also by the Japanese Americans who have just emerged from the collective nightmare of internment. Says Chizuye, one of the Japanese brides, "[Japanese Americans] are not our people. They hate us more than Americans because we remind them of what they don't want to be anymore."

Parts of *Tea* show the women enjoying the social ritual of sharing tea and visiting together. But Houston's script also emphasizes their sense of alienation from one another, and their loneliness in the face of being transplanted to this vast, boundless western space, where nuclear families are independent entities and a sense of community barely exists. This loneliness is especially acute for Himiko, who is stigmatized by her Japanese acquaintances because of her past as a dance-hall girl and shunned by whites because she is a foreigner. Her attachment to her daughter is her single vital link to another person.

In some respects, *Tea* bears feminist kinship with the much earlier play *Trifles* (1916), written by Eugene O'Neill's contemporary Susan Glaspell. In both works, we comprehend more about a woman's life by gradually understanding what led her to murder her husband. In each case, the woman has been emotionally (and probably physically) abused by her spouse, and isolated in a harsh, unfriendly western environment. For Himiko, this sort of oppression is much compounded by the cultural dislocation she endures in Kansas, and her feeling of being trapped in a hostile land – as many other Asian immigrants must have felt in a West which at first seduced, and later exploited them. Houston, however, makes it clear that the exploitation she addresses in *Tea* is specific to women. "I killed my husband because he laughed at my soy sauce just one time too many," Himiko remarks at one point, recalling with rueful humor the humiliation she endured daily. And at a later juncture she reflects: "I asked him once. I said, 'Why did you marry me?' And he said he wanted a good maid, for free."

Other plays by Asian American dramatists illuminate different dimensions of family life, in disparate families. One of the most enduring and often produced works in the genre is Wakako Yamauchi's *And the Soul Shall Dance* (1977), a haunting study of two Japanese American farm families in the Imperial Valley of California, during the Great Depression. Yamauchi pays special attention to the women in these traditionally male-dominated clans. Her most striking character is an alienated Japanese-born woman named Emiko, who is stuck in an arranged marriage on a remote farm far from the land she still considers home.

Like Himiko in *Tea,* Emiko cannot accept her stark surroundings. Nor can she meet the demands of her decent but insensitive
husband. Emiko longs to return to Japan, but has no money for the
trip, so she hides out in her own fantasy world, escaping through
drink and keeping the vision of an idealized Japan alive by listening
to old Japanese songs on the Victrola. Alone, after a dispiriting talk
with her frustrated husband, she pours a drink and tells herself:

> Because I must keep the dream alive . . . the dream is all I live
> for. I am only in exile now. Because if I give in, all I've lived
> before will mean nothing . . . will be for nothing. . . . Because
> if I let you make me believe this is all there is to my life, the
> dream would die . . . I would die . . .

This feeling of a lingering exile is a far cry from the sense of
boundless opportunity so often associated with immigration to the
American West in our national mythology. And yet the longing for
a lost culture comes up again and again in plays about Japanese
transplants to this country.

Other facets of family life are explored in the dozens of other
Asian American domestic dramas. Some well-known examples are
David Henry Hwang's 1981 comedy *Family Devotions* (which considers an affluent, Christian Chinese American family rattled by the
visit of a relative from mainland China); Ric Shiomi's *Uncle Tadao*
(1991), about a Japanese American clan struggling with the legacy
of their wartime internment in Western Canada; Filipino American
author Ernest Abuba's *An American Story* (1978), a look at a mixed
racial family led by a single mother in a waterfront slum of San
Diego; and Richard Haratani's *Inner Life* (1992), which considers
another group of newcomers to the American West − a circle of
South Vietnamese relations coming to terms with their new existence in San Francisco's rough Tenderloin district.

* * * * * *

Drawing from the rich reserves of traditional Asian mythology is
another frequent practice of Asian American dramatists. This has
also been a tactic of prominent Asian American prose writers (such
as the best-selling authors Amy Tan and Maxine Hong Kingston),
yet it has stirred heated debate within the Asian American literary
community. Frank Chin and his co-editors of *The Big AIIIEEEEE!:
An Anthology of Chinese American and Japanese American Literature*
(1991) have been harshly critical of what they feel are "Christian
assimilationist" distortions of traditional Chinese myths by Tan,
Kingston, Hwang, and others. Garrett Hongo, meanwhile, makes a

case for an imaginatively diverse, open-ended Asian American literature. In his foreword to the anthology *The Open Boat: Poems from Asian America*, Hongo writes, "Ethnic pride and an acceptance of our history do not necessarily militate against liberalities of thought."

Debate or no, mythic elements have added a heightened sense of theatricality to numerous plays by Asian American authors – even more so when images from Asian myths are presented in juxtaposition to myths of the American West. In such cases we are offered glimpses of life through double refractory lenses, glimpses which make us more aware of the complexity of our hybrid American culture.

F.O.B. (1980), a David Henry Hwang drama which preceded *The Dance and the Railroad,* makes fascinating use of a pair of mythic Chinese hero-figures in the context of modern Southern California. The play is set in a Chinese restaurant in the Los Angeles suburb of Torrance, and depicts the three-way cultural collision between Grace, a young woman minding the restaurant for her father, Grace's cousin Dale, and Steve, an F.O.B. – slang for a person who is "fresh off the boat" from China.

Steve wanders into the café seeking chong you bing (a kind of Chinese flatbread), and tells Grace he is really Gwan Gung, a fabled Chinese warrior and a hero of Cantonese operas (the same Gwan Gung whom Ma wants to play in *The Dance and the Railroad*). Grace does not believe Steve's arrogant, mysterious claims at first. But soon enough, in this energetically nonlinear script, Grace sees things differently. That's because Hwang freely alternates realistic passages with fantastic interludes, shifting and reshifting the identity of his characters and their relationships.

At several junctures Grace herself transforms into Fa Mu Lan, a young woman who (according to Chinese legend) courageously took her father's place in battle. (Hwang acknowledges borrowing his version of this female archetype from Maxine Hong Kingston's popular 1976 book, *The Woman Warrior.*) When she is not a fearless fighter, Grace shares her painful memories of growing up as a Chinese immigrant in WASP Southern California and trying unsuccessfully to "get in with the white kids" – to the point of bleaching her black hair blond. Steve slips in and out of three identities: the supremely confident Gwan Gung, a desperate and unsure Gold Rush era newcomer to America, and a stereotypical wealthy mogul from Hong Kong.

The odd person out here is Dale. A second-generation Chinese American, Dale reviles Steve, and lumps all F.O.B.s into one category of racial cliché: "Loud, stupid, four-eyed FOB. Big feet. Horny. Like Lenny of *Of Mice and Men.* . . . Someone you wouldn't want your sister to marry. If you are a sister, someone you wouldn't want to marry. . . . Before an ABC [American Born Chinese] girl would be seen on Friday night with a boy FOB in Westwood, she would rather burn off her face."

Grace is able to imagine herself in the heroic guise of Fa Mu Lan, and to eventually believe that Steve could be Gwan Gung. But the more assimilated Dale longs to succeed on purely American terms, fulfilling the Southern California myth of wealth, success, and glamour, and shedding whatever vestiges of the "F.O.B." may still cling to him. In a poignantly self-denying monologue he says:

> My parents – they don't know nothing about the world, about watching Benson at the Roxy, about ordering hors d'oeuvres at Scandia's, downshifting onto the Ventura Freeway at midnight. They're yellow ghosts and they've tried to cage me up with Chinese-ness when all the time we were in America. So, I've had to work real hard – real hard – to be myself. To not be a Chinese, a yellow, a slant, a gook. To be just a human being, like everyone else . . . I'm making it, you know? I'm making it in America.

But what is making it in America? And what kind of authenticity and depth are surrendered when you chop off all your roots and lose your ability to emulate the warriors of your ancestral collective consciousness? At the climax of the play, Grace and Steve go off to dance without Dale. But first the two share some chong you bing, in a moment of communion and cultural affirmation that honors immigrants as warriors:

> STEVE: Our hands are beautiful.
>
> GRACE: (She holds her hands next to his) What do you see?
>
> STEVE: I see the hands of warriors.
>
> GRACE: Warriors? What of gods, then?
>
> STEVE: There are no gods that travel. Only warriors travel.

Images interspersed throughout Philip Kan Gotanda's *Yankee Dawg You Die* (1986) are drawn from a mythic wellspring, one that originated in the American West: the movies. The interplay of these images gives *Yankee Dawg You Die* a double resonance. In format, it is yet another two-man encounter: a chronicle of the ambivalent friendship between two Japanese American actors in Hollywood. Vincent, in his sixties, has survived as a professional performer (and even been nominated for an Academy Award) by playing caricatured Asian American roles, getting a nose job, hiding his homosexuality, and even changing his surname from the Japanese "Nakada" to the Chinese "Chang" because it made him more saleable in Hollywood after World War II. The aspiring young turk Bradley, by contrast, came up through the politicized Asian American theater scene of the 1970s and 1980s and is out to conquer Hollywood – on his own terms, he thinks. Cocky and more than a little self-righteous, Bradley castigates the much older Vincent for selling out in "Charley Chop Suey roles," wearing "some god-damn monkey suit and kissing up to some white man" and "cutting up your face to look more white."

Vincent vigorously defends his compromises:

> "That's all there was, Bradley. That's all there was! But you don't think I would have wanted to play a better role than that bucktoothed, groveling waiter? I would have killed for a better role where I could have played an honest-to-god human being with real emotions. . . . Back then there was no Asian American consciousness, no Asian American actor, and no Asian American theaters. Just a handful of 'orientals' who for some god forsaken reason wanted to perform. . . . And we did. At church bazaars, community talent night, and on the Chop Suey Circuit playing Chinatowns and Little Tokyos around the country as hoofers, jugglers, acrobats, strippers – anything we could for anyone who would watch."

Vincent talks on, eager to put his own achievement, and the debt he believes Bradley and his peers owe pioneering Asian American actors like him, in clearer perspective: "You, you with that holier-than-thou look, trying to make me feel ashamed. You wouldn't be here if it weren't for all the crap we had put up with. We built something. We built the mountain, as small as it may be, that you stand on so proudly looking down at me."

A cross-generational dialogue as well as a pop-culture history lesson, *Yankee Dawg You Die* handles the sore subject of ethnic stereotyping with wit and adroitness. But what pushes it beyond a fairly predictable dramatic scheme (there's a role reversal at the end of this encounter, too), is Gotanda's frequent insertion of film iconography, scraps of fantasy from the Hollywood and Tokyo dream factories which have become enmeshed in the collective American psyche.

The conversations between Bradley and Vincent include frequent allusions to movie plots, and insider Hollywood gossip: it's the coin of the realm. The stage directions indicate a set with "two high-tech shoji [Japanese paper screens] for title and visual projections." In the Berkeley Repertory Theatre premiere production in 1986, some of those projections were stylized, modernistic cartoonlike paintings with Japanese themes, as well as photo images from Hollywood movies with stock Asian characters. Live action icons appear too. At one point, the destructive postnuclear dinosaur Gothra (a descendent of the Tokyo B-horror film star, Godzilla) charges on. The era of Fred Astaire and Ginger Rogers is recalled with a nostalgic song and dance tune from a fictive Asianized musical, *Tea Cakes and Moon Songs*.

Most insistent, however, is a brief scene of a broadly drawn Japanese soldier in World War II, "Sargeant Moto," speaking broken English: "You stupid American G.I. I know you try and escape. You think you can pull my leg. I speakee your language. I graduate UCLA, Class of '34. I drive big American car with big-chested American blond sitting next to . . . Heh? No, no, no, not 'dirty floor.' Listen carefully. Watch my lips. 34. 34! 34!!!"

This recurring monologue pushes a familiar racist media stereotype to the limit, but ultimately spins it around. At the play's end, Vincent repeats the speech in entirely clear English, adding plaintively, bluntly: "What is wrong with you? What the hell is wrong with you? I graduated from the University of California right here in Los Angeles. I was born and raised in the San Joaquin Valley and spent my entire life growing up in California. Why can't you hear what I'm saying? Why can't you see me as I really am?" Having just been through some humbling experiences himself in a Hollywood that has not really changed so much since Vincent's prime, Bradley comprehends the meaning of this cinematic analogy with a new maturity.

Chin, Gotanda, Hwang, Yep, Yamauchi, and Houston are part of the advance guard of modern Asian American playwrights. Newer writers (including the promising Filipino American dramatist Han Ong, and solo artist Brenda Wong Aoki, among others) are emerging in the early 1990s, with other stories to convey and different ways of imparting them. The immigrant sagas and family dramas will doubtlessly continue in some fashion. But third-, fourth-, fifth-generation Asian Americans, and newcomers who are arriving at the turn of the twentieth-first century, are facing a very different racial and social order than Asian Americans before them, and they cannot help but produce dramas of altered texture. Meanwhile, Hwang, Gotanda, and their contemporaries are moving on, away from the resurrection of history and the well-made family play, toward other comedic and dramatic explorations in theater, as well as in films and television. Hwang has pointed out that a topic which now demands urgent consideration is the strained relations and economic competition between different minority groups on the American scene. This was vividly exemplified in the African American–Asian American tensions which helped to fan the flames of the 1992 riots in South Central Los Angeles.

One thing that can certainly be expected from the current crop of Asian American dramatists, and from those that succeed them, is that many of their plays will be rooted in the American West – the American West of the imagination, the American West of desire and promise and disappointment, the American West of the twentieth century and the century before and beyond it. And for any comprehensive understanding of what that place is or was or will become, their stories must be told and their voices heard.

Works Cited

Chan, Jeffery Paul, Frank Chin, Lawson Fusao Inada, and Shawn Wong, eds. *The Big* AIIIEEEEE!: *An Anthology of Chinese American and Japanese American Literature*. New York: Meridian/Penguin, 1989, xi–xvi.

Chin, Frank. *The Year of the Dragon. The Chickencoop Chinaman and The Year of the Dragon: Two Plays by Frank Chin*. Seattle: U of Washington P, 1981, 67–142.

Gotanda, Philip Kan. Qtd. in Misha Berson. "Gotanda's Plays Explore Lives of Asian-Americans." *American Theatre Magazine* (September 1988), 54–55.

————. *The Wash*. In *Between Worlds: Contemporary Asian-American Plays*. Ed. Misha Berson. New York: Theatre Communications, 1990, 30–73.

————. *Yankee Dawg You Die*. New Dramatists' Plays. New York: Playwrights' P, 1986.

Hongo, Garrett. "Introduction." *The Open Boat: Poems from Asian America*. Ed. Garrett Hongo. New York: Anchor Books/Doubleday, 1993, xvii–xli.

Houston, Velina Hasu. *Tea*. Plays in Process Series. Vol. 9, no. 5. New York: Theatre Communications Group, 1987.

Hwang, David Henry. Qtd. in Patrick Pacheco, "David Hwang's 'M. Butterfly' Alights in S. F." *San Francisco Chronicle*. "Datebook," 4 August 1991, 20.

————. "David Hwang" (Interview). In *In Their Own Words: Contemporary American Playwrights*. Ed. David Savran. New York: Theatre Communications Group, 1988, 117–31.

————. *F.O.B. F.O.B. and Other Plays*. New York: New American Library, 1990, 1–50.

————. *The Dance and the Railroad. F.O.B. and Other Plays*, 51–86.

McDonald, Dorothy Ritsuko. "Introduction." Chin, *Chickencoop Chinaman and The Year of the Dragon*, ix–xxix.

Yamauchi, Wakako. *And the Soul Shall Dance.* In *Between Worlds*, 127–74.

———. *12-1-A.* In *The Politics of Life: Four Plays by Asian American Women.* Ed. Velina Hasu Houston. Philadelphia: Temple U P, 1993, 33–100.

Yep, Laurence. *Pay the Chinaman.* In *Between Worlds*, 176–96.

SELECTED BIBLIOGRAPHY

The following bibliography lists anthologies of western American literature and book-length critical studies (or important single essays) that address that writing. The anthologies listed that do not focus exclusively on some aspect of western writing do, nevertheless, include a significant representation of western American authors. Likewise, the critical works listed that do not focus exclusively on western writing contain meaningful discussions of some aspect of that writing. Historical works have been included only when they contain significant discussions of western literature.

Single-author studies and biographies have not been included unless their scope goes significantly beyond their individual subject. Nor have annotated bibliographies been listed below. Those looking for bibliographies on individual authors should consult Fred Erisman and Richard W. Etulain, eds., *Fifty Western Writers: A Bibliographical Sourcebook* (Westport, CT: Greenwood P, 1982); Geoff Sadler, ed., *Twentieth-Century Western Writers*, 2nd ed. (Chicago: St. James P, 1991); or the *Western Writers Series* published by Boise State University Press, which features short, comprehensive pamphlets on dozens of individual western writers. Yearly listings of current critical work on western writing can also be found in the winter issue of the journal *Western American Literature*. Richard W. Etulain and N. Jill Howard's *Bibliographical Guide to the Study of Western American Literature*, 2nd ed. (Albuquerque: U of New Mexico P, 1995) remains an extremely useful bibliographic sourcebook.

Because important criticism of western American literature appears in works classified by region as well as by multiethnic designations and by special subject matter (e.g., popular westerns and environmental writing), I have utilized several different bibliographical categories to suggest the full variety of critical approaches now being used to study the literature of the American West.

Reference Works

Lamar, Howard R., ed. *The Reader's Encyclopedia of the American West.* New York: Thomas Y Crowell Co., 1977.

Milner, Clyde A., et al., eds. *The Oxford History of the American West.* Oxford UP, 1994.

Tuska, John, and Vicki Piekarski. *Encyclopedia of Frontier and Western Fiction.* New York: McGraw-Hill, 1983.

Anthologies

Allen, Paula Gunn, ed. *Spider Woman's Granddaughters: Traditional Tales and Contemporary Writing by Native American Women.* Boston: Beacon, 1989.

Anaya, Rudolfo A., ed. *Voces: An Anthology of Nuevo Mexicano Writers.* Albuquerque: El Norte Publications, 1987.

Apple, Max, ed. *Southwest Fiction.* New York: Bantam, 1981.

Applegate, Shannon, and Terence O'Donnell, eds. *Talking on Paper: An Anthology of Oregon Letters and Diaries.* Corvallis: Oregon State UP, 1994.

Augenbraum, Harold, and Ilan Stavans, eds. *Growing Up Latino: Memoirs and Stories.* Boston: Houghton Mifflin, 1993.

Barclay, Donald A., James H. Maguire, and Peter Wild, eds. *Into the Wilderness Dream: Exploration Narratives of the American West, 1500–1805.* Salt Lake City: U of Utah P, 1994.

Barnes, Kim, and Mary Clearman Blew, eds. *Circle of Women: An Anthology of Contemporary Western Women Writers.* New York: Penguin, 1994.

Bartlett, Mary Dougherty, ed. *The New Native American Novel: Works in Progress.* Albuquerque: U of New Mexico P, 1986.

Beckham, Stephen Dow, ed. *Many Faces: An Anthology of Oregon Autobiography.* Corvallis: Oregon State UP, 1993.

Bergon, Frank. *The Wilderness Reader.* New York: New American Library, 1980.

Berson, Misha, ed. *Between Worlds: Contemporary Asian-American Plays.* Theatre Communications Group, 1990.

Blackburn, Alexander, Craig Lesley, and Jill Landem, eds. *The Interior Country: Stories of the Modern West.* Athens, OH: Swallow P/Ohio UP, 1987.

Blackburn, Alexander, and C. Kenneth Pellow, eds. *Higher Elevations: Stories from the West: A "Writers' Forum" Anthology.* Athens, OH: Swallow P/Ohio UP, 1993.

Bright, William, ed. *A Coyote Reader.* Berkeley: U of California P, 1993.

Busby, Mark, ed. *New Growth/2: Contemporary Short Stories by Texas Writers.* San Antonio, TX: Corona Pub. Co., 1993.

Carlson, Roy, ed. *Contemporary Northwestern Writing: A Collection of Poetry and Fiction.* Corvallis, OR: Oregon State UP, 1979.

Cattarulla, Kay, ed. *Texas Bound: 19 Texas Stories.* Dallas: Southern Methodist UP, 1994.

Caughey, John and Laree, eds. *California Heritage: An Anthology of History and Literature*. Los Angeles: Ward Ritchie, 1962.

Chan, Jeffery Paul, et al., eds. *The Big AIIIEEEEE!: An Anthology of Chinese American and Japanese American Literature*. New York: Meridian/Penguin, 1991.

Chock, Eric, et al., eds. *Talk Story: An Anthology of Hawaii's Local Writers*. Honolulu: Petronium P and Talk Story, 1978.

Chock, Eric, and Darrell H. Y. Lum, eds. *The Best of Bamboo Ridge: The Hawaii Writers' Quarterly*. Honolulu: Bamboo Ridge P, 1986.

Clow, Deborah, and Donald Snow, eds. *Northern Lights: A Selection of New Writing from the American West*. New York: Vintage, 1994.

Davidson, Levette Jay, ed. *Poems of the Old West*. Denver: U of Denver P, 1951.

Davidson, Levette Jay, and Prudence Bostwick, eds. *The Literature of the Rocky Mountain West, 1803–1903*. 1939. Rpt. Port Washington, D.C.: Kennikat P, 1970.

Day, A. Grove, ed. *Great California Stories*. Lincoln: U of Nebraska P, 1991.

Dodds, Gordon, ed. *Varieties of Hope: An Anthology of Oregon Prose*. Corvallis: Oregon State UP, 1993.

Hedin, Robert, and Gary Holthaus, eds. *Alaska: Reflections on Land and Spirit*. Tucson: U of Arizona P, 1989.

———, eds. *The Great Land: Reflections on Alaska*. Tucson: U of Arizona P, 1994.

Egli, Ida Rae, ed. *No Rooms of Their Own: Women Writers of Early California*. Berkeley: Heydey Books, 1992.

Eisen, Jonathan, and David Fine, eds. *Unknown California*. New York: Collier Books, 1985.

Evers, Larry, ed. *The South Corner of Time: Hopi, Navajo, Papago, and Yaqui Tribal Literature*. Tucson: U of Arizona P, 1980.

Faulkner, Virginia, ed. *Roundup: A Nebraska Reader*. Lincoln: U of Nebraska P, 1957.

González, Ray, ed. *After Aztlan: Latino Poets of the Nineties*. Boston: Godine, 1992.

———, ed. *Crossing the River: Poets of the Western U.S.* Sag Harbor, NY: Permanent P, 1987.

———, ed. *Mirrors Beneath the Earth: Short Fiction by Chicano Writers*. Willimantic, CT: Curbstone P, 1992.

Graham, Don, ed. *South by Southwest: 24 Stories from Modern Texas*. Austin: U of Texas P, 1986.

Grant, Lyman, ed. *New Growth: Contemporary Short Stories by Texas Writers*. San Antonio, TX: Corona Pub. Co., 1989.

Greenberg, Martin, ed. *Great Stories of the American West*. New York: Donald I. Fine, 1994.

Griffin, Shaun T., ed. *Desert Wood: An Anthology of Nevada Poets*. Reno: U of Nevada P, 1991.

Hagedorn, Jessica, ed. *Charlie Chan Is Dead: An Anthology of Contemporary Asian American Fiction*. New York: Penguin, 1993.

Haslam, Alexandra R., and Gerald W. Haslam, eds. *Where Coyotes Howl and Wind Blows Free: Growing Up in the West.* Reno: U of Nevada P, 1995.

Haslam, Gerald W., ed. *Many Californias: Literature from the Golden State.* Reno: U of Nevada P, 1991.

Hemesath, James B., ed. *Where Past Meets Present: Modern Colorado Short Stories.* Niwot, CO: UP of Colorado, 1994.

Hillerman, Tony, ed. *The Best of the West: An Anthology of Classic Writing from the American West.* New York: HarperCollins, 1991.

Hiura, Arnold, Stephen Sumida, and Martha Webb, eds. *Talk Story: Big Island Anthology.* Honolulu: Bamboo Ridge P and Talk Story, 1979.

Hongo, Garrett, ed. *The Open Boat: Poems from Asian America.* New York: Anchor Books/Doubleday, 1993.

Houston, James D., ed. *West Coast Fiction: Modern Writing from California, Oregon and Washington.* New York: Bantam, 1979.

Houston, Velina Hasu. *The Politics of Life: Four Plays by Asian American Women.* Philadelphia: Temple UP, 1993.

Huerta, Jorge, ed. *Necessary Theater: Six Plays About the Chicano Experience.* Houston: Arte Público P, 1989.

Jones, Suzi, and Jarold Ramsey, eds. *The Stories We Tell: An Anthology of Oregon Folk Literature.* Corvallis: Oregon State UP, 1994.

Jordan, Grace, ed. *Idaho Reader.* Boise: Syms-York, 1963.

Jordan, Teresa, and James R. Hepworth, eds. *The Stories That Shape Us: Contemporary Women Write About the West.* New York: Norton, 1995.

Kittredge, William, and Annick Smith, eds. *The Last Best Place: A Montana Anthology.* 1988. Rpt. Seattle: U of Washington P, 1991.

Kroeber, Theodora. *The Inland Whale: Nine Stories Retold from California Indian Legends.* Bloomington: U of Indiana P, 1959.

Lee, W. Storrs, ed. *Washington State: A Literary Chronicle.* New York: Funk & Wagnalls, 1969.

Lerner, Andrea, ed. *Dancing on the Rim of the World: An Anthology of Contemporary Northwest Native American Writing.* Tucson: U of Arizona P, 1990.

Lesley, Craig, and Katheryn Stavrakis, eds. *Dreamers and Desperadoes: Contemporary Short Fiction of the American West.* New York: Dell, 1993.

———, eds. *Talking Leaves: Contemporary Native American Short Stories.* New York: Laurel, 1991.

López, Tiffany Ana, ed. *Growing Up Chicana/o: An Anthology.* New York: William Morrow, 1993.

Love, Glen A., ed. *The World Begins Here: An Anthology of Oregon Short Fiction.* Corvallis: Oregon State UP, 1993.

Lucia, Ellis, ed. *This Land Around Us.* Garden City, NY: Doubleday, 1969.

Lyon, Thomas J., and Peter Stine, eds. *On Nature's Terms: Contemporary Voices.* College Station: Texas A & M UP, 1992.

Lyon, Thomas J., and Terry Tempest Williams, eds. *Great and Peculiar Beauty: A Utah Reader.* Salt Lake City: Gibbs Smith, 1995.

Maguire, James H., ed. *The Literature of Idaho: An Anthology.* Boise: Boise State University, 1986.

Margolin, Malcolm, ed. *The Way We Lived: California Indian Stories, Songs and Reminiscences.* Berkeley: Heyday Books, 1993.

Martin, Russell, ed. *New Writers of the Purple Sage: An Anthology of Contemporary Western Writers.* New York: Penguin Books, 1992.

Martin, Russell, and Marc Barash, eds. *Writers of the Purple Sage: An Anthology of Recent Western Writing.* New York: Penguin Books, 1984.

McFarland, Ronald E., and William Studebaker, eds. *Idaho Poetry: A Centennial Anthology.* Moscow, ID: U of Idaho P, 1989.

McNamee, Gregory, ed. *Named in Stone and Sky: An Arizona Anthology.* Tucson: U of Arizona P, 1993.

Michaels, Leonard, David Reid, and Raquel Scherr, eds. *West of the West: Imagining California.* New York: HarperPerennial, 1989.

Monaghan, Patricia, ed. *Hunger and Dreams: The Alaskan Women's Anthology.* Fairbanks, Alaska: Fireweed P, 1983.

Murray, John A., ed. *Nature's New Voices.* Golden, CO: Fulcrum, 1992.

———, ed. *A Republic of Rivers: Three Centuries of Nature Writing from Alaska and the Yukon.* New York: Oxford UP, 1990.

Niatum, Duane, ed. *Harper's Anthology of Twentieth-Century Native American Poetry.* San Francisco: Harper & Row, 1988.

Peery, William, ed. *21 Texas Short Stories.* Austin: U of Texas P, 1954.

Pukui, Mary Kawena, and Alfons L. Korn, eds. and trans. *The Echo of Our Song: Chants and Poems of the Hawaiians.* Honolulu: U of Hawaii P, 1973.

Ramsey, Jarold, ed. *Coyote Was Going There: Indian Literature of the Oregon Country.* Seattle: U of Washington P, 1977.

Rebolledo, Tey Diana, Erlinda Gonzales-Berry, and Teresa Márquez, eds. *Las Mujeres Hablan: An Anthology of Nuevo Mexicana Writers.* Albuquerque: El Norte Publications, 1989.

Rebolledo, Tey Diana, and Eliana S. Rivero, eds. *Infinite Divisions: An Anthology of Chicana Literature.* Tucson: U of Arizona P, 1993.

Riley, Patricia, ed. *Growing Up Native American: An Anthology.* New York: William Morrow, 1993.

Sarris, Greg, ed. *The Sound of Rattles and Clappers: A Collection of New California Indian Writers.* Tucson: U of Arizona P, 1994.

Schneider, Franz, et al., eds. *Deep Down Things: Poems of the Inland Pacific Northwest.* Pullman: Washington State UP, 1990.

Seelye, John, ed. *Stories of the Old West: Tales of the Mining Camp, Cavalry Troop, and Cattle Ranch.* New York: Penguin, 1994.

Simmen, Edward, ed. *North of the Rio Grande: The Mexican-American Experience in Short Fiction.* New York: Penguin, 1992.

Skelton, Robin, ed. *Five Poets of the Pacific Northwest.* Seattle: U of Washington P, 1964.

Smelcer, John E., and D. L. Birchfield, eds. *Durable Breath: Contemporary Native American Poetry.* Anchorage: Salmon Run P, 1994.

Smith, Anne M., ed. *Ute Tales.* Salt Lake City: U of Utah P, 1992.

Soto, Gary, ed. *California Childhood: Recollections and Stories of the Golden State.* Berkeley: Creative Arts Book Co., 1988.

————, ed. *Pieces of the Heart: New Chicano Fiction.* San Francisco: Chronicle Books, 1993.

Stewart, Frank, ed. *Passages to the Dream Shore: Short Stories of Contemporary Hawaii.* Honolulu: U of Hawaii P, 1987.

Stewart, Frank, and John Unterecker, eds. *Poetry Hawaii: A Contemporary Anthology.* Honolulu: U of Hawaii P, 1979.

Studebaker, William, and Rick Ardinger, eds. *Where the Morning Light's Still Blue: Personal Essays About Idaho.* Moscow, U of Idaho P, 1994.

Tatum, Charles M., ed. *New Chicana/Chicano Writing 1.* Tucson: U of Arizona P, 1992.

————, ed. *New Chicana/Chicano Writing 2.* Tucson: U of Arizona P, 1992.

————, ed. *New Chicana/Chicano Writing 3.* Tucson: U of Arizona P, 1993.

Thomas, James, and Denise Thomas, eds. *Best of the West 5: New Stories from the Wide Side of the Missouri.* New York: Norton, 1992.

————, eds. *Best of the West 4: New Stories from the Wide Side of the Missouri.* New York: Norton, 1991.

————, eds. *Best of the West 3: New Short Stories from the Wide Side of the Missouri.* Salt Lake City: Peregrine Smith, 1990.

————, eds. *Best of the West 2: New Short Stories from the Wide Side of the Missouri.* Salt Lake City: Peregrine Smith, 1989.

————, eds. *Best of the West: New Short Stories from the Wide Side of the Missouri.* Salt Lake City: Peregrine Smith, 1988.

Trafzer, Clifford E., ed. *Earth Song, Sky Spirit: Short Stories of the Contemporary Native American Experience.* New York: Anchor Books, 1993.

Tuska, Jon, ed. *The American West in Fiction.* 1982. Rpt. Lincoln: U of Nebraska P, 1988.

Valdez, Luis, and Stan Steiner, eds. *Aztlán: An Anthology of Mexican-American Literature.* New York: Knopf, 1972.

Wendt, Ingrid, and Primus St. John, eds. *From Here We Speak: An Anthology of Oregon Poetry.* Corvallis: Oregon State UP, 1993.

West, Ray B., Jr., ed. *Rocky Mountain Reader.* New York: Dutton, 1946.

Wild, Peter, ed. *The Desert Reader: Descriptions of America's Arid Regions.* Salt Lake City: U of Utah P, 1991.

Work, James C., ed. *Prose and Poetry of the American West.* Lincoln: U of Nebraska P, 1990.

General Criticism

Ainsworth, Len, and Kenneth W. Davis, eds. *The Catch-Pen: A Selection of Essays from the First Two Years of the National Cowboy Symposium and Celebration.* Lubbock, TX: The Ranching Heritage Center, 1991.

Allmendinger, Blake. *The Cowboy: Representations of Labor in an American Work Culture.* New York: Oxford UP, 1992.

Athearn, Robert G. *The Mythic West in Twentieth-Century America.* Lawrence: UP of Kansas, 1986.

Bakker, Jan. *The Role of the Mythic West in Some Representative Examples of*

Classic and Modern American Literature: The Shaping of the American Frontier. Lewiston, NY: Edwin Mellen P, 1991.

Bennion, Sherilyn Cox. *Equal to the Occasion: Women Editors of the Nineteenth-Century West.* Reno: U of Nevada P, 1990.

Berkhofer, Robert F. Jr. *The White Man's Indian: Images of the American Indian from Columbus to the Present.* New York: Vintage, 1978.

Billington, Ray Allen. *Land of Savagery, Land of Promise: The European Image of the American Frontier in the Nineteenth Century.* New York: Norton, 1981.

Bredahl, A. Carl, Jr. *New Ground: Western American Narrative and the Literary Canon.* Chapel Hill: U of North Carolina P, 1989.

Calder, Jenni. *There Must Be a Lone Ranger: The Myth and Reality of the American Wild West.* 1974. Rpt. London: Abacus, 1976.

Calvin, Ross. *Sky Determines: An Interpretation of the Southwest.* 1934. Rpt. Albuquerque: U of New Mexico P, 1975.

Dahood, Karen, ed. *The Golden West: The Literature of Comprehension.* Tucson: Arizona Historical Society, 1983.

Davidson, Arnold E. *Coyote Country: Fictions of the Canadian West.* Durham: Duke UP, 1994.

Durham, Phillip, and Everett L. Jones. *The Western Story: Fact, Fiction and Myth.* New York: Harcóurt Brace Jovanovich, 1975.

Engel, Leonard, ed. *The Big Empty: Essays on Western Landscapes as Narrative.* Albuquerque: U of New Mexico P, 1994.

Etulain, Richard W., ed. *The American Literary West.* Manhattan, KS: Sunflower UP, 1980.

Everson, William. *Archetype West.* Berkeley: Oyez, 1976.

Faas, Ekbert, ed. *Towards a New American Poetics: Essays and Interviews.* Santa Barbara: Black Sparrow P, 1978.

Fender, Stephen. *Plotting the Golden West: American Literature and the Rhetoric of the California Trail.* Cambridge: Cambridge UP, 1981.

Fiedler, Leslie. *The Return of the Vanishing American.* New York: Stein & Day, 1968.

Folsom, James K. *The American Western Novel.* New Haven: Yale UP, 1966.

Franklin, Wayne, and Michael Steiner, eds. *Mapping American Culture.* Iowa City: U of Iowa P, 1992.

Fussell, Edwin S. *Frontier: American Literature and the American West.* Princeton: Princeton UP, 1965.

Greenfield, Bruce. *Narrating Discovery: The Romantic Explorer in American Literature, 1790–1855.* New York: Columbia UP, 1992.

Grossman, James R., ed. *The Frontier in American Culture.* Newberry Library and Berkeley: U of California P, 1994.

Gurian, Jay. *Western American Writing: Tradition and Promise.* Deland, FL: Everett/Edwards, 1975.

Haines, John. *Living Off the Country: Essays on Poetry and Place.* Ann Arbor: U of Michigan P, 1981.

Harrison, Dick. *Crossing Frontiers: Papers in American and Canadian Western Literature.* Edmonton: U of Alberta P, 1979.

Haslam, Gerald, ed. *Western Writing*. Albuquerque: U of New Mexico P, 1974.

Hazard, Lucy Lockwood. *The Frontier in American Literature*. New York: Thomas Y. Crowell, 1927.

Heyne, Eric, ed. *Desert, Garden, Margin, Range: Literature on the American Frontier*. New York: Twayne, 1992.

Holthaus, Gary, et al., eds. *A Society to Match the Scenery: Personal Visions of the Future of the American West*. Niwot, CO: UP of Colorado, 1991.

Hyde, Anne Farrar. *An American Vision: Far Western Landscape and National Culture, 1820–1920*. New York: New York UP, 1990.

Kolodny, Annette. *The Land Before Her: Fantasy and Experience of the American Frontiers, 1630–1860*. Chapel Hill: U of North Carolina P, 1984.

Lee, L. L., and Merrill Lewis, eds. *Women, Women Writers, and the West*. Troy, NY: Whitston, 1979.

Lee, Robert Edson. *From West to East: Studies in the Literature of the American West*. Urbana: U of Illinois P, 1966.

Levin, David. *History as Romantic Art: Bancroft, Prescott, Motley and Parkman*. Stanford: Stanford UP, 1959.

Love, Glen A. *New Americans: The Westerner and the Modern Experience in the American Novel*. Lewisburg, PA: Bucknell UP, 1982.

Lutwack, Leon. *The Role of Place in Literature*. Syracuse: Syracuse UP, 1984.

Maguire, James H. "Fiction of the West." In *The Columbia History of the American Novel*. Emory Elliott, ed. New York: Columbia UP, 1991, 437–64.

Meldrum, Barbara Howard, ed. *Old West – New West: Centennial Essays*. Moscow, ID: U of Idaho P, 1993.

———, *Under the Sun: Myth and Realism in Western American Literature*. Troy, NY: Whitston, 1985.

Milton, John R. *The Novel of the American West*. Lincoln: U of Nebraska P, 1980.

———, ed. *Three West: Conversations with Vardis Fisher, Max Evans [and] Michael Straight*. Vermillion, SD: Dakota P, 1970.

Mitchell, Lee Clark. *Witnesses to a Vanishing America: The Nineteenth-Century Response*. Princeton: Princeton UP, 1981.

Mogen, David, et al., eds. *The Frontier Experience and the American Dream: Essays on American Literature*. College Station: Texas A & M UP, 1989.

Morris, Gregory L., ed. *Talking Up a Storm: Voices of the New West*. Lincoln: U of Nebraska P, 1995.

Namias, June. *White Captives: Gender and Ethnicity on the American Frontier*. Chapel Hill: U of North Carolina P, 1993.

Pearce, Roy Harvey. *Savagism and Civilization: A Study of the Indian and the American Mind*. 1953. Rpt. Berkeley: U of California P, 1988. Originally published as *The Savages of America: A Study of the Indian and the Idea of Civilization*.

Pilkington, William T., ed. *Critical Essays on the Western American Novel*. Boston: G. K. Hall, 1980.

Poulsen, Richard C. *The Landscape of the Mind: Cultural Transformations of the American West.* New York: Peter Lang, 1992.

———. *The Mountain Man Vernacular: Its Historical Roots, Its Linguistic Nature, and Its Literary Uses.* New York: Peter Lang, 1985.

Prown, Jules David, et al. *Discovered Lands, Invented Pasts: Transforming Visions of the American West.* New Haven: Yale UP, 1992.

Ring, Frances, ed. *A Western Harvest: The Gatherings of an Editor.* San Francisco: John Daniel, 1991.

Schlissel, Lillian, Vicki L. Ruiz, and Janice Monk, eds. *Western Women: Their Land, Their Lives.* Albuquerque: U of New Mexico P, 1988.

Simonson, Harold P. *The Closed Frontier: Studies in American Literary Tragedy.* New York: Holt, Rinehart & Winston, 1970.

———. *Writers, Western Regionalism and a Sense of Place.* Fort Worth: Texas Christian UP, 1989.

Slotkin, Richard. *The Fatal Environment: The Myth of the Frontier in the Age of Industrialization, 1800–1890.* New York: Atheneum, 1985.

———. *Gunfighter Nation: The Myth of the Frontier in Twentieth-Century America.* New York: Atheneum, 1992.

———. *Regeneration Through Violence: The Mythology of the American Frontier, 1600–1860.* Middletown, CT: Wesleyan UP, 1973.

Smith, Henry Nash. *Virgin Land: The American West as Symbol and Myth.* Cambridge: Harvard UP, 1950.

Sonnichsen, Charles L. *From Hopalong to Hud: Thoughts on Western Fiction.* College Station, TX: Texas A & M UP, 1978.

Stauffer, Helen Winter, and Susan J. Rosowski, eds. *Women and Western American Literature.* Troy, NY: Whitston, 1982.

Stegner, Wallace. *The Sound of Mountain Water: The Changing American West.* Garden City, NY: Doubleday and Co., 1969.

———. *Where the Bluebird Sings to the Lemonade Springs: Living and Writing in the West.* New York: Random House, 1992.

Stegner, Wallace, and Richard W. Etulain, *Conversations with Wallace Stegner on Western History and Literature.* Rev. ed. Salt Lake City: U of Utah P, 1990.

Steiner, Stan. *The Waning of the West.* New York: St. Martin's P, 1989.

Taylor, Cynthia Hinkel. "Out of Bounds: Women Writers and the Western Landscape." Dissertation, University of Minnesota, 1993.

Taylor, J. Golden, et al., eds. *A Literary History of the American West.* Fort Worth: Texas Christian UP, 1987.

Truettner, William H., ed. *The West as America: Reinterpreting Images of the Frontier, 1820–1920.* Washington, DC: Smithsonian Institution P, 1991.

Turner, Frederick. *Beyond Geography: The Western Spirit Against the Wilderness.* 1980. Rpt. New Brunswick, NJ: Rutgers UP, 1992.

———. *Spirit of Place: The Making of an American Literary Landscape.* Washington, DC: Island Press, 1989.

Udall, Stewart L., et al. *Beyond the Mythic West.* Salt Lake City: Peregrine Smith Books, in association with the Western Governors Association, 1990.

Whipple, T. K. *Study Out the Land.* Berkeley: U of California P, 1943.

White, G. Edward. *The Eastern Establishment and the Western Experience: The West of Frederic Remington, Theodore Roosevelt, and Owen Wister.* New Haven: Yale UP, 1968.

Worster, Donald. *Unsettled Country: Changing Landscapes of the American West.* Albuquerque: U of New Mexico P, 1994.

Popular Westerns

Bold, Christine. *Selling the Wild West: Popular Western Fiction, 1860–1960.* Bloomington: Indiana UP, 1987.

Cawelti, John G. *Adventure, Mystery, and Romance: Formula Stories as Art and Popular Culture.* Chicago: U of Chicago P, 1976.

———. *The Six-Gun Mystique.* Bowling Green, OH: Bowling Green U Popular P, 1971.

Davis, Robert Murray. *Playing Cowboys: Low Culture and High Art in the Western.* Norman: U of Oklahoma P, 1992.

Etulain, Richard W., and Michael T. Marsden, eds. *The Popular Western: Essays Toward a Definition.* Bowling Green, OH: Bowling Green U Popular P, 1974.

Folsom, James K., ed. *The Western: A Collection of Critical Essays.* Englewood Cliffs, NJ: Prentice-Hall, 1979.

Jones, Daryl. *The Dime Novel Western.* Bowling Green, OH: Bowling Green State U Popular P, 1978.

Klein, Marcus. *Easterns, Westerns, and Private Eyes: American Matters, 1870–1900.* Madison: U of Wisconsin P, 1994.

Robinson, Forrest G. *Having It Both Ways: Self-Subversion in Western Popular Classics.* Albuquerque: U of New Mexico P, 1993.

Tompkins, Jane. *West of Everything: The Inner Life of Westerns.* New York: Oxford UP, 1992.

Warshow, Robert. "Movie Chronicle: The Westerner." In *The Immediate Experience: Movies, Comics, Theatre and Other Aspects of Popular Culture.* Garden City, NY: Doubleday, 1962, 135–54.

Yates, Norris W. *Gender and Genre: Introduction to Women Writers of Formula Westerns, 1900–1950.* Albuqurque: U of New Mexico P, 1995.

The Great Plains

Fairbanks, Carol. *Prairie Women: Images in American and Canadian Fiction.* New Haven: Yale UP, 1986.

Faulkner, Virginia, and Frederick C. Luebke, eds. *Vision and Refuge: Essays on the Literature of the Great Plains.* Lincoln: U of Nebraska P, 1982.

Huseboe, Arthur R., and William Geyer, eds. *Where the West Begins: Essays on Middle Border and Siouxland Writing, in Honor of Herbert Krause.* Sioux Falls, SD: Center for Western Studies P, 1978.

Looney, Sandra, et al., eds. *The Prairie Frontier.* Sioux Falls, SD: The Nordland Heritage Foundation, 1984.

Olson, Steven. *The Prairie in Nineteenth-Century American Poetry.* Norman: U of Oklahoma P, 1994.

Quantic, Diane Dufva. *The Nature of the Place: A Study of Great Plains Fiction.* Lincoln: U of Nebraska P, 1995.

Thacker, Robert. *The Great Prairie Fact and the Literary Imagination.* Albuquerque: U of New Mexico P, 1989.

The Intermountain West

Bevis, William. *Ten Tough Trips: Montana Writers and the West.* Seattle: U of Washington P, 1990.

Ferril, Thomas Hornsby. "Writing in the Rockies." In *Rocky Mountain Reader.* Ray B. West, ed. New York: Dutton, 1946, 395–403.

González, Ray, ed. *Tracks in the Snow: Essays by Colorado Poets.* Arvada, CO: Mesilla P, 1989.

Robertson, Janet. *The Magnificent Mountain Women: Adventures in the Colorado Rockies.* Lincoln: U of Nebraska P, 1990.

The Southwest

Balassi, William, John F. Crawford, and Annie O. Eysturoy, eds. *This Is About Vision: Interviews with Southwestern Writers.* Albuquerque: U of New Mexico P, 1990.

Bennett, Patrick. *Talking with Texas Writers: Twelve Interviews.* College Station: Texas A & M UP, 1980.

Gaston, Edwin W. *The Early Novel of the Southwest.* Albuquerque: U of New Mexico P, 1961.

Gonzales-Berry, Erlinda, ed. *Pasó por Aquí: Critical Essays on the New Mexican Literary Tradition, 1542–1988.* Albuquerque: U of New Mexico P, 1989.

Graham, Don, James W. Lee, and William T. Pilkington, eds., *The Texas Literary Tradition: Fiction, Folklore, History.* Austin, TX: U of Texas and Texas State Historical Association, 1983.

Lensink, Judy Nolte, ed. *Old Southwest, New Southwest: Essays on a Region and Its Literature.* Tucson: Tucson Public Library, 1987.

Limerick, Patricia Nelson. *Desert Passages: Encounters with the American Deserts.* Niwot, CO: UP of Colorado, 1989.

Major, Mabel. *Southwest Heritage: A Literary History with Bibliography by Mabel Major, Rebecca W. Smith and T. M. Pearce.* Albuquerque: U of New Mexico P, 1938.

McMurtry, Larry. *In a Narrow Grave: Essays on Texas.* New York: Simon and Schuster, 1968.

Norwood, Vera, and Janice Monk, eds. *The Desert Is No Lady: Southwestern Landscapes in Women's Writing and Art.* New Haven: Yale UP, 1987.

Paredes, Americo. *Folklore and Culture on the Texas-Mexican Border.* Austin, TX: U of Texas P, 1993.

Pilkington, William T. *My Blood's Country: Studies in Southwestern Literature.*
Fort Worth: Texas Christian UP, 1973.

Powell, Lawrence Clark. *Southwest Classics: The Creative Literature of the Arid
Lands.* 1974. Rpt. Tucson: U of Arizona P, 1982.

Robinson, Cecil. *Mexico and the Hispanic Southwest in American Literature.*
Rev. ed. Tucson: U of Arizona P, 1977. Originally published as *With the
Ears of Strangers: The Mexican in American Literature* (1963).

———. *No Short Journeys: The Interplay of Cultures in the History and Literature
of the Borderlands.* Tucson: U of Arizona P, 1992.

Temple, Judy Nolte, ed. *Open Spaces, City Places: Contemporary Writers on the
Changing Southwest.* Tucson: U of Arizona P, 1994.

Turner, Teresa L., ed. *Down Mexico Way: The Literature of Conscience.* Tucson: Arizona Historical Society, 1984.

Weigle, Marta, and Kyle Fiore. *Santa Fe and Taos: The Writer's Era, 1916–
1941.* Santa Fe: Ancient City P, 1982.

The Pacific Rim

Bartlett, Lee. *The Sun Is But a Morning Star: Studies in West Coast Poetry and
Poetics.* Albuquerque: U of New Mexico P, 1989.

Berson, Misha. *The San Francisco Stage, Part 1: From Gold Rush to Golden
Spike, 1849–1869.* San Francisco: San Francisco Performing Arts Library & Museum Journal, 1989.

———. *The San Francisco Stage, Part 2: From Golden Spike to Great Earthquake, 1869–1906.* San Francisco: San Francisco Performing Arts Library & Museum Series, 1992.

Bingham, R. Edwin, and Glen A. Love, eds., *Northwest Perspectives: Essays on
the Culture of the Pacific Northwest.* Seattle: U of Washington P, 1979.

Chock, Eric, and Jody Manabe, eds. *Writers of Hawaii: A Focus on Our
Literary Heritage.* Honolulu: Bamboo Ridge P, 1981.

Crow, Charles L., ed. *Itinerary 7: Essays on California Writers.* Bowling
Green, OH: Bowling Green UP, 1978.

Davidson, Michael. *The San Francisco Renaissance: Poetics and Community at
Mid-century.* New York: Cambridge UP, 1989.

Day, A. Grove. *Books About Hawaii: Fifty Basic Authors.* Honolulu: U of
Hawaii P, 1977.

———. *Mad About Islands: Novelists of a Vanished Pacific.* Honolulu: Mutual
Publishing, 1987.

Ferlinghetti, Lawrence and Nancy J. Peters. *Literary San Francisco.* San
Francisco: City Lights Books and Harper & Row, 1980.

Fine, David, ed. *Los Angeles in Fiction: A Collection of Essays.* Rev. ed. Albuquerque: U of New Mexico P, 1995.

Hamilton, Ian. *Writers in Hollywood, 1915–1951.* New York: Caroll & Graf,
1990.

Haslam, Gerald. *The Other California: The Great Central Valley in Life and
Letters.* Santa Barbara: Capra P, 1990.

Johnson, Stephen, Gerald Haslam, and Robert Dawson. *The Great Central Valley: California's Heartland.* Berkeley: U of California P, 1993.

Jones, Margaret C. Jones. *Prophets in Babylon: Five California Novelists in the 1930's.* New York: Peter Lang, 1992.

Levy, Jo Ann. *They Saw the Elephant: Women in the California Gold Rush.* Norman: U of Oklahoma P, 1992.

Martin, Stoddard. *California Writers: Jack London, John Steinbeck, The Tough Guys.* London: Macmillan, 1983.

Maynard, John Arthur. *Venice West: The Beat Generation in Southern California.* New Brunswick: Rutgers UP, 1991.

O'Connell, Nicholas. *At the Field's End: Interviews with Twenty Pacific Northwest Writers.* Seattle: Madrona, 1987.

Pinsker, Sanford. *Three Pacific Northwest Poets: William Stafford, Richard Hugo, and David Wagoner.* Boston: Twayne, 1987.

Powell, Lawrence Clark. *California Classics: The Creative Literature of the Golden State.* 1971. Rpt. Santa Barbara: Capra P, 1982.

Robertson, David. *West of Eden: A History of the Art and Literature of Yosemite.* Berkeley: Yosemite Natural History Association, 1984.

Spatz, Jonas. *Hollywood in Fiction: Some Versions of the American Myth.* The Hague: Mouton, 1969.

Starr, Kevin. *Americans and the California Dream.* New York: Oxford UP, 1973.

————. *Inventing the Dream: California Through the Progressive Era.* New York: Oxford UP, 1985.

————. *Material Dreams: Southern California Through the 1920s.* New York: Oxford UP, 1990.

Stovall, Linny, ed. *Left Bank #1: Writing and Fishing the Northwest.* Hillsboro, OR: Blue Heron Publishing, 1991.

Sumida, Stephen H. *And the View from the Shore: Literary Traditions of Hawai'i.* Seattle: U of Washington P, 1991.

Walker, Franklin. *A Literary History of Southern California.* Berkeley: U of California P, 1950.

————. *San Francisco's Literary Frontier.* New York: Knopf, 1939.

Wallace, David Rains. *The Wilder Shore.* San Francisco: Sierra Club Books, 1984.

Wells, Walter. *Tycoons and Locusts: A Regional Look at Hollywood Fiction of the 1930s.* Carbondale: Southern Illinois UP, 1973.

Wyatt, David. *The Fall Into Eden: Landscape and Imagination in California.* New York: Cambridge UP, 1986.

Yalom, Marilyn, ed. *Women Writers of the West Coast: Speaking of Their Lives and Careers.* Santa Barbara: Capra P, 1983.

American Indian Writing

Allen, Paula Gunn. *The Sacred Hoop: Recovering the Feminine in American Indian Traditions.* Boston: Beacon, 1986.

Bruchac, Joseph, ed. *Survival This Way: Interviews with American Indian Poets.* Tucson: U of Arizona P, 1987.

Brumble, H. David III. *American Indian Autobiography.* Berkeley: U of California P, 1988.

Castro, Michael. *Interpreting the Indian: Twentieth-Century Poets and the Native American.* Albuquerque: U of New Mexico P, 1983.

Coltelli, Laura, ed. *Winged Words: Native American Writers Speak.* Lincoln: U of Nebraska P, 1990.

Fleck, Richard F., ed. *Critical Perspectives on Native American Fiction.* Washington, DC: Three Continents P, 1993.

Kroeber, Karl, ed. *American Indian Persistence and Resurgence.* Durham: Duke UP, 1994.

Krupat, Arnold. *For Those Who Come After: A Study of Native American Autobiography.* Los Angeles: U of California P, 1985.

———. *The Voice in the Margin: Native American Literature and the Canon.* Berkeley: U of California P, 1989.

Larson, Charles R. *American Indian Fiction.* Albuquerque: U of New Mexico P, 1978.

Lincoln, Kenneth. *Indi'n Humor: Bicultural Play in Native America.* New York: Oxford UP, 1993.

———. "Native American Literature: 'old like hills, like stars.'" In *Three American Literatures: Essays in Chicano, Native American, and Asian-American Literature for Teachers of American Literature.* Ed. Houston A. Baker, Jr. New York: Modern Language Association, 1982, 80–167.

———. *Native American Renaissance.* Los Angeles: U of California P, 1983.

McFadden, Steven. *Profiles in Wisdom: Native Elders Speak About the Earth.* Sante Fe: Bear and Co., 1991.

Murray, David. *Forked Tongues: Speech, Writing, and Representation in North American Indian Texts.* Bloomington: Indiana UP, 1991.

Owens, Louis. *Other Destinies: Understanding the American Indian Novel.* Norman: U of Oklahoma P, 1992.

Pearce, Roy Harvey. *Savagism and Civilization: A Study of the Indian and the American Mind.* Berkeley: U of California P, 1988.

Ramsey, Jarold. *Reading the Fire: Essays in the Traditional Indian Literatures of the Far West.* Lincoln: U of Nebraska P, 1983.

Sarris, Greg. *Keeping Slug Woman Alive: A Holistic Approach to American Indian Texts.* Berkeley: U of California P, 1993.

Swann, Brian, and Arnold Krupat, eds. *I Tell You Now: Autobiographical Essays by Native American Writers.* Lincoln: U of Nebraska P, 1987.

———, eds. *Recovering the Word: Essays on Native American Literature.* Berkeley: U of California P, 1987.

Tedlock, Dennis. *The Spoken Word and the Work of Interpretation.* Philadelphia: U of Pennsylvania P, 1983.

Velie, Alan R. *Four American Indian Literary Masters: N. Scott Momaday, James Welch, Leslie Marmon Silko, and Gerald Vizenor.* Norman: U of Oklahoma P, 1982.

Vizenor, Gerald, ed. *Narrative Chance: Postmodern Discourse on Native American Indian Literatures.* Albuquerque: U of New Mexico P, 1989.

Wiget, Andrew, ed. *Critical Essays on Native American Literature*. Boston: G. K. Hall & Co., 1985.

———. *Dictionary of Native American Literature*. Hamden, CT: Garland, 1994.

———. *Native American Literature*. Boston: Twayne, 1985.

Wong, Hertha Dawn. *Sending My Heart Back Across the Years: Tradition and Innovation in Native American Autobiography*. New York: Oxford UP, 1992.

Latino/Latina Writing

Anaya, Rudolfo A., and Francisco Lomeli, eds. *Aztlán: Essays on the Chicano Homeland*. Albuquerque: Academia/El Norte Publications, 1989.

Anzaldúa, Gloria. *Borderlands/La Frontera: The New Mestiza*. San Francisco: Spinsters/Aunt Lute, 1987.

Binder, Wolfgang, ed. *Partial Autobiographies: Interviews with Twenty Chicano Poets*. Erlangen: Palm & Enke, 1985.

Bruce-Novoa. *Chicano Authors: Inquiry by Interviews*. Austin: U of Texas P, 1980.

———. *Chicano Poetry: A Response to Chaos*. Austin: U of Texas P, 1982.

———. *Retrospace: Collected Essays on Chicano Literature, Theory, and History*. Houston: Arte Público P, 1990.

Calderón, Héctor, and José David Saldivar, eds. *Criticism in the Borderlands: Studies in Chicano Literature, Culture, and Ideology*. Durham, NC: Duke UP, 1991.

Candelaria, Cordelia. *Chicano Poetry: A Critical Introduction*. Westport, CT: Greenwood P, 1986.

Fabre, Genevieve, ed. *European Perspectives on Hispanic Literature of the United States*. Houston: Arte Público P, 1988.

Gutiérrez, Ramón, and Genaro Padilla, eds. *Recovering the U.S. Hispanic Literary Heritage*. Houston: Arte Público P, 1993.

Hernández, Guillermo E. *Chicano Satire: A Study in Literary Culture*. Austin, TX: U of Texas P, 1991.

Herrera-Sobek, María, ed. *Beyond Stereotypes: The Critical Analysis of Chicana Literature*. Binghamton, NY: Bilingual P, 1985.

Herrera-Sobek, María. *Reconstructing a Chicano/a Literary Heritage: Hispanic Colonial Literature of the Southwest*. Tucson: U of Arizona P, 1993.

Herrera-Sobek, María, and Helena María Viramontes, eds. *Chicana Creativity and Criticism: Charting New Frontiers in American Literature*. Houston: Arte Público P, 1988.

Huerta, Jorge A. *Chicano Theater: Themes and Forms*. Ypsilanti, MI: Bilingual P, 1982.

Jiménez, Francisco, ed. *The Identification and Analysis of Chicano Literature*. Binghamton, NY: Bilingual P, 1979.

Kanellos, Nicolás. *The History of Hispanic Theatre in the United States: Origins to 1940*. Austin: U of Texas P, 1990.

Lattin, Vernon E., ed. *Contemporary Chicano Fiction: A Critical Survey*. Binghamton, NY: Bilingual P, 1986.

Limón, José Eduardo. *Mexican Ballads, Chicano Poems: History and Influence in Mexican-American Social Poetry.* Berkeley: U of California P, 1992.

Mora, Pat. *Nepantla: Essays from the Land in the Middle.* Albuquerque: U of New Mexico P, 1993.

Padilla, Genaro M. *My History, Not Yours: The Formation of Mexican American Autobiography.* Madison: U of Wisconsin P, 1993.

Paredes, Raymund A. "The Evolution of Chicano Literature." In *Three American Literatures: Essays in Chicano, Native American, and Asian-American Literature for Teachers of American Literature.* Ed. Houston A. Baker, Jr. New York: Modern Language Association, 1982, 33–79.

Pettit, Arthur G. *Images of the Mexican American in Fiction and Film.* College Station, TX: Texas A & M UP, 1980.

Promis, José. *The Identity of Hispanoamerica: An Interpretation of Colonial Literature.* Trans. Alita Kelley and Alec E. Kelley. Tucson: U of Arizona P, 1991.

Rocard, Marcienne. Trans. Edward G. Brown, Jr. *The Children of the Sun: Mexican-Americans in the Literature of the United States.* Tucson: U of Arizona P, 1989.

Saldívar, Ramón. *Chicano Narrative: The Dialectics of Difference.* Madison: U of Wisconsin P, 1990.

Sánchez, Marta Ester. *Contemporary Chicana Poetry: A Critical Approach to an Emerging Literature.* Berkeley: U of California P, 1985.

Shirley, Carl R., and Paula W. Shirley. *Understanding Chicano Literature.* Columbia, SC: U of South Carolina P, 1988.

Sommers, Joseph, and Tomás Ybarra-Frausto, eds. *Modern Chicano Writers: A Collection of Critical Essays.* Englewood Cliffs, NJ: Prentice-Hall, 1979.

Tatum, Charles M. *Chicano Literature.* Boston: Twayne, 1982.

Vallejos, Tomás. *Mestizaje: The Transformation of Ancient Indian Religious Thought in Contemporary Chicano Fiction.* Ann Arbor: U Microfilms, 1980.

Asian American Writing

Chan, Jeffrey Paul, et al., eds. "An Introduction to Chinese-American and Japanese-American Literatures." In *Three American Literatures: Essays in Chicano, Native American, and Asian-American Literature for Teachers of American Literature.* Ed. Houston A. Baker, Jr. New York: Modern Language Association, 1982, 197–228.

Cheung, King-Kok. *Articulate Silences: Hisaye Yamamoto, Maxine Hong Kingston, Joy Kogawa.* Ithaca, NY: Cornell UP, 1993.

Kim, Elaine H. *Asian American Literature: An Introduction to the Writings and Their Social Context.* Philadelphia: Temple UP, 1982.

Lim, Shirley Geok-lin, and Amy Ling, eds. *Reading the Literatures of Asian America.* Philadelphia: Temple UP, 1992.

Ling, Amy. *Between Worlds: Women Writers of Chinese Ancestry.* New York: Pergamon, 1990.

Nomura, Gail M., et al., eds. *Frontiers of Asian American Studies: Writing, Research, and Criticism.* Pullman, WA: Washington State UP, 1989.

Wong, Sau-ling Cynthia. *Reading Asian American Literature: From Necessity to Extravagance.* Princeton: Princeton UP, 1993.

Environmental Writing

Abbey, Edward. *The Journey Home: Some Words in Defense of the American West.* New York: E. P. Dutton, 1977.

Cooley, John. *Earthly Words: Essays on Contemporary American Nature and Environmental Writers.* Ann Arbor: U of Michigan P, 1994.

Halpern, Daniel, ed. *On Nature: Nature, Landscape, and Natural History.* San Francisco: North Point P, 1986.

Hepworth, James, and Gregory McNamee, eds. *Resist Much, Obey Little: Some Notes on Edward Abbey.* 1985. Rpt. Tucson, AZ: Harbinger House, 1989.

Kolodny, Annette. *The Lay of the Land: Metaphor as Experience and History in American Life and Letters.* Chapel Hill: U of North Carolina P, 1975.

Lankford, Scott. "John Muir and the Nature of the West: An Ecology of American Life." Dissertation, Stanford University, 1991.

Love, Glen A. "*Et in Arcadia Ego:* Pastoral Theory Meets Ecocriticism." *Western American Literature* 27 (Fall 1992): 195–207.

———. "Revaluing Nature: Toward an Ecological Criticism." *Western American Literature,* 25, No. 3 (November 1990): 201–15.

Lyon, Thomas J. "A History [of American Nature Writing]." In *This Incomperable Lande: A Book of American Nature Writing.* Thomas J. Lyon, ed. New York: Penguin, 1989, 1–91.

Marx, Leo. *The Machine in the Garden: Technology and the Pastoral Ideal in America.* New York: Oxford UP, 1964.

McClintock, James I. *Nature's Kindred Spirits: Aldo Leopold, Joseph Wood Krutch, Edward Abbey, Annie Dillard, and Gary Snyder.* Madison: U of Wisconsin P, 1994.

McDowell, Michael J. "Finding Tongues in Trees: Dialogical and Ecological Landscapes in Henry David Thoreau, Robinson Jeffers, and Leslie Marmon Silko." Dissertation, University of Oregon, 1992.

Nash, Roderick. *Wilderness and the American Mind.* 3rd ed. New Haven: Yale UP, 1982.

Norwood, Vera. *Made from This Earth: American Women and Nature.* Chapel Hill: U of North Carolina P, 1993.

O'Grady, John P. *Pilgrims to the Wild: Everett Ruess, Henry David Thoreau, John Muir, Clarence King, Mary Austin.* Salt Lake City: U of Utah P, 1993.

Paul, Sherman. *For Love of the World: Essays on Nature Writers.* Iowa City: U of Iowa P, 1992.

———. *In Search of the Primitive: Rereading David Antin, Jerome Rothenberg and Gary Snyder.* Baton Rouge: Louisiana State UP, 1986.

Raglon, Rebecca Sue. "American Nature Writing in the Age of Ecology:

Changing Perceptions, Changing Forms." Dissertation. Queen's University at Kingston, 1990.

Sauer, Peter, ed. *Finding Home: Writing on Nature and Culture from Orion Magazine*. Boston: Beacon P, 1992.

Scheese, Donald Frederick. "Inhabitors of the Wild: Henry David Thoreau, John Muir, Aldo Leopold, and Edward Abbey." Dissertation, University of Iowa, 1991.

Servid, Carolyn, ed. *Reflections from the Island's Edge: On Nature, Values, and the Written Word*. St. Paul, MN: Graywolf P, 1994.

Slovic, Scott. *Seeking Awareness in American Nature Writing: Henry Thoreau, Annie Dillard, Edward Abbey, Wendell Berry, Barry Lopez*. Salt Lake City: U of Utah P, 1992.

Snyder, Gary. *The Practice of the Wild*. San Francisco: North Point P, 1990.

Stewart, Frank. *A Natural History of Nature Writing*. Covelo, CA: Island P, 1994.

Turner, Frederick. *Rediscovering America: John Muir in His Time and Ours*. New York: Viking, 1985.

CONTRIBUTORS

SHANNON APPLEGATE has been an historical researcher for twenty years and has an intimate knowledge of Oregon's past, its historical collections, and its archives. Several thousand letters and many diaries formed the basis for the narratives comprising her book *Skookum: An Oregon Pioneer Family's History and Lore* (1988), which was a nonfiction bestseller in the Pacific Northwest and an Oregon Book Award Finalist in 1989. She was the co-editor of *Talking on Paper: An Anthology of Oregon Letters and Diaries* (1994). A past member of the Oregon Committee for the Humanities' Publications and Editorial Advisory Boards, she has taught courses in regional history and writing, and has lectured and conducted workshops throughout the United States. She is currently working on a collection of short stories and her first novel.

MISHA BERSON is an arts journalist and educator who has taught in the School of Drama at the University of Washington and the Inter-Arts Center at San Francisco State University. She is presently the drama critic for the *Seattle Times*. For ten years she was the principal theater critic for the *San Francisco Bay Guardian*. Her work has appeared in *American Theatre Magazine*, the *Los Angeles Times*, the *San Francisco Chronicle*, *The Drama Review*, and in the *Cambridge Guide to American Theater*. She has written two books – *The San Francisco Stage: From Gold Rush to Golden Spike* (1990) and *The San Francisco Stage: From Golden Spike to Great Earthquake* (1992) – in a three-volume series for the San Francisco Performing Arts Library and Museum. For Theatre Communications Group, she has edited the first anthology of contemporary Asian American plays, entitled *Between Worlds* (1990).

WILLIAM W. BEVIS has taught English at the University of Montana,

Missoula, since 1974. He served on the editorial board of the Montana anthology, *The Last Best Place* (1988), and has published *Mind of Winter: Wallace Stevens, Meditation and Literature* (1988) and *Ten Tough Trips: Montana Writers and the West* (1990). *Borneo Log*, his book on native resistance to the logging trade between Sarawak and Japan, was published in 1995.

PHILIP BURNHAM, an independent scholar and freelance journalist, has written widely on perceptions of minority cultures for publications like *American Heritage, Transition,* and *The St. Louis Journalism Review*. His dissertation at the University of New Mexico concerned early contact between native and European cultures, and he has lectured widely in Africa and elsewhere on Native American history and literature as a Fulbright scholar. He lived and taught for several years on the Rosebud Sioux Reservation in South Dakota.

MARGARET GARCÍA DAVIDSON is completing a doctoral study entitled "Borderlands and Issues of Cultural/Ethnic Identity in Early Mexican American Writers" at the University of California, Davis. She is an assistant professor of English at Southern Methodist University in Dallas.

LINDA HAMALIAN is the author of *A Life of Kenneth Rexroth* (1991). She edited Kenneth Rexroth's *An Autobiographical Novel* (1991) and her essays and reviews have appeared in *The New York Times Book Review, The Literary Review, American Literature, African American Review,* and *North Dakota Quarterly*. She is an associate professor of English at William Paterson College in New Jersey.

JAMES D. HOUSTON is the author of a dozen works of fiction and nonfiction, including the novels *Love Life* (1985) and *Continental Drift* (1978). Among his nonfiction works are the award-winning *Californians: Searching for the Golden State* (1982; 1992), and *Farewell to Manzanar* (1973), both book and teleplay, co-authored with his wife, Jeanne Wakatsuki Houston. He is Visiting Professor of Literature at the University of California, Santa Cruz.

MICHAEL KOWALEWSKI is an associate professor of English at Carleton College. He is the author of *Deadly Musings: Violence and Verbal Form in American Fiction* (1993) and editor of *Temperamental Journeys: Essays on the Modern Literature of Travel* (1992). His essays have appeared in *Raritan, American Literary History, Texas Studies in Language and Literature, Northwest Review,* and *California History*. He is currently at work on a book about California writers, painters, and photographers.

THOMAS J. LYON is a professor of English at Utah State University, where he has edited *Western American Literature* since 1974. He was senior editor of *A Literary History of the American West* (1987), and editor of *This Incomperable Lande: A Book of American Nature Writing* (1989). He is co-editor of *Great and Peculiar Beauty* (1995), a Centennial Anthology of Utah writing.

LEE MITCHELL is a professor of English and chair of the department at Princeton University. He is the author of *Determined Fictions: American Literary Naturalism* (1989) and *Witnesses to a Vanishing America: The Nineteenth-Century Response* (1981). He has also edited *New Essays on "The Red Badge of Courage"* (1986). His recent essays have appeared in *Critical Inquiry, Prospects,* and *Nineteenth-Century Fiction.* He is presently at work on a book about the western.

SUSAN J. ROSOWSKI is Adele Hall Professor of English at the University of Nebraska at Lincoln. She is the author of *The Voyage Perilous: Willa Cather's Romanticism* (1986) and the editor of *Women and Western American Literature* (1982) and *Approaches to Teaching Cather's "My Ántonia"* (1989). She is editor-in-chief of the biennial series, *Cather Studies* and the general editor of the Nebraska scholarly edition of Willa Cather. Her essays and reviews have appeared in *Novel, Genre, Modern Fiction Studies, Western American Literature,* and *Great Plains Quarterly.*

DAVID RAINS WALLACE is a nature writer, novelist, and critic whose work has appeared in *Harper's, Sierra, Wilderness, The Los Angeles Times,* and *The New York Times Book Review.* His nonfiction books include *The Untamed Garden and Other Personal Essays* (1986), *The Klammath Knot: Explorations in Myth and Evolution* (1983; awarded the John Burroughs Medal for Nature Writing), *The Wilder Shore* (1984), and *Bulow Hammock: Mind in a Forest* (1989; awarded the Martha Kinney Cooper Library Association Literature Medal for Non-Fiction). His novels are "eco-thrillers": *The Turquoise Dragon* (1985) and *The Vermilion Parrot* (1991). His latest book is *The Quetzal and the Macaw: The Story of Costa Rica's National Parks* (1992).

PETER WILD is a professor of English at the University of Arizona. He is the author of more than one hundred articles and has written or edited forty books of poetry, nonfiction, and literary criticism, including *Cochise* (1973), *Pioneer Conservationists of Western America* (1979), and *The Desert Reader* (1991). He has done individual volumes on Clarence King, James Welch, Barry Lopez, John C. Van Dyke, Cabeza de Vaca, and others in the Western Writers Series of Boise State University Press. He was nominated for a Pulitzer Prize in 1973.

INDEX

The following titles are out of print:

8. Mitchell Breitwieser, *Cotton Mather and Benjamin Franklin: The Price of Representative Personality*
7. Peter Conn, *The Divided Mind: Ideology and Imagination in America, 1898–1917*
6. Marjorie Perloff, *The Dance of the Intellect: Studies in Poetry of the Pound Tradition*
5. Stephen Fredman, *Poet's Prose: The Crisis in American Verse,* first edition
4. Patricia Caldwell, *The Puritan Conversion Narrative: The Beginnings of American Expression*
3. John McWilliams, Jr., *Hawthorne, Melville, and the American Character: A Looking-Glass Business*
2. Charles Altieri, *Self and Sensibility in Contemporary American Poetry*
1. Robert Zaller, *The Cliffs of Solitude: A Reading of Robinson Jeffers*